CRADLE OF REDEEMING LOVE

JOHN SAWARD

CRADLE OF REDEEMING LOVE

The Theology of the Christmas Mystery

IGNATIUS PRESS   SAN FRANCISCO

Cover art: *The Nativity, at Night*
Geertgen tot Sint Jans
National Gallery, London
Copyright National Gallery
Cover design by Roxanne Mei Lum

© 2002 Ignatius Press, San Francisco
All rights reserved
ISBN 0-89870-886-9
Library of Congress Control Number 2001091855
Printed in the United States of America ∞

Ad honorem

Beatae Mariae

semper virginis

Matris pulchrae dilectionis

In memory of
George John Saward
Marjorie Elizabeth Saward
Robert John Thomas
Muriel Ivy Thomas

Agnus Dei, qui tollis peccata mundi,
dona eis requiem sempiternam.

CONTENTS

ABBREVIATIONS

Unless otherwise noted, quotations from Scripture are generally taken from Bishop Challoner's revised version of the Douay Bible (The Holy Bible, Douay Version, new ed. [London, 1956]). Psalms are numbered according to the Latin psalter. However, the spelling of Biblical names follows the conventions of the Revised Standard Version: for example, Hosea is called 'Hosea', not 'Osee'.

References to Papal encyclicals are in most cases to the paragraph numbers in the collection of translations edited by C. Carlen IHM, *The Papal Encyclicals* (Raleigh, 1981).

Bethlehem   Frederick William Faber, *Bethlehem* (London, 1860).

CA   *Catena Aurea*: commentary on the four Gospels collected out of the works of the Fathers by St Thomas Aquinas; English translation edited by John Henry Newman; new edition with an introduction by Aidan Nichols OP, in four volumes (Southampton, 1997). (In some places I have modified the translation. The number refers to the volume, and therefore the Gospel: thus CA 1 is the *Catena* on St Matthew, CA 2 on St Mark, and so on.)

CCC   *The Catechism of the Catholic Church.*

CCCM   *Corpus Christianorum: continuatio mediaevalis.*

CCSL   *Corpus Christianorum: series latina.*

CSCO   *Corpus scriptorum Christianorum orientalium.*

9

DCOO	*Doctoris ecstatici D. Dionysii Cartusiani opera omnia.*
DS	*Enchiridion symbolorum definitionum et declarationum de rebus fidei et morum,* ed. H. Denzinger and A. Schönmetzer SJ, 36th ed. (Rome, Freiburg and Barcelona, 1976).
EH	W. J. Birkbeck et al., eds., *The English Hymnal,* new ed. (London, 1933). (References are to hymn numbers.)
ET	= English translation.
FT	= French translation.
Greene	R. L. Greene, ed., *The Early English Carols,* new ed. (Oxford, 1977).
GT	= German translation.
L-R	J. Leclercq OSB and H. Rochais, eds., *Sancti Bernardi opera* (Rome, 1957–).
Ledit	J. Ledit, *Marie dans la liturgie de Byzance* (Paris, 1976).
LG	Second Vatican Council, Dogmatic Constitution on the Church, *Lumen gentium.*
Menaion	*The Festal Menaion,* trans. from the original Greek by Mother Mary and Archimandrite Kallistos Ware (London, 1977).
OCB	François Bourgoing, ed., *Oeuvres complètes de De Bérulle,* new ed. (Paris, 1856).
PG	J. P. Migne, ed., *Patrologia graeca.*
PL	J. P. Migne, ed., *Patrologia latina.*
Q	St Bonaventure, *Opera omnia,* ed. Franciscans of Quaracchi (1882–1902). (In the notes, the volume numbers are given as Roman numerals.)
Rationale	William Durandus, *Rationale divinorum officiorum.* (This work is cited by book, chapter, and paragraph

	from the critical edition in CCCM, vols. 140 and 140A.)
RSPT	*Revue des sciences philosophiques et théologiques.*
RSR	*Recherches de science religieuse.*
SC	*Sources chrétiennes.*
SCG	St Thomas Aquinas, *Summa contra gentiles.*
Sent.	St Thomas Aquinas, *Scriptum super libros Sententiarum.* (The number preceding *Sent.* refers to the particular book of Peter Lombard's *Sentences* being expounded.)
ST	St Thomas Aquinas, *Summa theologiae.*
Suppl.	Supplement to part three of the *Summa theologiae.*
Triodion	*The Lenten Triodion,* translated from the original Greek by Mother Mary and Archimandrite Kallistos Ware (London, 1978).
WH	D. Mathew et al., eds., *The Westminster Hymnal* (London, 1939). (References are to hymn numbers.)

PREFACE

Time was, with most of us, when Christmas Day, encircling all our limited world like a magic ring, left nothing out for us to miss or seek; bound together all our home enjoyments, affections, and hopes; grouped everything and everyone around the Christmas fire; and made the little picture shining in our bright young eyes, complete.[1]

As I grow older, the Christmas mystery seems ever greater, or rather the sense I had of its greatness when I was young and my eyes were still bright is, with every year's passing, more and more confirmed. When I was a child, Christmas did indeed encircle all my limited world: it was the goal of the year, the glorious summation of everything that was good. Even when Christmas began to be something I could remember from what little past I possessed, it still seemed each time altogether new, like the very first Christmas of all. When I looked up at the jewels in the black cope of the sky, I was sure I could see the beaming brightness that guided the Magi and hear the angels bringing glad tidings to the shepherds. This strange intuition was renewed twenty, thirty, forty years later when I was the father of a family. Our little ones were like icons of the Child–God of Bethlehem: in them I could see the likeness of His littleness and hear the echo of His preaching: 'Such I became for you, and such you

---

[1] Charles Dickens, 'What Christmas Is, As We Grow Older', in *The Christmas Stories*, ed. R. Glancy (London, 1996), p. 19.

must become if you want to enter my Kingdom.' Now, decades after my own and my children's first Christmases, I remain convinced that the Christmas mystery, in both its liturgical solemnities and its familial festivities, recapitulates the whole of the Catholic religion, inaugurates Easter, anticipates the Parousia and contains within it the source of the world's restoration.

Cradle of Redeeming Love is the sequel to *Redeemer in the Womb*.[2] The first volume was an Advent book, a study of the nine months that God-made-man spent in His Blessed Mother's womb. The second goes on to consider the Nativity and Epiphany of the Lord; it is a systematic theology of the Christmas mystery, the first to be written in many years. Although no author of recent times has done what I am trying to do here, I make no claim to originality. Self-consciously original theology tends always to be heretical theology. Orthodox theology has, by contrast, a blessed familiarity, for it does no more than assist the faithful in understanding what they already believe; its surprises are the outcome not of human ingenuity but of divine infinitude, the sign of a Truth that is ever ancient and ever new. My intention is to draw on the Christmas doctrine of the saints; of the Church's Doctors, mystics and poets; and in particular of that Doctor, Mystic and Poet whom the Church commends above all others as a teacher: St Thomas Aquinas, the Angel of the Schools.[3] With the help of St Thomas, and following the order of his discussion in the Third Part of the *Summa theologiae*, I shall try to shed some light on the 'great and

---

[2] John Saward, *Redeemer in the Womb: Jesus Living in Mary* (San Francisco, 1993).

[3] 'We therefore desired that all teachers of philosophy and sacred theology should be warned that if they deviated so much as a step, in metaphysics especially, from Aquinas, they exposed themselves to great risk' (Pope St Pius X, *Doctoris Angelici*, in J. Maritain, *St. Thomas Aquinas*, ET, new ed. [London, 1933], p. 217).

mighty wonder' once enacted when the Virgin bore an Infant 'with virgin-honour pure'.[4]

What follows is a work that is theological in the strict
sense: it is concerned with God and other things in relation
to God,[5] in this case, God the Son born of Mary according to
the flesh. The object at every stage is the truth about Christmas as expounded by the Doctors, not the truth about the
Doctors and the way they wrote their books. The reader will
find no tortured and tortuous post-modernist discussions
about the possibility of theology. Instead, I have taken the
risk of actually doing theology, of simply talking and talking
simply about God in His human infancy, the Creator in the
cradle. I have written, not as an historian or literary critic,
surveying trends and determining influences, but as a man
who, to his astonishment, has been given the privilege of
teaching dogmatic theology in the name of the Catholic
Church. In conformity, therefore, to my calling, the subject
of this book is no more and no less than the Christmas
dogma, the objective and divinely revealed truth of the Nativity of Christ, as proclaimed by His infallible and immaculate Bride. It is the splendour of this truth, of 'Love's noon in
Nature's night',[6] which for two millennia has captivated the
intelligence of Fathers and Schoolmen; activated the genius
of poets, painters and musicians; and, in even the bleakest of
midwinters, brightened the eyes of little ones when they
have knelt by the Crib.

> It is the dogma that is the drama—not beautiful phrases, nor
> comforting sentiments, nor vague aspirations to loving-kind-
> ness and uplift, nor the promise of something nice after

[4] J. M. Neale's translation of the hymn *Mega kai parádoxon thauma*, by St
Germanus of Constantinople (EH 19).

[5] Cf ST 1a q. 7.

[6] Richard Crashaw, 'In the Holy Nativity of Our Lord God', *Carmen Deo
nostro*, new ed. (London, c. 1897), p. 15.

death—but the terrifying assertion that the same God who made the world lived in the world and passed through the grave and gate of death. Show that to the heathen, and they may not believe it; but at least they may realize that here is something that a man might be glad to believe.[7]

19 March 2002
Solemnity of St Joseph

[7] Dorothy L. Sayers, 'The Dogma Is the Drama', in *Creed or Chaos? And Other Essays in Popular Theology* (London, 1947), p. 24.

ACKNOWLEDGEMENTS

I must thank His Eminence Christoph Cardinal Schönborn of Vienna for having invited me, four years ago, to join the faculty of the International Theological Institute in Gaming. *Cradle of Redeeming Love* is the fruit of these four happy years and of the intellectual fellowship of colleagues who are also dear friends. I am also grateful to Donald J. Uitvlugt of the University of Notre Dame for reading some of the chapters, and for his unfailing support and encouragement of my work.

Quotations from the works of G. K. Chesterton are made with the permission of A. P. Watt Ltd on behalf of the Royal Literary Fund. Quotations from *The Festal Menaion* and *The Lenten Triodion*, both works translated by Mother Mary and Archimandrite Kallistos Ware, are made with the permission of the publisher, Faber and Faber Ltd.

ART CREDITS

INTRODUCTION

Christ Is Born Today!

This day the King of Heaven has deigned to be born
   of a Virgin,
that He might bring back to Heaven man who was
   lost.
This day true Peace has descended from Heaven.
This day, through all the world, the skies have
   dropped down their sweetness. This day is the
   dawn of a new redemption, of the restoration of
   the old, and of everlasting joy.
This day Christ is born.
This day the Saviour has appeared.
This day the angels sing on earth, and the archangels
   rejoice.
This day the righteous exult, saying: 'Glory to God in
   the highest, alleluia!' [1]

In the liturgy of His Church, the eternal Word incarnate
works wonders with the calendar. The things He accomplished in the past once and for all He brings into the
present with all their vital force, so that the Church can in
truth sing on every Christmas Day: 'This day the King of
Heaven has deigned to be born of a Virgin.' Since Christ
rose from the tomb, time has ceased merely to run away into

[1] First and Second Responsories of the Matins of Christmas Day; Antiphon
of the Second Vespers of Christmas Day, *Breviarium romanum* (1962).

death. 'This is the Holy One', says St Bernard, 'who is not suffered to see corruption, this the New Man who can never become old, who brings into true newness of life those whose bones have all grown old.'[2] When God the Son ascended to the Father's right hand, He did not cast off His human flesh, nor did He consign to oblivion the stages of His earthly life. '[A]ll that Christ is—all that he did and suffered for all men—participates in the divine eternity, and so transcends all times while being made present in them all.'[3] Jesus Christ is 'the same yesterday, today, and for ever' (Heb 13:8). The flesh that God took, He keeps, and the deeds He did in time live on. The Redeemer of man is the redeemer of time (cf Eph 5:16).

It is above all on her altars that the Church receives the grace of time redeemed. By His activity as Priest and His presence as Victim, the risen Jesus in the Holy Eucharist embraces past, present and future. 'O sacred banquet', sings St Thomas Aquinas, 'in which Christ is received, the memory of His Passion renewed [past], the mind filled with grace [present], and a pledge of future glory given unto us [future].'[4] The Sacrifice once offered on Calvary is not locked away in the chronicles of yesteryear but is rather daily made present and applied to all the needs of the living and the dead, granting to wayfarers on earth the grace of repentance and to the poor souls in Purgatory a remission of their punishments that will the more swiftly lead them to glory.[5] Moreover,

[2] *In vigilia nativitatis Domini, sermo* 6, no. 6; L-R 4:239.
[3] CCC 1085.
[4] Magnificat Antiphon, Second Vespers of Corpus Christi.
[5] Council of Trent, Twenty-Second Session, *Doctrine on the Sacrifice of the Mass*, cap. 1 (DS 1740); cap. 2 (DS 1743); Twenty-Fifth Session, *Decree on Purgatory* (DS 1820). The Sacrifice of the Mass, as offered 'for sins, for punishments for sins, and for expiations' (cf DS 1753), 'does not remit the guilt of sins immediately as do the sacraments of Baptism and Penance, but mediately by the conferring of the grace of repentance' (L. Ott, *Fundamentals of Catholic Dogma*, ET, new ed. [Cork, 1963], p. 413).

since Christ's self-offering on the Cross consummated all His previous human acts, the Eucharistic re-presentation of the Passion gives the members of the Mystical Body a certain contact with *all* the mysteries of their Head, including the mystery of His temporal birth. 'Just as He is daily immolated in a certain manner when we "show forth His death", so He seems to be newly born when in faith we represent His Nativity.'[6] On the Cross, when He offered Himself to the Father, the eternal Son gathered up and handed over to Him all He had been and done as man, all the merits of His earlier earthly life: *Consummatum est* (Jn 19:30). Therefore, when now the consummating Sacrifice is re-presented in the Mass, the treasures of all the other mysteries are poured out from the Sacred Heart. It is because we stand day by day with Mary and John at the Cross that year by year we can kneel with Mary and Joseph round the crib, crying out with the angels, in breathless excitement, *Hodie Christus natus est,* 'Christ is born today.'

Christmas and Christ-Mass

Through the Eucharistic Sacrifice, the human conception and birth of the divine Prince of Peace are not only annually but also perpetually present in the life of the Church and her sons. Through the Christ-Mass mystery, the Christmas mystery is ever in our midst. There are both material continuity and formal resemblance between what took place once and for all in Nazareth and Bethlehem and what is daily repeated at Catholic altars. There is material continuity, because, as St Paschasius Radbertus reminded his fellow monks in the ninth century, the body really present in the Sacrament is the very body that was born of Mary, crucified under Pontius Pilate,

---

[6] St. Bernard of Clairvaux, *In vigilia nativitatis Domini, sermo* 6, 6; L-R 4:239.

and resurrected on the third day: 'What is confected at the word of Christ by the Holy Spirit is His body from the Virgin.'⁷ This is the truth expressed in the hymn that has inspired so many of Christendom's composers: *Ave verum corpus natum de Maria Virgine*, 'Hail true body born of the Virgin Mary'. The same doctrine is echoed in all the rites of the Church. Before the Copts receive Holy Communion, they make a confession of faith that identifies the Body in the Sacrament with the Body in the Crib: 'I believe, I believe, I believe, and confess till my last breath, that this is the life-giving body which thine only-begotten Son, our Lord, God, and Saviour Jesus Christ, took from our Lady, the mistress and queen of all, the holy sinless Virgin Mary, Mother of God.'⁸ In the Byzantine Churches, at every serving of the Divine Liturgy, a star-shaped cover is placed over the Sacred Host as a sign that here, really present, is the Child-God whom the Magi sought and worshipped. The star has six points, because it is the Star of David and thus signifies the presence of David's Son and Lord, the divine King of the Jews.⁹ As he places the star over the Lamb-Host, the priest repeats the words of the Evangelist: 'And behold, the star came and stood over where the Child was' (Mt 2:9). Around the large unconsecrated Host, representing the Christ-Child, the priest places smaller pieces in honour of the Mother of God ('On the right hand stood the Queen'), the angels and saints and all the living and the dead. These recall the presence by the Manger of the same all-holy Mother, the hosts of high Heaven and the herdsmen of humble Bethlehem. 'The shepherds were the chosen ones at Bethlehem; now the

⁷ Cf *Liber de corpore et sanguine Domini* 4, 3; PL 120:1279C.
⁸ *Liturgia S. Basilii alexandrina*; PG 31:1651.
⁹ Cf C. Kucharek, *The Byzantine-Slav Liturgy of St John Chrysostom: Its Origin and Evolution* (Allendale, 1971), pp. 314f.; Nicolas Cabasilas, *Liturgiae expositio*, cap. 11; PG 150:389C.

chosen are the members of Christ's Church, militant, triumphant, and suffering.'[10] Hieromonk Gregory of Mount
Athos, in his commentary on the Divine Liturgy, invokes St
Germanus of Constantinople in support of his claim that 'the
whole course of the Divine Liturgy follows the course of the
life of Christ.' At the beginning, during the offertory rite (or
prothesis), 'Christ is born anew. . . . And having been born,
Christ takes up again His infancy: "The divine body is placed
in the *prothesis* [the part of the church building where the rite
of *prothesis* is celebrated], as it was in Bethlehem, where
Christ was born."'[11] Even when unconsecrated, the Host is
treated as a symbol of the Word incarnate: it is called the
'Lamb' and is pierced with a spear. Later, after the consecration, when what lies on the paten is no longer a mere symbol
of Christ but the very reality of Christ substantially present
beneath the sacramental veil, the choir sings a hymn to extol
the divine motherhood and virginity of our Lady. As the
awful Sacrifice of Calvary is reenacted, so the miraculous
birth in Bethlehem is remembered:

> In thee rejoiceth, O thou who art full of grace, every created
> being, the hierarchy of the angels, and all mankind, O conse-
> crated Temple and supersensual Paradise, Glory of Virgins, of
> whom God, who is our God before all the ages, was incar-
> nate and became a little child. For He made of thy womb a
> throne, and thy belly did He make more spacious than the
> heavens. In thee doth all creation rejoice, O thou who art full
> of glory: Glory to thee.[12]

The Latin Church likewise does not venerate the Saviour's
glorious body in the Sacrament without saluting the generous womb of which He is the fruit. In the Roman Canon,

---

[10] Kucharek, p. 315.

[11] Hieromonk Gregory, *I theia leitourgía*, new ed. (Athens, 1985), p. 83.

[12] I. F. Hapgood, *Service Book of the Orthodox-Catholic Apostolic Church*, new
ed. (New York, 1922), p. 75.

moments before consecrating, the priest, in the name of the whole Church on earth, 'joins in communion and venerates the memory, in the first place, of the glorious Ever-Virgin Mary, Mother of our God and Lord Jesus Christ' (author's translation). On those days when a procession of the Blessed Sacrament is customary, as the priest carries the Sacred Host, the choir again recalls the Virgin Birth, in the words of the Angelic Doctor: *Nobis natus, nobis datus,* 'Born for us, given for us,/ Of a Virgin undefiled'.[13] Even on Maundy Thursday and at Corpus Christi, the wonder of Christmas Day absorbs the Church's mind. In all the incarnate mysteries, whether in the Virgin's womb or at the Father's right hand or on the altars of the Church, one and the same 'Christ and Son and Lord',[14] in one and the same flesh, glorifies the Father and sheds His grace upon Adam's sons. Dom Guéranger of Solesmes, in his meditations on the Masses of Christmastide, reminds the priest that after the consecration 'the divine Lamb, the Son of the Virgin, rests on the altar', and that, as he kisses the altar, the celebrant should 'greet it like the Crib in which slept, wrapped in swaddling clothes, the Word who said to men, "I am the Bread of Life"'.[15]

There is also a kind of formal resemblance between the Eucharist, on the one hand, and the Incarnation and human birth of the Son of God, on the other. They are not comparable in all respects; indeed, they are far more unlike than like each other, for human nature is not transubstantiated into the Word, nor is bread hypostatically united to the Body of Christ. Nevertheless, despite the differences, Catholic theology and piety persist in affirming a similarity between the

[13] From the hymn of St Thomas Aquinas *Pange lingua gloriosi,* sung both at the procession to the altar of repose on Holy Thursday and as the Office hymn for Vespers on the feast of Corpus Christi.

[14] Cf *Symbolum Chalcedonense*; DS 302.

[15] P. Guéranger OSB, *L'Année liturgique: Le Temps de Noël,* vol. 1, new ed. (Tours, 1922), p. 88.

assumption of flesh by the Word and the conversion of bread into flesh by the Spirit, and between the Godhead's dwelling bodily in the sacred humanity and the presence of the whole Christ in the Sacrament. Just as the Holy Spirit once fashioned a body for the Son of God from the Virgin's pure blood,[16] so now, when the priest utters the words of consecration, the same Holy Spirit comes down to change the whole substance of bread into the whole substance of the same Virgin-born body.[17] During His infancy the divinity of the Word was hidden beneath the littleness of His human form, and now, in the Sacrament, the whole Christ—Body, Blood, Soul and Divinity—is substantially present, though not sensibly perceptible, beneath the lowly accidents of bread.[18] Thus Altar and Tabernacle are an extension of the Manger, the place where God the Son, humbled in the flesh, can be visited and adored.[19]

[16] Cf ST 3a q. 31, a. 5.

[17] 'Why do you look for the order of nature in Christ's body [in the Sacrament],' asks St Ambrose, in a text quoted by St Thomas (ST 3a q. 75, a. 4), 'since the Lord Jesus Himself was born of the Virgin in a way that surpasses nature?' Later, St Thomas compares the act of omnipotence by which God preserves the accidents of bread in existence without a subject in which to inhere to that other most wonderful act by which He forms a body for His Son in the Virgin's womb without male seed (see ST 3a q. 77, a 1).

[18] As St Francis of Assisi says in his *Letter to the Entire Order*: 'O admirable heights and sublime lowliness! O sublime humility! O humble sublimity! That the Lord of the universe, God and the Son of God, so humbles Himself under the little form of bread': *Francis and Clare: The Complete Works*, ed. and trans. R. J. Armstrong OFM Cap and I. C. Brady OFM (New York, 1982), p. 58.

[19] According to Cardinal Bérulle, the Blessed Trinity, the Incarnation of God the Son, and the Holy Eucharist together form a great chain connecting God and man: '[I]n the first of these mysteries, the Father gives and communicates His essence to His Son; in the second, the Son gives and communicates His person to our humanity; in the third, the same Son gives and communicates His body and His humanity to men' (*Grandeurs de Jésus* 7, 4; OCB 268).

The 'Cosmic Value' of Christmas

The human birth of the Son of God is at all times alive in the Church's memory, but at certain times it becomes the chief object of her meditation—every year for a season, and at the beginning of a new millennium for twelve months of jubilee. Both observances, the annual and the millennial, testify to the grandeur of the saving event. As the Holy Father, John Paul II, said when he promulgated the most recent Great Jubilee: 'The fact that in the fulness of time the eternal Word took on the condition of a creature gives a unique cosmic value to the event which took place in Bethlehem two thousand years ago.' [20] If the Child born of the Virgin is the Father's Word, through whom all things were made, then the birth of that Child—the Christmas mystery—must indeed have a 'cosmic value', a truth large enough for an eternity of contemplation and a power sufficient to transform 'the sky, and stars, and sea's abyss'. [21]

The Season of Christmas

The world-transforming magnitude of the Christmas mystery is proved by the relative immensity of the veneration it receives from the Church in her liturgy, from the saints in their lives and from Christian artists in their works. Throughout Christendom, the liturgical privileges of Christmas are second only to those of Easter. In the Greek Church the feast is preceded by a forty-day fast and by five days of fore-feast. In the Latin Church, after four weeks of Advent, [22] including the seven days of the 'O antiphons', the birthday of the

[20] *Tertio millennio adveniente*, no. 3.

[21] From *Christe, Redemptor omnium* (Office for Christmas), in the translation by J. M. Neale (EH 17).

[22] The four weeks of Advent symbolize the four millennia of waiting from Adam to the Incarnation. See Guéranger, *L'Année liturgique*, p. 9.

Saviour is observed as a Solemnity (or 'Double of the First Class', as it was known in the old rite) with three thematically distinct Masses[23] and is followed by an octave dense with diverse feasts. The twelve days of Christmas lead from the Nativity to the even more ancient feast of the Epiphany (or 'Theophany'), which in the West chiefly celebrates the manifestation of the newborn Christ to the Gentiles and in the East the manifestation of the grown-up Christ at His Baptism. The Baptism of the Lord is commemorated in the Roman Missal of 1962 on the octave day of the Epiphany and in the 1970 Missal on the Sunday immediately following the Epiphany. Already on the sixth of January the later manifestations of the Son of God, in the Jordan and at Cana, are remembered, alongside the manifestation at Bethlehem, in the Office hymn *Hostis Herodes impie*, and in the *Benedictus* antiphon at Lauds.[24] According to certain ancient opinions, all three events took place on the same date.[25] The calendar of the older Roman rite provides a whole season of 'Sundays after Epiphany'. During this 'Epiphanytide', other revelations of our Lord's divinity are remembered: the changing of water into wine (cf Jn 2:1–11), the healing of the leper and the centurion's servant (cf Mt 8:1–13), and the calming of the

[23] Cf ST 3a q. 83, a. 2, ad 2.

[24] 'Lo, sages from the East are gone/ To where the star hath newly shone:/ Led on by light to Light they press,/ And by their gifts their God confess./ The Lamb of God is manifest/ Again in Jordan's water blest,/ And He who sin had never known/ By washing hath our sins undone./ Yet he that ruleth everything/ Can change the nature of the spring,/ And gives at Cana this for sign—/ The water reddens into wine': from the hymn *Hostis Herodes impie*, written by Sedulius (c. 450) and translated by Percy Dearmer; EH 38. In the *Benedictus* antiphon, we see how in each of these mysteries Christ is manifested as Bridegroom of the Church: 'This day the Church is joined to her heavenly Spouse, for Christ has washed away her crimes in the Jordan; with gifts the Magi hasten to the royal nuptials, and the guests are gladdened with wine made from water. Alleluia.'

[25] Cf P. Guéranger OSB, *L'Année liturgique: Le Temps de Noël*, vol. 2, new ed. (Paris and Poitiers, 1912), pp. 90f.

waves (cf Mt 8:23–27).²⁶ On these Sundays, says a medieval commentator on the liturgy, 'the Church wants to show us the appearing of the Lord, so that a star may arise within us to lead us to the Bethlehem above'.²⁷ In both editions of the Roman Missal, the Christmas cycle of feasts comes to a climax of light on the fortieth day with the feast of Candlemas (called the 'Purification of our Lady' in the 1962 Missal and the 'Presentation of our Lord' in 1970). During the Middle Ages the festivities of Christmas continued without interruption till Candlemas.²⁸ Throughout January, holly and ivy decked the halls, wassail was quaffed and carols rang out in praise of the successive mysteries of the infant God. 'Make we myrth/ For Crystes byrth,/ And syng we Yole tyl Candelmas.' ²⁹ Only on the second of February, with an eye on the approaching rigours of Lent, did medieval man dowse the Yuletide log.

The Saints of Christmas

During the season of Christmas, the Church is unsparing not only in the adoration she gives to Christ but also in the

---

²⁶ 'Two seasons of the Church's year show us our God in the depths of our humanity. As a child He lies in the Crib, so that we can rock Him in our arms, and then, as a poor suffering man, He trembles with fear in Gethsemane, so that we can lay our hand on His shoulder to console Him. Is it not a truly divine wisdom on the part of the Church, between these two seasons, to make the sublimity of the divine majesty to shine forth from Epiphany to Quinquagesima, so that in the Babe of Bethlehem and the Sufferer of Gethsemane and Golgotha we do not forget—to our detriment—the hidden God?': E. Przywara SJ, 'Epiphanie und Septuagesima', *Frühe religiöse Schriften* (Einsiedeln, 1962), p. 291.

²⁷ *Rationale* lib. 6, cap. 18, no. 1; 140A:210.

²⁸ 'The commemoration of the Purification of Mary is . . . indissolubly tied to that of the Birth of the Saviour; and the practice of celebrating these holy and joyous forty days appears to be of great antiquity in the Roman Church' (Guéranger, *L'Année liturgique: Le Temps de Noël*, vol. 1, p. 2).

²⁹ A fifteenth-century carol, in Greene, p. 4, n. 8.

veneration she directs to His saints. The Star of Jacob shines amidst a constellation of what the medievals call His 'companions' (*comites*).[30] St Bonaventure suggests an analogy between the sacred feasts and the secular festivities: 'On great feasts it is the custom to invite other people to the banquet, and if this is done to show charity, it is praiseworthy. Christ, therefore, did not want to be on His own at the banquet of joy, and so He invited His companions, friends, and servants to share in the joy.'[31] In the Byzantine rite, the Sundays before Christmas commemorate not only all the ancestors of Christ according to the flesh but also all the righteous from Adam to Joseph, the spouse most chaste of the holy Mother of God. St Joseph, together with King David, 'the ancestor of God', and St James, the 'brother of God', is also remembered on the Sunday after Christmas.[32] 'Approaching Christmas in this way', says a modern Orthodox theologian, 'the worshipper is enabled to see the Incarnation, not as an abrupt and irrational intervention of the divine, but as the culmination of a long process extending over thousands of years.'[33]

On the second day of Christmas, the Latin Church remembers St Stephen, the servant who was clothed with immortality by the King who was wrapped in swaddling clothes.[34] The third day is dedicated to St John, the virginal disciple specially loved by the divine Son of the Virgin, and

[30] Cf *Rationale*, 7, 42; 140B:107. 'A most magnificent constellation of saints, holy men and holy women, is scattered around the cradle of the Infant-God' (Guéranger, *L'Année liturgique: Le Temps de Noël*, vol. 1, p. 16).

[31] St Bonaventure, *De sancto Stephano, sermo* 1; Q IX:478BC.

[32] In the Tridentine Breviary the holy men of the past, both before and under the Law, are commemorated in the First and Second Nocturns of Matins.

[33] Archimandrite Kallistos Ware, introduction to *The Festal Menaion*, new ed. (London, 1977), p. 53.

[34] 'Yesterday we celebrated the temporal birth of our eternal King; today we celebrate the triumphal Passion of His soldier': St Fulgentius, Lesson at Matins in the *Breviarium romanum* (1962).

the fourth, 'Childermas', to the Holy Innocents, who by blood bore witness to the newborn Son of God, their kinsman in race and equal in age. Stephen was a martyr in both will and act, John in will alone and the Innocents in act alone.[35] On the twenty-ninth of December the Church remembers the holy blissful martyr St Thomas of Canterbury, who died during Christmastide 1170 in defence of the liberty of the Church militant. Even on Christmas Day itself, at the Second Mass, there is a commemoration of the martyr Anastasia, who died in the persecution of Diocletian. The Roman Martyrology also calls to mind the thousands of martyrs put to death by Diocletian in Nicomedia: 'Thus they had the good fortune to be born for Heaven on the very day on which Christ desired to be born on earth as its Redeemer.'[36] But why are the martyrs so prominent among the saints who shine around the Crib? Abbot Guéranger supplies the answer: '[A]ll this strength [of the martyrs], their whole triumph, came from the Crib of the Infant-God. That is why Thomas here meets Stephen. It took a self-emptied God, this exalted manifestation of humility and weakness in the flesh, to open the eyes of men to the nature of true strength.'[37] The saints draw their strength from the weakness of the cradled and crucified God.

Glorious above all the other Christmas companions of Christ is the Blessed Maiden who gave Him human birth. At the Matins of Christmas Day, the Church cries out: 'Blessed Mary, the Mother of God, whose womb abideth intact, hath this day given birth to the Saviour of the world.'[38] Each day of the octave, in the Canon of the Mass, the Latin Church venerates the 'inviolate virginity' that 'brought the Saviour

[35] Cf Guéranger, L'Année liturgique: Le Temps de Noël, vol. 1, p. 384.
[36] The Roman Martyrology.
[37] Guéranger, L'Année liturgique: Le Temps de Noël, vol. 1, p. 427.
[38] Fifth responsory.

into this world' and dedicates the whole of the eighth day to
the divine motherhood—in the old rite in the content of the
prayers and in the new rite in name as well as content.[39] Our
Lady's conceiving and carrying of God the Son in her virginal womb are remembered throughout Advent, especially
during the week of the O antiphons and, in the *novus ordo
Missae*, on the fourth Sunday. The Immaculate Conception is
celebrated on the eighth of December as the first, pre-
redemptive flowering of the grace for whose restoration
Christ was born and crucified in the flesh. In the liturgical
books of the Greek Church, the Mother of God is seemingly
omnipresent on every day of the liturgical year,[40] but during
the twelve days of Christmas, she receives special honours in
canticles of outstanding praise, and on the second day she has
a feast all of her own, the Synaxis of the Most Holy Theotokos, instituted after the Council of Ephesus in 431. On this
second day of the Byzantine Christmas, the Mother of God
appears before the Church as the Mystical Vine carrying in
the branches of her arms 'the bunch of grapes that was never
husbanded'. In the ecstasy of love she sings to her Child,
'Thou art my fruit, thou art my life; from thee have I learned
that I remain what I was. Thou art my God: for seeing the
seal of my virginity unbroken, I proclaim thee to be the
unchangeable Word, now made incarnate.'[41]

Among the saints of Advent and Christmastide are several
of the champions of Catholic Faith in the consubstantial
Trinity during the fourth century: St Nicholas of Myra (6

[39] In the *novus ordo* of the West, the first of January is called the 'Solemnity of
Mary, the Mother of God'. In the Missal of 1962 it is called, as it had been for
many centuries, the 'Circumcision of Our Lord' because of the passage read as
the Gospel. However, both the Collect and the Postcommunion place most
emphasis on the divine motherhood of our Lady.

[40] See S. Eustratiadès, *Theotokarion* (Chennevières-sur-Marne, 1931), and J.
Ledit, *Marie dans la liturgie de Byzance* (Paris, 1976).

[41] *Menaion*, p. 292.

December), who was one of the Fathers of the First Council of Nicaea (325) and as zealous in orthodox faith as he was generous in fraternal love; St Ambrose (7 December), who would not surrender his cathedral to the Arians; St Damasus (11 December), the Pope whose 'tome' condemned the chief Trinitarian and Christological heresies of the fourth century; St Eusebius (16 December), the Bishop of Vercelli, who suffered exile for his fidelity to Nicaea and the just cause of St Athanasius; St Sylvester (31 December), the Pope who sent legates to Nicaea; and St Basil the Great (1 January in the East, 2 January in the *novus ordo* of the West), who, among many other heroic works as pastor, liturgist and father of monks, defended the true divinity of the Son against the Eunomians and the true divinity of the Holy Spirit against the Macedonians. It is splendidly appropriate that our Lord should invite the heroes of Nicene orthodoxy to the Christmas feast, for these are the men who confessed the truth at the centre of the Christmas faith: the Virgin's Child is 'very God of very God'.[42]

God grants certain of His saints the grace of a special devotion to the human birth and infancy of the Son of God. Among the Fathers we should single out St Jerome, whose lionlike anger gave way to lamblike joy when he knelt before the Crib. He called Bethlehem 'the most glorious place on earth'[43] and selected it as the most gloriously suitable place on earth for a monastic life of poverty embraced in imitation of the poor and infant Christ. St Íte of Killeedy, in sixth-century Ireland, lived at a great geographical distance from Bethlehem, but she received from the Holy Child the grace of the utmost intimacy: He visited her and drank from her breast. 'The nursing done by me in my house', she said, 'is no

---

[42] As the hymn *Adeste fideles* reminds us: 'God of God,/ Light of Light,/ Lo, He abhors not the Virgin's womb;/ Very God, Begotten, not created' (EH 28).

[43] *Epistola* 58, no. 3; PL 22:581.

nursing of a base churl: Jesus with Heaven's inhabitants is against my heart every night.'[44] In the Middle Ages, the lifelong devotion of St Bernard of Clairvaux to the Christmas mystery began one Christmas Eve when, as a sleepy little boy, he was given a vision of 'the infant Word . . . being born of the Virgin His Mother, fairer in form than all the sons of men'.[45] One Christmas Day, four centuries later, St John of the Cross, while at ease with his brethren at recreation, took the image of the Holy Infant from the Crib and danced round the room, singing all the while: *Mi dulce y tierno Jesús*, 'My sweet and tender Jesus,/ If thy dear love can slay,/ It is today.'[46]

Foremost among the apostles of Christmas is St Francis of Assisi, who said that 'the birthday of the Child Jesus . . . was the feast of feasts, on which God, having become a tiny infant, clung to human breasts.'[47] When one of the friars felt tempted to fast on the day when Christmas fell on a Friday, the Fool of God replied by saying that, far from being inclined to fast, he had the urge to honour the Infant God by smearing the very walls with meat![48] Francis could not even utter the name 'Bethlehem' without stammering with emotion, 'like the bleating of a sheep'.[49] Three years before his death, ever the faithful son of the Roman Church, he obtained the Pope's permission for the making of a replica of the Manger, in order to arouse devotion to the Child Jesus and His birth.

[44] 'Jesus and Saint Íte', a poem dating from about 900, in *Early Irish Lyrics: Eighth to Twelfth Century*, ed. G. Murphy (Oxford, 1956), p. 27.

[45] William of St Thierry, *Sancti Bernardi vita prima* cap. 2; PL 185:229A.

[46] See Father Bruno ODC, *St John of the Cross*, ET (London, 1936), p. 226.

[47] Thomas of Celano, *The Second Life of St Francis*, bk. 1, chap. 151, no. 199; Marion A. Habig, ed., *St Francis of Assisi: Writings and Early Biographies* (London and Chicago, 1973), p. 521.

[48] Habig, *St Francis of Assisi*, pp. 521f.

[49] Habig, *St Francis of Assisi*, 'The First Life', p. 301, n. 86.

He has a crib made ready, hay brought in, and an ox and an
ass led to their places. The friars are summoned, the people
arrive, the forest resounds with voices, and the venerable
night is rendered solemn and radiant by a multitude of bright
lights and by resonant and harmonious hymns of praise. The
man of God stands before the crib, filled with devotion,
bathed in tears and overflowing with joy. Solemn Mass is
celebrated over the crib, with Francis, the levite of Christ,
chanting the Holy Gospel. Then he preaches to the people
standing about concerning the birth of the Pauper King,
whom, when he wished to name Him, he called, out of
tender love, the 'Babe of Bethlehem'.

The local squire, Sir John of Greccio, a 'virtuous knight
and true', said that he saw 'a beautiful little boy asleep in the
crib', whom 'the blessed Father Francis embraced in his arms
and seemed to wake from sleep'.[50] Having thus received the
Child-God from Heaven by miracle, Francis passed Him on
to later generations by example. '[H]e gave into the arms of
his followers that most precious of all babies, the *Bambino
Gesù*. The magnitude of the gift can be judged of in the
subsequent art, and from that moment there appears in in-
tensified form the cult of the Christ Child; the Infant King is
the *Gran Piccolino Gesù*, our Beloved, whom St Anthony
holds in his arms, the one baby who is everybody's brother.'[51]

The Arts of Christmas

The iconography of the Nativity, and indeed of all the other
mysteries of Christ, has been shaped both by the dogmatic
Faith of the Church and by the mystical contemplation of her

---

[50] *Legenda maior* 10, 7; Q VIII:535.
[51] N. de Robeck, *The Christmas Crib* (London, 1937), p. 54. St Francis was
probably not the sole originator of the Christmas Crib: see L. Gougaud, 'La
Crèche de Noël avant St François d'Assise', RSR 2 (1922), 26–34.

saints, their Mary-like pondering of the things of Jesus in their hearts (cf Lk 2:19, 51).[52] The first representations of the Madonna and Child and of the Adoration of the Magi, whether carved in stone on sarcophagi or painted on the walls of the catacombs,[53] coincide with the heroic endeavours of St Helena to protect the sacred places of the Saviour's life on earth. Through the preaching and example of St Bernard and St Francis, from the thirteenth century onwards the Child-God begins to appear as a real and lovable baby. In the sculpted Nativity in the rood screen at Chartres, the Mother of God lies, as she does in Byzantine icons, on a couch beside the Manger, in a posture of divinely contemplative repose, but now, doubtless through the new devotion to the incarnate mysteries, she shows humanly tender affection towards the Divine Infant and loosens the swaddling clothes around His neck.[54] In Giotto's 'Presentation in the Temple' [see art plate 1], the *Gran Piccolino* seems frightened by Simeon's words about the sign and the sword (cf Lk 2:34f.) and stretches out His arms for reassurance from His Mother.[55]

The Nativity of our Lord has inspired Christian poets in every age of the Church. The lyrics of St Ephrem and St Romanos have been incorporated into the official liturgies of the Syriac and Byzantine Churches. So admired was Romanos's hymn, with its refrain, 'He is born for us, a young child, God before the ages', that for many years it was chanted each Christmas Day at a special performance for the delight of the Byzantine Emperor.[56] In every period, all the great poets of

---

[52] Cf Second Vatican Council, Dogmatic Constitution on Divine Revelation, *Dei Verbum* (1965), no. 8.

[53] Cf G. Schiller, *Iconography of Christian Art*, vol. 1 (London, 1971), fig. 245.

[54] Ibid., fig. 181.

[55] Cf G. Basile, *Giotto: The Arena Chapel Frescoes*, ET (London, 1993), p. 122.

[56] *Prooimion* to *Hymn 1 on the Nativity*; SC 110:50. On the annual performance, see E. Wellesz, *A History of Byzantine Music and Hymnography*, new ed. (Oxford, 1961), p. 190.

Christendom have laid their gifts at the Crib. During his imprisonment in Toledo, St John of the Cross composed a ballad on the Trinity, Incarnation and Nativity, which, on the day of his escape, 'haggard, unshaven, and dirty' and leaning on the grille of the parlour, he recited to the nuns who gave him refuge.[57] Some Christian poets even made the Christmas mystery the chief matter of their art. This was true of St Robert Southwell, a Jesuit martyr of Elizabethan England. Time and again, however much the terrors of Tyburn shocked his imagination, the joys of Bethlehem seemed to embolden his heart. On a 'hoarie Winters night', while the hunted missionary stands 'shivering in the snow', he is 'surpris'd . . . with sodaine heate' by the 'Burning Babe'.[58] The martyr has made his choice: for love of the Child-God and His true Church he will suffer the freezing hatred of the world: 'Almightie babe, whose tender armes can force all foes to flie,/ Correct my faultes, protect my life, direct me when I die!'[59]

If we follow the opinion of certain of the Fathers and most of the medievals, then, by some kind of charism of prophecy, the Birth of Christ was even honoured with an eclogue by the greatest poet of pagan Rome. Virgil, 'the Father of the West',[60] looked forward to the coming of Jesus, the infant King of the Jews: 'Begin, auspicious Boy, to cast about/ Thy Infant Eyes, and, with a smile, thy Mother single out.'[61] The poem is prophetic not just in its striking details

[57] Cf Crisógono de Jésus OCD, *The Life of St John of the Cross*, ET (London, 1958), pp. 115f.
[58] 'The Burning Babe', in *The Poems of Robert Southwell SJ*, ed. J. H. McDonald CSC and N. P. Brown (Oxford, 1967), p. 15.
[59] 'A childe my Choyce'; ibid., p. 13.
[60] See Theodor Haecker, 'Betrachtungen über Vergil, Vater des Abendlandes', in *Essays* (Munich, 1958), pp. 433–74.
[61] Virgil's 'Fourth Eclogue' in the version in *The Works of John Dryden*, vol. 5 (Berkeley, 1987), p. 97.

(the return of the 'Virgin', the 'Boy' who will 'end the iron race at last'), but also, as Chesterton noticed, in its 'tone and incidental diction', in which we feel a 'potential sympathy with the great event'.[62] No wonder, then, that Constantine should read the poem to the Fathers assembled at Nicaea,[63] or that Dante should call its noble Roman author, with his *pietas* and reverence for the 'tears of things', the 'glory and light of other poets'[64] and be willing to follow his courteous Mantuan shade through the terrors of the underworld.

Of modern English writers none devoted more of his thinking to the 'cosmic value' of Bethlehem than the man whose judgment of Virgil we have just invoked, Gilbert Keith Chesterton. According to his friend and biographer Maisie Ward, each of Chesterton's Christmas writings 'goes to the heart of his thought'. 'Some men, it may be, are best moved to reform by hate, but Chesterton was best moved by love, and nowhere does that love shine more clearly than in all he wrote about Christmas.'[65] In his Christmas articles and poems, Chesterton turns calmly from holly to the Hypostatic Union, from turkey and plum pudding to the Persons of the Trinity and then back again. Such surprising juxtapositions are very Catholic, evidence of a sacramental mind. Chesterton wanted to prove that the comforting delights of Christmas, all the warmth of families around the fire and the tree, come directly from the colossal dogmas of Christmas. 'Definite doctrines' bear fruit in 'general humane festivals',[66] because what is definitely true is that God is so humane that, for the love of man, He assumed human nature. Such orthodoxy,

[62] Ibid.
[63] Cf *Oratio ad sanctorum coetum* cap. 21; PL 8:403B.
[64] Cf *Inferno* 1, 82.
[65] Cited in G. K. Chesterton, *The Spirit of Christmas: Stories, Poems, Essays*, ed. Marie Smith (London, 1984), p. 7.
[66] *The Illustrated London News*, 7 Jan. 1911; new ed., in The Collected Works of G. K. Chesterton, vol. 29 (San Francisco, 1988), p. 18.

said Chesterton, is revolutionary. The dramatic dogmas of the Incarnation and Nativity put down the mighty from their seat and exalt the lowly. 'There is in this buried divinity an idea of *undermining* the world.' [67] Belief in a God 'born like an outcast or even an outlaw' re-casts from top to bottom 'the whole conception of law and its duties to the poor and outcast'. Even the human merriments of the feast have an apologetical power, the capacity to work a spiritual revolution in the poor fool who has said that there is no God: 'Any agnostic or atheist whose childhood has known a real Christmas has ever afterwards, whether he likes it or not, an association in his mind between two ideas that most of mankind must regard as remote from each other; the idea of a baby and the idea of an unknown strength that sustains the stars.' [68]

If ever he wonders why no other anniversary so cheers the human heart, the atheist will have to consider the Christian claim that no other anniversary is the birthday of the God in whom all human hearts find their rest. Even the imagination of Thomas Hardy, whom Chesterton once described (to his later regret) as 'a sort of village atheist brooding and blaspheming over the village idiot',[69] made the Christmas connection and expressed a nostalgia for childhood's faith that, by God's mercy, may have been for him a saving *fides implicita*:

> So fair a fancy few would weave
> In these years! Yet, I feel,
> If someone said on Christmas Eve,
> 'Come; see the oxen kneel
> In the lonely barton by yonder coomb
> Our childhood used to know',

[67] G. K. Chesterton, *The Everlasting Man*, new ed., in The Collected Works of G. K. Chesterton, vol. 2 (San Francisco, 1986), p. 313.
[68] Ibid., p. 302.
[69] *The Victorian Age in Literature* (London, 1913); new ed., in The Collected Works of G. K. Chesterton, vol. 15 (San Francisco, 1989), p. 483.

> I should go with him in the gloom,
> Hoping it might be so.[70]

Paul Claudel, the greatest French poet and dramatist of the modern age, was converted through the Christmas mystery, that is, by the Child-God and His Blessed Mother. The date was the twenty-fifth of December 1886, 'the gloomiest day of winter, and the blackest afternoon of rain over Paris, Vespers in the half-night of Christmas'. The place was the cathedral of Notre Dame. Claudel was eighteen, confused and without faith, the victim of the scientific positivism of his age and schooling. As he listened to the choir singing Vespers, our Lady showed him the Blessed Fruit of her womb, that is, by her prayers manifested to his mind the truth of her Son. All at once, as the smoke of the incense 'rose up and spread out', Claudel saw Mary in the Church, the Church in Mary, and Jesus in both: '*Notre-Dame*, the Woman-Church, with loud voice, full of God, setting up her Magnificat'. The shadows of scientific doubt were scattered. 'Nothing to be done against this eruption, like the world, in the very depths of my entrails, of the Faith!'[71] That same Christmas, after Midnight Mass, in the town of Lisieux, a girl, just five years younger than Claudel, received her own grace of conversion, not from unbelief to faith but from a natural childishness of emotion to a supernatural childlikeness of mind. 'Jesus, who became a child for me, deigned to bring me forth from the swaddling clothes and imperfections of childhood.'[72] St Thérèse thereby learned one of the fundamental principles of her spiritual doctrine: to follow the

---

[70] 'The Oxen', in *The Complete Poems of Thomas Hardy* (London, 1976), p. 468.

[71] Paul Claudel, 'Le 25 décembre 1886', in *Oeuvre poétique* (Paris, 1957), p. 771.

[72] *Lettres* 201; in *Oeuvres complètes: Textes et dernières paroles*, ed. Jacques Longchampt (Paris, 1992), p. 559.

Little Way, it is not enough to be by age the youngest in the family. Even little sisters must convert and conform to the Infant Word in the Manger if they want to enter the Kingdom of Heaven.

The Christmas Revolution

This book has been written in the conviction that, through the mystery of His human birth and infancy, the King of Heaven can work a royal revolution in the souls of men, giving them new graces of conversion, of return to His gentle rule. 'For a Child is born to us, and a Son is given to us, and the government is upon His shoulder. . . . His empire shall be multiplied, and there shall be no end of peace' (Is 9:6f.). In the restless hearts of men, the Child who is wonderful shall hold sway, the Prince of Peace put an end to strife. When a man is first incorporated into Christ through faith and Baptism, or when the believer is restored to a living union with Christ by Penance, then indeed the Virgin's Child is born in him anew. Thus the birth of Christ, once accomplished in the flesh, can be repeated again and again in the Spirit, in the heart and the womb of the Church. By tradition, this 'spiritual birth' is the theme of the second Mass of Christmas Day, the Mass of the Dawn, but in fact on every day of human history, through the 'invisible mission' of the Son,[73] it can be said *Hodie Christus natus est*. . . . 'Today is the dawn of a new redemption, of the restoration of the old, and of everlasting joy.' To us this day, by the grace of the Holy Spirit, God the Father sends His Son, making new Nazareths and Bethlehems of our souls.

The primary goal of this book is theological and therefore more speculative than practical.[74] Before all else, it seeks

---

[73] Cf ST 1a q. 43, a. 5, ad 2.
[74] Ibid., q. 1, a. 4.

understanding, through the wisdom of the Church's Fathers and Doctors, of the human birth of the Only-Begotten of the Father. Now the wisdom to be found in the sermons and *Summae* of the saints was not merely acquired by study but also infused by the Spirit. Through the intimacy of their union with Christ by charity, through their high endowment with the Holy Spirit's Gift of Wisdom, they had a 'connatural' familiarity with the realities of the Faith. They did not just 'know about' the things of God; in the words of Blessed Denys the Areopagite, often quoted by St Thomas, they 'suffered' them, experienced them at first hand.[75] Thus the Christ Child whom they contemplated with faith-enlightened minds, they embraced with love-enkindled hearts. By their poverty and purity, a Jerome or a Francis understood the Manger with connatural depth.

In the spirit of the Fathers, then, this book proposes the Christmas mystery as a treasury of truth for instruction and of grace for imitation. I am urging Christians to awake to the unsuspected power of this most familiar and beloved feast: 'Acknowledge, O Christian man, your dignity—it is God's nature you share; do not, by an ignoble life, fall back into your old baseness.'[76] The Christmas Gospel, anticipating the Paschal proclamation, contains everything Christendom needs, everything the individual Christian needs, for spiritual restoration. Such was the claim of a poet in the last of England's Catholic centuries, those happy years before Tudor lust and greed laid bare the choirs. With his eyes fixed on the Child-God and His Virgin Mother, he imitates the Fathers and makes of the Christmas dogma a charter for human dignity.

> Out of your slepe aryse and wake,
> For God mankynd nowe hath ytake

---

[75] Ibid., 2a2ae q. 45, a. 2.
[76] St Leo the Great, *In nativitate Domini, sermo* 1, no. 3; SC 22B:130D.

Al of a maide without eny make;
Of al women she bereth the belle.
Nowel!

And thorwe a maide faire and wys
Now man is made of ful grete pris;
Now angelys knelen to mannys seruys,
And at this tyme al this byfel.
[Nowel!]

Now man is brighter than the sonne;
Now man in heuen on hye shal wone;
Blessyd be God this game is begonne,
And his moder emperesse of helle!
[Nowel!][77]

No wonder that a Puritan parliament should have banned
the birthday of Christ,[78] for the Christmas feast, even in a
Protestant country, is a loud re-assertion of the Catholic
Creed, the confounding of Calvinism and of every other
heresy of despair. The world of time, it says, is not a prison.
By His birth from the undefiled womb and His Resurrection
from the intact tomb, the eternal Word has broken the cycle
of decay. Man, in Christ, can be brighter than the sun. He
can even share in the brightness of the Son. Not only in its

[77] Greene, p. 16, n. 30.

[78] 'The House spent much Time this Day about the businesse of the Navie,
for settling the Affairs at sea, and before they rose, were presented with a
terrible Remonstrance against Christmas Day, grounded upon divine Scriptures: 2 Cor 5:16; 1 Cor 15:14, 17; and in honour of the Lord's Day, grounded
on these Scriptures: John 20:1; Rev 1:10; Ps 108:24; Lev 23:7; Mk 15:8; Ps
84:10; in which Christmas is called Anti-Christ's-masse, and those Masse-
mongers and Papists who observe it etc. In consequence of which, Parliament
spent some Time in Consultation about the Abolition of Christmas Day, pass'd
orders to that Effect, and resolv'd to sit on the following Day, which was
commonly called Christmas Day': *The Flying Eagle Gazette*, 24 Dec. 1652, cited
in *A Christmas Book: An Anthology for Moderns*, ed. D. B. Wyndham Lewis and
G. C. Heseltine (London, 1928), pp. 10f.

glorious finality but even in its humble present moments, human history bids welcome to its Lord. '*This day* the King of Heaven has deigned to be born of a Virgin, that He might bring back to Heaven man who was lost.'

I

'HOW GREAT THE MYSTERY!'

The Mysteries of the Life of Jesus

O magnum mysterium,
et admirabile sacramentum
ut animalia viderent Dominum natum,
iacentem in praesepio.
Beata Virgo,
cuius viscera meruerunt portare Dominum Christum.
Ave Maria, gratia plena, Dominus tecum.

How great the mystery
and wondrous the sacred sign,
that beasts should look upon the Lord
lying lowly in the stall!
O Blessed Virgin,
whose womb was found worthy to bear Christ the Lord.
Hail Mary, full of grace, the Lord is with thee.[1]

The human birth of the Son of God is a mystery in the strict theological sense: a divinely revealed reality that little ones can understand but not even learned ones can comprehend.[2]

---

[1] Responsory at Matins on the fifth, sixth, and seventh days of the Octave of the Nativity of our Lord, *Breviarium romanum* (1962).

[2] R. Garrigou-Lagrange OP, 'The mysteries of the supernatural are incomprehensible and indemonstrable, but the testimony to them is analogically

Theological mysteries are truth and therefore light for the mind, but the truth is so vast, the light of such intensity, that the mind is dazzled and amazed. When a man meets a mystery of the faith, he finds not a deficiency but an excess of intelligibility: there is just too much to understand.[3] Reverence for supernaturally revealed mystery is therefore not reason's abdication, but reason's recognition, through faith, of a grandeur transcending its powers. 'If it searches diligently, piously, and soberly,' say the Fathers of the First Vatican Council, 'reason, enlightened by faith, attains, by God's gift, a certain most fruitful understanding of the mysteries . . . but it never becomes adequate to investigating them in the way it does the truths that constitute its proper object.'[4] Like the ocean, the revealed mysteries of God have a visible surface, beneath which lie hidden and unfathomable depths.

After that of the Blessed Trinity, the mystery par excellence is the Incarnation of God the Son. 'Of all the works of God', says St Thomas, 'this surpasses reason more than any other, since one cannot conceive of God doing anything more wonderful than that true God, the Son of God, should be made true man.'[5] When 'the Incomprehensible willed to be comprehended',[6] He confirmed His divine incomprehen-

---

intelligible': De revelatione, vol. 1, new ed. (Rome, 1950), p. 169. To comprehend something is to know it as fully as it is knowable. But God is infinitely knowable. Therefore, God can be comprehended by a created intellect only if created intellects can know infinitely. But no created intellect can know God infinitely. Therefore, no created intellect can comprehend God (cf ST 1a q. 12, a. 7).

[3] 'As the eyes of bats are in relation to daylight, so is the intellect of our soul in relation to those things which are by nature the most evident of all' (Aristotle, Metaphysics 2, 1; 993b).

[4] First Vatican Council, Dogmatic Constitution on the Catholic Faith, Dei Filius, chap. 4; DS 3016.

[5] SCG 4, 27.

[6] [I]ncomprehensibilis voluit comprehendi (Pope St Leo the Great, Epistola dogmatica ad Flavianum; DS 294).

sibility by the very fact of His human comprehension, for, in His infinite intelligence, He did something far surpassing any act that unaided finite intelligence could have expected of Him. Thus, as St Thomas goes on to say, 'whoever diligently and piously considers the mysteries of the Incarnation will find a depth of wisdom so great that it surpasses all human knowledge. . . . To the man who considers it piously, more and more wonderful aspects of this mystery are manifested.'[7] When he looks into the Crib, he sees something tiny and seemingly as easy for his mind to grasp as for his arms to embrace—a newborn baby. But then faith recalls that this newborn baby is the eternal God, that the Creator of the universe has become small in humanity while remaining great in Divinity, and the pious student falls astonished to his knees: 'How great the mystery and wondrous the sacred sign!' Wonder, which is the beginning of philosophy, is also the prerequisite for theology. In the exercise of his science, as in the conduct of his life, the theologian must convert and become like a child, recovering and preserving a sense of astonishment at the grandeur of what God has revealed in His Son.[8] Just as Peter and John 'went out' to see the Empty

[7] SCG 3, 54. Origen said that 'the explanation of this mystery [of the Incarnation] is beyond the capacity of the whole creation of the heavenly powers' (De principiis 2, 6, 2; PG 11:211A). Matthias Scheeben points out that one of the things that make the Hypostatic Union so hard for our minds to grasp is the absence of any suitable analogy. The closest we get to an analogy would seem to be the unity of man as a composite of body and soul, but that suggestion 'presents great difficulties': Handbuch der katholischen Dogmatik, vol. 2, new ed. (Freiburg, 1933), p. 884.

[8] 'In their early years, we tell little children about "Baby Jesus", and then we say, "He is God", and this image of the Baby Jesus, who is God, is enough to awaken in their hearts great acts of faith and love. These acts are very silent, they take place in a kind of spiritual night, but the night is lit up by this beautiful name "Jesus", which enables them to enter into the highest mystery of Christian revelation, the mystery of the Trinity, the mystery of a plurality of persons within the Godhead': Charles Journet, Entretiens sur la Trinité (Saint-Maur, 1999), p. 17.

Tomb (cf Jn 20:3), so, according to the Angelic Doctor, 'the man who wants to explore the mysteries of Christ must somehow *go out of himself*'.[9] This movement outwards, this Christological ecstasy, is an intellectual as well as a moral conversion. The theologian must be ready to break away from the dull conventions of his conceptuality, as well as from the deadly habits of his carnality, and to conform himself to the ever fresh wisdom and wonder of the Church. Year by year, after the high drama of Holy Week and Easter and the calm contemplation of the weeks after Pentecost, she insists that her children go back to the humble beginning, to share the prophets' yearning for Christ to come and the Virgin's joy at His birth. Thus, by the law of her praying, the Church establishes the law of believing and therefore of theologizing. The liturgy's ceaseless return to Advent and Christmas proves beyond doubt that these and all Christ's other mysteries are unsearchably rich in meaning, repaying unceasing contemplation.

In this chapter I shall try to explain why the mysteries of the Word Incarnate, especially those of His birth and infancy, are so great, both in themselves and in what they can do for the poor sons of Adam for whose salvation He was born. Here, as throughout this book, I shall try to understand the revealed truth to be found in the Gospels with the help of the Fathers, the liturgy and, as the Church herself recommends,[10] St Thomas Aquinas.

[9] *Lectura super Ioannem*, cap. 20, lect. 1.

[10] In recent centuries, the Angelic Doctor has been commended to the students and teachers of philosophy and theology in a long line of Papal documents beginning in the Middle Ages and reaching as far as Pope John Paul II's encyclical *Fides et ratio* (1998). Pope Leo XIII's encyclical *Aeterni Patris* (1879) only sets out in programmatic detail what is commonly taught by all.

1. The Mysteries of Christ in Scripture and Tradition

The Greek word *mystêrion* means something secret or hidden.[11] However, the very naming of a thing as 'mystery' indicates that it is not altogether unknown, even if it is never fully grasped, for the altogether unknown is the altogether unnamed. Thus, in the Epistles of St Paul, the 'mystery' is first of all God's plan for man's salvation, which, having been hidden 'for ages and generations', has now been revealed and accomplished through the Incarnation of the Son (cf Col 1:26).[12] According to St Thomas, the reason why the mystery of the Incarnation was hidden 'for ages and generations' is that it proceeds from that most hidden of things, the loving will of God: 'The things also that are of God no man knoweth but the Spirit of God' (cf 1 Cor 2:11). 'Therefore, the cause of the Incarnation was hidden from everyone except those to whom God revealed it through the Holy Spirit: "But to us God hath revealed them, by His Spirit. For the Spirit searcheth all things, yea, the deep things of God" (1 Cor 2:10).'[13] The mystery of the love of God in Christ Jesus cannot be known at all without divine revelation and, even when revealed, cannot be comprehended (cf Eph 3:19); as St Thomas says, in its immensity it 'surpasses every created intellect and the knowledge of all'.[14] Thus, the mystery *is* Christ Himself, or rather it is 'the whole Christ', the Head and Bridegroom in union with His Mystical Body and Bride.

[11] A mystery, says St Thomas, is a 'hidden thing' (*res abscondita*); see *Super epistolam ad Colossenses*, cap. 1, lect. 6.

[12] 'For Paul, the mystery is the wonderful revelation of God in Christ. God, hidden in eternal silence, "who dwells in inaccessible light, whom no man has ever seen or can see" (1 Tim 6:16), has revealed Himself in the flesh. . . . Christ is the personal mystery, since He reveals the invisible Godhead in the flesh': Odo Casel OSB, *Das christliche Mysterium*, new ed. (Regensburg, 1960), p. 23.

[13] *Super epistolam ad Ephesios,* cap. 1, lect. 3.

[14] Cf ibid., cap. 3, lect. 5.

'This mystery (*mystêrion*) is a profound one, and I am saying that it refers to Christ and the Church' (RSV, Eph 5:32; cf Col 1:27). It is through the incorporation of Jews and Gentiles into the one Body of Christ that the Trinity's mysterious plan of love is fulfilled (cf Eph 3:4–6).

The Greek word *mystêrion* was rendered in early Christian Latin as *mysterium*, though also as *sacramentum*, a word that, according to classical usage, means in general a sacred thing or action and in particular the sacred oath taken by the soldiers of the Roman Empire, the *sacramentum militiae*. Tertullian was the first to use it for the purposes of Christian theology, a usage for which St Augustine gave the definition that became classical: 'sacred sign'.[15] For many centuries, the two words, *mysterium* and *sacramentum*, were used interchangeably in the Latin Church, since either of them could be used to mean a visible reality with invisible depths of sacred meaning and power, *sacramentum* emphasizing more the visible aspect, *mysterium* the invisible.[16] In the liturgical text with which this chapter began, *sacramentum* is used as a synonym of *mysterium* taken in the broad sense. By the twelfth century *sacramentum* had been narrowed in meaning to signify one of the seven efficacious signs of grace instituted by Christ. *Mysterium* continued to have a broader range of meaning, including both the revealed mysteries of the Faith (for example, the *mysterium incarnationis*) and the sacramental mysteries (the *sacra mysteria*). In the Byzantine Church, the proper name for the Sacraments has always been *mystêria*. That is why the Greek Fathers used the name *mystagôgía* for the teaching that the bishop gave to the newly baptized

---

[15] On Tertullian's use of *sacramentum*, see E. de Backer in *Pour l'histoire du mot 'sacramentum'*, ed. J. de Ghellinck SJ, vol. 1, *Les Anténicéens* (London, 1924), pp. 59–152.

[16] Pope St Leo the Great speaks of the *sacramentum incarnationis* and the *sacramentum resurrectionis* (ibid., p. 17).

during Easter Week about the Sacraments that they had just received. St Cyril of Jerusalem (†386) begins his *Mystagogical Lectures* by saying, 'Long have I wished to speak to you . . . of these spiritual and heavenly mysteries.'[17]

The word *mysterium* has been used in the Tradition not only of the Person of the Incarnate Word and the seven Sacraments of His Church but also of the successive stages and states, actions and sufferings, of the Word in His human nature, from His conception in the Virgin's womb to His ascent to the Father's right hand: the *mysteria vitae Iesu*.[18] Each of these is a particular event, in its circumstances fixed in time and space, but, according to the teaching of the Church, it also has a universal efficacy, the capacity to touch men of all times and places. From the beginning, the saints, both the unlettered and the learned, have regarded the mysteries of the life of Jesus as fathomless stores of truth and grace, somehow ever present and active in the liturgy of the Church.

In the early years of the second century, St Ignatius of Antioch speaks of the virginity of Mary, the birth of her Son and His death on the Cross as 'three mysteries of proclamation'. They were 'wrought in the silence of God', but now they speak with a divine eloquence, though their true meaning is lost on 'the prince of this world'.[19] St Irenaeus, in the second century, invokes the mysteries of Christ as part of his defence of the Faith against the Gnostics. Taking up and developing a word and idea of St Paul's, he argues that the Divine Word Incarnate 'recapitulates' and thus inaugurates the renewal of the whole life of man from conception to

[17] *Catecheses* 19 [*Mystagogica* 1], no. 1; PG 33:1065A.

[18] On the theology of the mysteries of Christ, see A. Grillmeier SJ, *Mit Ihm und in Ihm*, new ed. (Freiburg, 1976), pp. 716–35; and *Die Mysterien des Lebens Jesu und die christliche Existenz*, ed. Leo Scheffczyk (Aschaffenburg, 1984).

[19] St Ignatius of Antioch, *Epistola ad Ephesios* 19; in *The Apostolic Fathers*, ed. J. B. Lightfoot, vol. 2, sec. 1 (London, 1885), pp. 76ff.

death (cf Eph 1:10). 'He . . . passed through every age, becoming an infant for infants, a child for children . . . a youth
for youths . . . [and so on] . . . that He might be a perfect
master for all.' [20] St Irenaeus gives most emphasis to the physical effectiveness of the mysteries in our salvation. Origen
(†254), by contrast, gives greater prominence to their power
as moral examples. Despite his many errors, the great
Alexandrian displays a touching devotion to the humanity of
the One he calls 'my Jesus' and presents the whole life of the
Lord as a kind of 'parable', a pedagogical instrument employed by the divine Logos in order to communicate His
truth to men.[21]

In the fourth century those Fathers who defended the true
divinity of the Word also expounded the infinite dignity and
effects of His human acts. In his youthful work *De incarnatione*, St Athanasius shows that the 'achievements' (*katorthô-
mata*) of the eternal Logos in the flesh are 'of such a kind and
so great that anyone wishing to expound them would be like
men who gaze at the vast expanse of the ocean and try to
count its waves'. The goal of these mysteries is immense,
nothing less than the deification of man: 'He was made man
that we might be made God, and He made Himself seen
through a body that we might have a sense of the unseen
Father.' [22] In his preaching on the several feasts of the Church's
year, St Gregory Nazianzen urges his congregation 'to know
the power of the mystery',[23] to be more than mere spectators
and instead to play a personal role in the divine drama reenacted at the altar. In some way, the sacred liturgy enables the
members of the Mystical Body to re-live the mysteries of

[20] *Adversus haereses* 2, 22, 4 (PG 7:784A); cf 3, 18, 7 (PG 7:938B).
[21] See Hans Urs von Balthasar, *Origen: Spirit and Fire*, ET (Washington, D.C.,
1984), pp. 120ff.
[22] *De incarnatione*, no. 54; PG 25:192C.
[23] Cf *Oratio* 1, no. 4; PG 35:397B.

their Head. On Easter Day, every Christian can be a Joseph of Arimathea and 'beg the Body from him that crucified Him', thereby laying hold of 'that which cleanses the world'.[24] On the feast of the 'Theophany', remembering how 'God was manifested to man by [temporal] birth', Gregory calls on those who are still of the Gentiles to 'run with the Star and bear your gifts with the Magi'. The birth in Bethlehem, though an event in the past, is not a mere thing of the past: 'Even now the angels are rejoicing, the shepherds are startled by the blinding light; even now the star is coming from the East towards the great and inaccessible Light.'[25] Every man can partake of the mysteries of Christ, because, in assuming the form of a servant, the Son of God in a certain manner united Himself to every man, 'bearing all me and mine in Himself'.[26] He assumed a complete human nature and lived out a complete human life, because 'what is not assumed is not healed, but what has been united to God is saved.'[27]

The theology of the mysteries is not exclusive to the Greek Fathers. St Augustine speaks famously of 'the whole Christ, Head and Body'.[28] Christ and His Church are together like one flesh, one person, one man, one Son. Therefore, what the members endure, the Head, for their salvation, makes His own, and all that He is and does in the flesh He communicates to them as a grace. Thus when Christ was tempted by the devil in the wilderness, 'we were tempted in Him, [and] in Him we overcome the devil'.[29] The mysteries of the Saviour's life offer an external grace of good example, a *disciplina morum*,[30] but each of them also

[24] Cf ibid., 45, no. 24; PG 36:656C.
[25] Ibid., 19, nos. 12 and 13; PG 35:1057C.
[26] Cf *Oratio* 30, no. 6; PG 36:109C.
[27] *Epistola* 101, no. 32; SC 208:50.
[28] Cf *Enarratio in psalmum 54*, no. 3; PL 36:629.
[29] *Enarratio in psalmum 60*, no. 3; PL 36:724.
[30] Cf *De vera religione* cap. 16, no. 32; PL 34:135.

contains the secret of an inward grace, the hidden and abid-
ing power to sanctify.

In his sermons on the Church's year, Pope St Leo the
Great continues the same doctrine: '[J]ust as the totality of
the faithful, born of the baptismal font, has been crucified
with Christ in His Passion, resurrected with Him in His
Resurrection, and placed at the Father's right hand in His
Ascension, so it is likewise born with Him in [His] Nativity.'[31] 'Christ's Ascension is our elevation, and where the
Head has gone before in glory, there the Body is called to
follow in hope. . . . For the Son of God, having made them
one body with Himself, has now placed at the right hand of
the Father those whom the poisonous enemy threw out of
their first blissful habitation.'[32] Now while all men have the
potentiality for participation in our Lord's Ascension and
other mysteries, that potentiality must be actualized, by the
working of the Holy Spirit, through faith, charity, and the
Seven Sacraments. The effects the Son of God achieved by
His human actions performed once for all on earth are now
communicated through the sanctifying rites of His Church:
'[W]hat was visible in our Redeemer [in the mysteries of His
life] has passed over into His [sacramental] mysteries.'[33] The
graces He acquired for us by His visible human actions on
earth are now communicated to us by the visible signs of the
Sacraments of His Church. Thus, in the Sacrament of Baptism, we share in His temporal birth by being reborn in water
and the Holy Spirit, and we plunge into His death and
Resurrection by dying to sin and being raised up to new life.

The Cistercians of the twelfth century, seeking to follow
the poor Christ in poverty, anticipate the Franciscans of the
next century in their devotion to the sacred humanity and its

[31] *In nativitate Domini, sermo* 6, no. 2; SC 22B:138.
[32] *De ascensione Domini, sermo* 2, no. 2; SC 74:140.
[33] Ibid., *sermo* 1, no. 4; SC 74:138.

mysteries of infirmity and glory. In the theology of St Bernard of Clairvaux, Blessed Guerric of Igny and the rest, the dogmatic faith of Nicaea and Chalcedon lays the foundation for monastic meditation on the Gospels and the feasts of the liturgical year:

> He was incomprehensible and inaccessible, invisible and altogether beyond all our conceiving. But now He wanted to be comprehended, He wanted to be seen, He wanted to be reached by our conceptions. How was this to be, you may ask? Well, to be sure, by lying in the Manger, sleeping on the Virgin's lap, preaching on the mountain, spending the night in prayer, hanging on the Cross, pallid in death, "free among the dead" (Ps 87:6) and triumphant over Hell, rising on the third day and showing the Apostles the places of the nails, the signs of His victory, and at the end, in their presence, ascending to the heights of Heaven. Which of these cannot be considered in truth, piety, and holiness? And whichever of them I consider, it is God I am considering, and in every one of them my God Himself is there.[34]

In directing the devotion of his brethren to the mysteries of the sacred humanity, St Bernard makes them recall the principal object of that devotion, namely, the Divine Person of the Son of God, to whom the sacred humanity is hypostatically united. Remember, he says, the Divine Agent of these human actions, the Divine Subject of these human sufferings:

> I beg you to look and to see how perceptive is faith; consider more carefully the keenness of its sight. It recognizes the Son of God sucking at His Mother's breast, recognizes Him hanging on the Tree, recognizes Him dying. Yes, the thief recognizes Him on the gibbet, the Magi in the stable, the one seeing Him fixed by nails, the others wrapped in swaddling clothes; as for the centurion, he recognized Life in death. The Magi saw the Power of God in the infirmity of the

[34] St Bernard of Clairvaux, *In nativitate B. Mariae sermo*, no. 11; L-R 5:282.

infant's tender body; the centurion saw the Supreme Spirit in
the yielding of the spirit.[35]

William of St Thierry adds a Trinitarian perspective: in the
redeeming mysteries of the Son, we hear the loving voice of
the Father:

> And whatever He did, whatever He said on earth, even the
> insults, the spitting, the buffeting, even the Cross and the
> tomb, was nothing but you yourself [O Father] speaking in
> your Son, appealing to us by your love and stirring up our
> love for you.[36]

Contemplation of the mysteries of Christ is by no means
restricted to the Latin Middle Ages. A great Armenian con-
temporary of St Bernard, St Nerses Shnorhali, expounded
their healing power in a poem of four thousand verses, *Jesus,
the Father's Only Son.* Like many of the saints, Nerses was
convinced that he was the chief of sinners, his wickedness
exceeding that of every other man since Adam, and so in his
misery he addresses Jesus in each of His mysteries, both
divine and human, in the Old Testament and in the New. In
every case he invokes the mystery as a motive for the Lord to
show mercy. For example, in a stanza on the Gadarene
swine, he says, 'Rebuke also in me the wicked demon,/ As
once you did in them,/ And throw him into the deepest
abyss/ As you did with the herd of swine.'[37] Two centuries
later in the Latin West, the *Meditationes vitae Christi*, long

---

[35] *In Epiphania sermo* 2, no. 4; L–R 4:4.

[36] *De contemplando Deo* cap. 6, no. 13; PL 184:374B. 'When He handed the
Sacrament of His Body and Blood to His disciples, He said to them, "Do this
in remembrance of me".' For this reason festivals were instituted in the Church,
so that, as we re-present His Nativity, Passion, Resurrection, and Ascension, all
the kindness, sweetness, and charity that He shows us in all these things may
always be recent in our memory' (St Aelred of Rievaulx, *Sermo 8 in
Annuntiatione B. Mariae*; PL 195:251BC).

[37] *Jésus Fils unique du Père*, no. 336; SC 203:106.

thought to be the work of St Bonaventure but now attributed to another medieval Franciscan,[38] did in prose what Nerses had done in verse: it told the story of the life of the Lord, providing for each event a forceful moral application. Thus the anguish that precedes our Lady's finding of her Son in the Temple can be a consolation to the soul that has to endure aridity and apparent abandonment by God: 'It should not lose heart but rather earnestly seek Him by persevering in sacred meditation and good works, and then it will find Him again.'[39] In the fourteenth century, the *Vita Christi* of Ludolph the Carthusian serves a similar purpose; it is intended to move the reader to take up his cross and follow the Lord. Reading it helped to convert St Ignatius Loyola: 'While reading the life of our Lord and of the saints, he stopped to think, reasoning within himself: "What if I were to do what Francis did, or to do what Dominic did?"'[40] In his own *Spiritual Exercises*, Ignatius places 'contemplation' of the mysteries of the life of Jesus at the centre of the retreat. Employing the imagination as well as the intellect and affections, we look at the God-Man in order, by His light, to make a good 'election', that is, a decision about the state of life to which He is calling us. As the retreatant thinks about the Crib and the Cross and all the other humiliations taken upon Him by the Lord, he should say to himself, '[A]ll this for me.'[41]

In the Third Part of the *Summa theologiae*, St Thomas raises up the Patristic and medieval tradition of devotion to the mysteries of the life of Jesus to a new dogmatic plane. He follows his discussion of the Hypostatic Union with an

[38] John de Caulibus of San Gimignano.

[39] *Meditationes vitae Christi*, cap. 14; CCCM 153:64.

[40] J Tylenda, ed., *A Pilgrim's Journey: The Autobiography of Ignatius of Loyola* (San Francisco, 2001), p. 47.

[41] *Spiritual Exercises*, no. 30.

exposition of the successive episodes of the life of Jesus.[42] In the Prologue of the Third Part he states his intention to speak, first, of the 'mystery of the Incarnation' and, secondly, of '*the things that our Saviour, that is, God Incarnate, did and suffered*'.[43] And all the things that God Incarnate did and suffered, from the Virgin's womb to the right hand of the Father, are dealt with in thirty-three questions, one for each year of His earthly sojourn.[44] The human life of the Son, sent by the Father and returning to Him, follows a circular course, like that of the cosmos, indeed like that of the *Summa* itself.[45] St Thomas considers in turn the Son of

---

[42] St Thomas also sketches a Christology of the mysteries in his little work *De humanitate Christi*. In his Eucharistic hymn *Verbum supernum prodiens*, he sums up the Lord's mysteries in a single verse: 'In birth man's fellow-man was He,/ His meat while sitting at the board;/ He died, his ransomer to be,/ He reigns to be his great reward' (trans. J. M. Neale, E. Caswall et al., EH 330). Blessed Denys the Carthusian says of this verse: 'The Son did indeed give Himself to us, by offering Himself to us as our Saviour, and advocate. In other ways, too, He communicated Himself to us, because, by being born and living in the world, He made Himself the fellow [*socium*] of men; at the Last Supper He gave Himself to us as food; by dying as the price of our deliverance; at last in our heavenly homeland He will give Himself to us as our objective and beatifying reward' (*Enarratio in evangelium secundum Lucam*, cap. 1, a. 5; DCOO 11:404D).

[43] In the prologue to the first of the questions of the life of our Lord, St Thomas says that he is going to 'consider those those things which the incarnate Son of God did or suffered in the human nature united to Him' (ST 3a q. 27). As for what inspired St Thomas to write this systematic theology of our Lord's life, Father J.-P. Torrell OP has made the following suggestion: 'In all probability, Thomas found the idea for it in a text of St John Chrysostom when he was writing the *Catena aurea* and took it up again in his commentary on St Matthew's Gospel. It is therefore once again Thomas's Biblical and Patristic formation which is at the origin of the construction of this treatise. It is particularly striking to note that Thomists neglect to comment on it; the only exception here is Suarez, though his perspective is more an exhortation than a dogmatic exposition' (J.-P. Torrell OP, 'Le Thomisme dans le débat christologique contemporain', in *St Thomas au XXe siècle* [Paris, 1999], p. 390).

[44] ST 3a qq. 27–59.

[45] Cf ST 1a q. 2, prol.

God's entry (*ingressus*) into the world,[46] the progress (*progressus*) of His human life on earth,[47] His departure (*exitus*) from this world to the Father (cf Jn 13:1)[48] and His exaltation after this life.[49] When he comes to the question of the kind of life our Lord lived on earth, he states a fundamental principle for any theology of the mysteries: the way the Divine Word lives as man must be in harmony with the threefold purpose of His Incarnation, namely, the manifestation of truth, deliverance from sin and the opening up of access to God.[50]

Throughout the treatise on the life of our Lord, the Angelic Doctor shows that, since its subject is a Divine Person, this life develops in a different way from that of any mere man. Because of its Hypostatic Union with the Divine Word, the sacred humanity is endowed with certain wonderful perfections, especially in grace, knowledge and power.[51] As the Gospel tells us (cf Lk 2:52), the Lord Jesus grows both in body and at one level of His human mind, in His natural 'experimental knowledge', but at the higher, supernaturally bestowed levels of human knowledge, the beatific and infused, there is no growth.[52] By the beatific knowledge, from His conception, He knew in the Word all reality, past, present and future,[53] while by the infused knowledge He knew, at least habitually, everything knowable by man through natural knowledge as well as everything made known to man through Divine Revelation.[54] The Son of

[46] ST 3a qq. 27–39.
[47] Ibid., qq. 40–45.
[48] Ibid., qq. 46–52.
[49] Ibid., qq. 53–59.
[50] Cf Ibid., q. 40, a. 1. See also chap. 4 on the purpose of the Nativity (pp. 234f.).
[51] ST 3a qq. 7–13.
[52] Ibid., q. 12, a. 2.
[53] Ibid., q. 10, a. 2.
[54] Ibid., q. 11, a. 1.

God has to be perfect in His human nature, because He has assumed human nature in order to bring the whole race of man back to perfection.[55] Likewise, as the God-Man grows up, there is no increase in His grace.[56] 'Nothing can be greater, or can be thought to be greater, than someone being the Only-begotten of the Father. Hence nothing can be greater, or can be thought to be greater, than the grace with which Christ was full.'[57] Even as an unborn child resting in His Mother's womb, or as a young man sweating over the carpenter's bench, Jesus is 'full of grace and truth' (cf Jn 1:14). Such plenitude, though proper to Him as God-made-man, is not, so to speak, a merely private privilege. The habitual grace that He has as an individual man (*singularis homo*) is really identical with the grace He has as Head of the Church.[58] One of the reasons why as man He receives the grace of the Holy Spirit in such fullness is 'so that somehow it might be poured out from [His soul] to others'.[59] 'And of His fulness we all have received, and grace for grace' (Jn 1:16). If Christ and His Church are in this way like 'one mystical person', then it should not surprise us to learn that the grace-filled 'works of the Head are in some way the works of the members'. The merits of Christ profit us 'by causing grace in us through the Sacraments, by which grace we are stirred to meritorious works'.[60]

If the sacred humanity has certain perfections because of the person who assumed it, it has certain defects because of the purpose for which it was assumed. Not only is there an

[55] Ibid., q. 9, a. 1.
[56] Ibid., q. 7, a. 12.
[57] Ibid., q. 7, a. 12, *sed contra*.
[58] 'The personal grace by which Christ's soul is justified and the grace that is His as Head of the Church, justifying others, are the same in essence, though different in reason' (ST 3a q. 8, a. 5).
[59] Ibid., q. 7, a. 9.
[60] Cf *De veritate* q. 29, a. 7, ad 11.

ineffable union of the divine and human natures in the one
Person of the Word, there is also a strange mingling of
sublimity and lowliness in the assumed human nature. From
conception to the Cross, the Incarnate Son is both 'beholder
and wayfarer'.[61] His soul is blissful through gazing on the
Father, yet both soul and body are passible for the purposes
of redemption. Other men *contract* suffering and death as a
consequence of Original Sin, but the Son of God *assumes* a
body subject to suffering and death in order to suffer and die
in that body for our salvation.[62] He could have become man
in an entirely glorious way without infirmity, dazzling men
into submission by the radiance of His countenance, but
instead He chose to live out His human life in a condition
similar to our own, 'in the likeness of sinful flesh' (Rom 8:3).
He is absolutely sinless, indeed impeccable, free from all spark
of sin and from ignorance,[63] and yet, in love, He took upon
Himself the weaknesses of body that we endure as a penalty
for the sin of Adam, so that, in our place, He might make
atonement for our sin.[64] He wanted to be not just human but
believably human, someone whom other men would recognize as their fellow and an accessible example of virtue.[65] His
soul, too, was passible, though His passions never ran ahead
of reason or dragged it in their tow.[66] Such subjection to
reason did not make His spiritual pains less than any other
man's but rather greater, just as His bodily suffering, too, was
greater than anything any other man has suffered or ever will
suffer. The Saviour suffers knowingly and willingly with the
full engagement of His human intellect. His mind ensures

[61] Cf ST 3a q. 15, a. 10; M. J. Scheeben, *Handbuch der katholischen Dogmatik*,
vol. 3, new ed. (Freiburg, 1933), p. 275.
[62] Cf *Compendium theologiae*, lib. 1, cap. 226.
[63] Cf ST 3a q. 15, a. 1–3.
[64] Cf ibid., q. 14, a. 1.
[65] Ibid.
[66] Ibid., q. 15, a. 4.

that His grief goes unrelieved by any encouraging consideration or consoling distraction.[67]

The Christology of the mysteries, rooted in the contemplation and exposition of the Gospels, was common among the Fathers, but it was unusual in the age of Scholasticism and not developed by many of St Thomas's later disciples.[68] Perhaps the purest expression of the Thomistic doctrine is to be found not in a book but in the paintings of the Dominican *beatus* Fra Angelico, Brother John of Fiesole.[69] In his images of the life of Jesus, Dominican and other saints of later Church history appear alongside the original actors of the Gospel drama. When Christ is cradled by His Mother's love or mocked by the world's hatred, Dominic and his sons and daughters contemplate and adore Him, drawing upon His light and mercy. When the friars woke up each morning in San Marco, the radiant frescoes in their cells confirmed what they had learned from the articles of the *Summa*, namely, that what Jesus once did and suffered could even now touch and transfigure the souls of men.

During the Baroque age, Cardinal Bérulle and his disciples in the French School, with their mysticism of the 'states' of Jesus, kept the traditional doctrine of the mysteries alive. 'He wanted', says Bérulle, 'to pass through all the degrees, conditions, and lowlinesses of our humanity, and make Himself like the children of men except for ignorance and sin, and

[67] Ibid., q. 46, a. 6.

[68] One later theologian who did follow St Thomas's example was the Jesuit Cardinal Billot. The first part of his *De Verbo incarnato* is devoted to 'the mystery of the Incarnation itself', while the second considers 'the things God incarnate did and suffered' (new ed. [Rome, 1927], pp. 13ff., 383ff.).

[69] See my book *The Beauty of Holiness and the Holiness of Beauty: Art, Sanctity, and the Truth of Catholicism* (San Francisco, 1997); and A. Hertz, *Fra Angelico* (Freiburg, 1981). On medieval Dominican devotion to Christ in His sacred humanity, see the essays in *Christ among the Medieval Dominicans: Representations of Christ in the Texts and Images of the Order of Preachers*, ed. K. Emery and J. Wawrykow (Notre Dame, 1998).

thereby to restore, sanctify, and deify in His own person all the miseries and lowlinesses He wanted to take for our salvation.'[70] While their external, material circumstances pass away, the grace of each of the mysteries remains alive and effective in the glorified Christ in Heaven. In the seventeenth century, and indeed in every age, the doctrine of the mysteries of Christ was given practical expression in the lives of those saints who, while worshipping Jesus as true God and true man in one person, as every Christian does, had the special vocation of drawing the attention of the faithful to one of the mysteries of His humanity in particular: the Sacred Heart (St Margaret Mary and St John Eudes), 'Jesus living in Mary' (St Louis-Marie de Montfort, 'the last of the great Bérullians'), the Holy Infancy (the Carmelites of Beaune), the Sacred Passion (Louis Chardon OP), Jesus in the Blessed Sacrament and Jesus in the persons of the poor (St Vincent de Paul).

In the nineteenth century, Matthias Scheeben, inspired by St Thomas and the Greek Fathers, incorporated the doctrine of the *mysteria vitae Iesu* into his great *Dogmatik*. In the Apostles' Creed he finds eight mysteries of Christ's humanity: 'born of the Virgin Mary', 'suffered under Pontius Pilate', 'died', 'was buried', 'He descended into Hell', 'He rose again from the dead', 'He ascended into Heaven' and He 'is seated at the right hand of God the Father almighty'. He divides the eight into two groups of four, of which the first enacts 'a descending movement from the height of Heaven into the depths of the earth' and the second 'an ascending movement, which, beginning with the glorious Descent of Christ's soul, continues from the underworld into the glorious height of Heaven'.[71] This pattern of descent and

[70] Pierre de Bérulle, *Opuscules de piété*, new ed. (Grenoble, 1977), p. 183.

[71] *Handbuch der katholischen Dogmatik*, vol. 3, p. 262.

ascent can be seen in the Christmas hymn of St Ambrose, *Veni, Redemptor gentium*:

> From God the Father He proceeds,
> To God the Father He speeds;
> His course He runs to death and Hell,
> Returning on God's throne to dwell.[72]

The mighty Word, in the human nature He assumed, traversed the heights and depths of the cosmos that in His divine nature He created. He came down so low, so that we who lie prostrate may be raised up aloft with Him in Heaven.

At the beginning of the twentieth century, a great son of Ireland and St Benedict, Blessed Columba Marmion, opened up the rich graces of *Christ in His Mysteries* for the sanctification of a wide readership of priests, religious and laity. 'Our Lord being God,' he said, 'the least circumstances of His life, the least features of His mysteries, are worthy of attention. Nothing is little in the life of Jesus. The Eternal Father looks upon the smallest action of Christ with more delight than He looks upon the whole universe.'[73] Building on the doctrine of St Thomas and the French School, Marmion argued that we contemplate the mysteries not only 'to see how Jesus lived and strive to imitate Him' but also 'that our souls may participate in each special state of the Sacred Humanity and draw forth from it the proper grace that the Divine Master attached to it, in meriting this grace as the Head of the Church for His Mystical Body'.[74] Since Head and members together make up the one 'whole Christ', all of Christ's mysteries are in some way *our* mysteries: He wants us to partake of each of the states of His life and to draw from it the special grace it contains. Such participation can be

[72] The translation is by J. M. Neale, in EH 14.
[73] Columba Marmion, *Christ in His Mysteries*, new ed. (London, 1939), p. 7.
[74] Ibid., p. 25.

achieved through meditation on the Gospels, but above all by 'uniting ourselves, in the Liturgy, to the Church, the Bride of Jesus'.[75]

Between the two world wars, the German Benedictine Odo Casel proposed a controversial theory, brilliant in its intuitions and attractive to the supporters of the Liturgical Movement but somewhat muddled in its metaphysics, about how the mysteries of Christ live on in the liturgy. While rightly arguing for a more than merely 'intentional' or 'subjective' mode of presence (the mysteries are present in a way that is higher than the presence of an idea in the mind), Casel offered no clear account of the higher, 'objective' mode of presence other than to affirm, again rightly, that it was a work of the God-Man in cooperation with the Church.[76] He also drew too sharp a distinction between 'the historical man Jesus' and 'the *Kyrios Christos*', even though he affirms that 'this twofold figure [*Doppelgestalt*] . . . is one and the same Jesus Christ'.[77]

Thank God, the Church does not depend for the exposition of Christ's mysteries on the insights of her theologians, however learned and pious. She has a teaching office, exercised by the Pope and the bishops with and under him, through which the Spirit of Truth takes the things of Jesus and manifests them to us (cf Jn 16:15). Since the middle of the twentieth century, the doctrine of Christ's mysteries has entered the documents of the Spirit-guided Magisterium. In his encyclical *Mediator Dei*, Pope Pius XII showed how, in the course of the ecclesiastical year, the faithful can 'take their

[75] Ibid., p. 19.

[76] See A. Schilson, *Theologie als Sakramententheologie: Die Mysterientheologie Odo Casels* (Mainz, 1982), pp. 271ff. Some critics have also challenged Casel's high esteem for the Hellenistic mystery religions, which seems to be accompanied by a correspondingly low view of the Old Testament (ibid., pp. 265ff.).

[77] Odo Casel OSB, 'Mysteriengegenwart', *Jahrbuch für Liturgiewissenschaft* 8 (1928), 155.

part in Christ's mysteries' so that 'the divine Head of the Mystical Body may live in all the members with the fulness of His holiness.' The mysteries are present and active through the celebration of the sacred liturgy as 'examples to imitate' and 'treasures of sanctity for us to make our own':

> In the sacred liturgy, the whole Christ is proposed to us in all the circumstances of His life, as the Word of the eternal Father, as born of the Virgin Mother of God, as He who teaches us truth, heals the sick, consoles the afflicted, who endures suffering and who dies; finally, as He who rose triumphantly from the dead, and who, reigning in the glory of Heaven, sends us the Holy Paraclete, and who abides in His Church forever. . . . [T]he liturgy shows us Christ not only as a model to be imitated but as a Master to whom we should listen readily, a Shepherd whom we should follow, as Author of our salvation, the Source of our holiness, and the Head of the Mystical Body whose members we are, living by His very life. . . . Hence, the liturgical year, devotedly fostered and accompanied by the Church, is not a cold and lifeless representation of the events of the past, or a simple and bare record of a former age. It is rather Christ Himself, who is ever living in His Church. Here He continues that journey of immense mercy which He lovingly began in His mortal life, 'going about doing good' (cf Acts 10:38), with the design of bringing men to know His mysteries and in a way live by them. These mysteries are present and active, not in a vague and uncertain way,[78] as some modern writers hold, but in the way that Catholic doctrine teaches us. According to the Doctors of the Church, they [the mysteries of Christ's life] are shining examples of Christian perfection, as well as sources of divine grace, due to the merit and prayers of Christ. They still influence us because each mystery brings its own special grace for our salvation.[79]

[78] Pope Pius XII may be gently criticizing Dom Odo in this sentence.

[79] *Mediator Dei*, nos. 151–53, 163–65, in C. Carlen IHM, ed., *The Papal Encyclicals 1939–1058* (Raleigh, N.C., 1981), pp. 143–45.

This simple statement is a precious clarification of the doctrine of mysteries: Christ's mysteries 'still influence us', not in their historical circumstances, which are a thing of the past, but in their spiritual fruits, which abide for ever. The Pope emphasizes that they can be sources of grace by reason of 'the merit and prayers of Christ'. On earth, at each moment of His human life, our Lord merited grace for us. Now in Heaven, where He lives to make intercession for us at the right hand of the Father, He confers, through the Sacraments, the graces that before His death He merited for us.

Pope Pius's teaching was continued and extended by the Fathers of the Second Vatican Council in their Constitution on the Liturgy. In line with the decision of Blessed Pope John XXIII that the Council should present its teaching in the form of pastoral exhortation rather than dogmatic definition, *Sacrosanctum concilium* speaks in an uncomplicated way about how the mysteries of Christ continue to be efficacious throughout the ecclesiastical year:

> [Holy Mother Church] unfolds the whole mystery of Christ through the course of the year, from the Incarnation and Nativity to the Ascension, the day of Pentecost, and the expectation of a blessed hope and the coming of the Lord. Recalling thus the mysteries of redemption, she opens up to the faithful the riches of her Lord's powers and merits, so that these are in some way [*quodammodo*] made present for all time; the faithful lay hold of them and are filled with the grace of salvation.[80]

Towards the end of the twentieth century, *The Catechism of the Catholic Church* gave Christ's faithful the most detailed exposition of the subject ever found in a document of the Holy See. It insists that nothing in the life of God-made-man is futile or trivial. Everything—'from the swaddling clothes

---

[80] *Sacrosanctum concilium*, no. 102.

of his birth to the vinegar of his Passion and the shroud of his Resurrection'—is 'a sign of his mystery'.[81] The whole life of Christ is, in fact, an efficacious mystery of 'revelation . . . , redemption, and recapitulation'.[82] The riches of Christ belong to all, can be shared in by all. Not only does Jesus in all His life present Himself as our model, He also 'enables us to live in him all that he himself lived' and indeed *'he lives it in us'* [83] Himself. As an authority the *Catechism* quotes one of the saints of the French School, St John Eudes:

> We must continue to accomplish in ourselves the stages of Jesus' life and his mysteries and often to beg him to perfect and realize them in us and in his whole Church. . . . For it is the plan of the Son of God to make us and the whole Church partake in his mysteries and to extend them to and continue them in us and in his whole Church. This is his plan for fulfilling his mysteries in us.[84]

2. The Power of the Mysteries

According to the common doctrine of the Fathers and St Thomas, which is the doctrine re-asserted by the Church's Magisterium during the twentieth century, each of the mysteries of Christ, every human action and suffering of the Son of God on earth, makes its own special contribution to our salvation. Even now our souls receive light and mercy from the Birth in Bethlehem and the Finding in the Temple, the Agony in the Garden and the Crowning with Thorns, as well as from the supreme events of the Crucifixion, Descent into Hell and Resurrection.

[81] CCC 515.
[82] CCC 516ff.
[83] CCC 521.
[84] CCC 521, quoting St John Eudes, *Liturgy of the Hours*, Week 33, Friday, Office of Readings.

The Subject of the Mysteries

The proper subject of the mysteries of the sacred humanity is a Divine Person, the Father's eternal Word. Thus, while being finite in themselves, these human sufferings and actions acquire, through the Hypostatic Union, an infinite dignity and power. This is the earthly odyssey of God, the human biography of One of the Trinity. These events and deeds therefore hide within them a limitless abundance of truth and grace.

As man, but because He is God, Christ is the Head of the Church, the Head of all men. Moreover, as we have learned already from St Thomas,[85] Head and members are together 'like one mystical person', so that what belongs to the former can be poured out as a gift on the latter. What Jesus is or does in His human nature is for sharing—His merits and satisfaction, His Resurrection and Ascension. By the grace of the Holy Spirit, we can even share in the Sonship of God the Son, for 'by the act of [our] adoption a likeness of the natural Sonship is communicated to men'.[86] All of Christ's mysteries are meant to become *our* mysteries. This is the doctrine that Blessed Columba Marmion loved to preach in his conferences:

> [A]ll the graces that [our Lord] merited by each of His mysteries, He merited them in order to distribute them to us. He received the fullness of grace from His Father: *Vidimus eum plenum gratiae*; but He did not receive it for Himself alone; for St John at once adds that it is of this fullness we have all received: *Et de plenitudine eius nos omnes accepimus*; it is from Him that we receive it, because He is our Head, and His Father has made all things subject to Him.[87]

In a certain way, then, the subject of the mysteries is *the whole Christ*, Head and Mystical Body together.

[85] See p. 62.
[86] ST 3a q. 23, a. 1, ad 2.
[87] Marmion, *Christ in His Mysteries*, p. 15.

Trinitarian Mysteries

The Christological mysteries are also Trinitarian. Only God
the Son assumed human nature in the Virgin's womb, but
the operation of fashioning that human nature and uniting it
to the Son was common to the three Divine Persons.[88] The
proper subject of the incarnate mysteries is the Son alone,
but the whole Trinity is at work within them and by some of
them is explicitly revealed. When the angel Gabriel comes to
the Virgin Mary at the Annunciation, he opens up for her
the Trinitarian life of God: she is to conceive the Son of the
Father Most High through the overshadowing of the Spirit
(cf Lk 1:26ff.). At the Baptism and Transfiguration, the voice
of the Father acclaims the beloved Son, whether humbled in
the river or glorified on the mountain, and the Holy Spirit is
manifested in visible form, in the dove and the luminous
cloud (cf Mt 3:16f.; 17:5ff.). Some of the human actions of
the Son rise up from His sacred manhood to the Godhead
and display the reality of that manhood as well as the distinction of the Divine Persons. The Incarnate Son worships,
merits, offers sacrifice. With His human will, He does the
will of the Father (cf Jn 6:38) in perfect docility to the Holy
Spirit (cf Lk 4:1), and He prays to the Father, rejoicing in the
Holy Spirit (cf Lk 10:21). Other human actions of Christ
bring down blessings from Heaven and reveal more clearly
the Son's consubstantiality in divinity with the Father and the
Holy Spirit. In His miracles and in the forgiveness of sins,
our Lord, while still operating in His human nature, produces effects that surpass the powers of human nature.[89] Here
the Son acts together with the Father and the Holy Spirit,

[88] See pp. 185f.

[89] The distinction I am making here between two kinds of 'theandric' action
in Christ is based on one made by Cardinal Journet in *L'Église du Verbe incarné*,
vol. 2, *La structure interne de l'Église: Le Christ, la Vierge, l'Esprit Saint*, new ed.

employing the actions of the humanity (the thoughts and words and bodily gestures), as we shall see later,[90] as an instrument of the divinity.

Just as the whole Trinity was at work in the mysteries of our Lord's earthly life, so now in Heaven, by their common operation, all three Divine Persons communicate to men a share in the graces of the mysteries. It is God the Father who, in the Holy Spirit, draws us into the mysteries of the Son. Of the role of the Father, Dom Marmion says: '[W]hat makes Christ's mysteries ours is, above all, because the Eternal Father saw us with His Son in each of the mysteries lived by Christ and because Christ accomplished them as Chief of the Church.'[91] Another Benedictine, the polymathic abbess St Hildegard, likewise ascribes these words to the Father: 'What my Son, for love of man, suffered in the world appears before my eyes, for the Nativity, Passion, Burial, Resurrection, and Ascension of my Only-begotten did to death the death of the human race. And so [these mysteries] shine brightly in my presence, for I have not forgotten them, but to the end of the age they will make their appearance before me in all their radiance.'[92] We can relive the mysteries of our Head, because the Father has them—and us—eternally in mind. He sees the adopted sons in the true and natural Son, blessing them with all the blessings of the Spirit that pour forth from the Son's Most Sacred Heart (cf Eph 1:3).

(Paris, 1999), pp. 359f. In the first case, the human nature of our Lord serves as a 'secondary principal [efficient] cause', while in the second, it is an instrumental efficient cause (ibid.). Of the first set of actions we can and must say that the person of the Son *alone* is the agent: only He in His humanity, not the Father or Holy Spirit, worships, merits, offers sacrifice. However, with regard to the second set, we must affirm that the effect (e.g., raising Lazarus) is the work of the whole Trinity, of the Son with the Father and the Holy Spirit, using the human actions (words, gestures, etc.) as an instrument.

[90] See pp. 88f.

[91] Marmion, *Christ in His Mysteries*, p. 14.

[92] St Hildegard of Bingen, *Scivias*, visio 6, cap. 17; CCCM 43:245.

It is by the mission of the Holy Spirit that we are given access to the mysteries of the Son. 'But when the Paraclete cometh, whom I will send you from the Father, the Spirit of Truth, who proceedeth from the Father, He shall give testimony of me' (Jn 15:26). As Pope John Paul II has said, the Holy Spirit, through the teaching and Sacraments of the Church, 'unceasingly continues the historical presence on earth of the Redeemer and His saving work'.[93] What the Holy Spirit did once in the Incarnation, He does in similar fashion, again and again, in the Holy Sacrifice of the Mass. In the womb of our Mother Mary, He formed a fleshly body for the Son of God. On the altars of our Mother the Church, the Holy Spirit transubstantiates bread into that same fleshly body, the body that was born of the Virgin, nailed to the Cross, placed in the tomb, and raised in glory on the third day.[94] That is why in many of the Eucharistic prayers of Catholic Chris-

---

[93] Cf *Dominum et vivificantem*, no. 7.

[94] 'Although the Holy Spirit is sent by the Son and comes to us in the Son, He is, by the strongest of all appropriations, also the channel through which the Son is brought to us. As the aspiration terminating the Son's love, He urges the Son to deliver Himself up to us in the Incarnation and the Eucharist. As the flame issuing from the mighty ardour of the Son in His work of sanctification and unification in the womb of the Virgin, He brings about the origin, the hypostatic union, and the resulting holiness of the Son's human nature, and in the Eucharist effects the conversion of earthly substances into the Son's flesh and blood. After the hypostatic union and transubstantiation have been wrought, He lives on in the Son's flesh and blood with His fire and His vitalizing energy, as proceeding from the Son, and fills the sacred humanity with His own being to sanctify and glorify it. Particularly in the Eucharist, He glorifies and spiritualizes the Son's human nature like a flaming coal, so that it takes on the qualities of sheer fire and pure spirit. Straightway He makes use of the Eucharist as an instrument to manifest His sanctifying and transforming power to all who come into contact with it, and as a channel to communicate Himself to all who receive it and feast upon it. The body of Christ, as a spiritual gift which God presents to us and which we offer in sacrifice, has its origin from the fire of the Holy Spirit; it is permeated and encompassed by the Holy Spirit, who so transfigures and spiritualizes it that both the fire and the coal which the fire pervades with white heat seem to be one and the same

tendom, the priest calls expressly upon the Holy Spirit (in the so-called *epiklêsis*). The mission of the Paraclete is always the same: to unite us to the flesh-and-blood reality of the eternal Son made man. The living streams of the grace of the Holy Spirit flow forth, with the water and blood, from the pierced side of the Incarnate Son, and to that Incarnate Son His streams never cease to carry us on their tide, and only thus do we reach the Father. The principle stated by St John in his first epistle knows of no exceptions: 'And there are three that give testimony on earth: the Spirit and the water and the blood. And these three are one' (1 Jn 5:8). Neither in the Incarnation nor after Pentecost can we have the Son without the Spirit or the Spirit without the Son.[95] His work is not one of abstraction but of, as it were, an unending conversion to the phantasms, that is, to the flesh-and-blood reality of the mysteries of Christ. The Holy Spirit is, as St Cyril of Alexandria insisted against Nestorius, Christ's 'very own' Holy Spirit, not only the Spirit of the Father, but also the Spirit of the Son.[96] In His eternal procession, He proceeds from the Son, as well as from the Father, as from one principle.[97] And in His temporal mission, He is sent from the Father by the incarnate, crucified and risen Son to complete His work on earth, 'to transform us', as Pope John Paul says, quoting St Cyril, 'into His own risen image'.[98] He is not a Spirit of disincarnation; He does not alienate us from our Lord's incarnate reality but rather admits us unceasingly to its secrets.

---

object, and finally, it is flooded with the Holy Spirit, thus yielding up His fragrance in sacrifice, and His vitalizing energy in Holy Communion' (M. J. Scheeben, *The Mysteries of Christianity*, ET [St Louis, 1946], pp. 529f.).

[95] As the *Catechism* says: 'In their joint mission, the Son and the Holy Spirit are distinct but inseparable' (CCC 689).

[96] Cf *Adversus Nestorium* 4, 1; PG 76:172f.

[97] Cf the Second Council of Lyons, Constitution on the Blessed Trinity and on the Catholic Faith (1274); DS 850.

[98] Cf *Dominum et vivificantem*, no. 24.

The Power of Outward Example

The first way in which the mysteries of Christ contribute to our salvation is by offering us a pattern for our imitation. Jesus is our first and greatest Teacher (cf Mt 23:10), and like every good teacher, He teaches first by example.[99] By assuming our infancy, the divine Logos calls us to convert and become like little children.[100] His circumcision according to the prescription of the Law exhorts us to be obedient.[101] His efforts at the carpenter's bench reveal the dignity of labour.[102] In submitting to Satan's temptations, He warns us that no man in this life is safe from the devil's wiles.[103] By withdrawing to lonely places, He shows His disciples the need to give rest to their bodies, to dedicate certain times to prayer and to shun public acclaim.[104] The thinking in the Word's human mind and the love in His human heart, displayed in words but also in gesture and silence, are the model to which all men must conform if they are to be holy.

In all that He says and does as man, the Lord Jesus is a moral example and teacher in a way that infinitely surpasses the utterances and actions of His saints. The nobility of the lesson He teaches derives from the dignity and particular property of His Divine Person. He is the eternal *Word* of God, and so His 'whole earthly life—his words and deeds, his silences and sufferings, indeed his manner of being and speaking—is *Revelation* of the Father'.[105] Everything He says and does as man, even His silence before His accusers (cf Mk

[99] In each mystery, says Pope Pius XII, our Lord is 'a master to whom we should listen readily' (cf *Mediator Dei*, no. 163).
[100] See pp. 252f.
[101] Cf ST 3a q. 37, a. 1.
[102] See Pope John Paul II, *Laborem exercens*, nos. 118ff.
[103] Cf ST 3a q. 41, a. 1.
[104] Ibid., q. 40, a. 1.
[105] CCC 516.

15:4f.; Lk 23:9; Jn 8:6), is an instrument of ultimate prophecy, the means by which God the Father speaks that complete truth of which the utterances of the earlier prophets were but fragments (cf Heb 1:1). Whatever the Logos does in the flesh speaks volumes, volumes for which the cosmos itself has insufficient shelf room (cf Jn 21:25). However much they may be enlightened by the charism of prophecy, other teachers speak out of the obscurity of faith, but the human words of the Incarnate Son express the truth that He knows, even as man, by clear vision (cf Jn 1:18; 6:46).[106] By His personal property as Word, and by the perfections and achievements of His sacred humanity, the Lord Jesus is 'at once the mediator and the plenitude of the whole of revelation'.[107]

In each of His mysteries, Jesus, who is God and man in one Person, reveals not only God to man but man to man. Such is the teaching of Pope John Paul II and the Second Vatican Council:

> Only in the mystery of the Word Incarnate does the mystery of man truly become clear. For Adam, the first man, was a type of Him who was to come (cf Rom 5:14), namely, Christ the Lord. Christ, the New Adam, in the very revelation of the mystery of the Father and His love, fully manifests man to himself and brings to light his most high calling. . . . He who is the 'image of the invisible God' (cf Col 1:15) is Himself the perfect man who has restored in the sons of Adam that likeness to God which had been disfigured ever since the first sin.[108]

The poets and philosophers of the ancient world taught important truths about the nature of man and the purpose of

[106] See pp. 61f.

[107] See the Second Vatican Council's Dogmatic Decree on Divine Revelation, *Dei Verbum* (1965), no. 2.

[108] Second Vatican Council, Pastoral Council on the Church in the Modern World, *Gaudium et spes* (1965), no. 22.

human life, but only when God Himself had become man and lived a human life, from conception to death, only when He had conquered death by rising again in the flesh, was man able to decipher the enigma of his nature and to move towards a destiny surpassing all the imaginings of the poets and all the reasonings of the philosophers. It took God as man to show man what he truly is and to make him what he is meant to be. In everything that the Incarnate Word does in His human nature, both as child and as adult, the light of divine revelation shines upon the stages of human life, disclosing a grandeur unsuspected even by the wisest of the ancients. The most ordinary of earthly situations become, in Christ, occasions and instruments of heavenly illumination: the dependency of infancy upon the womb and the breast of a mother; childhood and youth; manual labour; fasting and praying, eating and drinking; the fellowship of friends; anguish of mind and agony of body; the act of dying and the state of being dead.[109]

The Power of Inward Grace

But the mysteries of the life of Jesus are more than just a series of dogmatic instructions and moral lessons. They provide not only a model for outward imitation but also a source of inward transformation, a treasury of divine grace. To use the jargon of the Schools, they sanctify us by an efficient as well as an exemplary causality; they not only show us how to

[109] In one of the few authentic sermons of St Thomas that have survived, a sermon for the First Sunday after Epiphany, he begins by saying that 'all the things that our Lord did or suffered in the flesh are salvific teachings and examples for us' (*Sermones*, no. 1, pars 1). Taking as his text, 'The Child Jesus advanced in wisdom and age and grace with God and men' (Lk 2:52), the Angelic Doctor says that 'since no age [of human life] is deprived of the way of salvation, especially the one that attains the age of reason, the adolescence of Christ is proposed as an example for adolescents' (ibid.).

be holy in the likeness of our Saviour but reproduce that likeness in our souls. From the fleshly birth of the Head comes the spiritual rebirth of the members.[110] When the divine Messiah takes on the Old Law at His Circumcision, He lifts the burden from other men.[111] The immersion of His body in the Jordan gives a new sacramental vocation to water.[112] His victory over Satan in the wilderness strengthens His faithful against temptation.[113] His Passion saves us by merit, satisfaction, sacrifice and redemption.[114] His Resurrection from the tomb is the source and model of our own resurrection, in soul and in body.[115] 'Redemption', says the *Catechism*, 'comes to us above all through the blood of his cross,[116] but this mystery is at work throughout Christ's entire life.'[117] As Pope Pius XII said, in each mystery, Christ is the 'Author of our salvation'.[118]

Everything the Incarnate Son does or undergoes in His human nature, even from His conception, is of saving benefit to us, because, even from His conception, He is exercising His priestly office of sanctification and salvation. The priesthood of Christ reached its finest hour on the Cross, but it began at the first moment of the Incarnation. The womb of the Virgin was the temple in which God became a priest. Even in the Manger, then, our Lord was acting as a priest, anticipating that supreme sacerdotal deed that He performed when He poured out His precious blood in atonement for our sins. As we have learned from St Thomas, the human

[110] Cf the text quoted from the Sermons of St Leo the Great on p. 277.
[111] Cf ST 3a q. 37, a. 1.
[112] Ibid., q. 39, a. 1.
[113] Ibid., q. 41, a. 1.
[114] Ibid., q. 48, a. 1–4.
[115] Ibid., q. 56.
[116] See Eph 1:7; Col 1:13–14; 1 Pet 1:18–19.
[117] CCC 517.
[118] Cf *Mediator Dei*, no. 163.

nature of Christ, from the first moment of His conception, enjoys certain perfections, including the beatific knowledge of God and the use of free will.[119] Since what is willed must first be known, St Catherine of Siena argues that the obedience to the Father in the Saviour's human will flows from the direct vision of the Father in His human intellect. 'What caused the great obedience of the Word?' She answers herself in the voice of the Father: 'The love which He had for me and your salvation. Whence proceeded this love? From the clear vision with which His soul saw the divine essence and the Eternal Trinity, thus always looking on me, the Eternal God.' [120] As soon as our Lord has a human intellect, He gazes with it upon the face of the Father: 'I speak that which I have seen with the Father' (Jn 8:38). Once equipped with a human will, He offers it up in loving obedience to the Father's saving plan: 'I came down from Heaven, not to do my own will but the will of Him that sent me. Now this is the will of the Father who sent me that of all that He hath given me I should lose nothing; but should raise it up again in the last day' (Jn 6:38f.). Having become a priest at the moment of His conception, He is able from that moment to act as priest, to offer Himself to the Father in atoning sacrifice for the sins of mankind. *'When He cometh into the world*, He saith: "Sacrifice and oblation thou wouldest not; but a body thou hast fitted to me. . . . Behold, I come to do thy will, O God"' (Heb 10:5ff.; cf Ps 39:7ff.).

In seeing and loving God the Father of Heaven, the Incarnate Son also sees and loves the sons of earth. Long taught within the Schools, this doctrine was incorporated into the Papal Magisterium by the Venerable Pope Pius XII:

---

[119] Cf ST 3a q. 34, a. 2 and 4. See pp. 61f.

[120] *The Dialogue of the Seraphic Virgin, Catherine of Siena*, chap. 135; ET by A. Thorold (London, 1925), p. 302.

[H]ardly was He conceived in the womb of the Mother of God when He began to enjoy the Beatific Vision, and in that vision all the members of His Mystical Body were continually and unceasingly present to Him, and He embraced them with His redeeming love. . . . In the Crib, on the Cross, in the unending glory of the Father, Christ has all the members of the Church present before Him and united to Him in a much clearer and more loving manner than that of a mother clasping her child to her breast, or that by which a man knows and loves himself.[121]

The *Catechism of the Catholic Church* refers to this text in a footnote in support of its teaching that 'Jesus knew and loved us each and all during his life, his agony, and his Passion and gave himself up for each one of us.'[122] This is the mystery that so haunted the Apostle: 'The Son of God . . . loved me and gave Himself for me' (Gal 2:20). When He was on earth, our Lord could not, by a natural human knowledge, know every single human being that has ever existed,[123] but by a supernatural human knowledge, by the Beatific Vision, He could and did know each one of us as an individual. The blessed see in God those things of which God is the origin. How much they see of creatures depends on how perfectly they see the Creator. At the very least we can be sure that they perceive 'those things that concern them'.[124] No soul sees God more perfectly than the soul of Christ does, because it is united to the Divine Word and therefore 'receives more fully than any other creature the influence of that light

[121] *Mystici corporis*, no. 75.

[122] CCC 478, note 118 (cf DS 3812).

[123] 'By this [experimental] knowledge the soul of Christ did not know all things simply, but all such as are knowable by the light of man's active intellect. Hence by this knowledge He did not know the essences of separate substances, nor past, present, or future singulars, which, nevertheless, He knew by infused knowledge' (ST 3a q. 10, a. 1, ad 3).

[124] Cf ibid., q. 10, a. 2.

in which God is seen by the Word Himself'.[125] The Incarnate
Word is the Head and Judge of all men, and so He has a truly
boundless interest in things human. Through the Beatific
Vision, therefore, our Lord knew all reality, past, present and
future, including the secrets of every human conscience. In
beholding the Father, the Son, even as man and on earth,
bore each of us in His mind and could thus keep each of us
in His heart.

From His conception, the human will of Christ is not
only on fire with love for us, but also, out of love, meriting
our salvation.[126] In each of His mysteries, from Mary's womb
to the hill of Golgotha, He merits for men a grace specifi-
cally designed for the state of human life which at that
moment He is sharing. The earthly life of Jesus is like one
long liturgy:

> [T]he whole life and conversation of Christ in mortal flesh,
> [says Blessed Dionysius the Carthusian] from the first mo-
> ment of the Incarnation to the moment of His giving up the
> ghost on the Cross, was like a continuous Mass and celebra-
> tion, by which He unceasingly offered Himself for us to the
> Father by a most ready will and prayed for us with the utmost
> affection, and whatever He prayed for by His deliberate will
> He obtained.[127]

'A single drop of blood'

But if our Lord was meriting our salvation in all of the
previous mysteries of His human life, why did He need to
suffer and die for our salvation? Why does the 'hour' of the
Passion (cf Jn 17:1) surpass all the previous moments of His

[125] Ibid., q. 10, a. 4.
[126] Cf ibid., q. 34, a. 3.
[127] Blessed Denys the Carthusian, *Elementatio theologica*, propositio 119;
DCOO 33:202.

temporal life? Why is it only as He gives up the ghost that He says, 'It is consummated' (Jn 19:30)? St Thomas answers the question as follows. First, he argues that there is no contradiction in the same thing belonging to the same person for different reasons. To take an example from British politics, a man might sit in the House of Lords as both a hereditary peer and a bishop of the established Church. Christ was likewise 'able to merit by later acts and sufferings the glory of immortality that He merited in the first moment of His conception, not so that it might be owed to Him more, but that it might be owed to Him through different causes'.[128] Secondly, if we are to understand why our Lord still needed to suffer after He had already merited so much for us by the earlier mysteries of His life, we must remember the exact sense in which His Passion is necessary for our salvation. It is not necessary by an unconditional necessity, as if it were absolutely impossible for God to save man in another way, though it does have a conditional necessity, that is, on the presupposition that God has decreed that His Son should suffer for our salvation. Again, our Lord did not have to suffer because of any kind of compulsion, for the Triune God willed it with the freedom of the divine will, and He Himself embraced it with the freedom of His human will. However, the Passion is necessary by a necessity of purpose and suitability as the means best suited for attaining the goal of man's salvation.[129] In the

[128] ST 3a q. 34, a. 3, ad 3.

[129] Cf ibid., q. 46, a. 1. St Thomas Aquinas's teacher, St Albert the Great, shows how the various kinds of necessity correspond to the various kinds of cause. Necessity by way of efficient causality is the necessity of coercion, where we have to do something because someone, an agent, forces us to do it. Necessity by way of material causality is the kind of necessity proper to material substances, which, by the physical laws of the visible cosmos, have to behave in a certain way (e.g., apples falling on to Newton's head by gravity). Necessity by way of formal causality is the necessity of nature; thus man is by necessity rational. Finally, there is necessity by way of final causality, where

De rationibus fidei, St Thomas points out that, in considering
the works of God, we must take into account the suitability
(*convenientia*) of the works, their contribution to the harmony
of the created order, as well as the omnipotence of the
Creator. For example, God created the great quantity of the
heavens and the vast number of the stars, not because it was
impossible for Him to act otherwise, but because it was
fitting for Him to act in this way—it was an enhancement of
the beauty of the universe, a lovely thing to do.[130] Similarly,
the atoning Sacrifice of Christ on the Cross, while surpassing
all His previous acts of self-oblation to the Father, crowns
and consummates them, thus perfecting the spiritual beauty
of His whole human life in the state of mortality.

Speculation about the necessity of the Passion for man's
salvation must not be allowed to obscure the 'foolishness of
God' (cf 1 Cor 1:18, 25), the prodigal excess of His charity
for fallen mankind (cf 1 Jn 4:10). 'O loving Madman!' cries
St Catherine of Siena in her own folly of love, 'Was it not
enough for thee to become incarnate, that thou must also
die?'[131] In this respect, theological meditation on the preceding mysteries of Christ's life serves a valuable purpose: it
makes the wise folly of the Passion stand out with even
greater clarity. In divine freedom with the Father and the
Holy Spirit, and in human freedom in the human nature that
is proper to Him, the Son willed man's salvation through the
endurance of a suffering exceeding by far what was strictly
necessary for man's salvation. In 1343, in the bull *Unigenitus*

---

something is necessary as a means to an end (for example, a man has to be just
if he wants to attain beatitude). St Albert concludes: 'By this kind of necessity,
which we call the necessity of fittingness (*congruentia*), we say that it was
necessary for God to become incarnate. This was supremely congruous with
our most beautiful [*decentissimam*] redemption' (*De incarnatione*, tract. 1; *Opera
omnia*, vol. 26 [Münster, 1958], p. 171).

[130] Cf *De rationibus fidei*, cap. 7.

[131] Catherine of Siena, *Dialogue*, chap. 30; ET by Thorold, p. 59.

Dei Filius, Pope Clement VI declared that, even though, because of the Hypostatic Union, just one drop of the Precious Blood would have been sufficient for man's salvation, Christ chose to pour it forth in superabundant streams.[132] St Thomas likewise sings of 'that blood whose least drops sovereign be/ To wash my worlds of sin from me'.[133] Each of the Saviour's sufferings (for example, His Circumcision), because of the Divine Person who was suffering it, had an infinite moral value and so, in itself, was more than sufficient to save us. But, in obedience to the Father and in the love of His Sacred Heart for us, Christ was ready to suffer more, immeasurably more.

St Thomas speaks for the whole Tradition when he argues that the human suffering of the Son of God, both in body and in soul, is greater than anything any other man in this life has ever suffered or could ever suffer.[134] He suffered not only alongside us, presenting an example of noble patience, but in our place, by making vicarious atonement for our sins; as St Thomas says, He 'ascribed them to Himself'.[135] The sinless Son of God endured an immensity of pain proportionate to the immensity of the wickedness for which He was making satisfaction. By 'patiently sustaining the evils of punishment', says St Bonaventure, He destroys 'in us the evils of guilt'.[136] Ours were the infirmities and sorrows that He bore, for ours was the iniquity that had been laid upon Him (cf Is 53:4ff.). 'Him who knew no sin [God] hath made sin for us, that we might be made the justice of God in Him' (2 Cor 5:21). The blessings of grace and glory that flow from the Cross of the New Adam exceed by far the curses of sin and death that

[132] Cf DS 1025.

[133] J. Austin's adaptation of R. Crashaw's translation of the *Adoro te devote* (WH 73).

[134] Cf ST 3a q. 46, a. 6.

[135] Ibid.

[136] Cf *Dominica 20 post Pentecosten, sermo* 2, no. 3; Q IX:432.

come from the fall of the Old Adam. 'Wherever sins increase, there grace has become superabundantly copious' (Rom 5:20). The Passion surpasses the other acts of our Lord's human life not because of any defect in the earlier mysteries but because of the excess of the final hour, the magnitude of the charity, divine and human, that it displays, and of the atoning effects that it delivers.

The foolishness of God is a hidden and transcendent wisdom. There is real reason in His seeming madness. The totality of our Lord's human sufferings is in harmony with the divine logic of the Incarnation, by which the Word makes His own everything that is human. The Triune God wants the Son to share as man in all the disabilities of sinful men—apart, of course, from those that imply a deficiency of grace. 'He bears the whole punishment of sin, so that He might wholly atone for sin.' [137] That is why He presses on to the end (cf Jn 13:1). From the afternoon of Good Friday to the early hours of Easter Sunday morning, His body lies in the tomb, and His soul descends into the Limbo of the Fathers, so that 'in both ways He might be like His brethren'.[138] The Holy Saturday mystery is, therefore, in St John Damascene's words, 'the culmination of the divine economy'.[139] He comes to seek and to save the lost and, in the divine folly of His love, is ready to pursue the search even into the depths of Hades.

The great final hour of the Saviour's Passion does not rob the preceding moments of His life of their power; on the contrary, as Cardinal Charles Journet says, it 'contained in itself the virtue of all His previous actions'. To help us understand this mystery, he suggests an analogy with language: 'We must picture to ourselves His entire life as a sentence where

---

[137] Cf St Thomas Aquinas, *In symbolum apostolorum*, a. 5.
[138] Cf St Thomas Aquinas, *3 Sent.* d. 2, q. 2, a. 1.
[139] *Homilia in sabbatum sanctum* 2; PG 96:601D..

each of the words has its own importance, but only receives its significance with the last of them.'[140] For example, all the words of institution are necessary for the Eucharistic consecration, but only when the last word is uttered does transubstantiation take place.[141] Journet quotes Dominic Soto in support of his interpretation:

> If, therefore, by reason of the person of Christ, each of His acts had in itself an infinite value, nevertheless, in effect, each of them was offered as a part of the whole that the Passion was to accomplish. That is why, though *de iure* His merits were all infinite, *de facto* the more numerous they were, the richer the grace the Passion pours out in the Sacraments. What I mean is that if God had suffered only the Passion without carrying out the acts that preceded it, the grace by which we become His members would be less ample. It would be absurd to deny that a particular effect of grace in us corresponds to each of the works of Christ. Were that not true, His works would be of no benefit to us, whereas we know that He gave His whole life for us. Now we can see that the power of the Sacraments can result from the whole life of Christ, even though it flows in a special way from His Passion.[142]

From 'Lo, I have come to do thy will, O God' to 'Father, into thy hands I commend my spirit', the Incarnate Son surrenders Himself, yields His human will, to the Father. The final act of obedience contained but also consummated His whole life of obedience.[143] Moreover, what the Passion gathered up, the Resurrection made perpetual. By raising

---

[140] Charles Journet, *L'Église*, vol. 2, p. 326.

[141] Cf ST 3a q. 78, a. 6.

[142] *4 Sent.* d. 1, q. 3, a. 5 (Venice, 1584), p. 74, cited by Journet, *L'Église*, pp. 327f.

[143] '[A]ll the mysteries of His existence are recapitulated in a supreme mystery, the mystery of His redemptive Death on the Cross' (Journet, *L'Église*, p. 324).

Him from the dead, the Father accepts the Incarnate Son's
sacrifice, His total gift of Himself, and sets the seal of the
Spirit on the great movement of self-oblation from conception to the Cross. By the mission of the Holy Spirit in the
Church, the mission of the Son in its totality is made present,
'renewed in the midst of the years' (Hab 3:2), and opened up
for participation by all the faithful. The chief means by
which the Holy Spirit makes Christ's mysteries present are
the Seven Sacraments and above all the Eucharistic Sacrifice,
to which all the others are directed.

The Instrumental Power of the Mysteries

St Thomas describes the humanity of Christ as an 'instrument' of His divinity.[144] Without losing anything of their
natural integrity, the human actions of Christ receive from
the divine nature, in the Person of the Word, a power surpassing the resources of any created person. 'His divine operation
employs His human operation, and the human operation
shares in the power [virtutem] of the divine.'[145] As man, but
because He is God, the God-Man can do things that no mere
man by his own might and main can do, such us 'cleansing
sins, illuminating minds by grace, and leading people into the
perfection of eternal life'.[146] When our Lord performs

[144] 'As Damascene says, the humanity of Christ was a kind of instrument of
the divinity, and so His actions could be salvific for us' (De veritate q. 29, a. 5, ad
9). In his study of the Greek Patristic sources of St Thomas's Christology,
I. Backes says that Damascene is the 'mediator' to Aquinas of the Athanasian
and Cyrillian doctrine of the instrumentality of Christ's humanity (Die
Christologie des heiligen Thomas von Aquin und die griechischen Kirchenväter [Pader-
born, 1931], p. 271). In his De incarnatione, St Athanasius writes: 'Though
powerful and the Creator of the universe, He fashioned for Himself in the
Virgin a body as a temple and made it His own as an instrument in which to
dwell and be known' (no. 8; PG 25:109C).
[145] ST 3a q. 19, a. 1, ad 1.
[146] SCG 4, 41

miracles, His human words and gestures (the shout to Lazarus, the making of paste from spittle, the touching of the deaf mute's tongue) become instruments of divine power in order to produce strictly divine effects.[147] The divine nature, says Thomas, quoting Leo the Great, 'shines forth in miracles', and the human nature 'submits to insults', yet 'each [of the natures] acts in communion with the other'. 'The human nature is an instrument of the divine action, and the human action receives power from the divine nature.'[148]

Like every doctrine of the Faith, the instrumentality of Christ's humanity can be misinterpreted and fall from the beauty of truth into the ugliness of error. To protect it from heretical abuse, St Thomas draws on his study of St Cyril of Alexandria in order to make some important clarifications. He says that the human nature of our Lord is not, as Nestorius thought, a 'separated' instrument, as if it were a human person inhabited and directed by the Divine Person of the Word. The assumed human nature is a 'conjoined' instrument, united to the divinity in the one Person of the Word, and therefore belongs as much to the Son of God as my hand belongs to me.[149] Again, we must not fall into the Apollinarian heresy and regard the sacred humanity as an inanimate, passive tool, like Michelangelo's hammer and chisel; it is an 'animate' organ, not only a material body but a spiritual soul endowed with intellect and will, with consciousness and freedom.

---

[147] Cf ibid. 'His touching of the leper was an action of the humanity, but the fact that that touch cured the leper from leprosy was due to the power of the divinity' (*Compendium theologiae* lib. 1, cap. 212).

[148] Cf ST 3a q. 43, a. 2.

[149] See *De veritate* q. 27, a. 4; ST 3a q. 13, a. 2; SCG 4, 41. St Thomas's theology of the instrumentality of the sacred humanity is 'formulated in such a way as to avoid the criticism that Cyril of Alexandria directed against the theme . . . as used by Nestorius': Édouard-Henri Weber OP, *Le Christ selon saint Thomas d'Aquin* (Paris, 1988), p. 180.

St Thomas is adamant that '*all* the actions and sufferings of Christ operate instrumentally, in the power of the Godhead, to effect our salvation'.[150] They are all, in a broad sense, 'theandric' (divine-human) acts, the human actions and sufferings of a Divine Person, the Second Person of the Blessed Trinity. Not all of them draw upon the power of the Godhead in the way that the more strictly theandric acts do, to produce immediate effects that surpass the capacity of human nature— for, example, raising Lazarus from the dead.[151] However, even humble human pains and deeds, when endured or performed by the Divine Person of the Son with His human will, can bring about the ultimate effect of human salvation. Through the instrumentality of each of our Lord's ordinary human actions, the Trinity produces a grace adapted to a particular

[150] ST 3a q. 48, a. 6; cf *Compendium theologiae* lib. 1, cap. 212.

[151] It is of divine and Catholic faith for us to hold, according to the definition of the Third Council of Constantinople (680–681), that our Lord Jesus Christ possesses two natural operations, the divine and the human, just as He possesses two true and perfect natures. There are purely divine operations of the Son, namely, those He performs as God, with the Father and the Holy Spirit, outside of the sphere of the assumed human nature (e.g., creating the world). Then there are the human operations of the divine Person of the Son, the 'theandric' actions, in the broad and narrow sense described on this page. The term *theandric* comes from the writings of Blessed Dionysius the Areopagite. It does not mean, as the Monoenergist heretics claimed, that the divine operation completely overwhelms an entirely passive human nature. St Thomas gives us the authentic interpretation of the Dionysian phrase: 'Dionysius posits a theandric operation in Christ, i.e., a God-manlike, or divine-human, operation, not by any confusion of the operations or powers of both natures, but inasmuch as His divine operation employs the human, and His human operation shares in the power of the divine. Hence, as he says in a letter, "what is of man He works beyond man; and this is shown by the Virgin conceiving supernaturally and the water bearing the weight of the earthly feet." Now it is clear that to be conceived belongs to human nature, and likewise to walk; yet both were in Christ supernaturally. So, too, He did divine things humanly, as when He healed the leper with a touch. Hence in the same epistle he adds: "He performed divine works not as God does, and human works not as man does, but, God having been made man, by a new operation of God and man"' (ST 3a q. 19, a. 1).

human need. So, for example, from the infancy of the Son of God flow all the graces of 'spiritual childhood'.[152] The Son as man merits the graces, by a moral causality, while the Son as God, with the Father and the Holy Spirit, by a physical causality, produces and confers the graces.[153]

A Power Ever Present

The mysteries of Christ, including the Christmas mystery of His human birth and infancy, are instrumental causes of grace, but does their instrumentality work in the past or in the present? The Triune God, as principal efficient cause, sanctifies us through the instrumentality of the assumed nature, in which all the human actions and sufferings of the Son of God once took place, but does He sanctify us through the instrumentality of those actions and sufferings as taking place or as having taken place? It is evident that we are given the grace of rebirth through *Jesus who once was born of Mary*, but less clear that we receive it through *Jesus in the very act of being born*. Is it *the then rising Christ*, or only *the now risen Christ*, who is the cause of our resurrection in body and soul? St Thomas leaves us in no doubt: 'As God and rising man (*homo resurgens*), Christ is the proximate and, as it were, univocal cause of our resurrection.' [154] But how can Christ's birth or His rising from the dead, which took place two thousand years ago, continue to act upon us? We must make a distinction between the movements or actions that make

[152] See pp. 263f.

[153] According to St Thomas, the efficacy of the theandric operations is physical and not merely moral: '[Christ's] actions were salvific for us by the power of the Godhead, that is, by causing grace in us, *both by merit and by a certain efficiency*' (ST 3a q. 8, a. 1, ad 1). See Journet, *L'Église*, pp. 361f, on the Headship of Christ in its two aspects, physical and moral.

[154] *4 Sent.* d. 43, q. 1, a. 2, sol. 1. 'The life of the rising Christ [*Christi resurgentis*] will be poured out in the general resurrection' (*In Iob* cap. 19).

up the mystery as an event and the power or virtue (*virtus*) that emanates from it as an effect. The first, the event in its historical circumstances, is a thing that passes away, but the second, the virtue, is a reality that abides forever. St Thomas says of the mystery of the Cross, that, 'though Christ's Passion and Death are not to be repeated, yet the *virtue* of that Victim endures for ever, for, as it is written "by one oblation He hath perfected for ever them that are sanctified" (Heb 10:14).' [155] As we have seen, Pope Pius XII likewise teaches that the mysteries live on through their imperishable virtue or fruits. [156]

The mysteries of the life of Jesus are perpetually present in the Church because of the perpetual presence of the body of the Church's Head, in which all these mysteries were lived out. In the Church Triumphant, the true, individual body of Jesus is present in its natural form at the Father's right hand, and in the Church Militant, it is present in its sacramental form in the Holy Eucharist. According to the Fathers and Doctors, the wounds in the risen body of the Son in Heaven are like an enduring supplication on our behalf to the Father. The teaching of St Bede the Venerable on this matter has shaped the thinking of most of the great theologians who follow him: Christ preserves the sacred wounds in His glorious body, 'so that as a suppliant before the Father for us, He may show for all eternity the kind of death He underwent for the life of man'. [157] In the *Dialogue* of St Catherine of Siena, God the Father Himself propounds the same doctrine: '[T]he scars of His body are preserved and continually cry for mercy for you to me, the Supreme and Eternal Father.' [158]

[155] ST 3a q. 22, a. 5, ad 2. Cf 3a q. 52, a. 8.

[156] See pp. 68f.

[157] *In Lucae evangelium expositio* lib. 6, cap. 24, no. 40; PL 92:630C. Cf ST 3a q. 54, a. 4.

[158] Catherine of Siena, *Dialogue*, chap. 41; ET by Thorold, p. 75.

Now, if the wounds in the Son's risen body address an objective appeal for mercy to the Father, the body itself is a
permanent plea for the pouring out of the merits of all the
incarnate mysteries. As St Thomas says, our Lord 'makes
intercession' for us in Heaven, not by offering up petitions,
but 'by making present (*repraesentando*) in the sight of the
Father the humanity assumed for us and *the mysteries celebrated
in that humanity*'.[159]

The mysteries of Christ are also perpetually present
through the perpetuity of the soul of Christ and its several
powers. As Cardinal Bérulle says, if our Lord can take the
wounds of His body into glory, He can also 'preserve something in His soul in the definitive state of His glory. . . . What
remains in Him of these mysteries forms on earth a kind of
grace, which pertains to those souls chosen to receive it.'[160]
The dispositions of the soul of Jesus, corresponding to His
several states, live on for ever and continue to have a salvific
effect upon us.

[The mysteries] are past with regard to execution, but present
with regard to their virtue, and their virtue never passes away,
nor will the love ever pass away with which they were accomplished. The spirit, then, the state, the virtue, the merit
of the mystery is ever present. The Spirit of God, by whom
this mystery was effected, the interior state of the interior
mystery, the efficacy and the virtue which makes this mystery
alive and operative in us, this state and virtuous disposition,
the merit by which He acquired us for His Father and merited Heaven, life and Himself; even the actual taste, the living
disposition by which Jesus effected this mystery—[all this] is
ever alive, actual, and present to Jesus. So much so that if it
were necessary, or agreeable to God His Father, He would be
ready to go off and carry out this work anew, this action, this

[159] *Super epistolam ad Romanos*, cap. 8, lect. 7.
[160] Bérulle, *Opuscules de piété*, p. 242.

mystery. This obliges us to treat the things and mystery of
Jesus not as past and extinguished, but as living and present,
and even eternal, the source from which we can reap a fruit
that is present and eternal.[161]

As we have seen, the humanity of Christ is an instrument
united to the Divinity in the Person of the Word and as such,
without any confusion of the two natures, partakes of the
power of the Divinity. Now the Divinity is eternal and ubiq-
uitous, and so, in partaking of the divine power, the human
action also in some way partakes of the divine eternity and
ubiquity; in other words, it can reach men of all times and
places.[162] Cardinal Journet makes this argument in relation to
the Passion: 'The motion of the Godhead conferred on this
transient and localized act an instrumental influence reaching
the whole sequence of time and the whole extension of
space.'[163] The argument is taken up by *The Catechism of the*

[161] Ibid., p. 241.

[162] 'Just as all the other things which Christ did and endured in His humanity
are profitable to our salvation through the power of the Godhead . . . so
Christ's Resurrection is also the efficient cause of ours, through the divine
power whose office it is to quicken the dead; and this power by its presence is
in touch with all places and times; and such *virtual* contact suffices for its
efficiency' (ST 3a q. 56, a. 1, ad 3). 'Every instrument participates, in a
"tendential" and transitory way, in the dignity of the principal cause that
employs it: in the service of God, the created instrument participates, in its
activity as instrument, in the divine eternity and ubiquity to the point that its
past action, its efficiency, still endures': Jean Gaillard OSB, 'Chronique de
liturgie', *Revue thomiste* 57 (1957), 539.

[163] *L'Église*, p. 335. Thus also J.-P. Torrell OP: '[T]he instrument is moved to
produce its effect by the principal cause, and it espouses the conditions that
cause, including its temporal conditions. Inasmuch as it operates *in virtute
divina*, the act performed by Christ is not subject to time, for God in His
eternity has the privilege of reaching as present beings that for us are past or
future. He therefore will be able to unite the efficiency of an instrument with
its destination when that comes into existence, without the proper operation of
the instrument reaching it itself. In other words, the Resurrection of Christ
will truly produce its actual effect in each of its beneficiaries at the moment
chosen by God': *St Thomas d'Aquin: Maître spirituel* (Fribourg, 1996), p. 182.

Catholic Church: '[A]ll that Christ is—all that he did and suffered for all men—participates in the divine eternity, and so transcends all times while being made present in them all.'[164] There are no passing moments, no sequential stages, in the eternal Now of God. Everything that on earth is successively unfolded, from the creation and fall of Adam at the beginning to the general Resurrection and Judgment at the end, is serenely enfolded in one simple and eternal act of the divine intellect. God the Father looks eternally on the several incarnate mysteries of His only-begotten Son, on the Babe of Bethlehem and Man of Sorrows as well as on the risen and ascended Lord, and in seeing the Son in His human states, He sees us, for we are the members of the Son and are called to share His states and only thus His Sonship. This is the truth perceived by St Hildegard in the text quoted above: the mysteries 'shine brightly in [the Father's] presence, for [He has] not forgotten them, but to the end of the age they will make their appearance before [Him] in all their radiance'.[165] Since they are everlastingly present in the sight of God, the mysteries can be everlastingly effective in the salvation of men.

3. Participation in the Mysteries of Christ

Christ, by His mysteries, has objectively and in principle renewed all of human life, but individual human beings must still subjectively and in person make that newness their own—'through faith and charity and the Sacraments of faith'.[166] Salvation takes place not in an automatic process but through a personal encounter of the whole man with the whole God-Man, by the spiritual acts of the theological virtues and the corporeal signs that are the Sacraments.

[164] CCC 1085. See also pp. 21f.
[165] St Hildegard of Bingen, *Scivias*, visio 6, cap. 17; CCCM 43:245.
[166] Cf ST 3a q. 49, a. 3, ad 1.

> The humanity of Christ is the instrumental cause of justification, which cause is applied to us in a spiritual way through faith and in a bodily way through the Sacraments. For the humanity of Christ is both spirit and body, so that we [who are also spirit and body] may receive within us the effect of the sanctification that comes to us through Christ.[167]

He who created us without us will not save or sanctify us without us. Therefore, as Blessed Columba Marmion says, 'Participation in the mysteries of Jesus requires the cooperation of the soul.'[168] True, infants are not consulted before they are plunged into the Easter mystery in Baptism, but even then there are cooperative human acts of intention and faith, on the part not of the sleeping or crying baby, but of the parents and godparents who bring him to the font.[169] In a sense, it is Holy Mother Church herself who lends these little ones her own mouth to renounce the Devil and profess their faith in the Trinity.[170]

The Mysteries of Christ and the Sacraments

The historical mysteries of Christ's life are prolonged in the sacramental mysteries of His Church, for, as the Catechism says, 'what was visible in our Savior has passed over into his mysteries.'[171] Just as, in the historical mysteries, the actions of Christ's visible human nature served as the signs and instruments of His invisible divine nature, so now, in the sacramental mysteries, material things and human actions become the visible signs and instruments of invisible grace. As Cardinal

[167] De veritate q. 27, a. 4. 'Grace is channeled into us from Christ not by means of human nature, but by Christ's personal action alone' (ST 3a q. 8, a. 5, ad 1).

[168] Christ in His Mysteries, p. 19.

[169] Cf ST 3a q. 68, a. 9, ad 1.

[170] Ibid.

[171] CCC 1115, quoting St Leo the Great, Sermo 74, 2; PL 54:398.

Newman said, it is the Incarnation itself that 'establishes in the very idea of Christianity the sacramental principle as its characteristic'.[172] This is the joyful truth announced by the priest when he sings the Preface of the Nativity: 'Through the mystery of the Incarnate Word, the new light of thy radiance has shone into the eyes of our mind, so that, while knowing God in a visible way, we are transported into love of the invisible.'[173] The Sacraments are an extension of the Incarnation.

The Sacraments and the Mysteries are connected not only by exemplary causality, in the sense that the Sacraments are modelled on the Mysteries, but also by efficient instrumental causality, because sanctifying grace passes from the Triune Godhead into the Sacraments through the instrumentality of Christ's human nature and actions.[174] Now, as we have seen, the virtue of the past mysteries has a perpetual influence, which comes to men through the Sacraments. The same power that once passed from Christ's body in its mortal state to heal the woman with the flow of blood now pours into the Sacraments from His body in its glorious state in order to heal fallen man from all the wounds in his nature.[175] The Sacraments are, as it were, the hands of the glorified Christ extended in space and time in order to touch and thus to

[172] John Henry Newman, *An Essay on the Development of Christian Doctrine*, new ed. (Notre Dame, 1989), p. 325.

[173] The Preface of the Nativity of our Lord, *Missale romanum* (1962 and 1970).

[174] Cf ST 3a q. 62, a. 5.

[175] 'The sacraments of the Church now continue the works which Christ had performed during his earthly life (cf. §1115). The sacraments are as it were "powers that go forth" from the Body of Christ to heal the wounds of sin and to give us the new life of Christ' (CCC, commentary on the fresco from the catacomb of SS. Marcellinus and Peter, which serves as a frontispiece for the second part of the *Catechism*). In its teaching on the Anointing of the Sick, the *Catechism* says that 'in the sacraments Christ continues to "touch" us in order to heal us' (CCC 1504).

heal, to sanctify and thereby to deify, the wounded sons of
Adam.[176]

It is above all in the Sacrament of Sacraments, in the
Eucharistic Sacrifice, that the mysteries of Christ's life are
relived and their virtue poured out. This is symbolized in the
Mozarabic rite by the breaking of the Host into nine parts
corresponding to the nine mysteries of the life of the Lord:
the Incarnation, Nativity, Circumcision, Epiphany ('Apparition'), Passion, Death, Resurrection, Glory and Reign. The
fragments are then assembled in the shape of a cross, at the
centre of which is the Nativity.[177] The medievals believed
that the rites and ceremonies of the Mass represented the
whole of Christ's life, indeed the whole history of salvation.
The drama begins with the yearning of the Patriarchs and
Prophets for Christ's first coming (articulated in the Introit)
and reaches its climax with the Ascension and Second Coming (symbolized by the final blessing, for Christ blessed His
disciples when He ascended into Heaven [Lk 24:50], and
when He comes again, He will bless the elect, saying,
'Come, ye blessed of my Father' [Mt 25:34]).[178]

The presence of the mysteries of our Lord's earthly life in
the liturgy is subordinate to, and indeed dependent upon, the
unique way in which He with His central mystery—the
Sacrifice on the Cross—is made present in the Sacrament.
The Church believes that the whole Christ—Body, Blood,

[176] 'To continue to reach us with the same intimacy as in the days of His
mortal life, He leaves in our midst hierarchical powers and sacramental rites
which prolong His sensible contact in space and duration, and by which He
will send the fullness of His grace and truth' (Journet, L'Église, p. 301).

[177] Cf Concelebratio Eucharistica ritu Hispanico veteri seu Mozarabico (Salamanca,
1976), pp. 81f.

[178] 'By the ordinance of providence, the office of the Mass is so arranged that
it contains many of those things that were done by Christ or to Christ, from
the time He descended from Heaven to His Ascension into Heaven, and
represents them, by words as well as signs, in a wonderful form' (Rationale lib. 4,
cap. 1, no. 11; 140:242).

Soul and Divinity—is contained in the Sacrament, not merely by sign, figure or power but 'truly, really, and substantially'.[179] And she teaches that the Sacrifice of the Cross is 'represented', that is, made present with all its saving power, in the Sacrifice of the Mass. If we consider the divine Victim-Priest and the purpose for which He offered Himself, then we must conclude that the Sacrifice of the Cross and the Sacrifice of the Mass are essentially one and the same. He who offered Himself then, in adoration and thanksgiving to God and in propitiation and petition for men, is the very same One who offers Himself now for the same glorious ends. The difference is the manner of offering: on Calvary, Christ offered Himself without the assistance of priests, whereas in the Mass He offers Himself through their ministry; then He offered Himself in a bloody way and in His own natural appearance, whereas now He offers Himself in an unbloody way under the appearances of bread and wine.[180] On the Cross His Body and Blood were separated by violence in the physical order, but in the Mass a separation takes place in the sacramental order, through the separate consecration of bread to be His Body and of wine to be His Blood. Thus 'Jesus Christ is symbolically shown by separate symbols to be in a state of victimhood.'[181] In the Mass, the Redeemer revives His work 'in the midst of the years' (cf Hab 3:2).

The Christ who is substantially present in the Eucharist is the very same Christ who undertook or underwent the diverse mysteries of His earthly life. The body and blood are

[179] Cf Council of Trent, Thirteenth Session, Decree on the Most Holy Eucharist (1551), chaps. 1, 3, and 4, cans. 1–3; DS 1636-37, 1639–41, 1642, 1651–53.

[180] Cf Council of Trent, Twenty-Second Session, Doctrine on the Most Holy Sacrifice of the Mass (1562), chaps. 1–2, cans. 1–2; DS 1739–43, 1751–52; Pope Pius XII, *Mediator Dei*, nos. 70–83.

[181] Pope Pius XII, *Mediator Dei*, no. 70.

the same, as are the soul and the Divine Person to whom
body, blood and soul alike belong. In every historical mystery
and finally in the Eucharistic mystery, the heart of the same
Son shows the same filial love to the Father. Moreover, the
'virtue' of each of the mysteries, though available outside the
Sacraments according to the good pleasure of the Lord, is
primarily attached to the corresponding feast and to the
celebration of Mass on that day. This is evident from an
inspection of the liturgical books. For example, in the Secret
for the Feast of the Transfiguration, the priest, speaking in
the person of the Church, asks God the Father to 'hallow the
gifts we offer *by the glorious Transfiguration of [His] only-begotten
Son*' and to 'cleanse us from the stains of our sins *by the
splendours of His illumination*'.[182] Finally, if the Sacrifice Christ
offered on Calvary continued and brought to their perfection
all His previous acts of self-oblation, then, through the re-
presentation of the Passion, the other mysteries, too, are
made efficaciously present. In the Mass the specific graces of
the mysteries are poured out upon our souls.

Meditation on the Mysteries of Christ

We dispose ourselves to receive the graces of the mysteries of
Christ's life through the practice of prayer, and especially
through that prayerful act of mind and heart which is known
as *meditation*. '[B]y beholding Him often in meditation, your
whole soul will be filled with Him; you will learn His disposition, and you will form your actions after the model of
His.'[183] The medievals regarded meditation as an act of the
whole man. It is an act of the intellect: thinking, pondering,
going over something in one's mind. But the thinking is

[182] *Missale romanum* (1962).
[183] St Francis de Sales, *Introduction to the Devout Life*, ET by A. Ross, Congregation of the Oratory, new ed. (London, 1948), p. 75.

often of the practical order and therefore engages the will: a man meditates on something before he does it; to meditate is to plan a course of action. In this sense, the word can be used, both in classical and medieval Latin, in reference to any kind of mental rehearsal or practice. Before the general dispatches his troops and the orator makes his speech, they 'meditate', go over what they have to do or say in their mind. But *meditari* is also an act of the body: you meditate by murmuring the words you are reading. *Os iusti meditabitur sapientiam* (cf Ps 36:30); the *mouth*, the very lips, of the just man will meditate on wisdom. He repeats the words of the sacred text, either out loud or under his breath, in order to fix them in his mind. He learns by heart through learning by mouth.[184] The sound of the words of Scripture has a kind of sacramental significance: it shows that, when the Christian meditates, he is not turned inwards, in absorption with himself, but outwards, in a Spirit-moved response to the resounding reality of the Word. St Thomas, summarizing the common teaching of all the masters of the Middle Ages, whether in the monasteries or in the Schools, says that meditation stands in the middle between reading and prayer. First of all, we read the Scriptures and hear God speaking to us. Secondly, we meditate, and the God whom we have heard becomes present to us in our understanding and affections, and we become present to Him. Thirdly, we address God in prayer.[185] Some authors, including St Thomas himself, use the metaphor of 'chewing' (*masticatio* or *ruminatio*) to describe the nature and purpose of meditation. 'Just as food is not nourishing unless it is first chewed, so you cannot make progress in knowledge except by chewing the things you

---

[184] On the medieval meaning of *meditari*, see the classic work of Dom Jean Leclercq OSB, *The Love of Learning and the Desire for God: A Study of Monastic Culture*, ET, new ed. (New York, 1974), pp. 20f.

[185] Cf *4 Sent*. d. 15, q. 4, a. 1B, ad 1.

hear by frequent meditation.'[186] Meditation releases the flavour and food of the Divine Word from the dry husk of the text.

The supreme exemplar of meditation on the mysteries of the life of Jesus is Mary, His Ever-Virgin Mother. Twice St Luke tells us that our Lady kept and pondered in her heart the realities of her Son's birth and childhood (cf Lk 2:19, 51). St Thomas says that this meditation of Mary's was 'integral' and 'profound': she kept *all* the words, the totality of the realities of Jesus, in her heart, and, as David says, she meditated with her heart; she was 'exercised and . . . swept [her] spirit' (cf Ps 76:7). In the *Catena aurea*, St Thomas quotes St Bede's interpretation of the words of St Luke: '[The Blessed Virgin] pondered upon both His divine words and works, so that nothing that was said or done by Him was lost upon her, but as the Word itself was before in her womb, so now she conceived the ways and words of the same, and in a manner nursed them in her heart.'[187] When a 'certain woman of the crowd' cries out to our Lord, 'Blessed is the womb that bore thee', and He replies, 'Yea, rather, blessed are they who hear the word of God, and keep it' (cf Lk 11:28f.), He reveals the true blessedness of His Mother: '[S]he was the Mother of God, and indeed blessed, in that she was made the temporal minister of the Word becoming incarnate; yet therefore much more blessed that she remained the eternal keeper of the same ever to be beloved Word.'[188]

The school of Christian meditation is permanently under the patronage of our Lady. By her earthly example and heavenly intercession, she enables Christ's faithful to preserve and ponder His mysteries in their hearts. In the Holy Rosary, we greet 'Mary, full of grace' and implore her to help

[186] *Sermo* 1, part 3. See Leclercq, *Love of Learning*, p. 90.
[187] CA 3, 103.
[188] CA 3, 409 (St Bede).

us to know and love Jesus in His mysteries of joy, sorrow and glory, and thereby to do the will of 'our Father in Heaven' and to give glory to Him and to the Son and to the Holy Spirit. It is almost, says Pope Leo XIII, 'as though [we] were listening to the very voice of the Blessed Mother explaining the mysteries and conversing with [us] at length about [our salvation]'.[189] To help us 'diminish distractions of the imagination', St Louis-Marie de Montfort recommends adding a word or two after the Holy Name of Jesus in the Hail Mary as a reminder of the mystery being contemplated. For example, in the joyful mysteries, we can speak of Jesus successively as 'incarnate', 'sanctifying [the Baptist] in the womb', 'poor infant', 'sacrificed' and 'holy of holies'.[190] We can even direct each individual Hail Mary towards a different mystery. So, for example, in the fifth joyful mystery, it is a good idea to meditate on all the mysteries from the humble work and obedience of the Saviour's hidden life in Nazareth to the final act of His public ministry, 'the institution of the Holy Eucharist'.[191] The effects of this meditation on the mysteries can be truly revolutionary—both in the individual Christian and in Christendom as a whole. Through the Rosary, the Albigensian heresy was overcome in France and the Turk defeated at Lepanto. In every age, the Christian mysteries of joy, sorrow and glory 'humiliate an old and most subtle enemy in the spread-out array of his power'.[192]

The Western tradition of the litany also keeps devotion alive to the mysteries of Christ, both of His divinity and of His humanity. For example, in the Litany of the Holy Name, we ask our Lord to deliver us through 'the mystery of [His]

[189] *Magnae Dei Matris* (1892), no. 17.

[190] 'Méthodes pour réciter le Rosaire', in St Louis-Marie Grignion de Montfort, *Oeuvres complètes* (Paris, 1966), p. 397.

[191] Ibid., p. 411.

[192] Pope Leo XIII, *Superiore anno*, no. 2.

holy Incarnation ... Nativity ... Infancy ... Most Divine Life
... Labours ... Agony and Passion ... Cross and Dereliction
... Languors ... Death and Burial ... Resurrection ... Ascension ... [and] Institution of the Most Holy Eucharist'.[193]
Litanies were particularly popular in Ireland during the penal
times. The mysteries they invoke are generally greater in
number than those to be found in the standard Roman form.

> By the heavenly Father, by the Holy Spirit, and by
> thine own Divinity;
> By thy great compassion, by thy great affection for the
> human race from the beginning of the world to its
> end;
> By thy coming humbly from the heavenly places in the
> form of a servant to help it and rescue it from the
> dominion of the devil;
> By thy Conception in the womb of Mary the Virgin;
> By thy Humanity which grew in unity of person with
> thy Divinity;
> By the loving Mother from whom thou didst receive it;
> By thy birth from her, without opening of the womb;
> By the offering and willing gift which thou madest of
> thyself to Cross and Passion for the sake of the
> human race;
> By thine ineffable compassion toward the seed of
> Adam;
> By the deliverance that thou broughtest to the just man
> of the five ages from the murk and darkness of
> Hell;
> By thy Resurrection from the dead after three days;
> By thine Ascension into heaven in the presence of
> thine Apostles and thy disciples;

[193] *Rituale romanum.*

By the beauty and great glory in which thou abidest
eternally at the right hand of God the Father in
Heaven;

By thy coming to the judgement of doom to gather
together the just to dwell for ever in the eternal life,
and to drive away the sinners to the sorrow and
torments of Hell.[194]

All prayers and devotions addressed to Christ in His mysteries involve the worship of *latria*, which is due to God alone.
Strictly speaking, worship is given always to a particular *Person*. Now in Christ only one Person subsists in the two
natures, namely, the Divine Person of the Word. That single
Person is, therefore, to be worshipped, as St Cyril of Alexandria says, 'by a single worship'.[195] The sacred humanity cannot
be excluded from the worship of the Divine Person, because
it is inseparably united to that Person. It is not adored for its
own sake, but for the sake of the Divinity to which it is
united.[196] As St Thomas says, 'To worship the flesh of Christ is
nothing other than worshipping the enfleshed Word of God,
just as worshipping the clothing of the king is to adore the
clothed king.'[197] Moreover, if adoration is given to the whole
of Christ's human nature because of the Hypostatic Union, it
can and must be given for the same reason to each of that
nature's parts (for example, to the Sacred Heart) and, by
analogy, to each of its historical states. Devotion to the mysteries of Christ is therefore an act of divine worship.[198]

---

[194] 'Litany of the Saviour' in *Irish Litanies*, ed. Charles Plummer, text and
translation, vol. 62 (London: Henry Bradshaw Society, 1925), p. 21 (translation
slightly adapted).

[195] *Anathematismi*, no. 8; DS 259.

[196] Cf ST 3a q. 25, a. 2, ad 2 and 3.

[197] Ibid., q. 25, a. 2.

[198] 'So, then, this same truly precious and august tree, on which Christ
offered Himself as a sacrifice for our sakes, is to be worshipped because it has

The Book of the Mysteries of Christ

'All Sacred Scripture', says the *Catechism*, 'is but one book, and this one book is Christ, "because all divine Scripture speaks of Christ, and all divine Scripture is fulfilled in Christ".' [199] The Bible is therefore the great book of the mysteries of the Incarnate Word. In the Old Testament the things that the Messiah would suffer and do are foretold, while in the New Testament the things He did suffer and do are recorded and their saving effects declared. [200]

The theology of the mysteries of Christ presupposes the Catholic doctrine of Biblical inerrancy, that is, the freedom of Scripture from error of all kinds—not only on religious and moral matters but also concerning historical fact, including the events of the earthly life of our Lord. If the sacred authors of Scripture were mistaken in reporting that certain mysteries would or did take place, then the Church would be mistaken in praying for the grace of those mysteries. But the Church cannot be mistaken, and so we can be sure that the sacred authors, too, were neither misled nor

---

been sanctified through its contact with His holy body and blood. We likewise worship the nails, the spear, the clothes, those sacred tabernacles of His which are the manger, the cave, salvific Golgotha, the life-giving tomb, Zion, the chief stronghold of the Churches, and the like. In the words of David, the forefather of God, "We shall go into His tabernacles, we shall worship at the place where His feet stood". It is clear that it he means the Cross when he adds: "Arise, O Lord, into thy rest." For the Resurrection comes after the Cross. For if we long for those things that we love (house and couch and garment), how much the rather should we long for what belonged to God, our Saviour, by means of which we are saved' (St John Damascene, *De fide orthodoxa* lib. 4, cap. 11; PG 94:1132A).

[199] CCC 134, quoting Hugh of St Victor, *De arca Noe* 2, 8: PL 176:642; cf. ibid., 2, 9: PL 176:642–43.

[200] After His Resurrection from the tomb, our Lord reminds His disciples of the things 'written in the law of Moses and in the Prophets and in the Psalms, concerning [Him]' (Lk 24:44).

misleading. In his encyclical *Providentissimus Deus*, Pope Leo XIII states the Church's teaching on this matter with the utmost vigour: '[I]t is absolutely wrong and forbidden, either to narrow inspiration to certain parts only of Holy Scripture, or to admit that the sacred writer has erred.'[201] All the books of the Bible, in their every part, are wholly free from error. Moreover, within each book, we cannot restrict inspiration and thus inerrancy to the religious and moral teachings; under the inspiration of the Holy Spirit, the sacred authors make no statement, on any subject, that contradicts the truth of reality. As St Thomas says, 'Nothing false can ever underlie the literal sense of Sacred Scripture.'[202] If the literal sense concerns some historical matter, that is, if the sacred author intends to tell us what some really existing subject once said or did, we can be sure that he is telling us without error what that person said or did. As conscious and free instruments, the sacred authors act under the inspiration of the Spirit of Truth. The Holy Spirit cannot err, nor can they, despite their human imperfections, when they write beneath His gentle sway. Inspiration, Pope Leo goes on to say, 'not only is essentially incompatible with error, but excludes and rejects it as absolutely and necessarily as it is impossible that God Himself, the supreme Truth, can utter that which is not true'.[203] The Holy Spirit, by His supernatural power, 'so moved and impelled' the sacred authors that they wrote down all and only the things that He commanded. First, they 'rightly understood [them], then willed faithfully to write [them] down, and finally expressed [them] in apt words and with infallible truth'.[204] God revealed Himself in history by performing mighty deeds for His people

[201] *Providentissimus Deus*, no. 20.
[202] ST 1a q. 1, a. 10, ad 3.
[203] *Providentissimus Deus*, no. 20.
[204] Ibid.

and above all by sending His Son in human nature.[205] He therefore guaranteed all the truth to be found in the sacred texts, the historical facts as well as the religious and moral doctrine.

In his teaching on inerrancy, Pope Leo presents, not a speculative thesis from the Schools, but 'the ancient and unchanging faith of the Church, solemnly defined in the Councils of Florence and Trent, and finally confirmed and more expressly formulated by the [First] Council of the Vatican'.[206] On this matter the consensus of the Fathers, that sure indication of the mind of the Church,[207] is strikingly evident. As Pope Leo says, the Fathers and Doctors were so 'emphatically agreed' that the Scriptures were free from all error, even on matters of historical detail, that they 'laboured earnestly, with no less skill than reverence, to reconcile with each other those numerous passages which seem at variance'. The sacred authors did not deceive or lie, nor did they make mistakes. Where their narratives appear to clash, the fault must lie elsewhere, in the scribe or in the reader. The Pope cites the opinion of St Augustine: 'On my part I confess . . . that it is only to those Books of Scripture which are now called canonical that I have learned to pay such honour and reverence as to believe most firmly that none of their writers has fallen into any error. And if in these books I meet anything which seems contrary to truth, I shall not hesitate to conclude either that the text is faulty, or that the translator has not expressed the meaning of the passage,

---

[205] As the Fathers of the Second Vatican Council say, 'This economy of revelation takes place in deeds and words that are so intrinsically connected with each other that the works accomplished by God in the history of salvation manifest and confirm the doctrine and realities signified by the words, while the words proclaim the works and shed light on the mystery they contain' (*Dei Verbum*, no . 2).

[206] *Providentissimus Deus*, no. 20.

[207] Cf First Vatican Council, *Dei Filius*, chap. 2; DS 3007.

or that I myself do not understand.'[208] The seeming contradictions of Scripture are my problem, not the sacred authors'.

What is true of the Scriptures in general applies to the Gospels in particular: they teach, without error, the truth about Jesus, not only general timeless truths about His Divinity, but also particular historical truths abut His humanity, for it was through the mysteries of His human life that He revealed His Divinity to us. The Fathers and Doctors find truth and grace, not in mere fictions, but in massive facts, the tremendous realities that God Incarnate suffered and did for man's salvation. The theology of the *mysteria vitae Iesu* is utter vanity, a self-indulgent riot of the imagination, unless there be true mysteries whose meaning theology can contemplate. No graces were merited by actions that were never performed. Only if the Gospels tell us the objective truth about what our Lord said and did, without any admixture of error, can they be instruments of salvation. At the Second Vatican Council, Pope Paul VI, through the mediation of Cardinal Bea, intervened to ensure that this fundamental principle of Catholic doctrine was not endangered.[209] Exercising his Petrine authority and freedom of action, the Holy Father asked the theological commission to strengthen what to him seemed a dangerously weak statement about the historical reliability of the Gospels. In the end, the text approved by the Fathers contained this clear and robust statement of Catholic truth:

> Holy Mother Church . . . firmly and most constantly has held and holds that the Four Gospels, whose historicity she unhesitatingly affirms, faithfully hand on what Jesus, the Son of God, while He lived among men, really did and taught for their eternal salvation, until the day when He was taken up.[210]

---

[208] *Providentissimus Deus*, no. 21.
[209] See S. Schmidt, *Augustin Bea: The Cardinal of Unity* (New Rochelle, N.Y., 1992), pp. 549ff.
[210] *Dei Verbum*, no. 19.

The Servants of the Mysteries

One of the ways in which the Church gives us contact with the mysteries of her Head is through the Gospels, which she reads solemnly within the liturgy, and therefore through the Gospel writers, whom she commemorates during the liturgical year. Sadly, Liberal Protestant and Modernist Biblical scholars have seemed, for a large part of the last two centuries, to be determined to separate the evangelists as far as possible, in space and time as well as in direct contact, from the Jesus whose life and teaching they set forth. First, the critics 'prescind' from the dogmatic faith and Tradition of the Church, in order, so they allege, to attain a scientific reading of the texts.[211] Secondly, they give prominence to what they take to be contradictions of fact or opinion between the sacred authors, or between the Bible and natural science.[212] Thirdly, they destroy the historical identity of the evangelists. The Gospels—so they claim—were written, not by recognized disciples of Truth but by unknown and unknowable devisers of myth. The evangelists composed their narratives not in order to tell the honest truth about the Lord but to promote the religious interests (or 'theologies', as the critics like to say) of particular communities in the early Church. The Higher Critics are embarrassed by every physical marvel in the life of Jesus—His miracles, His bodily Resurrection, and the virginity of His Blessed Mother; like the Gnostics of old, they seem repelled by the Word's deep descent into the world of matter. Whatever its motivation, the upshot of this spiritualizing scepticism is catastrophic: 'It leaves us practi-

---

[211] A leading radical exegete, J. P. Meier, writes as follows: 'My method follows a simple rule: it prescinds from what Christian faith or later Church teaching says about Jesus, without either affirming or denying such claims' (*A Marginal Jew: Rethinking the Historical Jesus*, vol. 1 [New York, 1991], p. 1).

[212] Meier claims that in their infancy narratives 'Matthew and Luke diverge from or even contradict each other on certain key points' (ibid., p. 210).

cally with a heap of ruins, the destruction of the figure
attested to by the New Testament.'[213]

By contrast, the Catholic Church, the undeceiving
Mother of Christ's faithful, commemorates the evangelists on
their feast days as named men who were either disciples or
disciples of disciples of the Lord, and at every celebration of
the Holy Sacrifice she solemnly proclaims the Gospel 'according to' one or other of the four named evangelists. Since
the Holy Spirit leads the Church into all the truth, we can
trust the Church's daily assertions of the authorship and authenticity of the Gospels. It is Holy Mother Church, the
Bride of the Word, 'to whom it belongs to judge of the true
sense and interpretation of Holy Scripture'.[214] The Bible is
the Church's book. It is she who made the canon of Scripture, she who discerned, with the Holy Spirit's assistance, the
inspiration He once gave to the sacred writers. In the person
of Mary, the Church meditated on the mysteries of Jesus
long before any of the evangelists had lifted his pen (cf Lk
2:51).[215] It is therefore to the Church, both to her Tradition
and to her Magisterium, that we should turn for enlightenment concerning the identity and mission of the evangelists,
the servants of the mysteries. Consider, for example, what
the Tradition teaches us about St Luke, who records so many
of the mysteries of our Lord's birth and infancy. In the *Catena
aurea*, St Thomas quotes Eusebius of Caesarea, who says that

[213] Hans Urs von Balthasar, *Does Jesus Know Us—Do We Know Him?* ET (San
Francisco, 1983), p. 65.

[214] First Vatican Council, Dogmatic Constitution on the Catholic Faith, *Dei
Filius* (1870), chap. 2; DS 3007. Cf Second Vatican Council, Dogmatic Constitution on Divine Revelation, *Dei Verbum* (1965), no. 12.

[215] In the beautiful words of Marie-Dominique Philippe OP: 'Christian
Tradition was born in the heart of Mary' (*Wherever He Goes: A Retreat on the
Gospel of John*, ET [Laredo, Tex., 1998], p. 67). The Fathers of the Second
Vatican Council likewise refer to our Lady's pondering of the mysteries in her
heart when they explain the nature of Tradition (see *Dei Verbum*, no. 8).

Luke was a physician, originally from Antioch. He can be trusted as a 'sure witness' to Christ, because 'he obtained his knowledge of the truth either from St Paul's instructions, or from the instructions and traditions of the other Apostles, who were themselves eyewitnesses from the beginning.'[216] In the opening lines of the Gospel, he declares his intention to pass on to his friend Theophilus, not his own speculations or imaginative reconstructions, but the 'verity of those words in which thou hast been instructed' (Lk 1:4). He refers to the '*things* that have been accomplished among us' (v. 1), using the strong Greek term *pragmatôn*, 'realities', in order to indicate, as Titus Bostrensis says, that it was 'not by shadows, as the heretics say, that Jesus accomplished His advent in the flesh'; no, 'since He was the Truth, so in very truth He performed His work.'[217]

St Luke's Gospel displays that quiet and sober attention to the truth which distinguishes all four of the canonical Gospels from the apocrypha and indeed from all legendary or mythic literature. Curiously, this elephantine difference has escaped the notice of the higher critics. C. S. Lewis argues that blindness to the obvious is a fatal deficiency in these would-be men of science:

> [W]hatever these men may be as Biblical critics, I distrust them as critics. They seem to me to lack literary judgement, to be imperceptive about the very quality of the texts they are reading. . . . A man who has spent his youth and manhood in the minute study of New Testament texts and of other people's studies of them, whose literary experience of those texts lacks any standard of comparison such as can only grow from a wide and deep and genial experience of literature in general, is, I should think, very likely to miss the obvious things about them. If he tells me that something in a

[216] CA 3, 6.
[217] Ibid.

Gospel is legend or romance, I want to know how many legends and romances he has read, how well his palate is trained in detecting them by the flavour; not how many years he has spent on that Gospel.[218]

Turning to St John's Gospel, Lewis presents this challenge to the critics:

I have been reading poems, romances, vision-literature, legends, myths all my life. I know what they are like. I know that not one of them is like this. Of this text there are only two possible views. Either this is reportage—though it may no doubt contain some errors[219]—pretty close up to the facts; nearly as close as Boswell. Or else, some unknown writer in the second century, without known predecessors or successors, suddenly anticipated the whole technique of modern, novelistic, realistic narrative. If it is untrue, it must be narrative of that kind. The reader who doesn't see this has simply not learned to read.[220]

The Higher Critics do not see it, and so we can safely conclude that they cannot read and therefore cannot teach us how to read the Holy Gospels.

Mysteries Manifesting Mysteries

The richness of the mysteries of Christ is demonstrated by the tradition of spiritual exegesis of the Scriptures, of which the *Catechism* speaks as follows:

---

[218] C. S. Lewis, 'Fern-seed and Elephants', in *Fern-seed and Elephants: And Other Essays on Christianity*, new ed. (London, 1975), p. 107.

[219] Lewis is not denying the inerrancy of Scripture. He is arguing apologetically, according to natural reason, and therefore does not want to presuppose any supernaturally determined estimate of the dignity of the Gospels. The critic ought to see, again simply by natural reason, that the Gospel of St John, with all its detailed dialogues and descriptions, must be either close to the facts or a work of the imagination.

[220] Lewis, 'Fern-seed and Elephants', p. 108.

According to an ancient tradition, one can distinguish between two *senses* of Scripture: the literal and the spiritual, the
latter being subdivided into the allegorical, moral, and
anagogical senses. The profound concordance of the four
senses guarantees all its richness to the living reading of
Scripture in the Church.[221]

The doctrine of the fourfold sense of Scripture is concerned in the first place not with the sacred texts themselves,
but with the sacred history that the texts narrate, with the
revealed realities of holy persons, institutions and events, and
with their multiple, divinely willed interconnections. Man, as
a rational creature, can make *words* signify things, even several
things at the same time, but only the Creator, the provident
Author of all things, can arrange for *things* to signify things,
mysteries that manifest further mysteries.

[T]ruth is manifested in Sacred Scripture in two ways: in one
way, by things being signified by words (this constitutes the
literal sense); in another way, by things being figures of other
things (and this constitutes the spiritual sense).[222]

The *allegorical sense* is the Christological sense, the meaning
that some reality in Scripture and salvation history has in
relation to the Lord Jesus Christ and His mysteries, more
exactly to 'Christ as Head of the Church militant, justifying
and infusing grace into her'.[223] Allegory, a way of speaking in
which one thing is understood by another,[224] tells us what to
hold by *faith* in the Incarnate Word. The *moral or tropological
sense*, by contrast, is the meaning that something has in relation to the conduct of Christ's members; it tells us how to act
in *charity*. The *anagogical sense* is eschatological, the meaning

[221] CCC 115.
[222] St Thomas Aquinas, *Quaestiones quodlibetales* 7, q. 6, a. 1.
[223] Ibid., a. 2, ad 4.
[224] Cf St Augustine, *De Trinitate* lib. 15, cap. 9, no. 15; CCSL 50A:481.

that something has in relation to Christ as 'Head of the Church Triumphant, glorifying her';[225] it tells us what to look forward to in *hope*. The literal sense of the Bible's many references to Jerusalem is the earthly city in Palestine. The allegorical sense is Christ's Church or Blessed Mother. The moral sense is the Jerusalem of the soul, whether besieged by Satan in temptation or delivered by God in grace. The anagogical sense is the heavenly city, 'Jerusalem the golden, with milk and honey blest'.

Spiritual exegesis is not restricted to texts of the Old Testament. The events recorded in the Gospels also have layers of rich meaning deposited in them by the Holy Spirit. According to St Thomas, 'what is said literally about Christ the Head can be set forth allegorically in reference to His Mystical Body, morally, in reference to our acts that have to be reformed according to [Christ]; and anagogically, inasmuch as the way of glory is shown to us in Christ.'[226] It is these deep levels of meaning in the mysteries of Christ that Christian meditation, both in theology and in prayer, seeks to uncover.

Saving Mysteries and Sacred Icons

In both Christian West and East, the mysteries of the life of our Lord are depicted, for contemplation and veneration, in the sacred images of the Church. Christian iconography in all its forms, whether icons or altarpieces, sculpture or stained glass, constitutes the Bible of the poor and therefore the Gospel of the illiterate. Even the educated Christian probably first met the mysteries in the beauty of the Church's sacred art, when his mother showed him Baby Jesus in the Crib, with Mary and Joseph kneeling nearby.

[225] St Thomas Aquinas, *Quaestiones quodlibetales* 7, q. 6, a. 2, ad 4.
[226] Ibid., q. 6, a. 2, ad 5.

It is the Incarnation of the invisible Word in visible human nature, together with the things He did and suffered in that human nature, which both justify the making of images and reveal their saving power when the images are displayed. This is the teaching of St John Damascene in his defence of the holy icons against the Iconoclasts:

> How can the Invisible be depicted? How can we draw what is boundless, immeasurable, infinite? How can form be given to the formless? How do we paint the bodiless? How can you describe a mystery? Quite clearly, when you behold God becoming man, *then* you can depict Him clothed in human form. When the Invisible is made visible to the flesh, then you may draw His likeness. When He who is bodiless and without form, immeasurable in the boundlessness of His own nature, existing in the form of God, empties Himself and assumes the form of a servant in substance and in stature, and is found in a body of flesh, *then* you may draw His image and show it to anyone willing to have a look at it. Depict His wondrous condescension, His Birth from the Virgin, His Baptism in the Jordan, His Transfiguration on Tabor, His Sufferings, which have freed us from passion, His Death, His Miracles, which are signs of His divine nature, since by divine power He worked them in the flesh. Show His saving Cross, the Tomb, the Resurrection, the Ascension into Heaven. Describe all these things, in words or in colour. Do not be afraid; have no anxiety; distinguish the different kinds of veneration.[227]

4. The Mysteries of Christ and the Mystery of Christmas

By the 'mysteries of Christ' we mean all the things the Incarnate Word suffered and did for man's salvation, or, as Denys the Carthusian put it, 'the most holy Incarnation of

---

[227] *De sacris imaginibus* 1, no. 8; PG 94:1240A.

the eternal Word and the other sacred things which Christ assumed, did, and endured for our salvation, such as the Birth, the Circumcision, the Oblation in the Temple, the Institution of the Sacraments, especially of the Eucharist, the Passion etc.'.[228] By the 'Christmas mystery' we mean the human birth and infancy of the Son of God, including such early events and experiences as His circumcision, manifestation to the Gentiles, presentation in the Temple, and flight into Egypt. These mysteries belong in the first place to Christ, to the Head, but since, in becoming man, He unites Himself by human bonds with men, the mysteries belong also to others, to those of His members, angels or men, who at the first Christmas were specially united to Him. St Bonaventure provides a comprehensive list:

> The mysteries are these: the blessed fecundity of the undefiled Virgin; the humility, at once sublime and singular, of the superblessed Child; the courteous devotion of Blessed Joseph; the devout credulity of the simple shepherds; the new mirth of the angelic spirits; the beginning of the happiness of the whole human race; the beginning of the radiance of the Christian religion.[229]

What the mysteries of Christ in general are and do, the Christmas mystery in particular is and does: it has a power of both outward example and inward grace, it is perpetually present through the sacred liturgy of the Church, and it can be shared in by the sons of the Church. The specific virtue of the Christmas mystery is the power to transfigure human souls in the likeness of the Holy Infant, to make them partakers by grace of His divine Sonship and nature, and to form within them dispositions of heart resembling His own. This was the message preached by Cardinal Bérulle:

---

[228] *Expositio hymnorum aliquot ecclesiasticorum*; DCOO 42:86f.

[229] *In vigilia nativitatis Domini, sermo* 6; Q IX:95.

The infancy of the Son of God is a passing state. The circumstances of this infancy are past, and He is no longer an
infant, but there is something in this mystery which continues in Heaven. It effects a similar kind of grace in those souls
on earth which it pleases Jesus Christ to dedicate to this
humble and first state of His person.[230]

Each year, at Christmastide, the Church prays that her
children may share in 'this humble and first state' of the
Person of her Head. In *Mediator Dei*, Pope Pius XII has left us
a beautifully exact description of this Christmas grace:

On the anniversary of the birthday of the Redeemer, [the
Church] invites us to return in spirit to the cave of Bethlehem, and there learn that it is necessary for us to be born
again and thoroughly to reform ourselves; and this happens
only when we come into close and vital touch with the
Incarnate Word of God and receive a share of His divine
nature, to which we have been elevated.[231]

St Gregory Nazianzen invites each member of his flock to
play his own peculiar role in the drama of the Nativity,
which is made present through the liturgical mysteries of the
Christmas season. Gregory, Christendom's first dramatist,[232]
insists that we cannot be mere spectators of the starlit stable:

Run with the star and offer your gifts with the Magi, gold
and frankincense and myrrh, as to a king and a god and One
who died for you. With shepherds glorify Him, with angels
sing hymns, with archangels join in chorus. . . . Travel fault-
lessly through every stage and faculty of the life of Christ. Be
purified, be circumcised; strip off the veil that has covered
you from your birth.[233]

---

[230] Bérulle, *Opuscules de piété*, new ed., p. 242.
[231] *Mediator Dei*, no. 155.
[232] Gregory wrote a verse-drama of the Passion, *Christus patiens* (SC 149).
[233] *Oratio* 38, nos. 17–18; PG 36:332AB.

We are given a share in the human birth of the Son of God by being reborn into Him in Baptism. Thereafter, all the other Sacraments plunge us, through the Easter mystery of death and Resurrection, into the Christmas mystery of second birth and new childhood.[234] When Christ, through the power He gave His priests on the first Easter Sunday, absolves us from our sins, He truly renews our innocence in the likeness of His own immaculate infancy. By the power of the keys, we become like *the* Little Child. The unlikeness of our relative purity to His absolute and incandescent purity is far greater than the likeness, and yet, through the lesser likeness, we are in truth made partakers and followers of the Lamb. In the nineteenth century, Father Faber of the English Oratory meditated at great length on Bethlehem's capacity to rejuvenate the souls of men:

> Bethlehem exists as a living power in its continual production of supernatural things in the souls of men. It is for ever alluring them from sin. It is for ever guiding them to perfection. It is for ever impressing peculiar characteristics on the

[234] Pope St Leo the Great: 'Now the triumph of His Passion and Resurrection has been accomplished, the humble deeds He undertook for us have passed away. Nevertheless, today's feast renews for us the sacred beginnings [*sacra primordia*] of Jesus born of the Virgin Mary, and as we worship the birth of our Saviour, we discover that we are celebrating our own origin. For the birth of Christ is the origin of the Christian people, and the birthday of the Head is the birthday of the Body. Although each is called in turn, and all the sons of the Church are distinct by succession of time, nevertheless, the whole mass of the faithful spring from the font of Baptism. Just as they are crucified with Christ in His Passion, raised with Him in His Resurrection, and placed at the Father's right hand in the Ascension, so they are born with Him in this Nativity. Every believer, . . . from whatever part of the world he comes, is regenerated in Christ, and having broken with the ways of original oldness, is re-born and becomes a new man. From now on, he is counted, not among the offspring of his fleshly father, but among the race of the Saviour, who became Son of Mary, so that we might become sons of God. Had He not descended to us by His humility, no one could reach Him by any merits of his own' (*In nativitate Domini, sermo* 6, 2; SC 22B:138ff.).

holiness of different persons. It is a divine type, and is moulding souls upon itself all day long, and its works remain, and adorn the eternal home of God.[235]

* * *

The rest of this book will consider, in turn, the nature of our Lord's human birth, the person of the Blessed Virgin who bore Him, the purpose for which He was born, the time and place in which He was born, and finally His manifestation to His newfound brethren in human nature. In each chapter I shall strive to imitate the Church in the reverent wonder with which she approaches the cradle of Redeeming Love:

> How great the mystery
> and wondrous the sacred sign,
> that beasts should look upon the Lord
> lying lowly in the stall!

[235] *Bethlehem*, p. 164.

II

'BEGOTTEN ALL INEFFABLY'

The Two Births of the One Person of Christ

Jesu, the Father's only Son,
Whose death for all redemption won,
Before the world, of God most high,
Begotten all ineffably.

The Father's Light and Splendour thou,
Their endless hope to thee that bow;
Accept the prayers and praise today
That through the world thy servants pay.

Salvation's author, call to mind
How, taking the form of humankind,
Born of a Virgin undefiled,
Thou in man's flesh becamest a child.[1]

The Nativity in Bethlehem is not the only birth of our Lord
Jesus Christ. Two thousand years ago, He was born in time,
'in man's flesh', of 'a Virgin undefiled', but, 'before the
worlds', He was—is—born eternally, according to His Divinity, of God the Father. The same Divine Person, the
Second Person of the Blessed Trinity, 'the Father's only Son',

---

[1] The hymn *Christe, Redemptor omnium* (in the version of J. M. Neale, EH 17)
is the office hymn for Vespers during Christmastide, in both the *Breviarium
romanum* of 1962 and the post-conciliar *Liturgia horarum*.

is the subject of two births, the divine and the human, the eternal and the temporal. Jesus is the 'twice-born' Son.[2] This revealed truth, confessed by the Church in her Creeds and the definitions of her Councils,[3] is the foundation upon which the whole structure of the Christmas mystery, indeed of the dogma of the Incarnation itself, is built. We cannot understand the saving purpose for which the Son of God was born as man until we have considered that human birth both in itself and in relation to the divine birth, the eternal begetting by the Father, for the human birth reveals to us, and in a sense prolongs, the divine.[4] Such a consideration is the task of the chapter that follows. First, we shall consider birth in general, then the eternal birth of God the Son and finally His birth in the fullness of time.

1. Nativity and Nature

Nature and nativity are connected as words, as concepts, and as realities. In both Greek and Latin, the nouns translated as 'nature' are derived from verbs meaning 'to be born'. Nature

[2] In the *Purgatorio*, Dante calls the Griffin, the mythical beast whose dual bodily form symbolizes the two natures of Christ, *l'animal binato*, 'the beast twice-born' (32, 47). 'Birth is the only event in Christ's career of which it can be said that it took place twice, once in eternity, and once in time' (Anscar Vonier OSB, *The Divine Motherhood*, in The Collected Works of Abbot Vonier, vol. 1 [London, 1952], p. 355).

[3] In the Niceno-Constantinopolitan Creed, we affirm our faith 'in one Lord Jesus Christ, only-begotten Son of God, born of the Father before all the ages . . . who . . . was incarnate by the Holy Spirit of the Virgin Mary and was made man' (DS 150). The Council of Chalcedon in 451 included the two births in its definition of Christological faith: 'The same was begotten from the Father before the ages as to the divinity and in the latter days, for us and our salvation, was born as to His humanity from Mary the Virgin Mother of God' (DS 301).

[4] This statement depends upon the principle that the temporal missions of the Divine Persons manifest and prolong the eternal processions. '[T]he mission includes the eternal procession and adds something, namely, a temporal effect' (ST 1a q. 43, a. 2, ad 3).

is what the Schoolmen call the 'term' of birth; it is where you end up when you are born. Aristotle puts it rather elegantly: birth, he says, is the 'road to nature', the way you arrive at being what you are.[5] It is by birth, as it is by nature, that 'a man's a man for a' that.' Nature is not the subject of birth, the one that is born: it is persons (or, in the case of nonrational creatures, hypostases) who are born; nature is *that in or into which one is born*. Thus, if someone had more than one nature, he would have more than one birth. (See the discussion of birth in relation to conception, pp. 152–54 below.)

> Nature is related to birth as term to movement or change. However, as the Philosopher makes clear, there are as many different movements as there are different terms. Now in Christ there are two natures, the divine and the human, one of which He receives eternally from the Father, the other He receives temporally from His Mother. It is, therefore, necessary to attribute two births to Christ, one in which He is eternally born of the Father, the other in which He is temporally born of the Mother.[6]

In God-made-man there are two births, as there are two natures, but only one person, the Divine Person of the Word, is born by those births in those natures. The Blessed Virgin does not give temporal birth to a human person in whom a Divine Person dwells, but to the Divine Person Himself, the eternally begotten Son of the Father, albeit in His human, not divine, nature. It is one and the same 'God the Word, who before all ages was begotten of the Father, [that] was in these last days made flesh and born of [the Virgin Theotokos]'.[7] Moreover, according to St Thomas, there is only

---

[5] Cf ST 3a q. 35, a. 1; Aristotle, *Physics* 2, 1; 193b13; *Sententia super Physicam*, lib. 2, lect. 2.

[6] ST 3a q. 35, a. 2.

[7] The Second Council of Constantinople (553), *Anathematismi de tribus Capitulis*, can. 6; DS 427.

one real relationship of Sonship (*filiatio*) in Christ, just as there is only one person. It is important to remember this truth because of the subtle heresy of the Spanish adoptionists who taught that there were two Sonships in Christ, one natural and one adoptive: as God, they said, He was the natural Son of God, but as man the adopted son. But this leads directly to the Nestorian heresy of two persons in Christ, which was condemned by the Council of Ephesus in 431. Therefore, the Church teaches that, not only as God but also as man, Jesus is the natural Son of God. The one person of the natural Son of God subsists in the two natures, the human as well as the divine.[8]

Sonship is indissolubly bound up with personhood. If you have Sonship, then you have *someone* who is Son. In the Trinity, Sonship is the personal property of the Second Person, belonging to Him alone and distinguishing Him from the other two Divine Persons; indeed, it is the real relation that constitutes Him as the person He is, for Divine Persons are subsisting relations.[9] Thus, in God, Sonship *is* the Son, just as Fatherhood *is* the Father. The Father is not a separately constituted person who enters into the relation of Fatherhood; He only exists in His relation to the Son; to be the Father is to be towards the Son, eternally begetting Him in Divinity. Likewise, to be the Son is to be towards the Father, eternally begotten of Him in Divinity. Now in

[8] Cf ST 3a q. 16, a. 11. The Council of Frankfurt (794) poses the rhetorical question: 'If . . . He who is born of the Virgin is true God, how can He be adopted or a servant?' (DS 612–15).

[9] 'Just as the Godhead is God, so the divine Fatherhood is God the Father, who is a divine person. Hence "divine person" signifies relation as subsistent' (ST 1a q. 29, a. 4). 'These three relations—Fatherhood, Sonship, and Procession—are called "personal properties", as constituting, so to speak, the persons, for Fatherhood is the person of the Father, Sonship the person of the Son, and procession the person of the Holy Spirit, who proceeds' (ibid., q. 30, a. 2, ad 1; cf q. 32, a. 3).

Christ there is only one person, and that person is the Divine Person of the eternal Son, the person constituted by Sonship of the Father. Therefore, Sonship, too, must be one in Christ. There is only one real relation of Sonship in Christ, and that is His eternal relation of being begotten by the Father.

But what, then, do we say of our Lord's Sonship of Mary? Does He not have a real relation to her who supplied Him with His flesh and blood, who carried Him in her womb and nursed Him at her breast? St Thomas's answer is at first sight disconcerting. He argues that the relation of God the Son to the Mother who gave Him temporal birth is like every other relation of the eternal God to the temporal world: it is a relation not according to reality but only according to reason.[10] It is the kind of relation where there is change on one side of the relation but not on the other, like, for example, my relation to St Peter's basilica when I first see it with my own eyes: I am changed, but St Peter's basilica is not. This principle is exemplified first of all in creation in general: creation is the one-sided relation in which the creature depends upon God for everything, for its being and activity, while God depends upon the creature for nothing.[11] To say that God is related to His creatures only 'according to reason', not 'according to reality', does not mean that He is not related to them at all, but describes the particular kind of relation that He has. In being related to the creature, God does not cease to be God. Now God is 'He Who Is', self-subsisting being (*ipsum esse subsistens*); He exists by essence,[12] of necessity. By contrast, the creature, as our Lord

---

[10] Cf ST 1a q. 13, a. 7.

[11] 'Creation is not a change but the very dependence of created being on the principle by which it is established; it therefore belongs to the genus of relation' (SCG 2, 18, 2).

[12] Cf ST 1a q. 3, a. 4.

told St Catherine, is 'she who is not',[13] created out of nothing; she exists by participation, in utter dependence upon the
gift of existence freely bestowed on her by God.[14] Any relation of God and creature will, therefore, be marked by a
fearful lack of symmetry.

What is true in general of the Triune God's relation to
creatures is true in particular of the Son's relation to His
created human nature and to the Virgin from whom He
assumes it. She is really related to Him as His Mother, for it is
she who conceived Him and gave Him His flesh, but 'the
Sonship by which Christ is related to His Mother cannot be
a real relation, but only a relation of reason'. If we linked
Sonship with birth and nature, then we should have to conclude that there are two real Sonships, as there are two really
distinct births and natures. But if, as we ought rather to do,
we link Sonship with person, then we must affirm, that
Christ's eternal Sonship of the Father is the only Sonship in
Him that is a real relation.

> He does have the relation of Son in regard to His Mother,
> because it is implied in the relation of motherhood to Christ.
> Thus God is called Lord by the relation that is implied in the
> real relation by which the creature is subject to God. And
> although lordship is not a real relation in God, yet He is really
> Lord through the real subjection of the creature to Him. In
> the same way, Christ is really the Son of the Virgin Mother
> through the real relation of her motherhood to Christ.[15]

Far from making our Lady remote from her Son, this doctrine should instill a new sense of reverence for her intimacy

[13] Blessed Raymond of Capua, *The Life of Catherine of Siena*, chap. 10, ET
(Dublin, 1980), p. 85.

[14] Cf ST 1a q. 44, a. 1.

[15] ST 3a q. 35, a. 5. 'Christ can be called the Son of the Virgin, not by a real
Sonship existing in Him, but by real Motherhood existing in the Mother, and
because He was really born from her' (Blessed Dionysius the Carthusian,
Elementatio theologica, prop. 129; DCOO 33:207).

with Him. The Child born of the Virgin is God *in all His
uncompromised deity*. If Christ's Sonship of Mary had been a
real relation in Him, it would have altered Him, added something or taken something from Him. But then it would not
have been true God who was born of Mary as true man, for
God is infinite in His perfections, without need of enhancement and incapable of diminution. And so, as Pope St Leo
the Great says in his Tome, 'The birth that took place in time
took nothing from, and added nothing to, the divine and
eternal birth, but was dedicated entirely to the restoration of
man who had been deceived.' [16] The Nativity in Bethlehem
does not change God, but it does change man, at least in
principle and by way of hope, for the temporal birth of God
is the dawn of mankind's redemption from sin and death and
the deceiving wiles of Satan. The Son of God did not need
to have a temporal birth from our Lady in addition to His
eternal birth from the Father. No, 'it was for us and for our
salvation that He united humanity hypostatically to Himself
and came forth from a woman. For this reason He is said to
be born in the flesh.' [17] Everything God does through the
Incarnation, as in creation, is outward going, an act of
infinite liberality, of transformation and elevation in the creature without any loss or gain in the changeless Creator. This
truth is beautifully expressed in Byzantine icons of our Lady:
the Child in her arms bears within His halo the name revealed to Moses on Sinai, the name that, according to the
Fathers and St Thomas, is 'the supreme proper name of God'
(cf Ex 3:14): *ho ôn*, 'He Who Is'.[18] Real human baby though

[16] *Tomus Leonis*; DS 291.

[17] St Cyril of Alexandria, cited by St Thomas in ST 3a q. 35, a. 2, ad 2.

[18] St Thomas quotes Damascene (*De fide orthodoxa* lib. 1, cap. 9; PG 94:836B)
as saying that '"He Who Is" is the most important of all the names attributed
to God, for, comprehending all in itself, it contains being itself as an infinite
and indeterminate sea of substance' (ST 1a q. 13, a. 11; cf St Gregory
Nazianzen, *Oratio* 38, no. 7; PG 36:317B–319A).

He now is, He is still, without alteration, the God of the 'metaphysics of the Exodus'.[19]

Born without Change

Conception in human nature and birth in time do not, therefore, change the only-begotten and eternal Son. He sleeps on His Mother's breast without leaving the bosom of the Father.[20] Without ceasing to be the great and almighty God, He is born as a tiny and defenceless infant. 'Lo, He who lay in the manger became small,' says St Augustine, 'but He did not destroy Himself. He took to Himself what He was not, but He remained what He was.'[21] Human infancy is exalted through its assumption by God the Son, but divine majesty is not injured by His condescension.[22] The self-emptying manifested on Christmas Day is a taking by God of our childhood's weakness, not a loss of His Godhead's strength.[23] Thus the changeless grandeur of divinity

[19] See Étienne Gilson, *Le Thomisme*, new ed. (Paris, 1972), pp. 99ff.

[20] *Oratio* 15, 5; PG 65:804B.

[21] *Sermo* 196, cap. 3, no. 3; PL 38:1020. 'In a wonderful way, He began to be what we are without ceasing to be what He was, assuming our nature in such a way that He Himself would not lose what He was' (St Bede, *Homelia* I, 5, *In vigilia nativitatis Domini*; CCSL 122:34).

[22] 'May the Lord be honoured in His infancy, and let not His bodily beginnings be seen as an injury to His divinity' (Pope St Leo, *In nativitate Domini*, sermo 9, no. 3; SC 22B:184). 'Therefore, the Word of God, Himself God, the Son of God who "in the beginning was with God", through whom "all things were made" and "without" whom "was nothing made", with the purpose of delivering man from eternal death, became man. Bending Himself to take on Him our humility without any diminution of His own majesty, He remained what He was and assumed what He was not, so that He might unite the true form of a slave to that form in which He is equal to God the Father, and join both natures together by such a covenant that the glorification should not swallow up the lower nor the assumption lessen the higher' (*In nativitate Domini, sermo* 1, no. 2; SC 22B:70).

[23] According to the Athanasian Creed, our Lord is 'one, not by the conversion of Godhead into flesh, but by the taking up of manhood into God' (DS 76).

and the fragile littleness of humanity are united without confusion in the one Person of the Word. In Pope St Leo's words, Christmas is 'a mystery of strength united with infirmity'.[24] The baby in the Crib, says St Augustine, is the almighty Creator: 'While ruling the stars, He nurses at His Mother's breast. He is great in the nature of God and small in the form of a servant, and yet His greatness is not diminished by the smallness nor His smallness overwhelmed by His greatness.'[25]

2. The Eternal Birth

The Midnight Mass of Christmas is by tradition devoted to the divine and eternal birth of the Son of God.[26] According to Durandus, it is fitting that this procession within the Godhead should be commemorated 'in deepest night', because it is 'hidden from us', a vast mystery.[27] A reference to our Lord's eternal begetting can be found in the Introit of the Mass: *Dominus dixit ad me: Filius meus es tu, ego hodie genui te,* 'The Lord hath said to me: Thou art my Son; this day have I begotten thee' (Ps 2:7). 'This day' is not an item in any earthly calendar, but the day of the divine eternity, the day that is the eternal Godhead Itself. Of this day David speaks in the Psalm, sung at Christmas Matins, when he cries out, 'Sing ye to the Lord and bless His name: bless His salvation from day to day *(de die in diem)*' (cf Ps 95:1–3). 'What is this "day from day"', asks St Augustine, 'if not the Son born of the Father, Light from Light?'[28] One of Augustine's later disciples develops the argument further: 'The one "day" of

---

[24] *In nativitate Domini, sermo* 3, no. 2; SC 22B:98.

[25] *Sermo* 187, cap. 1, no. 1; PL 38:1001.

[26] Cf ST 3a q. 83, a. 2, ad 2.

[27] *Rationale* lib. 6, cap. 13, no. 23; 140A:189f.

[28] St Augustine, *Sermo* 189, cap. 1, no. 1; PL 38:1095.

eternity is acknowledged by us as at once the Father and the Son, but in the day of time only the Son is found. The eternal day, the Father and the Son, made our body and soul; on the day of time, the Son alone assumed our body and soul.'[29]

Ineffable Generation

The Eunomian heretics claimed to have exhaustive comprehension, even in this life, of the divine generation of the Son.[30] To confound such presumption, the Fathers invoke the prophet's reverence for the mystery: 'Who shall declare His generation?' (Is 53:8). The Fathers like to point out that these words apply to the two births, human as well as divine.[31] If the human and temporal birth from the Virgin eludes the full grasp of our minds, how much more so does the divine and eternal birth. We know *that* the Son of God is begotten of the Father, but we cannot grasp *what* such begetting is and must resort to the way of negation, removing from it the imperfections of all creaturely birth. The Father's begetting of the Son is eternal and therefore surpassing all succession, without beginning or end. It is immaterial, incorporeal, utterly free of the flesh and its passions. It is simple, lacking all composition of parts or elements or stages. The Father's only Son is indeed, as the Christmas hymn says, 'before the worlds, of God most high, begotten all *ineffably*'.[32]

[29] St Fulgentius, *Sermo 2 de duplici nativitate Christi*, no. 4; PL 65:727BC.

[30] See the anti-Eunomian treatises of St Basil the Great (*Adversus Eunomium*, PG 29:497ff.) and his brother, St Gregory of Nyssa (*Contra Eunomium*, PG 45:248ff.).

[31] Cf Pope St Leo, *In nativitate Domini*, sermo 9, no. 1; SC 22B:176.

[32] St Athanasius says that the Word is begotten of the Father in Heaven 'ineffably, inexplicably, incomprehensibly, and eternally' (*De incarnatione Dei Verbi et contra Arianos*, no. 8; PG 26:996A).

Generation, Not Creation

According to the Creed, the eternal Son is 'begotten, not made'.[33] His generation is not creation, nor is the world's creation a generation. The Son is Son, not work, and the world is work, not Son. Even in the created order, a son is not 'made' by his father's act of conception. 'How can you compare a father's function with that of a maker? . . . A work is external to the nature, but a son is the proper offspring of the substance.'[34] The universe is produced out of nothing, but the Son is begotten out of the very substance of the Father.[35] As Matthias Scheeben says, summarizing the teaching of the Fathers:

> Creation is a free act of the divine will, whereby God calls into being things which of themselves were nothing and communicates to them an existence which is essentially different from His own. But God brings forth His interior Word by communicating to Him His own being, His own substance. The Word proceeds from the Father's innermost substance, which passes over to the Word and places Him in full possession of the very nature that is proper to the Father.[36]

The personal being of the Father is Fatherhood, not Creatorhood. Far from being creature, the Son is Himself Creator, the eternal Word, 'through whom all things were made' (cf John 1:3).[37] Were He a creature, He could not by His Incarnation and redemptive work 'deify' us, for only

[33] The Church confesses our Lord to be 'true and natural Son of God, eternal, equal with the Father, and true God, of the same essence and nature with the Father, begotten, not created or made' (SCG 4, 7).

[34] *Oratio 1 contra Arianos*, no. 29; PG 26:72AB.

[35] According to the Creed of the First Council of Nicaea, the Son of God is 'begotten of the Father, only-begotten, that is, out of the substance [*ousías*] of the Father' (DS 125).

[36] M. J. Scheeben, *The Mysteries of Christianity*, ET (St Louis, 1946), p. 87.

[37] Cf St Augustine, *De Trinitate* lib. 1, cap. 6, no. 9; CCSL 50:38.

One who is God and Son of God by nature can make others
gods and sons of God by grace.

> If he were joined to a creature, man could not be deified. Man
> cannot be deified unless the Son is true God. Man would
> never have been brought into the Father's presence, had it not
> been His natural and true Word who put on the body. And
> just as we would not have been delivered from sin and the
> curse of sin if the flesh assumed by the Word had not been by
> nature human flesh (for we can have nothing in common with
> a being that is alien to us), so, likewise, man would not have
> been deified if He who was made flesh had not been by nature
> from the Father and His true and proper Word.[38]

Incorporeal Generation

The eternal generation of the Son by the Father is incorporeal,[39] wholly transcending the order of the flesh, and therefore without passion, marriage or pregnancy.[40] The Fathers
of East and West dismiss with a righteous intolerance the
pagan and Gnostic ideas of a divine Son born of a divine
Father and divine Mother.[41] They are unanimous: the Son
who is born in His humanity of a Mother without a father
is begotten in His Divinity of the Father *without a mother*.[42]

[38] *Oratio 2 contra Arianos*, no. 70; PG 26:296AB.

[39] Cf the Second Council of Constantinople II (553), *Anathematismi*, no. 2;
DS 422.

[40] Cf St Gregory Nazianzen, *Oratio* 29, no. 4; PG 36:77C.

[41] Cf St Augustine, *De Trinitate* lib. 12, cap. 5, no. 5; CCSL 50:359f.

[42] We can cite St John Damascene as a representative of the Greek Fathers:
'We worship His two births: one before the ages and eternal, without cause,
from the Father without a mother; and the other from the Virgin Mother
without a father for our salvation' (*Contra Iacobitas* 79; PG 94:1476C). St Augustine can speak for the Latins: 'The birth of Christ from the father without a
mother, and from the Mother without a father. Both are wonderful. The first is
eternal, the second temporal' (*Sermo* 189, cap. 4, no. 4; PL 38:1096; cf *Sermo*
194, cap. 1, no. 1; PL 38:1015).

There is no motherhood in the Godhead. Occasionally, the *metaphor* of motherhood may be used to describe some essential attribute or operation of the Godhead, but nowhere, neither in Scripture nor in the Fathers, do we find an *analogy* of motherhood used to name any of the Divine Persons and the relations by which they are constituted. The Father and the Spirit do not generate the Son; the Father and the Son spirate, breathe forth, the Spirit. The Spirit is neither generated nor generating, neither a second offspring nor a second parental principle, but rather the One who proceeds from the Begetter and the Begotten as their immanent bond of love. There is only one generation in God, and that is the eternal generation of the Word, which is motherless, just as His temporal conception is fatherless. If the temporal motherhood of Mary is virginal, so, too, is the eternal Fatherhood of God. God the Father needs no wife to enable Him to be Father. He is the eternal Father of the co-eternal Son by an immaterial generation of transcendent purity. Thus the First Person of the Blessed Trinity is the primal source and model of all virginity, just as He is the Father from whom all earthly and heavenly fatherhood takes its name (cf Eph 3:15).[43]

The Father's generating of the Son is incorporeal and therefore simple, entirely without parts or division. This was

---

[43] This insight, which we find first in St Gregory of Nyssa (see *De virginitate*, cap. 2; PG 46:321C), was developed in the seventeenth century by the theologians of the French School. For example, the learned dogmatician, Louis Thomassin, says that in His two births the Son of God is born of 'a Virgin Father [God] and a Virgin Mother [Mary], in both cases virginally and without corruption' (*Dogmata theologica*, vol. 3, new ed. [Paris, 1866], p. 186). Père Bourgoing refers to the way in which our Lady, by the virginal integrity of her child-bearing, 'adores and imitates' God the Father, who is the 'primary virgin' (*Méditations sur les divers estats de Jésus-Christ, Nostre Seigneur* [Paris, 1648], p. 56). Father Louis Bouyer, also of the French Oratory, made the same point in *Le Trône de la sagesse: Essai sur la signification du culte marial*, new ed. (Paris, 1987), pp. 146ff, 215ff.

a truth that the Fourth Lateran Council reasserted against the Trinitarian errors of the early thirteenth century:

> [T]he Father, in generating the Son from eternity, gave Him His substance. . . . One cannot say that He gave Him a part of His substance and kept a part for Himself, since the substance of the Father is indivisible, being entirely simple. Nor can one say that in generating, the Father transferred His substance to the Son, as though He gave to the Son in such a way as not to retain it for Himself, for then He would have ceased to be substance. It is therefore clear that the Son, in being born, received the substance of the Father without any diminution, and thus the Father and the Son have the same substance.[44]

The Council here merely unfolds the meaning of the words addressed by our Lord to the Father on the evening of Holy Thursday: '[A]ll my things are thine, and thine are mine' (Jn 17:10). The Son is the 'All' of the Father.

Eternal Generation

The begetting of the Father's Son and Word is eternal, that is, altogether free of succession, without before or after, beginning or end.[45] The Byzantine Church expresses the dogmatic truth in words that match metaphysical precision with poetical beauty: 'The Virgin draws nigh to bear thee, O Lord, who, shining timelessly from the Father, hast now come to be in time, setting us loose from the temporal passions of our souls.'[46] The Word is the co-eternal Son of the eternal Father. Whenever the Father was, the Son was. In the

---

[44] DS 805.

[45] '[T]he action by which the Father produces the Son is not successive, because then the Son would be generated successively, and His generation would be material and involve motion, which is impossible. What remains, then, is that whenever the Father was, the Son was, and in this way the Son is co-eternal with the Father, as is the Holy Spirit with Them both' (ST 1a q. 42, a. 2).

[46] The Forefeast of the Nativity, *Menaion*, p. 211.

agelessness of the Godhead, the Son is as old as the Father and the Father as young as the Son. The Father simply does not exist without the Son.[47] Since the Father is always the Father, the Father is never without the Son. Had there once been no Son, there once would have been no Father.[48] With the satirical sharp edge that so often marks the rhetoric of the Fathers when they are dealing with the Arians, St Gregory of Nyssa asks them what we should call the Father in the period before He became Father: Was He 'child, infant, baby, or youth'?[49] As I have said, Fatherhood, the active generation of the Son, is not a relation into which the Father enters, but the relation by which the Father exists, that which constitutes Him as Father, just as the relation of Sonship, the Son's passive generation, is constitutive of the Son. ' "Father" is not the name of an essence or of an operation, but of the relation that the Father has towards the Son and the Son towards the Father.' [50] What distinguishes the Son from the Father is not being God but being Son. The very thing that relates Him to the Father distinguishes Him from the Father. 'All things [in the Trinitarian Godhead] are one where there is no opposition of relation.' [51]

To be the Father is eternally to be begetting the Son, and to be the Son is eternally to be begotten.[52] Thus the Son never outgrows the bosom of the Father, nor is His eternal birth ever a thing of the past. As the One whom the Greek Fathers call the 'offspring' (*gennêma*) of the Father, the eternally begotten Son is the first and most perfect model of

[47] As St Gregory of Nyssa says: '[W]ithout the Son, the Father has neither existence nor name' (*Contra Eunomium* lib. 2, no. 4; PG 45:477B).

[48] Cf St Athanasius, *Oratio 3 contra Arianos*, no. 6; PG 26:333AB.

[49] Cf *Contra Eunomium* lib. 1, no. 38; PG 45:433AB.

[50] St Gregory Nazianzen, *Oratio* 29, no. 16; PG 36:96A.

[51] The Council of Florence, Decree for the Jacobites (1442); DS 1330.

[52] Cf John of St Thomas, *Cursus theologicus in summam theologicam D. Thomae*, t. 4 (in 1a q. 27, disp. 12, a. 3, no. 45) (Paris, 1884), p. 65.

childhood, though we must add immediately that He is offspring and child of the Father without any suggestion of
imperfection or growth into maturity. He is eternal Child
because He receives everlastingly the whole of the divine
essence, all that He is, from the Father.

Intellectual Generation

According to St Thomas, St John the Evangelist was inspired
by the Holy Spirit to call the Son of God 'the Word' (*Logos*)
in order to exclude any suggestion that generation in God
was carnal.[53] The Greek word *logos* means not only the spoken word but the thought the spoken word expresses, the
'word of the mind [or heart]' or the 'concept of the intellect', the 'inner word' as distinct from the 'outer' or spoken
word.[54] Thus, by calling the Son 'Logos', St John indicates
that the begetting of the Son in the Godhead should be
understood by analogy with the forming of a concept in the
mind. 'Since God is above all things, the things said about
God are not to be understood in the manner of the lowest
creatures (which are bodies), but by likeness to the highest
creatures (which are spiritual substances).'[55] God is spirit (cf

[53] 'Hence it is that in the rule of the Catholic faith we are taught to confess
the Father and the Son in the Godhead, when it says *Credo in Deum Patrem et
Filium eius*. And lest anyone, on hearing the names "Father" and "Son", suspect
there was a carnal generation, as with us when we say "father" and "son", St
John the Evangelist, to whom the heavenly mysteries were revealed, says
"Word" instead of "Son", so that we might know that the generation was of
the intellectual order' (*Compendium theologiae*, lib. 1, cap. 40).

[54] Cf ST 1a q. 34, a. 2; SCG 4:11. As in all analogies, the creaturely image is
more unlike than like the divine model: 'In the Godhead, the Son is in a
certain way represented, *albeit deficiently*, by the word of our mind' (*Super
epistolam ad Colossenses*, cap. 1, lect. 2). On the definition of *verbum*, see B. J.
Lonergan SJ, *Verbum: Word and Idea in Aquinas* (London, 1968), p. 1 and passim.

[55] ST 1a q. 27, a. 1. 'Now the generation of God is different from the
generation of other things. We cannot, therefore, reach the generation of God

Jn 4:24), and so processions in God are best understood by
comparison with the spiritual acts of intellectual creatures,
namely, with acts of intellect and will. The Son is begotten
of the Father by way of intellect as Word, just as the Holy
Spirit proceeds from the Father and the Son by way of will
as Love. 'The Son of God is the Word and conception of
God understanding Himself.'[56] On this matter all the
Schoolmen are in agreement. Bonaventure speaks in complete harmony with his friend Thomas: 'When the mind
understands itself, it conceives an idea [*speciem*] of itself in
itself. Were it to understand itself from eternity, it would
generate an idea [of itself] from eternity. Now since . . . God
never existed without understanding Himself, God never
existed without uttering the Word, was never Father without generating the Son.'[57]

---

except through the generation of what in creatures gives more access to the
likeness of God. Now nothing is so like God as the soul of man. The mode of
generation in the soul is that a man thinks [*cogitat*] something through his soul
which is called the conception of the intellect. And conception of this kind
arises out of the soul as from a father, and is called the word of the intellect or
man. The soul, when it thinks, generates its word. In this way also the Son of
God is none other than the Word of God, not like a word externally uttered,
because that passes away, but like a word internally conceived. And therefore
the Word of God Himself is of one nature with God and equal with God' (St
Thomas Aquinas, *In symbolum apostolorum expositio*, art. 2). The Roman Catechism makes a similar statement: 'Of all examples which are adduced with a
view to an explanation of the nature and manner of this eternal generation,
that appears most nearly to approach the matter, which is taken from the
intellectual activity of our soul, for which reason St John calls the Son of God
the "Word". For just as our spirit, knowing itself, produces a picture of itself,
which theologians have called a "word", so God also, insofar as human can be
compared to divine, knowing Himself, generates the eternal Word' (*De 2
symboli articulo*).

[56] SCG 4, 12. We must add this important qualification: 'The divine Word is
not only an intention understood, as our word is, but also a reality existing and
subsisting in nature, for God is a true subsisting reality, since He is the being
that exists *per se* to the highest degree' (ibid.).

[57] *In nativitate Domini, sermo* 2; Q IX:106B.

Begetting in God resembles intellectual knowledge: the Father is, as it were, God Understanding, and the Son is God Understood.[58] God knows Himself in the Word—all that He is, all that He does and all He can do. This transcendent Trinitarian knowing or understanding is properly called 'begetting', for, where you have begetting, you find one living thing coming from another, the one resembling the other, and both existing in the same nature.[59] To understand this mystery a little more deeply, we need to remember that ' "knowing" constitutes and establishes the most intimate relationship conceivable between two beings (a fact that is expressed and confirmed through the age-old usage of "knowing" to indicate sexual intercourse)'.[60] Somehow the thing I know or understand comes into me, becomes part of me. More exactly, the *form* of the thing is communicated to me.[61] To know what a dog is is to have within oneself the form of a dog, what makes a dog to be a dog. In dear old Rover on my hearth rug, the dog form exists 'materially', as informing the matter, whereas in my mind the dog form exists 'intentionally', as informing my mind with the intention or idea of a dog. Thus, through the form, the object known shapes the knowing subject. The soul is form in relation to the matter of its body, but in relation to the form of the thing it understands, it is matter. In this sense, the intellect appears to be, as it were, feminine and maternal,

[58] Cf SCG 4, 11.

[59] Cf ST 1a q. 27, a. 2. 'The Second Person receives the Father's nature in order to exhibit and manifest it in Himself. What then is to prevent us from saying that He is truly generated, nay, that His generation is the perfect ideal of all generation, and that, in accord with the words of Holy Scripture, all fatherhood in heaven and on earth is so called after the generating fatherhood of His principle?' (Scheeben, *Mysteries of Christianity*, p. 91).

[60] Josef Pieper, *Living the Truth: The Truth of All Things and Reality and the Good*, ET (San Francisco, 1989), p. 37.

[61] Cf ST 1a q. 14, a. 1.

insofar as it is receptive of reality and bears the concept within itself, while the thing understood, shaping the mind as it does, might appear to be more active and therefore analogously masculine and paternal. However, when the intellect understands *itself*, when the object that is understood and the subject that understands are essentially the same thing, then the concept, the likeness of the thing understood, relates to the intellect as offspring to the Father.[62] According to this analogy, therefore, the Word, God's perfect Idea of Himself, is properly called 'the Son', the Father's beloved Only-Begotten, distinct from Him in person but one with Him in essence. The Word is 'begotten Wisdom', for 'He is nothing but the concept of the Wise One [the Father].'[63] He is called 'Word', not 'Thought' (*cogitatio*), because a thought is something incomplete, a search for truth, whereas the interior word is the attainment of understanding, a perfect contemplation of the truth, what 'the intellect conceives by knowing'.[64]

The reasonableness of this so-called psychological analogy for understanding the Divine Processions is confirmed by the other names of the intellectual order that the Scriptures predicate of God the Son. For example, St Paul calls Him the 'Wisdom of God' (cf 1 Cor 1:24) for the good reason that, as Word of the Father, He is like the concept in the

[62] 'Since that which is conceived by the intellect is a likeness of the thing understood, representing its species, it seems to be a kind of offspring of the intellect. When, therefore, the intellect understands something other than itself, the thing understood is like the father of the word conceived in the intellect, whereas the intellect itself bears more of a likeness to a mother, within whom the conception takes place. But when the intellect understands itself, the word conceived is related to the understanding [mind] as offspring to father. Since, therefore, we speak of the Word in terms of God understanding Himself, the Word Himself must be related to God, whose Word He is, as Son to Father' (*Compendium theologiae*, lib. 1, cap. 39).
[63] Cf ST 1a q. 34, a. 1, ad 2.
[64] Ibid.

mind of a wise man.[65] Again, He is fittingly named the 'Image of the invisible God' (cf Col 1:15) and 'figure of [the Father's] substance' (cf Heb 1:3), because the concept of a thing is a kind of likeness of that thing, an icon in the mind, while the Word, the Father's consubstantial concept, perfectly reflects all His essential attributes. However, He is the kind of image that only a true Son can be, for 'that which proceeds from a living thing in the likeness of the species is called "Son"'.[66] Of course, an idea or likeness in my mind is not a person distinct from myself, nor does it have anything except intentional existence. By contrast, the eternal Word and Son has true natural existence and is distinct from the Father in person, while being one with Him in essence.[67]

According to St Thomas, in knowing Himself in the Word, the Father knows all the ways in which the infinite perfections of the Godhead can be mirrored by the finite perfections of creatures. Thus the Word expresses not only the Father but creatures as well.[68] All the ideas in the divine mind are summed up in the one great, consubstantial Idea, the eternal Logos. The Father's uncreated Image within the Godhead is the model for everything that the Triune God creates to resemble Him outside the Godhead. '[J]ust as the Word of God is that which God conceives of Himself,' says Blessed Denys the Carthusian, 'so He is also that which God conceives of everything else, for God, by one simple gaze,

[65] Ibid.; cf SCG 4, 12.

[66] SCG 4, 11.

[67] 'The Word of the divine intellect has an existence (*esse*) that is truly natural and substantially identical with the existence of the Father's intellect' (Blessed Denys the Carthusian, *De lumine christianae theoriae*, lib. 2, a. 25; DCOO 33:417BC).

[68] 'Because by the one act God understands both Himself and everything else, His single Word expresses not only the Father but creatures as well' (ST 1a q. 34, a. 3; cf St Bonaventure, *Collationes in Hexaëmeron* 1, 13; Q V:331).

contemplates Himself and all other things.'[69] Every creature corresponds to an idea, an eternal thought contained within the eternal Word and translated into reality in the act of creation. If this is so, then we can begin to understand a little of what the Evangelist means when he says that all things were created through the Word (cf Jn 1:3). Just as Michelangelo modelled his Pietà on an idea in his mind, an 'interior word', so the Divine Artist creates the world through His eternal Word.[70] The Son and Word of God is the Father's eternal 'Art', like that intellectual virtue in the mind of the human artist which encompasses all his artistic ideas.[71] St Thomas concludes that it is supremely fitting that it should be the uncreated Word and Wisdom, the Art of the Father, through whom the original artwork of the cosmos was created, who becomes incarnate in order to restore the canvas to its pristine beauty.

> Things have to be repaired by the very same thing by which they were made. Therefore, it is fitting that the things created by Wisdom should be restored by Wisdom. As it says in the book of Wisdom: '[B]y Wisdom they were healed, whosoever have pleased thee from the beginning' (9:19). Now this restoration was in a special way done by the Son, inasmuch as it is He Himself made man who, having restored the state of man, somehow restored all those things that were made for man's sake; as it says in the epistle to the Colossians, 'through Him reconciling all things unto Himself . . . both as to the

[69] *De lumine Christianae theoriae* lib. 2, a. 18; DCOO 33:408CD.

[70] 'When someone makes something, he pre conceives it in wisdom, which is the form and pattern of the thing made. The form conceived beforehand in the mind of the craftsman is the pattern of the chest to be made. Thus God does nothing except through the concept of His intellect, which is His Wisdom conceived from eternity, namely, the Word of God, the Son of God. And so it is impossible that He does anything except through the Son' (*Lectura super Ioannem*, cap. 1, lect. 2).

[71] 2 *Sent.* d. 1, q. 1, a. 6, ad 1.

things that are on earth and the things that are in Heaven'
(Col 1:20).[72]

For all the likeness of our thinking to the generation of the
Son, the unlikeness is greater. Our poor thoughts flit in and
out of our minds, but the Word is co-eternal with the Father,
eternally begotten, ever actual. The human idea is imperfect,
never adequately representing the thing it expresses, but the
eternal Word is the most perfect and entirely adequate expression of the Father, as infinitely perfect as He is. Our
'interior word' is not of the same nature with us, but the
Word is consubstantial with the Father in Divinity.[73]

The Love-Breathing Word

Just as love springs forth from the word or concept of a thing
in our mind, so the Holy Spirit proceeds from the Son, as
well as from the Father, as their mutual Love.[74] There is an
essential love that is common to the three Divine Persons,
but there is also a personal love, a Person-Love, that is God
the Holy Spirit Himself.[75] Thus God the Son is the 'Love-
breathing Word'.[76] This truth is manifested to us in Scripture
not only by those texts that attribute the works of love
outside of the Godhead to the Holy Spirit (cf Rom 5:5), but
also by the ways in which the sacred authors relate the Spirit,
inside the Godhead, to both the Father and the Son (cf Mt
10:20; Gal 4:6). It is precisely because He is the Spirit of the

[72] *1 Sent.* Prooemium. 'The first creation of the world was achieved by the
power of God the Father through the Word. Therefore, the re-creation of the
world had to take place by the power of God the Father through the Word, so
that creation and re-creation should correspond' (ST 3a q. 3, a. 8, ad 2).

[73] Cf *Lectura super Ioannem*, cap. 1, lect. 1.

[74] Cf ST 1a q. 36, a. 2.

[75] Cf ST 1a q. 37, a. 1.

[76] St Augustine, cited in ST 1a q. 43, a. 5, ad 2.

Son in the inner life of the Trinity that, in the economy of salvation, He can communicate a share by grace in the Sonship of the Son. The Holy Spirit's name is made up of two words that express attributes common to the Father and the Son: the Father and the Son are both holy, just as the Father and the Son are both spirit or immaterial. To use that most useful of American words, this 'commonality' of the Holy Spirit's by name expresses that commonality which is His very person: He is in Himself 'the communion and connection of the Father and the Son'.[77] Within the eternal Godhead, the Father and the Son 'spirate', breathe forth, that Love which connects Them.[78] This is beautifully expressed in the altarpiece of the charterhouse in Villeneuve-lès-Avignon.[79] As the Father and the Son crown our Lady as Queen of Heaven, the wings of the Spirit-Dove touch their mouths: He is the Love they breathe out in unison, the Kiss exchanged between the One who kisses and the One who is kissed (cf Song 1:1).[80] Moreover, it is by the Love-Kiss of the Holy Spirit that the Father and Son pour out the gifts of the Godhead upon creatures, including the grace and glory poured out on the Blessed Virgin. In the Holy Spirit, the Father and the Son love each other;[81] in the Holy Spirit They

[77] St Thomas, *De potentia* q. 10, a. 5, ad 11; cf ST 1a q. 36, a. 1; q. 36, a. 4, ad 1.

[78] As St Bonaventure says: 'The Father expresses Himself in the Word, that is, by declaring or expressing Himself He generates the Word, and by generating the Word He expresses Himself in the Word. Similarly, the verb "to love" [*diligere*] implies the act of connecting or harmonizing and breathing, so by reason of this act of connecting we can say: the Father and the Son love each other by the Holy Spirit. In other words, in harmony with each other, They breathe forth the Holy Spirit, and by breathing forth the Holy Spirit They are connected with each other' (*1 Sent.* d. 32, a. 1, q. 1, concl; Q I:558).

[79] See J. and Y. le Pichon, *Le Mystère du Couronnement de la Vierge* (Paris, 1982).

[80] Cf St Bernard, *Super Cantica canticorum, sermo* 8, no. 2; L-R 1:37.

[81] Cf ST 1a q. 37, a. 2; *Compendium theologiae* lib. 1, cap. 219; *Super epistolam ad Romanos* cap. 5, lect. 1.

love us; and in the Holy Spirit we love Them. This truth must be recalled whenever we consider the human birth of the Son. In His Divine Person, He is the Word who breathes forth uncreated Love, and in His human nature, according to His human conception and birth, He is filled with, and then pours out from His heart, all of the Holy Spirit's created gifts of love. The Holy Infant is the Love-breathing Word.

Revealed Generation

The eternal generation of the Son by the Father is one of 'the mysteries hidden in God that can only be known if divinely revealed'.[82] It is not a truth that unaided reason could have discovered or deduced.[83] We should never have heard of it had we not learned of it, through the apostles and evangelists, from the human mind and heart of the Son of God Himself.[84] 'Who shall declare His generation?' Plato spoke of God as 'Maker and Father of this universe',[85] by some act outside the Godhead, but before the eternal Son became man, neither Plato nor any other philosopher had so much as suspected that there were really distinct and eternal relations of Fatherhood and Sonship *inside* the one simple

[82] Cf First Vatican Council, Dogmatic Constitution on the Catholic Faith, *Dei Filius*, cap. 4; DS 3015.

[83] 'The philosophers did not know the mystery of the Trinity of the Divine Persons by their properties [*per propria*], such as Fatherhood, Sonship, and Procession, according to the Apostle's words, "We speak the wisdom of God which none of the princes of the world", that is, the philosophers, "knew" (1 Cor 2:6). Nevertheless, they knew some of the essential attributes appropriated to the Persons, such as power to the Father, wisdom to the Son, and goodness to the Holy Ghost' (ST 1a q. 32, a. 1, ad 1).

[84] We know of the temporal birth of Christ through St Matthew and St Luke and of the eternal birth through St John, who by the 'privilege of his singular chastity' merited to receive deep revelations concerning the Trinitarian Godhead when he leaned against the Heart of Jesus at the Last Supper (see St Bede the Venerable, *Homilia 8 in nativitate Domini*; CCSL 122:52f.).

[85] Cf *Timaeus* 28c.

Godhead. 'Jesus revealed that God is Father in an unheard-of sense: he is Father not only in being Creator; he is eternally Father in relation to his only Son, who is eternally Son only in relation to his Father.'[86] In the Old Testament, the Triune God had revealed many truths about Himself, but the Divine Processions, the generation of the Son and the spiration of the Holy Spirit, though indicated by remote signs, such as the visit of the three angels to Abraham, remained hidden.[87] Only through the human features of the Son was the divine countenance of the Father disclosed (cf Jn 14:9). Only when the Son has humbled Himself in Mary's womb to take the form of a servant, and in Jordan's waters to receive John's baptism of penance, only then, in the depths of the Son's self-emptying, do the voice of the Father ring out and the Dove descend from above. Cardinal Bérulle concludes that it is a great and wonderful privilege for Christian faith, after millennia of hiddenness, to receive at last the revelation of the Fatherhood of God: 'O Father unknown for the space of four thousand years in this Fatherhood'. The divine Fatherhood is 'so elevated . . . above our capacity, so full . . . of marvel', that 'the world in its darkness, and before the birth of the true Light in the universe, worshipped . . . the Godhead without worshipping the Fatherhood in the Godhead, even though it merited such great homage, for it is a marvel, the origin of all marvels created and uncreated.'[88]

Fatherhood—that is, the active generation of the Son—is

[86] CCC 240.

[87] Cf ST 2a2ae q. 2, a. 8, ad 2. 'In the Old Testament the Father was made known under the aspect of God Almighty. . . but not under the aspect of the Father. Therefore, though they did know Him as God, they did not yet know Him as Father of the consubstantial Son' (*Lectura super Ioannem*, cap. 8, lect. 2). 'Abraham did not know the Trinity expressly. He knew it as the rose is known in the bud: the essentials were already there' (Charles Journet, *Entretiens sur la Trinité* [Saint-Maur, 1999], pp. 35f.).

[88] Pierre de Bérulle, *Grandeurs de Jésus* 10, 4; OCB 338f.

not a figure of speech ascribed from below by human ingenuity or, as the feminists would claim, male perversity, but
the proper reality of God revealed by Divine Wisdom Incarnate Himself. As St Thomas says, the Son is 'is called "Son"
and His principle called "Father" properly and not metaphorically'.[89] When you use a metaphor of God (for example, when you call Him 'the rock of salvation'), the
metaphorical name belongs in reality to the creature first. By
contrast, when you use a name properly of God, it belongs,
in the order of reality, primarily to God and secondarily to
creatures; it is only in the order of naming and knowing, in
the way that words are used and understood, that they apply
first to creatures. Before a man can meaningfully call God
'Father', he must know what 'father' means among men, but
before any man was father or was named as father, God the
Father was Father in eternity. His Fatherhood is the source
and model of fatherhood among creatures; from Him 'all
paternity in Heaven and on earth is named' (Eph 3:14).[90]
God the Father is the perfect, the primordial Father, of
whom human fathers, even the holiest, are but a fragile
reflection. Fatherhood is not 'projected' onto God as an
imposition and presumptuous aspiration but rather proceeds
from Him as an image and priceless gift.

> Although we transfer the notion of generation to God from
> creatures [says Matthias Scheeben], since we form it from
> creatures, we perceive that the object of this concept in its
> purest, most perfect, and ideal sense is found originally in
> God alone, and therefore the corresponding production of
> creatures merits the name of generation only in a secondary
> and partial sense.[91]

[89] ST 1a q. 33, a. 2, ad 3.
[90] Ibid., q. 33, a. 2, ad 4; cf SCG 1, 34.
[91] Sheeben, *Mysteries of Christianity*, p. 91. Blessed Denys the Carthusian
likewise writes: '[I]n fatherhood, both spiritual and natural, the name of

Fatherhood has the same essential meaning (the same *ratio*, as St Thomas would say) in God that it has among creatures, namely, the active communication of nature: in the Trinity, as in humanity, the father gives to his son what he is. However, the sameness of meaning between the two is not, as the philosophers say, 'univocal' but 'analogical'.[92] Human sons do not receive the whole substance of their fathers, but only part, whereas God the Son receives the whole substance of the Father.[93] Among men, to father a son is to perform a bodily act, but God is spirit and generates the Son incorporeally. Again, men become fathers, having beforehand been themselves sons of their own fathers, but God the Father is eternally Father of the Son and has no source before or beyond Him from which He receives.[94] The case of fatherhood confirms the general law of the analogy of being: however much of a likeness there is between Creator and creatures, the unlikeness is always greater.[95] Human fatherhood was created in the image of the divine; indeed, it is one way in which the image of God in men is superior to the image of God in angels;[96] but in its creaturely finitude

---

fatherhood comes down to us from the Supreme Father. Therefore, Damascene says: "The names of Fatherhood and Sonship are not transferred from us to the blessed Fatherhood and Sonship in the Godhead; on the contrary, they are transferred from Them to us"' (*1 Sent.* d. 5, q. 1; DCOO 19:315).

[92] 'Fatherhood does not have univocally the same character (*eiusdem rationis*) in God and creatures, though it does have the same character by analogy, which has something of sameness of *ratio* and something of diversity' (St Thomas, *1 Sent.* d. 21, q. 1, a. 1b).

[93] *De veritate* q. 4, a. 4.

[94] As St Athanasius says: 'The generation of the Son surpasses and transcends the thoughts of men. . . . We become fathers of our own children in time, since we ourselves in the first instance do not exist and then come into existence. But God, since He always exists, is always the Father of the Son' (*De decretis Nicaenae synodi*, no. 12; PG 25:436C; cf *Oratio 1 contra Arianos*, no. 14; PG 26:41B).

[95] Cf Fourth Lateran Council (1215); DS 806.

[96] The fact that man proceeds from man, just as God proceeds from God, is one of the ways in which the image of God is more perfect in man than in the

it falls short of the infinite reality upon which it is modelled.

Jesus died for revealing the truth of His Divine Sonship. Peter's confession, 'Thou art the Christ, the Son of the living God' (Mt 16:16), expresses, as Cardinal Bérulle says, 'the truth on which the Christian Church is founded, and for which the Son of God exposed Himself to death'.[97] When our Lord calls God 'my Father', His persecutors recognize that He is not claiming to be a servant raised up from earth to be God's adopted son, but God's natural and coequal Son come down on earth to be servant.[98] 'Hereupon therefore the Jews sought the more to kill Him, because He did not only break the Sabbath but also said God was His proper Father (*Patéra ídion*), making Himself equal to God' (Jn 5:18). By a sad irony, those feminist theologians who take offence at the divine name of 'Father' place themselves in the company of the persecutors of Christ. The supposed scandal is different in each case: the persecutors in the past were shocked by the seeming blasphemy, whereas the feminists of today protest at the 'patriarchal oppression', but in both cases the truth revealed by Jesus is not recognized and instead rejected as false.

---

angels. However, this does not pertain to the nature of the divine image of man, 'unless we presuppose the first likeness, which is in the intellectual nature', which is why we have to conclude that, in their intellectual nature, angels are, absolutely speaking, more to the image of God than man is (cf ST 1a q. 93, a. 3).

[97] Bérulle, *Grandeurs de Jésus* 10, 6; OCB 341.

[98] Jesus reveals that He is the true and natural Son, not the Son by adoption. When He speaks to St Mary Magdalen after the Resurrection, He distinguishes between 'my Father and your Father' (Jn 20:17): God the Father is the Father of Jesus by nature and of the disciples by grace (see *Lectura super Ioannem* cap. 20, lect. 3).

3. The Temporal Birth in Relation to the Eternal

The revelation of the eternal birth is depicted very beautifully in the late medieval paintings in which God the Father looks down from Heaven upon God the Son in the manger, while God the Holy Spirit, in the form of a dove, holds His wings outstretched between Them.[99] The eternal birth comes before the temporal birth by the precedence of eternity, but were it not for the temporal birth we would not even know of the eternal birth. The temporal birth reveals the eternal birth. The divine mission of the Son manifests outside of the Godhead His divine procession within the Godhead. When the Father sends His Son, 'born of woman' (cf Gal 4:4), He opens up His own inner life, the life of the Trinity. The birth in Bethlehem, so human and humble, is like a door into the infinite abyss of God.

> It takes place in a village in Judea, but its emanation is from the eternal Father. A thing so humble in appearance as the birth of the Child Jesus in the stable in Bethlehem on the hay and straw, between the ox and the ass, has a very lofty and wonderful source . . . the bosom of the eternal Father. . . . For the Word as Son is enclosed within the bosom of the Father, and He only comes to earth and into our humanity through His sending by His Father, and the Father only sends Him to become incarnate by the same power by which He begets Him in Himself. Thus the principle of His eternal generation is the principle of His mission, of His birth, and of His Incarnation in the world.[100]

The eternal birth is the exemplary cause of the temporal birth; the temporal birth 'expresses and imitates' the

[99] Cf G. Schiller, *The Iconography of Christian Art*, vol. 1, ET (London, 1971), plates 196–99. These paintings reflect the influence of the revelations of St Bridget of Sweden.
[100] Bérulle, *Grandeurs de Jésus* 11, 2; OCB 353f.

eternal.[101] Thus, through the marvels of the fatherless birth
from the Virgin, the believing intellect is led to the glories
of the motherless birth from the Father. The Son's human
Mother has the singular privilege of a certain resemblance to
His heavenly Father: '[S]he is Mother as He is Father: she is
Mother without Father, just as He is Father without Mother,
and . . . she is alone Mother, just as He alone is the Father of
Jesus.' [102] St Augustine makes a series of contrasts between the
two births:

> Christ as God was born of His Father, as man of His Mother;
> of the immortality of His Father, of the virginity of His
> Mother; of His Father without a mother, of His Mother
> without a father; of His Father without time, of His Mother
> without seed; of His Father as the source of life, of His
> Mother as the end of death; of His Father, ordering every
> day, of His Mother, consecrating this particular day.[103]

Only when we contemplate the temporal birth in the light
of the eternal do we begin to discern a little of the infinite
magnitude of the gift that God our Father gives us in the
Christmas mystery. 'God so loved the world as to give His
only-begotten Son' (Jn 3:16). In His generous love, says St
Bonaventure, the Father gave us 'not pennies but a person,
not a servant but the Son', and, in giving His Son, He
lavished upon us 'all He was, all He had, all He could'. The
Son whom He gave us is His 'natural Son', and so, 'since
there is one nature of the Father and the Son, by giving the

---

[101] 'The source of this humble birth is the bosom of the Father. Its exemplar
is the eternal generation. Its end is the glory and grandeur of God, of God
exactly as Father. What is special about it is that it gives a new birth to God, a
new being to the eternal and immutable, to give a new essence to the only Son
of God. Its result is the salvation of the universe. . . . Its proper term and effects
is to make God be man, a Virgin be Mother of God, sinners be holy and
children of God for ever' (ibid., 11, 13; OCB 387; cf 11, 3; OCB 357).

[102] Ibid., 10, 6; OCB 343f.

[103] St Augustine, *Sermo* 194, cap. 1, no. 1; PL 38:1015.

Son the Father gave all that He was.' And, since the Father gave His natural Son to be our Brother, He gave Himself as Father and the Holy Spirit as Comforter, indeed He lavished upon us the whole of the Blessed Trinity. As the Apostle says, 'God sent His Son, made of a woman . . . that we might receive the adoption of sons, and because you are sons, God hath sent the Spirit of His Son into your hearts, crying, "Abba, Father!"' (Gal 4:4ff.). Thus, in sending His Son, born of the Virgin, the Father 'deified us', that is to say, opened up for us a share in His divine life, the 'power to be made the sons of God' (Jn 1:12). This tiny baby, lately born as man of the Virgin, is in truth the 'All' of the Father.[104]

From St Bonaventure's conclusion, St John of the Cross proceeds to a further argument. If, in the Virgin-born Son, God the Father has revealed and given us everything He is and has, it would be sinful folly to desire private revelations:

> God could respond as follows: If I have already told you all things in my Word, my Son, and if I have no other Word, what answer or revelation can I now make that would surpass this? Fasten your eyes on Him alone, because in Him I have spoken and revealed all, and in Him you shall discover even more than you ask for and desire. You are making an appeal for locutions and revelations that are incomplete, but if you turn your eyes to Him, you will find them complete. For He is my entire locution and response, vision and revelation, which I have already spoken, answered, manifested, and revealed to you, by giving Him to you as a brother, companion, master, ransom, and reward. . . . One should not, then, inquire of God in this manner, nor is it necessary for God to speak any more. . . . Anyone wanting to get something in a supernatural way . . . would as it were be accusing God of not having given us in His Son all that is required. . . . We must be guided humanly and visibly in all

---

[104] *In vigilia nativitatis Domini, sermo* 1: Q IX:89–91.

things by the law of Christ the man and that of His Church and of His ministers.[105]

Despite their obvious differences, Modernism, on the one hand, and the disordered desire for private revelations, on the other, have one attribute in common. Both imply that what God has revealed in His Son, the revelation that is here and now transmitted by the Catholic Church, is deficient and in need of supplementation. When Christ and His Blessed Mother appear to the saints on earth, to Margaret Mary, say, or to Bernadette, they do not add to the deposit of divine revelation, but rather shed a fresh light upon it, confirming its grandeur and power. It is significant that it is our Lady who is most frequently seen and heard on earth. Having been glorified in body as well as soul, she retains a special closeness to her brethren still struggling in mortal flesh. By her simple words, she draws us into her own contemplation of the things of Jesus (cf Lk 2:19, 51) and thus enhances our gratitude to the Father for the all-encompassing gift of His Son.

4. The Temporal Birth in Itself

Birth and Conception

The divine birth, as we have seen, is eternal and incorporeal and therefore simple. By contrast, the human birth is temporal and corporeal and therefore complex, a process made up of successive stages. When God begets God, conception and delivery are the same thing, without motion or succession, but childbirth among creatures involves conception, gestation and delivery.[106] The human child comes into being in-

---

[105] *The Ascent of Mount Carmel*, bk. 2, chap. 22, nos. 5ff; ET by K. Kavanaugh OCD and O. Rodriguez OCD, new ed. (Washington, D.C., 1979), pp. 180f.

[106] Cf SCG 4, 11. 'In the Godhead, the Father not only spiritually conceives His Son, but also truly and properly generates Him spiritually, that is,

side the womb, grows and is fed within it and then emerges into the light of day, breathing on his own and ready to drink his mother's milk. Since human childbirth is a complex process rather than a simple procession, the name 'birth' can be applied to its first as well as its last stage. Thus, when the angel Gabriel speaks to Joseph of the Virginal Conception of Jesus, he refers to it as a birth: 'That which is born in her [*en autê gennêthèn; in ea natum est*] is of the Holy Spirit' (Mt 1:20). 'He does not say *of her*', writes St Thomas, 'for to be born of a mother is to come forth into the light; to be born *in her* is to be conceived, which is of the Holy Spirit.' [107] It was this latter birth, the birth-conception in the womb, that was the Son of God's way into human nature and life: true God became true man at the first moment of His conception by the Holy Spirit.[108] Both human births are replete with miracles: the Son of God is born in the Virgin by the Holy Spirit and without seed, and then He is born from her, nine months later, without corruption or pain.

> In the interior birth [says Cardinal Bérulle] the Virgin receives the eternal Word from the bosom of the Father into her virginal womb, so that He may become incarnate. In the exterior birth she brings forth the Incarnate Word from her womb and gives Him to the world.[109]

The two births of the Lord turn out to be three: Jesus is born *before Mary* (by an eternal birth, as God), *in Mary* (by an

---

communicates the whole of the numerically identical divine nature, which cannot be divided or multiplied; He communicates this to Him from eternity, so that the only-begotten Son is already from eternity utterly perfect, "an adult", so to speak, in His divine "age" and entirely equal with the Father' (R. Garrigou-Lagrange OP, *De Deo trino et creatore*, new ed. [Rome, 1951], p. 139).

[107] St Thomas Aquinas, *Lectura super Matthaeum*, cap. 1, lect. 4.

[108] See my book *Redeemer in the Womb: Jesus Living in Mary* (San Francisco, 1993).

[109] Bérulle, *Grandeurs de Jésus* 11, 12; OCB 381f.

internal birth, or conception, as man), and *from Mary* (by an external birth, a coming forth from the womb, as man). 'The second and third have been shown to us on earth as a remedy; the first is reserved to us in Heaven as a reward.' [110] In the tradition of mystical exegesis of the liturgy, a another kind of threefold birth, corresponding to the three Masses of Christmas, is attributed to Christ: 'The one eternal, from the heart of the Father; the second fleshly, from the womb of the Virgin; the third spiritual, by which He is born in the minds of those who are converted to Him or re-born in Him'.[111]

The Paradoxes of the Temporal Birth

The divine birth of God the Son is ineffable and incomprehensible, but so too, in a certain way, is the human. 'Who shall declare His generation?' If the divine birth is mysterious because of the incomprehensibility proper to the divine essence, the human birth eludes capture by the mind because, though finite in itself, its subject is a Divine Person, who imparts to it an infinite plenitude of meaning and value. Moreover, it is accompanied by divine miracles, effects beyond the natural power of any created cause: the Mother is a virgin, who conceived by the Spirit and without seed and now gives birth without corruption. In the Byzantine liturgy, it is the Virgin Mother herself who makes the proper response to the ineffability of her Son's human birth:

> The Virgin was amazed, as she beheld a conception past telling and a birth past utterance. Rejoicing at once and weeping, she raised her voice and said: 'Shall I give my breast to thee, who givest nourishment to all the world, or shall I sing thy praise as my Son and my God? What manner of

[110] St Bonaventure, *In vigilia nativitatis Domini sermo* 12, 1; Q IX:99–100.

[111] Blessed Denys the Carthusian, *Expositio Missae*; DCOO 42, p. 28. Cf ST 3a q. 83, a. 2, ad 2.

name shall I find to call thee, O Lord whom none can name?'[112]

The Christmas preaching and poetry of the saints, like the Christmas liturgy of the Church, abound in paradox. One of St Bernard's sermons on the Nativity is a litany of the enigmas of the feast: the Child-God is 'short length, narrow width, low height, flat depth . . . unshining light, speechless Word, thirsting water, hungry bread'.[113] Such coincidences of opposites do not contradict the principle of noncontradiction. God is the First Truth, who can neither deceive nor lie. When the eternal Logos becomes incarnate and is born of the Virgin Mary, He perfects, does not destroy, human logic, for He created man's logical mind in His image, to be a word of the Word. In the Christian understanding, therefore, a paradox is not a contradiction but the capacity of a great truth to evoke wonder. As a master of paradox and Christian wisdom once said, '[W]henever we feel there is something odd in Christian theology, we shall generally find that there is something odd in the truth.'[114] Now, as we have seen, what is 'odd' about the truth of the Incarnation is that it is a becoming without change: it takes place 'not by the conversion of Godhead into flesh but by the taking up of manhood into God'.[115] Thus the descent of God into the Virgin's womb is not by local movement, a kind of evacuation of the

[112] Forefeast of the Nativity of Christ, *Menaion*, p. 199. St John Chrysostom likewise insists that, while the believing mind accepts the 'that' of the Virgin Birth, the 'how' lies beyond its grasp: 'Though I know that a virgin this day gave birth, and I believe that God was begotten before all time, yet the manner of this generation I have learned to venerate in silence, and I accept that this is not to be probed too curiously with wordy speech. For with God we look not for the order of nature, but rest our faith in the power of Him who is at work' (*In salvatoris nostri Iesu Christi nativitatem oratio*; PG 56:385).

[113] *Sermo 2 in laudibus Virginis Matris*, no. 9; L-R 4:27.

[114] G. K. Chesterton, *Orthodoxy*, new ed., in The Collected Works of G. K. Chesterton, vol. 1 (San Francisco, 1986), p. 286.

[115] The Athanasian Creed; DS 76.

Empyrean. The eternal Son begins to be on humble earth as man, but He does not cease to be in high Heaven as God. To quote Chesterton again, when Christian orthodoxy combines things, you do not get 'an amalgam or compromise, but both things at the top of their energy'. And when divinity and humanity are united in the hypostasis of the Word, you get neither confusion nor change, neither separation nor division, but the integrity of the two natures preserved undiminished in the union. That is why, as Father Faber argues in his treatise on the Christmas mystery, 'The deepest and most profitable devotion to the Incarnation is that which never loses sight for a single moment of our Blessed Lord's Divinity; and the richest as well as the safest devotion to the Divine Perfections is that which contemplates them in connection with the mysteries of the Incarnation.'[116]

The two natures, which are united without confusion in the Person of the Word, cannot be separated in reality, nor ought they to be separated in our thinking. In venerating the mysteries of the manhood, we must not forget the One whose human sufferings and actions these are, namely, the Divine Person of the eternal Son. As Cardinal Newman says of the Passion, 'it is [no] forgetfulness of His sacred humanity to contemplate His Eternal Person. It is the very idea that He is God which gives a meaning to His sufferings; what is to me a man, and nothing more, in agony, or scourged, or crucified? There are many holy martyrs, and their torments were terrible. But here I see one dropping blood, gashed by the thong and stretched upon the Cross, and He is God.'[117] Likewise, in contemplating the attributes of the Godhead, we ought not to forget that these are common to the three Divine Persons and were most marvellously manifested

[116] *Bethlehem*, pp. 236f.

[117] John Henry Newman, 'The Infinitude of the Divine Attributes', in *Discourses Addressed to Mixed Congregations*, new ed. (London, 1892), pp. 320f.

through the manhood of the Second Person, both by confirmation in that manhood's perfections and by contrast in its infirmities. If we remain faithful to the logic of the Church's Christological orthodoxy, then, as Father Faber says, the mystery of the Incarnation will unlock the treasures of the Godhead 'by a series of shocks or sweet surprises'.

> Thus the littleness of the Babe of Bethlehem, touched in our hearts by the faith in His Divinity, sends us by a kind of impulse far into the understanding of His infinity. . . . This is the characteristic of devotion to the Divine Perfections through the Incarnation, that it impels us by these shocks deeper into the hiding-places of the Immense Majesty than we should otherwise have been able to go.[118]

The Childhood of God

In the womb of the Blessed Virgin, God the Son, without ceasing to be true and perfect God, was made true and perfect man, a real and complete human being. Now man moves and grows in time, from infancy to maturity, and so too does the man who is God. He could have created for Himself a human body in adult form, as He did for Adam, but such was not His will.[119] He could have come, as Bérulle says, 'without birth and without genealogy, and without having a mother on earth, just as on earth He had no father',[120] but He did not choose that motherless path. By the

[118] *Bethlehem*, pp. 238f.

[119] 'He who had made Adam and brought him into being from non-being, without woman, man or birth, could have constructed an adult human nature for Himself and dwelt in it and thus lived in the world' (*Viae dux* cap. 13; PG 89:236A).

[120] *Oeuvres de controverse* 3, 9; OCB 723. Bérulle compares our Lord's decision to enter this world through Motherhood to His decision to leave this world only after giving His disciples the Holy Eucharist by which He remains with us to the end of the age: 'At the end of His days He could have separated Himself

wise and merciful decree of the Trinity, the Son took the slow way into the world of men, the low road of childhood; He chose to be mothered into humanity. Thus, for Him, as for us, the beginning of human life was conception in a mother's womb, though in His case the Mother was a virgin, and the active principle of the conception was not the material seed of any man but the immaterial Spirit of God. When we say that the Word was made flesh, we mean, of course, as St Bernard says, that He was made '*infant* flesh, young flesh, helpless flesh'.[121] Having been conceived, the Incarnate Word remained for a full nine months within His Mother's body, and then He came forth, again in a miraculous manner, but with all the essential littleness and weakness of infancy to human eyes displayed. 'For a *Child* is born to us' (Is 9:6). For God, becoming man means becoming a real baby:

[God] truly became a child [*bréphos*] and was born [says St Anastasius of Sinai]. . . . He hastened to [His Mother's] breasts as babies do [*nêpiotrepôs*], crying in accordance with the law of our baby nature, and in likeness to us, without any difference, suffered the circumcision of the flesh and rejection.[122]

God deemed no stage of human life unworthy of His presence. He did not abhor the Virgin's womb, nor did He despise the swaddling clothes and the manger. 'He dis-

from earth without uniting Himself with, and incorporating Himself into, His Apostles by this mystery. . . but in fact it pleased Him, at the hour of His departure, to unite His disciples to Himself in as real and intimate a way as He had been conjoined and united to his Mother at the time of His birth, and by this divine and wonderful Sacrament to extend to all His own, and to consummate with each of them, the holy union that He had accomplished with an individual nature through the Incarnation' (ibid.).

[121] *Sermo 3 in nativitate Domini* 2; L-R 4:259.
[122] St Anastasius of Sinai, *Viae dux* cap. 13; PG 89:217A.

dained', says Pope St Leo the Great, 'neither birth nor the
earliest stages of infancy [*primordia . . . infantiae*].'[123] The
Magi found and worshipped a child 'in size a baby, in need of
the help of others, incapable of speech, and in no way different from other human infants'.[124]

The Youth of the Ancient of Days

When God was born in Bethlehem, said Chesterton, He
'turned back eternity and was young'.[125] He assumed childhood's temporal brevity as well as its corporeal infirmity.
The Father's eternally begotten Son is pleased to be the
Virgin's newly born baby. To this great and mighty wonder
the Greek Church keeps returning through all the liturgical
hours of Christmas Day: '[U]nto us is born a young child,
the pre-eternal God.'[126] He who in His divine nature remains in the serenity of eternity, without motion or succession, in the bosom of the Father, enters in His human nature
into the mutability of time, coming forth from the Virgin's
womb and thereafter passing through all the divers stages of
human life. Thus, as a twelfth-century Cistercian preacher
put it, the one Christ is both 'Child and Ancient of Days, a
child in bodily form and age, Ancient of days in the incomprehensible eternity of the Word'.[127] 'Who has ever seen a
child older than his mother?' asks St Ephrem the Syrian and
then provides the answer: 'The Ancient of days entered and
became a child in [Mary]. As a newborn child He came
forth and grew through her milk. He entered and became

---

[123] *Sermo sive tractatus contra haeresim Eutychis*, no. 2; SC 22B:206.

[124] *Sermo* 34 (*In Epiphaniae solemnitate* 4), no. 3; SC 22B:244.

[125] 'A Little Litany', in The Collected Works of G. K. Chesterton, vol. 10A
(San Francisco, 1994), p. 14.

[126] The Feast of the Nativity, *Menaion*, p. 261.

[127] Guerric of Igny, *In nativitate Domini, sermo* 1, no. 1; SC 166:164.

small in her. He came forth and grew through her, a mighty wonder.'[128]

The Speechlessness of the Word

The principal actor in the 'theo-drama'[129] of Christmas does not have a speaking role. He cries when He is hungry, but He utters no words. He is a real baby, and babies cannot communicate by words, as the very name 'infant' suggests: *in-fans* in Latin means 'not speaking'. This is the day, says St Augustine, 'on which the Wisdom of God manifested Himself as a speechless Child, and the Word of God wordlessly uttered the sound of a human voice.'[130] Belonging as it does to the eternal Word, such speechlessness speaks volumes; in Him baby babble becomes enlightening eloquence, revealing the mercy of the Father. 'Coming down from the royal seat of the Father to the manger,' says Blessed Guerric of Igny, 'He speaks to us better by His silence.'[131] Just as music is made up of both notes and rests, so the Word Incarnate does His work of revelation through silence as well as words, by suffering as well as acting. Through its union with the Divine Person of the Logos, human nature serves as 'an instrument from which every melody can be enticed; even silence, the pause, can become a striking means of communication'.[132]

[128] *Des heiligen Ephraem des Syrers Hymnen de Nativitate (Epiphania)* 12, no. 1; GT by E. Beck, CSCO, *Scriptores Syri* (Louvain, 1959), p. 63.

[129] The phrase is von Balthasar's. The *Theodramatik* [ET: *Theo-Drama*] is the second part (San Francisco, 1989–1998) of his theological trilogy in which he considers Divine Revelation from the side of the good—and thus of end, action, and drama.

[130] St Augustine, *Sermo* 185, cap. 1, no. 1; PL 38:997.

[131] Guerric of Igny, *In nativitate Domini, sermo* 5, no. 2; SC 166:226.

[132] Hans Urs von Balthasar, *Das Ganze im Fragment*, new ed. (Einsiedeln, 1990), p. 273.

The Littleness of Immensity

God the Son, without ceasing to be immense and infinite in
His divinity, makes His own our infant littleness. When He
journeys into human nature, He takes the little way. 'He
without whom nothing was made', says Guerric, 'emptied
Himself to the point where He seemed almost to be nothing.' [133] When they are searching for prophetic testimonies to
the littleness of the infant Word, the Fathers quote a text from
Isaiah taken up by St Paul: 'A short Word shall the Lord make
upon the earth' (Rom 9:28; cf Is 10:22). The *Verbum incarnatum*
is the *verbum breviatum*, the Word abridged, the shortened
Logos.[134] The meaning of this title is shown in a lovely way in
the Nativity painted in the fifteenth century by Geertgen tot
Sint Jans and exhibited in London at the National Gallery: the
Holy Infant is a tiny mite, a real newborn (so unlike the
chubby toddler of the Italian Renaissance or the reduced adult
of Byzantium), and yet light streams upwards from Him on to
the faces of the Madonna and of the adoring angels [see art
plate 2]. There is no contradiction between divine illumination
and human abbreviation, as St Thomas explains: 'He is said to
be emptied or shortened, not because anything has been taken
away from the plenitude or magnitude of His divinity, but
because He has assumed our smallness and littleness.' [135]

The Poverty of the King

The infant God whom the Magi worship is, according to St
Bonaventure, 'a poor little boy (*puer pauperculus*)'.[136] 'The

[133] *In nativitate Domini, sermo* 1, no. 2; SC 166:168.

[134] 'The Lord made a short word on earth. And so "a child is born for us",
and remaining immense, "the Son is given to us"' (St Bonaventure, *In vigilia
nativitatis Domini, sermo* 12, no. 2; Q IX:101).

[135] *Super epistolam ad Romanos* cap. 9, lect. 15.

[136] *In Epiphania, sermo* 1; Q IX:146.

King of Kings and Lord of Lords has become the slave and
humble servant of men. . . . God, supremely glorious, dwelling in the heights of majesty, has dwelt in a lowly manger.
. . . God, the desire of the angels, has become a spectacle for
shepherds.'[137] In truth, as Peter Abelard sings in a Christmas
hymn, He is a 'pauper God, yea, the poorest of the poor'.[138]
He is born in obscurity, a little and lowly Messiah, not a
dazzling Davidic king and conqueror. His cradle is a manger,
because there was no room for Him in the inn (cf Lk 2:7).
The first to worship Him are shepherds, poor workingmen
(cf Lk 2:8). Mary and Joseph, when they present Him in the
Temple, make the offering of the poor (cf Lk 2:24; cf Lev
12:2–8). Within weeks of His birth, He is that poorest of
poor men, the refugee (cf Mt 2:13ff.), a 'waif upon His own
earth'.[139] He is the foster son of an artisan and spends long,
hidden years at the lathe.

But the poverty of the Christ Child is more than a mere
deficiency in physical comfort or social privilege. The material poverty is the outward sign of the metaphysical poverty
of the assumed human nature. Without losing the riches of
the divinity, God the Son takes on our humanity with all the
limitations intrinsic to what is created and bodily. 'Look at
the eternal Word,' says Father Faber, 'first in the bosom of
the Father, and then in the bosom of Mary, and say whether
a lower depth of poverty can be conceived.'[140] The Greek
Church, in her bold way, gives us access to the inmost heart
of the Theotokos as she looks upon this metaphysical poverty
of the Child-God at her breast:

> The undefiled Virgin, beholding the pre-eternal God as a
> child that had taken flesh from her, held Him in her arms and

[137] *In vigilia nativitatis Domini, sermo* 9, no. 2; Q IX:97.
[138] *Hymni solemnitatum divinarum, In nativitate Domini*; PL 178:1789C.
[139] *Bethlehem*, p. 378.
[140] Ibid.

without ceasing she kissed Him. Filled with joy, she said aloud to Him: 'O Most High God, O King unseen, how is it that I look upon thee? I cannot understand the mystery of thy poverty without measure.' [141]

The Son of God could have assumed a body already glorious, but instead, in His great love for sinful mankind, He freely chose to assume a passible and mortal human nature in which He could suffer and die in expiation for human sin. He voluntarily makes His own the dependency and helplessness of childhood, when He could have become man as an adult.

> [T]he first state [says Cardinal Bérulle] in which the Son of God enters human nature is the state of infancy, the lowest and most abject state of human nature after death. . . . [T]he thoughts of God are not the thoughts of men. . . . He seeks the abasement which is not proper to Him and not the grandeur proper and natural to Him. . . . He wants to exist, to live, and to appear to the world as a poor, powerless infant, in conformity to the properties of that state, without shortening for one moment the duration of that infancy, whether inside or outside His holy Mother, and without dispensing Himself in one part from the constraints, abasements, and poverty which that infancy involves.[142]

The Infant Word makes no outward display of His divine power; the only miracles of His childhood, indeed of the first thirty years of His human life on earth, are the Virginal Conception and Birth. St Thomas rejects the legends in the apocryphal gospels that tell of miracles performed by the boy Jesus. No, says Thomas, the changing of water into wine at Cana was His first sign. If He had worked miracles as a child, 'men would have thought that His Incarnation

---

[141] Forefeast of the Nativity, *Menaion*, p. 200.
[142] Pierre de Bérulle, *Opuscules de piété*, new ed. (Grenoble, 1977), pp. 199f.

was a fantasy'.[143] During His childhood He, so to speak, leaves the power to work miracles in the hands of His heavenly Father: He still possesses it as God, but He chooses not to draw upon it as man.

The Marriage of the Infant

Alone among the sons of men, the Son of God was already married when He was born. 'He hath set His tabernacle in the sun,' sings the Church on Christmas Day, 'and He, as a bridegroom coming out of His bridal chamber, hath rejoiced as a giant to run His way' (Ps 18:6).[144] St Thomas offers this commentary: 'The bridal chamber is the Virgin's womb, from which, like a bridegroom, He came forth, because in her He married human nature in a perpetual union, which is why in death His Godhead remained united to His soul and body.'[145] According to St Bonaventure, the newborn Christ is the husband of a threefold bride: He is wedded to the assumed human nature 'by an undivided love', to the Church 'by a benevolent love', and to the individual holy soul 'by a chaste love'.[146] St John of the Cross was likewise concerned with Christ's spousal union with humanity in its several stages. In a poem written during his captivity in Toledo, he even sketches, so to speak, the prehistory of the nuptial mystery: from all eternity, God the Father planned to give His only-begotten Son 'a lovely bride,/ And one who for your worth will merit/ To live forever by our side'. In order to draw the race of Adam into the nuptial embrace, the Bridegroom-Word takes flesh in Mary's womb at His con-

[143] ST 3a q. 36, a. 5, ad 3.

[144] Psalm 18, with the verse quoted as an antiphon, is sung during the Matins (or Office of Readings) for Christmas Day in both the 1962 and the 1971 editions of the Roman Breviary.

[145] *Postilla super Psalmos* 18, no. 3.

[146] *In nativitate Domini sermo* 26, no. 2; Q IX:125.

ception and then comes forth at His birth: 'Like a bride-groom from His chamber/ He emerged upon our earth.' As He lies in the manger, the Word 'cling[s] close to His be-loved/ Whom He brought along with Him', that is to say, to the human nature that He has espoused, and the 'jewels of the dowry' are the tears that flow from His infant eyes.

> The tears of Man in God alone,
> The joy of God in men was seen.
> Two things so alien to each other,
> Or to the rule, had never been.[147]

The comparing of the Incarnation to a marriage, and of the Nativity to a bridegroom's emergence from his chamber, is thoroughly orthodox and very ancient, going back to the earliest years of the Church. However, after the condemna-tion of the heresy of Nestorius, who claimed that there were two persons in Christ, the Fathers handle the spousal analogy with heightened delicacy and precision. They want to avoid any suggestion that the 'wedded' human nature is a human person. In an ordinary marriage, there is a union of two distinct human persons, but the spiritual marriage that is the Incarnation is the union of two distinct natures, the divine and the human, in the one Divine Person of the Word. Despite this difference, the hypostatic union can be likened to a marriage in two ways: first, because the two natures are united in a sort of 'indissoluble bond'; and secondly, because human nature is subordinated to the Word as the wife is subject to her husband (cf Eph 5:22).[148] Pope St Gregory the Great suggests that the safest interpretation of the divine nuptials is to identify the bride with the Church rather than with the assumed human nature:

---

[147] St John of the Cross, *Poems*, ET by R. Campbell (Harmondsworth, England, 1960), pp. 64ff.

[148] Cf St Thomas, *4 Sent.* d. 49, q. 4, a. 3, ad 2.

God the Father prepared a marriage for God the Son when He united the Son to human nature in the womb of the Virgin, since He wished Him who was God before the ages to become man at the end of the ages. Now, though such a union ordinarily requires two persons, far be it from our minds to think that the person of Jesus Christ, our God and the Redeemer of man, is made up of two persons. We do indeed affirm that He is made up of two natures and exists in two natures; but the belief that He is composed of two persons, we avoid as heresy. Therefore, speaking more plainly and safely, we may say that the Father arranged the marriage of His kingly Son by joining Holy Church to Him through the mystery of the Incarnation.[149]

Cardinal Journet urges caution about another aspect of the nuptial mystery. He reminds us that humanity in general, the human race as a whole, can be wedded to the Word only when its individual members are incorporated into the Church.

It is the whole of humanity that is espoused, in principle, by Christ; all of humanity is invited to the nuptial feast. But it is only as it responds to the invitation, only when the marriage is consummated, that humanity becomes the Bride in reality and takes the name of 'Church'. If we look not just at possibilities but at realities, not at the virtual but at the actual aspect, then we ought to say that the Bride is the Church alone and not all mankind.[150]

The Cardinal's point is well made. If there is to be a 'marriage' between divinity and humanity in the Person of the Word, there must be mutual consent, for it is consent that makes a marriage. Now divinity gives its consent in the Person of the Word, for He, with the Father and the Holy

---

[149] *Homiliarum in evangelia*, lib. 2, hom. 38, no. 3; PL 76:1283AB.

[150] C. Journet, *L'Église du Verbe incarné*, vol. 2, *La structure interne de l'Église: le Christ, la Vierge, l'Esprit Saint*, new ed. (Paris, 1999), p. 234.

Spirit, freely wills the Incarnation, and humanity gives its consent when it responds, in the Church, to the divine invitation. But where is the Church, humanity in the form of the Bride, at the very moment when the Word is made flesh, before a single apostle has been called? The answer of the Tradition is beyond doubt: bridal humanity, the consenting Church, exists already, even at the Incarnation, in the person of the Blessed Virgin Mary.

> In order to show that there is a certain spiritual wedlock between the Son of God and human nature [says St Thomas], in the Annunciation the Virgin's consent was sought in place of that of the entire human nature.[151]

In the created person of the Blessed Virgin, the race and nature of man says 'I will' to the uncreated Person of the Word, when He declares His intention to assume the nature and redeem the race. This espousal of humanity is an utterly immaterial and infinitely pure act, transcending altogether the sexual order of bodily creatures.[152] It is husbandly by analogy, for, like a husband, the assuming Divine Person takes the initiative in espousing, while the nature assumed allows itself to be espoused. At the Annunciation, the Virgin's bridal love is likewise spiritual and supernatural, an act of immaculate charity directed towards the Word as God, with the Father and the Holy Spirit. In the flesh, in relation to the Word as man and male, our Lady is, of course, Mother, not Bride. However, in the Spirit, as the representative of humanity and the type of the Church, she can be called *Sponsa Verbi*, the Bride of the Word. By her loving faith, the Blessed Virgin gave the Word the human nature He wedded to

---

[151] ST 3a q. 30, a. 1.

[152] In the words of the Holy Father, 'the nuptial quality of God's love has a completely spiritual and supernatural character' (General audience address, 2 May 1990). Cf *Redemptoris Mater*, no. 26.

Himself, and, by her fulness of grace and glory, she is the perfect 'image and beginning' of the Church, the Bride 'without spot or wrinkle' (cf Eph 5:27; Rev 21:1ff.).[153] Here is the most perfect model, for all who belong to the Church, of those dispositions that make the soul a spouse of Christ. Even as He lies in the manger, the heart of Jesus reaches out to the members of His Bride, and, as she kneels by His side, the heart of Mary, on their behalf, responds with devoted faith and love. Thus the Christmas mystery of the two births inaugurates that 'great mystery' (cf Eph 5:32) of which the Apostle speaks, the nuptial mystery of Christ and His Church. For the sake of the spotless Bride, the Son of the heavenly Father is born of the Virgin Mother.

> Jesu, the Father's only Son,
> Whose death for all redemption won,
> Before the world, of God most high,
> Begotten all ineffably.
>
> Salvation's author, call to mind
> How, taking the form of humankind,
> Born of a Virgin undefiled,
> Thou in man's flesh becamest a child.[154]

---

[153] Cf LG no. 65.

[154] The hymn *Christe, Redemptor omnium* (in the version of J. M. Neale, EH 17) is the office hymn for Vespers during Christmastide, both in the *Breviarium romanum* of 1962 and the post-conciliar *Liturgia horarum*.

III

'MOTHER AND MAIDEN'

The Ever-Virgin Mother of the Incarnate Son of God

> I sing of a maiden
> That is makeles;
> King of all kings
> To her Son she ches.
>
> He came all so still
> To His Mother's bowr,
> As dew in April
> That falleth on the flower.
>
> Mother and maiden
> Was never none but she;
> Well may such a lady
> Godes Mother be.[1]

Our blessed Lady is a matchless mystery, both as mother and maiden. Though in herself a creature and therefore finite, her divine motherhood is infinite in its dignity.[2] Not even the

---

[1] A fifteenth-century carol in *The Oxford Book of Carols*, ed. P. Dearmer et al., new ed. (London, 1964), pp. 390f., n. 183. *Makeles* means 'matchless'; *ches* means 'chose'.

[2] Cf ST 1a q. 25, a. 6, ad 4. 'The measure . . . of the divine motherhood is infinitude and eternity' (Anscar Vonier OSB, *The Divine Motherhood*, in The Collected Works of Abbot Vonier, vol. 1 [London, 1952], p. 337).

highest of angelic intellects can encompass the full truth of the Woman who gave birth to God. And as maiden, too, Mary is a mystery without peer. 'Mother and maiden was never none but she.' Two realities that nowhere coincide in nature meet, by supernatural power, in her lowly and lovely person. Our Lady receives the office of divine motherhood, yet does not forfeit the state of holy maidenhood: she conceives as a virgin, gives birth as a virgin, and remains a virgin for ever, her whole life long.[3] The Catholic can only bow the knees of his mind before such a profusion of wonders: 'Most glorious and beyond our understanding are all thy mysteries, O Theotokos: for with the seal of thy virginity unbroken, thou hast become in full reality a mother, giving birth to the true God.'[4]

This chapter will sing of the Maiden that is matchless. I shall try to come to her in faith, as her Son came to her in the flesh, with the quietness of reverence ('all so still') and without the clamour of curiosity. My goal is to let the

---

[3] The first Father of the Church to have used this formula seems to have been St Zeno of Verona in the fourth century: 'O great mystery! Mary conceived as an uncorrupted virgin; after conception, she gave birth as a virgin; and after birth she remained a virgin' (cf *Tractatus* lib. 2, tract. 8, no. 2; PL 11:414). St Augustine speaks in similar terms on many occasions: 'As a virgin she conceived: be amazed. As a virgin she gave birth: be amazed still more. A virgin she remained: who shall declare this generation?' (*Sermo* 196, cap. 1, no. 1; PL 38:1019). Doubtless St Augustine received it as a fixed formula expressing divine and Catholic faith. The Catechism sums up this faith as follows: 'From the first formulations of her faith, the Church has confessed that Jesus was conceived solely by the power of the Holy Spirit in the womb of the Virgin Mary, affirming also the corporeal aspect of this event: Jesus was conceived "by the Holy Spirit without human seed"' (CCC 496, quoting the Council of the Lateran [649]: DS 503). 'The deepening of faith in the virginal motherhood led the Church to confess Mary's real and perpetual virginity even in the act of giving birth to the Son of God made man (cf DS 291; 294; 427; 442; 503; 571; 1880). In fact, Christ's birth "did not diminish his mother's virginal integrity but sanctified it" (LG no. 57). And so the liturgy of the Church celebrates Mary as *Aeiparthenos*, the "Ever-Virgin"' (CCC 499).

[4] The Sunday of Orthodoxy, *Triodion*, p. 302.

splendour of truth shine forth from the Mother of Fairest
Love. Most of the chapter will, therefore, be a simple and
peaceful meditation on our Lady's divine motherhood and
virginity. However, in places, in the very cause of reverence,
a more martial note will be struck. The saints prefer to sing
in praise of God's Mother, but sometimes they are obliged to
argue in her defence. Then Mary's troubadours become her
knights, for this is an apologetic that concerns nothing less
than the honour of Heaven's Queen. Those who admire the
Church's Doctors for the clarity of their understanding of
Mary and the warmth of their love for her cannot fail to be
stirred by the just anger with which they fight against her
foes. Thus, when St Thomas Aquinas addresses the error of
Helvidius, who 'presumed to say that Joseph had carnal
knowledge of the Mother of Christ after she had given
birth', he forsakes his habitual placidity and declaims with
the chivalrous zeal of his crusader cousins that this error is
'indubitably detestable'.[5]

1. Matchless Motherhood

Theotokos

The name 'Mother of God' is the greatest of our Lady's titles,
and the office it denotes is the reason for all her other privileges. According to St John Damascene, *Theotokos* 'sums up
the whole mystery of the economy. If she who gave birth is
Mother of God, then He who was born of her is definitely
God and also definitely man. . . . This [name] signifies the

---

[5] Cf ST 3a q. 28, a. 3. Another saintly Thomas, St Thomas More, the
martyr, speaks with similar warmth of those, such as the heretic Tyndale, who
'would minish the worship of our most blessed Lady' (*The Confutation of
Tyndale's Answer*, bk. 3, ed. L. A. Schuster et al., The Complete Works of St
Thomas More, vol. 8, part 1 [New Haven, 1973], p. 287).

one hypostasis and the two natures and the two births of Our Lord Jesus Christ.'[6] To call Mary 'Mother of God' is to declare that Jesus is true God and true man in one person, begotten eternally in His Divinity of God the Father and born in time in His humanity of the Virgin Mother.[7]

When we say that our Lady is *Theotokos*, we mean that she furnished the sacred humanity of our Lord with everything that every other mother gives to the fruit of her womb. In fact, she did even more, because, as Virgin Mother, she was His only physical link with the race of Adam. It is on His Mother's side alone that the sons of men are kinsmen of the Son of God, flesh of His flesh. As St Leo says, Mary is the woman who supplies Him with His bodily substance (*corporeae ministra substantiae*).[8] The eternal Word did not bring His body down from Heaven, as some heretics thought, nor did He make it out of the dust of the earth, as He did in the case of Adam. No, 'it was taken from the Virgin Mother and fashioned from her most pure blood. . . . [T]his is all that is required for the notion of mother. Thus the Blessed Virgin is truly the Mother of Christ.'[9]

---

[6] *De fide orthodoxa* lib. 3, cap. 12; PG 94:1029CD. John Henry Newman argues along similar lines: 'And the confession that Mary is *Deipara*, or the Mother of God, is that safeguard wherewith we seal up and secure the doctrine of the Apostle from all evasion, and that test whereby we detect all the pretences of those bad spirits of "Antichrist which have gone out into the world". It declares that He is God; it implies that He is man; it suggests to us that He is God still, though He has become man, and that He is true man though He is God. . . . If Mary is the Mother of God, Christ must be literally Emmanuel, God with us' ('The Glories of Mary for the Sake of Her Son', in *Discourses to Mixed Congregations*, new ed. [London, 1892], pp. 347f.).

[7] 'To confess our faith in orthodox fashion . . . it is enough to confess that the Blessed Virgin is Theotokos' (St Cyril of Alexandria, *Homiliae diversae* 15; PG 77:1093C).

[8] *In nativitate Domini, sermo* 4, no. 3; SC 22B:104.

[9] ST 3a q. 35, a. 3. When St Thomas speaks of our Lord's body being formed from His Mother's 'blood', he is using the words and concepts of the obsolete biology of the ancient world. The ancients and medievals knew

The name 'Mother of God' also affirms the true Divinity of Christ. The person whom our Lady conceived and bore is a Divine Person, the Second Person of the Blessed Trinity, God the Son, not, of course, according to His divine nature, but according to the human nature that He assumed. The word *Theotokos* is not found in Scripture, but the truth it signifies is nothing less than the apostolic proclamation.[10] The whole New Testament teaches us that Jesus Christ is 'the true God' (cf 1 Jn 5:20). Now the sacred authors also tell us that the Blessed Virgin is the Mother of Jesus Christ (cf Mt 1:18). 'Therefore, it follows of necessity from the words of Scripture that [the Blessed Virgin] is Mother of God.'[11] This is the truth implicit in St Elizabeth's description of our Lady as 'Mother of my Lord' (cf Lk 1:43), for St Elizabeth's Lord is God.

Strictly speaking, it is only the body that the Son of God *takes* from our Lady. His rational soul, like that of every other man, is not taken from her or from anyone else, but is instead created immediately by God and infused into the body at the moment of conception, the complete human nature in the same instant being assumed. The Nestorians argued from this premise that Mary should not be called 'Mother of God', because she is only the mother of the flesh of Christ. St Cyril of Alexandria replied as follows: 'Although mothers produce only the body, they are nonetheless said to bring into the world the whole living being composed of soul and body, not just one of its parts.'[12] St Thomas quotes St Cyril and develops his reasoning.[13] The gist of the argument is as follows. My mother is the woman who supplies the matter for

---

nothing of ovulation. They believed that male seed acted upon a special secretion of blood in the body of the woman. See my book *Redeemer in the Womb: Jesus Living in Mary* (San Francisco, 1993), pp. 13ff.

[10] Cf St Cyril of Alexandria, *Epistola* 1; PG 76:13B.

[11] ST 3a q. 35, a. 4, ad 1.

[12] *Epistola* 1; PG 77:21BC.

[13] Cf ST 3a q. 35, a. 4, ad 2; *Compendium theologiae* lib. 1, cap. 222.

my conception. True, it is God alone who creates the form, the rational soul, but that does not make my mother just the 'mother of my matter'—though, if I were Bertie Wooster, I might affectionately dub her 'my old flesh and blood'. She is the mother of the *person* I am, the one who has both body and soul. It is persons who are born, just as it is persons who give birth. Mothers are mothers of persons, not of natures or bits of natures. The same is true of our Lord and our Lady. Mary gives Jesus what every mother gives her child: He is conceived of her blood, made flesh of her flesh, and on that basis a person-to-person relation, a mother–son relationship, is established. But the person to whom our Lady relates as mother is a Divine Person, God the Son. Therefore, she is rightly and properly called 'Mother of God'.[14] Our blessed Lady is the Mother of the Divine *Person* of God the Son, not of His divine nature. 'We must therefore say that the Blessed Virgin is called the Mother of God, not because she is the Mother of the divinity, but because she is the Mother, according to the humanity, of the Person who has divinity and humanity.' [15]

The Catholic believer can never take the title *Theotokos* for granted. If, as the Fathers insist, it contains within itself a complete confession of faith in Christ, then those who refuse or are reluctant to employ it cut themselves adrift from

[14] '[A] woman is not said to be someone's mother because the whole of what is in him is taken from her. For a man consists of soul and body, and man is more what he is according to his soul than what he is according to the body. The soul of no man, however, is taken from his mother, but is created immediately by God. . . . A woman is said to be the mother of a man because his body is taken from her; and so the Virgin Mary must be called the Mother of God if the body of God is taken from her. We must say that it is the body of God, since it is assumed into the unity of the person of the Son of God, who is true God. Confessing, therefore, human nature to have been assumed by the Son of God into the unity of the person, it is necessary to say that the Blessed Virgin Mary is the Mother of God' (*Compendium theologiae* lib. 1, cap. 222).

[15] ST 3a q. 35, a. 4, ad 2.

historical Christianity. It is a striking fact that, while the original leaders of the Protestant revolt continued to use the name 'Mother of God', their heirs and successors have shown it either open embarrassment or thinly suppressed contempt. Surveying the widespread departure from Christological orthodoxy among the Protestants of the nineteenth century, Matthias Scheeben made this telling observation:

> No one need fear that the honor of God and Christ will be infringed by stressing Mary's divine motherhood. But great danger threatens the honor of Christ, where His Mother is not gladly and loudly proclaimed Mother of God. As the Nestorians opposed this title because they did not acknowledge Christ as true God, so Protestantism has slowly lost the full knowledge of the divinity of Christ because it has refused to Mary the honor due to the Mother of God, supposedly for the sake of God and Christ.[16]

Newman in the same period held the same view: 'The Church and Satan agreed together in this, that Son and Mother went together; and the experiences of three centuries has confirmed their testimony, for Catholics who have honoured the Mother, still worship the Son, while Protestants, who now have ceased to confess the Son, began then by scoffing at the Mother.'[17]

The Gift of Motherhood

Motherhood is the privilege of the creature. Motherly love, like every other creaturely perfection, has its efficient and exemplary cause in God, in the whole Trinity, and as such may be appropriated to particular persons. However, as we have seen, there is no really existing *relation* of motherhood within the Godhead: none of the Divine Persons relates to

[16] M. J. Scheeben, *Mariology*, vol. 1, ET (St Louis, 1946), p. 139.
[17] Newman, 'The Glories of Mary', p. 348.

any of the others as mother to child or child to mother.[18] Motherhood belongs entirely on the side of the creature; indeed, it is the most beautiful expression of what it is to be a creature, for the fruitfulness of motherhood is the outcome of that receptivity of womanhood which is analogous to the dependence of every creature upon God. Motherhood, in the person of the Mother of God, is thus mankind's sweetest gift to God. Only in His human nature does He know a mother's love. The Byzantine liturgy expresses this great truth in one of its most exquisite hymns:

> What shall we offer thee, O Christ, who for our sakes hast appeared on earth as man? Every creature made by thee offers thee thanks. The angels offer thee a hymn; the heavens a star; the Magi, gifts; the shepherds, their wonder; the earth, its cave; the wilderness, the manger; and we offer thee *a Virgin Mother*.[19]

2. Mother in Faith

Our Lady is a mother to God not only with her body in all its parts but with her soul in all its faculties. Her connection with her Son by flesh and blood is a stupendous glory, but more glorious still is her communion with Him by the faith that perfects her intellect and by the hope and charity that perfect her will. Our Lord Himself points to this spiritual centre of the divine motherhood when a woman praises the womb that bore Him and the paps that gave Him suck: 'Yea, rather, blessed are they who hear the Word of God and keep it' (cf Lk 11:28). Above and before all others, the Blessed Virgin hears the Word of God and keeps it: 'Mary kept all these words, pondering them in her heart' (cf Lk 2:19). As St Augustine and St Leo say, she conceived the Word in her mind by faith before conceiving Him in her womb.[20] Indeed,

[18] See pp. 132f.
[19] Feast of the Nativity, *Menaion*, p. 254.

'the motherly relation would have had no profit for Mary, had she not borne Christ more gladly in her heart than in her flesh.'[21] Blessed, then, is she who believed (cf Lk 1:45).

God does not impose motherhood on Mary. He wants her to give Him His flesh not only from the substance of her body but through the surrender of her faith. 'The Fathers rightly see Mary not merely as passively engaged by God, but as freely co-operating in the work of man's salvation through faith and obedience.'[22] With 'her whole human and feminine person',[23] our Lady *welcomes* the Son of God into human nature; she offers Him, consciously and freely, the shelter of her womb and the comfort of her breast. As we saw above, the Virgin's *fiat* is spousal, like the deliberately uttered 'I will' of a bride to her groom. If the Incarnation is a wedding of human nature to the Divine Word, then it is in the person of our Lady that human nature consents to be wedded.[24] All of mankind, therefore, has an interest in these nuptials. St Bernard pictures the Fathers in Limbo, indeed the whole of the Old Adam's race, waiting breathless for the New Eve to plight her troth to God:

> Weeping Adam begs this of you, O loving Virgin. . . . Abraham and David, too, the holy fathers, your forefathers, those who dwell in the valley of the shadow of death, earnestly beg this of you. . . . The whole world, on bended knee before you, is waiting . . . for on your word depend consolation for the afflicted, redemption for captives, deliverance for the condemned, in short, salvation for all of Adam's sons. . . . O Virgin, give your answer quickly.[25]

---

[20] Cf St Augustine, *Sermo* 215, cap. 4, no. 4; PL 38:1074; St Leo, *In nativitate Domini, sermo* 1, no. 1; SC 22B:68.

[21] St Augustine, *De sancta virginitate*, cap. 3, no. 3; PL 40:398.

[22] LG no. 56.

[23] Cf Pope John Paul II, *Redemptoris mater*, no. 13.

[24] See pp. 167f.

[25] *In laudibus Virginis Matris, sermo* 4, no. 8; L-R 4:53.

Life and death, entry to Heaven and escape from Hell, everlasting bliss or unceasing torment: everything is poised on the word of a humble creature. Far from detracting from the prerogatives of the Creator, this cooperation exhibits His power. He does not compete with His creatures, as if the divine activity displaced the human. The truth is that God is at work in all the actions of His creatures in such a way that those actions are truly their own. We are distinct from Him, yet utterly dependent upon Him, in what we are and in what we do.[26] Even in the natural order, the secondary cause produces its effects in dependence upon the Primary Cause; God causes us to cause. And in the supernatural order our correspondence with grace is itself an outcome of grace: we can only be 'co-workers with God' (cf 1 Cor 3:9) because 'God is at work in [us], both to will and to work for his good pleasure' (RSV Phil 2:13). Our Lady's freely given Yes is therefore the wonderful flowering of her plenitude of grace. '[W]here the Spirit of the Lord is, there is liberty' (2 Cor 3:17). Mary is so full of the Spirit's grace that her will is free of any enslaving tendency to oppose the plan of the Father and resist the coming of the Son.[27]

Our Lady's cooperation with the person and work of the Redeemer began but did not end with her consent to His

---

[26] 'For God grants his creatures not only their existence, but also the dignity of acting on their own, of being causes and principles for each other, and thus of cooperating in the accomplishment of his plan' (CCC 306).

[27] In the opinion of Matthias Scheeben, Protestantism does not understand this marvel of divine condescension revealed in human cooperation: 'So far as Protestantism still believes in the divinity of Christ, it regards Mary only as the earth from which the second Adam has been taken, and not as a person who has the closest mutually spiritual relations with Christ. This fits in completely with the doctrine of the Reformation, according to which human nature in general is as a "lump of clay", which was not changed through grace to its essence and which could not co-operate in the reception of grace. According to the Catholic concept, however, Mary represents the living, passive, and active susceptibility to regenerating grace' (*Mariology*, vol. 1, pp. 5f.).

Incarnation. She renewed her acts of loving faith during the nine months of His residence within her body, at the blissful birth in Bethlehem and on the fearful Flight into Egypt, indeed throughout the whole of His earthly life. But her faith's finest hour was at the foot of the Cross. There, in the words of *Lumen gentium*, she 'united herself with a mother's heart to His Sacrifice and lovingly consented to the immolation of this Victim which she herself had brought forth'.[28] Pope Pius XII says that the sinless Mother offered her Divine Son to the eternal Father 'together with the holocaust of her motherly rights and motherly love, like a New Eve, for all the children of Adam contaminated through his unhappy fall. Thus she, who was the Mother of our Head according to the flesh, became by a new title of sorrow and glory the spiritual Mother of all His members.'[29]

By the decree of the Crucified Son (cf Jn 19:26f.), and by her own acts of obedience to Him, the Mother of God is a mother to all men 'in the order of grace'.[30] On Calvary, in the night of faith, she cooperates with her Son as He merits the grace of our adoption as God's children (the 'objective redemption'), and in Heaven, in the daylight of vision, she cooperates in the distribution of that grace among us (the 'subjective redemption'). In virtue of the first cooperation, certain of the Popes of the last century have called our Lady 'Co-redemptrix', and in virtue of the second, she is commonly hailed as 'Mediatrix of All Graces'. In both respects, our Lady's salvific influence upon us is 'wholly singular',[31] the unique act of a unique person, the incomparably glorious Mother of God. But it is also utterly subordinate to the work of her Son, a service performed by the supremely humble

[28] LG no. 58.
[29] *Mystici corporis*, no. 110.
[30] Cf LG no. 61.
[31] Ibid.

Handmaid of the Lord.[32] It 'flows from the superabundance
of the merits of Christ, is founded upon His mediation,
absolutely depends upon it, and draws all its efficacy from
it'.[33] In dependence upon the will of the Father, the merits of
the Son, and the indwelling presence of the Holy Spirit, our
Lady participates in the objective and subjective redemption.
Just as all the just are sons in the Son, so the Mother of God
is a Mediatrix in the Mediator, the *Co*-Redemptrix, not
equal to but working with the one and only divine Redeemer of the human race:

> No creature can ever be ranked with the Incarnate Word and
> Redeemer. But just as the priesthood of Christ is shared in
> various ways both by sacred ministers and by His faithful
> people, and as the one goodness of God is in reality poured
> out diversely among His creatures, so also the unique media-
> tion of the Redeemer does not exclude but rather gives rise
> among creatures to a manifold co-operation, which is but a
> sharing in this unique source.[34]

Contemplation of the icons of the Christmas mystery—
for example, of the 'Mystic Nativity' of Botticelli—helps to
ensure our adherence to the true Catholic doctrine of our
Lady as Mediatrix and Co-Redemptrix [see art plate 8]. The
Christ Child stretches out His arms to His Mother. He looks
up in love to her, and she looks down in love to Him. No
created person, neither angel nor man, is dearer to His Heart
than Mary is, none more intimately united to His person and
work. In her flesh and by her faith, with all the intelligence
of her mind and all the love in her heart, she has brought the
Redeemer into the world, mediated the Mediator to men.
But the Virgin is also kneeling in adoration, for this Child of

---

[32] Our Lady plays a 'subordinate role' (*munus subordinatum*; see LG no. 60).
[33] Ibid.
[34] LG no. 62.

hers is also her God, and what light streams from her is but a
reflection of His brightness. Her hands are joined, for
through her intercession, as through an aqueduct,[35] the waters of His grace are destined to flow out upon the parched
souls of men.

> All receive something from her fulness [says St Bonaventure]:
> the captive receives redemption, the sick their healing, the
> sorrowful consolation, the sinner forgiveness, the righteous
> grace, the angels happiness, the whole Trinity glory, the
> person of the Son the substance of human flesh.[36]

3. Matchless in Grace

As Mother of God, our Lady is without equal, surpassing by
far all other created persons, whether angels or men.[37] After
the human nature of the Son, no created entity is closer to
the Trinity. According to St Thomas, Gabriel's words at the
Annunciation, 'The Lord is with thee', express his recognition that the Jewish maiden is closer than he or any other
angel is to the Three-Personed God:

> She surpasses the angels in her familiarity with God. The
> angel indicated this when he said, 'The Lord is with thee', as
> if to say, 'I therefore show thee reverence, because thou art
> more familiar with God than I am, for the Lord is with thee.
> The Lord, the Father, is with thee, because thou and He have
> the same Son, something no angel or any other creature has.
> "And therefore the Holy which shall be born of thee shall be

---

[35] On the image of the aqueduct applied to our Lady, see St Bernard's
sermon on her nativity, *De aquaeductu* (L-R 5:279).

[36] *De annuntiatione Beatae Virginis Mariae, sermo* 4, no. 1; Q IX:673.

[37] 'It is impossible for a pure creature to be raised to a higher degree. By the
grace of her motherhood, she exhausts, so to speak, the very possibility of a
higher elevation' (Charles de Koninck, *Ego sapientia: La sagesse qui est Marie*
[Montreal, 1943], p. 39).

called the Son of God" (Lk 1:35). The Lord, the Son, is with thee, in thy womb. "Rejoice and praise O thou habitation of Zion, for great is He that is in the midst of thee, the Holy One of Israel" (Is 12:6).' The Lord is therefore with the Blessed Virgin in a different way than He is with the angel, for He is with her as Son, but with the angel as Lord. 'The Lord, the Holy Spirit, is with thee, as in a temple.' Hence she is called 'the temple of the Lord', 'the sanctuary of the Holy Spirit', because she conceived by the Holy Spirit. 'The Holy Spirit shall come upon thee' (Lk 1:35). In this way, therefore, the Blessed Virgin is more familiar with God than the angel is, for the Lord Father, the Lord Son, the Lord Holy Spirit are with her, in other words, the whole Trinity. That is why we sing of her: 'Noble resting-place of the whole Trinity'.[38]

Our Lady is without compare in her objective dignity, and so it is fitting that she should be unrivalled in her subjective sanctity. To prepare her for the task of being Mother to the Son, both physically and spiritually, God the Father bestows upon her an incomparable plenitude of sanctifying grace, the infused virtues and the Gifts of the Holy Spirit. St Thomas argues as follows. The nearer something is to any kind of source, the more it shares in the effects of that source. The part of the lawn nearest to the sprinkler will be greener than the more remote parts. Now Christ is the source of grace, as author in His Divinity and as instrument in His humanity, and the Blessed Virgin is closer to Him than any other creature is, because it was from her that He received His human nature. 'It was therefore necessary for her to receive from Christ a plenitude of grace greater than that of anyone else.'[39] Even from her conception, she was full of grace. By the anticipated merits of her Son, she was preserved from all stain of Original Sin in the first moment of

---

[38] *In salutationem angelicam*, a. 1.
[39] Cf ST 3a q. 27, a. 5.

her conception. Now Original Sin is the privation of sanctifying grace. If, therefore, our Lady was preserved from that
privation, if she lacked the lack of grace, she was—putting it
positively—endowed in the first moment of her existence
with the overflowing fulness of the redeeming grace of her
Son. She never lacked grace nor did she ever lose it. By a
special privilege she was free from all personal sin, mortal and
venial, even from the inclination to sin. All men are sinners,
says St Augustine, 'except the Holy Virgin Mary, whom, for
the sake of the honour of the Lord, I want to exclude
altogether from any talk of sin'.[40]

When, then, we contemplate all the actions that make up
our Lady's motherhood, ('Welcome in womb and breast,/
Birth, milk, and all the rest'),[41] we should remember that
these humble human realities are endowed, through Mary's
supernatural perfections, with a spiritual beauty surpassing
that of any other mother in human history. 'And she brought
forth her first-born son and wrapped Him up in swaddling
clothes and laid Him in a manger, because there was no room
for them in the inn' (Lk 2:7). St Luke's words, by their very
simplicity and sobriety, convey something of the supernatural
refinement of maternal affection in our Lady's heart. She
shows her Son and God that precious virtue which the
Middle Ages (including St Thomas) named as 'courtesy'
(curialitas), the delicacy of a loving intelligence, the opposite
of that crass lack of perception in the man without charity.[42]

---

[40] De natura et gratia cap. 42, no. 36; PL 44:267.

[41] Gerard Manley Hopkins SJ, 'The Blessed Virgin Compared to the Air We
Breathe', The Poems of Gerard Manley Hopkins, ed. W. H. Gardner & N. H.
Mackenzie, new ed. (London, 1970), p. 94.

[42] The anonymous author of the fourteenth-century poem Pearl calls our
Lady 'the Queen of Courtesy': see Sir Gawain and the Green Knight, Pearl, and
Sir Orfeo, trans. J. R. R. Tolkien, new ed. (New York, 1980), p. 111. 'Great is
the courtesy', says St Thomas, 'when the King of Kings and Lord of Lords
invites us to His nuptials' (Sermo 1, pt. 3).

These gestures, which other mothers do instinctively and which express their natural love in its most natural aspects, are done by Mary under the guidance of the Holy Spirit. For these gestures express a love that is not only motherly but virginal, a divine love for her God who is giving Himself to her in the weakness, the littleness of the Little One, handed over totally to His Mother. Under the movement of the Gifts of Fear, Piety, and Counsel, Mary carries out these actions in a divine way. It is with a chaste and loving fear, in perfect abandonment to the Father's will, that she clasps her Child to her heart, to warm the tiny and tender limbs of the only Son of the Father. . . . No mother has clasped her baby to her heart with more tenderness than Mary; no mother has had more delicacy and respect for the frailty of her baby.[43]

4. Matchless Maidenhood

Our Lady's Virginity in Conceiving Her Son

From the beginning, the Church has confessed, in the words of the Apostles' Creed, that the only Son of God was 'conceived by the Holy Spirit, born of the Virgin Mary'. At the Council of the Lateran in 649, she taught that 'at the end of the ages' the Mother of God 'conceived without seed by the Holy Spirit God the Word, who was begotten of God the Father before all ages'.[44] This is the fact prophesied by Isaiah and reported by St Matthew and St Luke:

---

[43] M.-D. Philippe OP, *Mystère de Marie: Croissance de la vie chrétienne* (Nice, 1958), p. 145. According to the *Revelations* of St Bridget of Sweden, when the Blessed Mother saw her newborn Son shivering with cold, she 'took Him in her arms and pressed Him to her breast, and with her face and breast warmed Him with great gladness and tender motherly compassion': *Revelationes*, lib. 7, cap. 21; new ed., vol. 2 (Rome, 1628), p. 231.

[44] DS 503.

Behold a Virgin shall conceive and bear a Son, and His name shall be called Emmanuel (Is 7:14).

When Mary His Mother was espoused to Joseph, before they came together, she was found with child by the Holy Ghost (Mt 1:18).

The Holy Ghost shall come upon thee, and the power of the Most High shall overshadow thee (Lk 1:35).

The Virgin conceives not by male seed but by the Holy Spirit.[45] 'Mankind's only Lover', says St John Damascene, 'was conceived in the immaculate womb of the Virgin, not by will or desire, not by congress with a man or generation joined with pleasure, but by the Holy Spirit.'[46] In other words, the effect naturally achieved through the corporeal act of a man was here supernaturally achieved, without seed or intercourse, through the incorporeal act of God. Like all other works outside the Godhead, the conception of the body of Christ is wrought by the whole Trinity. However, Scripture and the Creeds attribute it to the Holy Spirit with good reason. He is the Love-Person within the Godhead, the One in whom the Father and the Son love each other and all of us,[47] and so it is splendidly appropriate that He should be at work in the human conception of the Son, which is the highest manifestation of God's love for man: 'God so loved

[45] *Non ex virili semine, / Sed mystico spiramine* (from the hymn *Veni, Redemptor gentium*). 'Thy conceiving was above reason, thy giving birth above nature, O Mother of God, for it was of the Spirit, not of seed' (St Andrew of Crete, *Canones et triodia*; PG 97:1416). The Greek word *asporôs* is frequently used by the Byzantine liturgy (see Ledit, p. 171) and Greek Fathers (e.g., St Sophronius of Jerusalem, *Oratio* 2, no. 22; PG 87:3241C).

[46] *De fide orthodoxa* lib. 3, cap. 1; PG 94:984C. St Leo says that our Lady was made fruitful 'not by human intercourse, but by the Holy Spirit' (*In nativitate Domini, sermo* 2, 3; SC 22B:82). According to the Greek Fathers, the Virgin Mother is *apeirogamos*, 'without experience of the conjugal act' (e.g., St Proclus of Constantinople, *Oratio* 4, 2; PG 65:712C).

[47] Cf ST 1a q. 37, a. 1–2. See pp. 142f.

the world as to give His only-begotten Son' (Jn 3:16).[48] The
Spirit is also the Gift-Person in the Godhead, from whom,
through the Son, all the Father's gifts and graces are showered
upon creatures.[49] It is therefore appropriate that He should be
at work in the Incarnation, for the assumption of human
nature by the Son of God is a grace, the grace of graces, not
the reward of any human action that would in strict justice
be meritorious.[50] According to St Bernard, the Holy Spirit is
the kiss of peace exchanged between the Father and the
Son,[51] and so when William of Newburgh, who had close
connections with the Cistercians, reads the opening words of
the Canticle, 'Let Him kiss me with the kiss of His mouth'
(Song 1:1), he applies them to our Lady and the Holy Spirit.
This is the voice, says William, of 'the Virgin believing the
angel's announcement and conceiving her Child'. The kiss of
the Bridegroom's mouth is the Holy Spirit. The eternal
Word kisses the Virgin with His Holy Spirit, taking flesh
from her by the same Spirit's overshadowing. This is the
kissing of Justice and Peace of which the Psalmist speaks (cf
Ps 84:11), because through the assumption of human nature
into the unity of the Person of the Word comes, on the
Cross, the making of mankind's peace with God.[52]

Once the Blessed Virgin has uttered her *fiat*, a material
body is fashioned from her pure blood by the Holy Spirit,[53] a

[48] ST 3a q. 32, a. 1.

[49] ST 1a q. 38, a. 1–2.

[50] ST 3a q. 32, a. 1; cf 3a q. 2, a. 11. St Thomas admits, however, that 'the
holy Patriarchs merited the Incarnation congruously by their desires and petitions, for it was fitting that God should hear the prayers of those who obeyed
Him' (ST 1a q. 32, a. 1).

[51] *Super cantica canticorum, sermo* 8, no. 2; L-R 1:37.

[52] William of Newburgh, *Explanatio sacri epithalamii in matrem sponsi* (in 1.1),
ed. J. C. Gorman SM (Fribourg, 1960), pp. 78f.

[53] Cf ST 3a q. 31, a. 5. The ancients and medievals knew nothing of
ovulation. They believed that the woman's physical contribution to conception
was a special secretion of blood, upon which the male seed did its work (cf

rational soul is created out of nothing and infused into the body, and—all in the same instant—the complete human nature is assumed by God the Son into the unity of His divine person.[54] 'Be it done unto me according to thy Word. . . . And the Word was made flesh and dwelt among us' (Lk 1:38; Jn 1:14). The Son of God did not bring His body down from heaven,[55] nor did He make it out of the dust of the earth, as He did in the case of Adam. No, the matter of His body was fashioned from the Virgin's own immaculate blood. Since she conceives as a virgin, without male seed, our Lady is the only 'material principle' of the flesh of her Son, His one and only physical link with the race of Adam.

The Virginal Conception is a mystery, the work of the incomprehensible God. It is 'neither proved by reason nor demonstrated from precedent (*exemplo*). Were it proved by reason, it would not be miraculous; were it demonstrated from precedent, it would not be unique.'[56] The Church assures us *that* it took place as a bodily and historical reality, but our poor minds cannot determine exactly *how* the Holy Spirit, by His incorporeal and supernatural operation, made

Aristotle, *De generatione animalium* lib. 1, cap. 19; 727b31–33). Now, whereas in natural human conception male seed acts upon matter supplied by the woman (blood according to the ancients, the ovum according to the moderns), in the conception of Christ the 'active principle' that acts upon the matter supplied by the Blessed Virgin is the divine and supernatural power of the Holy Spirit (see ST 3a q. 32, a. 1). Thus, if we consider the matter supplied by Our Lady (blood or ovum), we can say that the conception of Christ was totally natural, but if we consider the active principle, the fertilizing power (the Holy Spirit), we have to conclude that it was totally miraculous (see ST 3a q. 33, a. 4).

[54] Cf ST 3a q. 33, a. 1 and 3. 'By the action [of the power of the Most High] instantly His body was fashioned, His soul created, and at once both were united to the divinity in the person of the Son, so that the same person was both God and man, with the properties of each nature preserved' (St Bonaventure, *Lignum vitae*, fructus 1, no. 3; Q VIII:71).

[55] Cf ST 3a q. 5, a. 2; q. 31, a. 1–2 and 4–8.

[56] The Eleventh Council of Toledo (675), Profession of Faith; DS 528.

the Virgin fruitful. St Bonaventure, 'like one stammering', tries to shed a little light by presenting an analogy based on that 'trace' (*vestigium*) which the Creator, the Triune God, has left upon all His creatures, even the lowliest. Consider, says Bonaventure, the way in which the earth is made fruitful by the influence of the heavens.

> Heaven makes things fruitful through the sun, the moon, and the nature of the stars. Its influence is threefold, because it pours in heat, moisture, and energy (*vigor*), which represent the Blessed Trinity. By pouring in heat, it makes things subtle, enflames, and elevates. By pouring in moisture, it penetrates, conciliates, and inebriates. By pouring in energy, it moves, forms, and germinates. In similar fashion, the Holy Spirit, when He causes holiness, is like the heat that makes things subtle. When He causes gladness, He is like the moisture that irrigates. When He causes fruitfulness, He is like the energy that works with power. These three things the Holy Spirit did in that blessed earth of ours, the glorious Virgin. First, as heat, He made her holy. Secondly, as spiritual moisture, He saturated her. Thirdly, as spiritual energy, He made her fruitful. On account of these three things, the Incarnation of Our Lord was prefigured in three miracles: the fire of the Bush (cf Ex 3:2ff.), the dew of the fleece (Judg 6:37ff.), and the rod of the flower (cf Num 17:8).[57]

Like the influence of the heavens upon the earth, the Holy Spirit comes upon the Virgin with strength and gentleness, 'as dew in April that falleth on the flower'. Thus, by an analogy that for all its apparent complexity remains essentially simple, St Bonaventure shows the beautiful harmony between the great works of the Trinity: in the creation and government of the visible world, in the revelation made to the Jews and in the Virginal Conception of the only-begotten Son.

[57] *Vigilia nativitatis Domini, sermo* 11; Q IX:97.

In the early Church the Church's faith in the Virginal Conception was denied, among others, by the Jewish sect known as the Ebionites, who accepted that Jesus was the Messiah but denied that He was the pre-existent Son of God; they claimed that He was a mere man and was conceived of the two sexes in the natural way.[58] The doctrine was also rejected and mocked by the pagan critics of Christianity.[59] During the last hundred and fifty years, Liberal Protestants and Modernists have repudiated the historical reality of the Virginal Conception by a number of fallacious arguments, several of which are mutually exclusive, and all of which emanate from post-Enlightenment prejudices against supernatural revelation and the possibility of miracle.[60]

I shall now consider some of the objections to the Virginal Conception raised by these ancient and modern opponents of the Church's Faith, and, in each case, I shall respond with the help of the Fathers and Doctors of the Church.

First, the critics claim that there is a difficulty about the origin of the doctrine. In pagan antiquity there were legends about great men being conceived by the gods—Perseus and Hercules in mythology, Plato and Alexander in history. Is it

[58] Cf St Irenaeus, *Adversus haereses* lib. 1, cap. 26, nos. 1–2; PG 7:686AB; Eusebius of Caesarea, *Historia ecclesiastica* lib. 3, cap. 27, no. 1; PG 20:273A.

[59] Cf Origen, *Contra Celsum* lib. 1, cap. 32; PG 11:720C–24A.

[60] Jose de Freitas Ferreira has applied historical criticism to the works of the Protestant historical critics and their rejection of the Virginal Conception. With the skill of a master detective, he reveals the undiscriminating dependency of one author on another and the lack of firsthand research. The thesis has been transmitted within Liberal Protestantism by 'the laws of inertia', through a kind of intellectual lethargy. Thus the 'scholarship' upon which the 'Catholic' Modernists Schillebeeckx and Küng base their critique of the Virginal Conception turns out to be 'already fourth- or fifth-hand' (*Conceiçao virginal de Jesus: Análise crítica da pesquisa liberal protestante, desde a 'Declaração de Eisenach' até hoje, sobre o testemunho de Mt 1.18–25 e Lc 1.26–38* [Rome, 1980], p. 453). 'In the final analysis . . . the decisive impulse always comes from philosophical *a priorism*, which is prior to, and ever present in, exegetical-historical criticism and subsequent mythical reconstruction' (ibid., p. 275).

not likely, argue the Liberal Protestants, that the Virginal
Conception is just such a legend, inserted into the Gospels
under Hellenistic influence? Even without such influence,
might it not be a 'theological construct', a fictional story
with a theological message, namely, that Jesus is the Son of
God? To both of these questions the answer is an unwavering
No. The Virginal Conception bears little resemblance to the
begetting of pagan demigods and heroes. These are never
virginal conceptions.[61] The women *lose their virginity* through
some kind of physical impregnation, whether by sexual intercourse or through a thunderbolt or shower of gold. True,
when he is explaining the faith for the pagans, St Justin
Martyr compares the Virginal Conception of Christ to the
conception of Perseus.[62] But he is merely making a debating
point: 'You claim [he says in effect] that the Virginal Conception of Jesus is incredible; is it any more incredible than
the stories you tell about the conception of your heroes and
demi-gods?' As C. S. Lewis argued, those who would place
the Gospels in the category of legends and myths prove only
their own lack of literary discernment. Even by the light of
reason, no reader should fail to see the difference between
the elaborate eroticism of the pagan legends and the simple
purity of the Christian Gospels.[63]

The claim that the Virginal Conception is a mere theological construct is another outcome of the same blindness.
After a century and a half of effort in the salt mines of
scepticism, the higher critics have not produced a single scrap
of solid evidence to show that any of the evangelists fabri-
cated facts, here or anywhere else. Matthew and Luke proclaim Jesus as Messiah and Son of David. It would, therefore,
make no sense for them to invent a story that denied His

[61] Cf Ferreira, *Conceiçao virginal de Jesus*, pp. 478f.
[62] *Apologia* 1, no. 22; PG 6:361B–64A.
[63] See pp. 112f.

PLATE 1
Giotto di Bondone (1266–1336), *Presentation of Christ in the Temple*

PLATE 2
Geertgen tot Sint Jans, *The Nativity, at Night*

PLATE 3
Tympanum of the right portal of West front of Chartres

PLATE 4
Joos van Cleve (1485–1540), *The Birth of Christ*

PLATE 5
Piero della Francesca, *The Nativity*

PLATE 6
Hugo van der Goes (c. 1420–1482), Nativity Scene
with Adoration of the Shepherds

PLATE 7
Andrei Rublev (or Pseudo-Rublev), *The Nativity*

PLATE 8
Sandro Botticelli, *Mystic Nativity*

bond by blood with Joseph 'of the house and family of
David' (Lk 2:4). As the *Catechism* says, 'Faith in the virginal
conception of Jesus met with the lively opposition, mockery,
or incomprehension of non-believers, Jews and pagans
alike;[64] so it could hardly have been motivated by pagan
mythology or by some adaptation to the ideas of the age.'[65] It
is the very evangelist who reports the Virginal Conception,
St Luke, who, in the preface to his Gospel, declares his
intention to tell the plain truth about Jesus. As St Ambrose
says, the evangelist writes 'in an historical manner', with the
aim of 'describing realities rather than formulating pre-
cepts'.[66] Luke even vouches for the reliability of his sources:
'those who from the beginning were eyewitnesses and ministers of the Word' (cf Lk 1:2). Now only one human person
was eyewitness of the Word from the *very* beginning, and
that was the Virgin Mother. It was doubtless, therefore, she
who was the evangelist's primary source for his infancy narrative, a conclusion confirmed by his insistence on her
memory: 'And His Mother kept all these words in her heart'
(Lk 2:51). Luke knew that Mary treasured the things of Jesus
in her heart, because she had opened up that treasury to him.

Behind the Liberal Protestant critique of the Virginal
Conception lies German Idealist contempt for historical revelation. The scepticism of David Strauss's *Leben Jesu* is directly indebted to Hegel:

> It is Hegel who furnishes [Strauss] with the definitive seman-
> tic key to the Scriptures that enables him to distinguish
> between the religious concept and its image or sensible ex-
> pression. The two are inseparable, but the true object of faith,
> the perennial, timeless reality, is not the historico-sensible

[64] Cf St Justin, *Pial.* 99, 7; PG 6:7, 708–709; Origen, *Contra Celsum* 1, 32, 69;
PG 11:720–721; et al.
[65] CCC 498.
[66] *Expositio evangelii secundum Lucam*, prol., no. 1; SC 45:39.

dimension of the Biblical narrative (for example, the miracles) but its religious-doctrinal content.[67]

The second difficulty concerns the prophecy of the Virginal Conception in the Old Testament. The critics like to point out that the Hebrew word *almah* used by Isaiah means not 'virgin' but 'young woman of marriageable age'. Moreover, from the context it would seem that the birth foretold by Isaiah is not of the Messiah in the distant future, but of the son of King Ahaz, Hezekiah, in the immediate future. In the strict sense, then, there would seem to be no prophecy of the Virginal Conception in the Old Testament. However, if we read the texts more closely with the help of the Fathers, we find that the Hebrew word *almah* means *more*, not less, than 'virgin'. An *almah* seems always to be not just a virgin, but a virgin whose purity has been carefully honoured and guarded.[68] Rebecca, for example, is described as 'an exceeding comely maid, and a most beautiful virgin, and not known to man' (Gen 24:16). That is why in the Septuagint version of Isaiah 7:14, the holy translators render the Hebrew word as *parthénos*. With regard to the argument that Isaiah's prophecy refers to Hezekiah and his mother, the wife of Ahaz, we should remember that the prophecy was delivered during the reign of Ahaz, and that, even if spoken during the first year of that reign, Hezekiah would have been at least nine years old. What is more, Hezekiah's wife did not conceive and give birth as a virgin, nor was her son called Emmanuel. It must be a *virginal* conception and birth that is prophesied, for, as St Irenaeus says, there would be no 'sign' if a young woman in an entirely natural way, after intercourse with a man, were to conceive and bear a son. No, Irenaeus goes on to say, it is precisely 'because the salvation that was to come was unex-

---

[67] Ferreira, *Conceiçao virginal de Jesus*, pp. 273f.

[68] Cf St Jerome, *Hebraicae quaestiones in Genesim* cap. 24, no. 43; PL 23:974AB; *Adversus Iovinianum* lib. 1, no. 32; PL 23:254C–255C.

pected that the unexpected childbirth of a Virgin took place, God giving the sign and man doing nothing towards it'.[69] Notice Irenaeus's words: 'the *unexpected* childbirth of a Virgin'. Although, by the charism of prophecy, Isaiah had expected the Virginal Conception, there is no evidence to suggest that Jews of the first century were expecting such a miracle and might therefore have been disposed to invent a story by way of fictional fulfillment.[70] St Matthew does not make up the fact to fit the texts; on the contrary, with the help of the Holy Spirit, he searches for texts to fit the fact, 'the unprecedented childbirth of a Virgin'.

The third difficulty is that the Virginal Conception seems to be mentioned explicitly only in the Gospels of St Matthew and St Luke. The other authors of the New Testament appear to be silent on the subject. Therefore, it is argued, the Virginal Conception was not part of the general preaching of the apostles, but at best a pious belief of particular individuals. However, when we read the Bible more closely with the help of the Church, under the guidance of her Fathers, we find that there are several other passages in the New Testament that teach the Virginal Conception. Take, for example, John 1:13: 'born, not of blood, nor of the will of the flesh, nor of the will of man, but of God'. In all of the Greek manuscripts, and in the Vulgate of St Jerome, the verb is in the plural and refers to the supernatural rebirth of God's adopted sons of God: 'But as many as received Him, He gave them power to be made the sons of God, to them that believe in His name, who are born, not of blood', etc.

---

[69] *Adversus haereses* lib. 3, cap. 21, no. 6; PG 7:953A. As Theodoret says: 'If the birth is not virginal but marital [the fruit of the marital act], why should nature's course be called a "sign"?' (*Interpretatio in Isaiam prophetam*, cap. 7, v. 14; PG 81:276D).

[70] See J. McHugh, *The Mother of Jesus in the New Testament* (London, 1975), pp. 282f.

However, in two Latin codices, and more importantly in the writings of, among others, St Irenaeus, the verb is in the singular and refers to the Virginal Conception of the Word: 'He gave them power to be made the sons of God, to them that believe in His name who is born, not of blood', etc. It has, therefore, been suggested that in the original Aramaic text of St John's Gospel, with which St Irenaeus may have been familiar, there was a singular reading rendered in the plural by a Greek translator working from a defective copy of the original.[71] Whatever we may think of the textual question, we cannot fail to see that St John's formulation is a most apt description of the Virginal Conception of Our Lord: Our Lord owes His human coming-to-be to God's will and direct operation, not to the will or operation of a man. Matthias Scheeben is surely right when he says, 'The temporal existence of a divine person must not . . . be determined through the will of a creature.'[72]

Another text referring to the Virginal Conception, at least implicitly, is St Paul's declaration that God sent His Son '*made of a woman* [*genómenon ek gynaikós, factum ex muliere*]' (Gal 4:4), a strange form of words, which, according to some commentators, is St Paul's way of affirming that the body assumed by the Son was not conceived by male seed but by the power of the Holy Spirit.[73]

[71] Ibid., pp. 255–68. St Irenaeus, the Asia Minor Greek who became a priest and bishop in Gaul, is adamant that one and the same apostolic faith is taught in all parts of the Christian world. 'Hence it follows of necessity that in the second half of the second century and the first half of the third, for vast areas of the Church (let us confine ourselves for the present to Irenaeus's itinerary), the singular was the authentic reading' (de Freitas Ferreira, *Conceiçao virginal de Jesus*, pp. 259f.). We should also add that St Irenaeus was a disciple of a disciple (St Polycarp) of the beloved disciple of the Lord, a man, moreover, who was always careful to show the continuity of the Tradition.

[72] M. J. Scheeben, *Handbuch der katholischen Dogmatik*, vol. 2, new ed. (Freiburg, 1933), p. 923.

[73] Cf St Thomas Aquinas, *Super epistolam ad Galatas*, cap. 4, lect. 2.

The Bible is the Church's book. It is she, the Bride of the Word, who places it in our hands and enables us to read it in the same Holy Spirit in whom it was composed.[74] When we heed the Church's wisdom and allow ourselves to be instructed by her Doctors and liturgy, we find many types and evidences of the Virginal Conception and Birth: the Burning Bush,[75] Aaron's Flowering Rod,[76] Gideon's Moist Fleece,[77] the Closed Gate,[78] the Stone Cut without Hands,[79] all examples of miraculous fertility and unspoilt integrity.

[74] Cf Second Vatican Council, Dogmatic Constitution on Divine Revelation, *Dei Verbum*, no. 12.

[75] Ex 3:2. 'There a bush burned and was not consumed; here a virgin gives birth to the Light and is not corrupted' (St Gregory of Nyssa, *In diem natalem Christi*; PG 46:1136BC). 'In the bush unburnt that Moses saw, we recognise thy praiseworthy virginity preserved: O Mother of God, intercede for us' (Antiphon at Vespers and Lauds, The Octave of Christmas, *Breviarium romanum* [1962]).

[76] Num 17:8. 'What is this rod of Aaron and Jesse? Mary, who without cultivation, flowered and bore fruit, to whom, for me, she gave birth as a virgin and after childbirth remains for ever a virgin' (St Romanus Melodus, *Canticum in Christi nativitate* 3, 4; SC 110:122) 'A bud has sprung forth from the root of Jesse; a star has arisen out of Jacob: a virgin has given birth to a Saviour: we praise thee, our God' (Antiphon at Vespers and Lauds on the Octave of Christmas, *Breviarium romanum* [1962]).

[77] Judg 6:37ff. 'She is the stainless fleece placed on the ground of the cosmos, upon which the rain of salvation came down from Heaven' (St Proclus of Constantinople, *Oratio* 6, 17; PG 65:756CD). 'When thou wast born of the Virgin in a manner beyond all telling, the Scriptures were fulfilled; thou didst descend like rain upon the fleece, to save the human race: we praise thee, our God' (Antiphon at Vespers and Lauds, The Octave of Christmas, *Breviarium romanum* [1962]).

[78] Ezek 44:2. 'Virginity's gate was closed. Through it the Lord God of Israel entered, and through it He came forth from the Virgin's womb. Her virginity was preserved, and the Virgin's gate remained closed for ever' (Rufinus, *Commentarius in symbolum apostolorum*; PL 21:349B).

[79] Dan 2:34. 'Daniel, foreseeing His coming, said that a stone cut without hands had come into this world. His coming into this world was not by the work of human hands, of the men whose job it is to cut stones. In other words, it took place not by the operation of Joseph, but by the co-operation of Mary alone with the divine plan of redemption' (St. Irenaeus, *Adversus haereses* lib. 3, cap. 21, no. 7; PG 7:953AB).

From Genesis to Revelation, if we read according to the mind of the Fathers and the liturgy, we shall meet the Ever-Virgin Mary, present or promised, on every page of the inspired text. We should add that, even if there be a relative silence in the New Testament concerning the Virginal Conception, it is a silence of reverence for a mystery great not only in power but also in purity. If the apostles and the Fathers maintained a certain reserve, the 'discipline of the secret', about the sacred mysteries of the liturgy, in order to protect them from pagan curiosity, how much more, and with what fervour of Christian chivalry, did they guard the immaculate mystery of the Virgin Mother from the curiosity of the world and its prince.

The fourth difficulty is not so much an objection as a confusion: If our Lord is 'conceived by the Holy Spirit', does it not follow that the Holy Spirit is the Father of Christ as man? The answer again is No. The work of the Holy Spirit in the Incarnation is not procreative but simply creative, not a begetting but a making, that is, the fashioning of the matter of Christ's body from the flesh and blood of His Mother. A father communicates his nature to his son, but the Holy Spirit does not communicate His own nature, the divine nature, to Christ, because Christ already possesses it from eternity through His generation by God the Father.[80] In any case, the whole Trinity is at work in the conception of Our Lord, and so in one sense the Son of God makes His own body from the flesh of His Mother. As St Gregory of Nyssa says, 'When he said, "Wisdom hath built herself a house" (Prov 9:1), he indicates obscurely by these words the construction of Our Lord's flesh, because true Wisdom did not dwell in a home belonging to someone else, but built a home for Himself out of the body of the

---

[80] Cf St Thomas, *Lectura super Matthaeum* cap. 1, lect. 4.

Virgin.'[81] When Scripture attributes the conception of Christ to the Holy Spirit, it does so, as we have seen, because that conception is an operation of God's love, and the Holy Spirit is the Love of the Father and the Son. The heavenly Father is the only Father of Jesus.

Having answered objections to faith in the Virginal Conception, let us now turn to its 'fittingness',[82] that is, the beauty of its harmony with the other mysteries of the Faith: with the personal properties of the three Divine Persons, the essential attribute of omnipotence manifested by the Triune God in His creation of the world, the perfection of the Son's sacred humanity and His Headship as New Adam, the dignity of womanhood and the purpose for which He, true God, was made true man.

First, the Virginal Conception is fitting because it reveals the personal property of God the Father, who sent the eternal Son into the world, and reveals our Lord's identity as that eternal Son who was sent, the true and natural Son of God. As St Thomas says, 'Since Christ is the true and natural Son of God, it was not fitting for Him to have any other father than God, lest the dignity of God be transferred to another.'[83] As we have seen, according to the Fathers of the Church, the Son of God's human conception in the womb of the Virgin imitates in a most wonderful way His divine generation in the bosom of the Father: He who is begotten

---

[81] *Contra Eunomium* lib. 3, cap. 4; PG 45:580D. The Power of the Most High that overshadows the Virgin is, according to many of the Fathers and Doctors, God the Son Himself, who, as the eternal Splendour of the Father, the Sun of Justice, 'made a shadow for Himself in the Virgin, through which He came down to us, so that He could be seen' (St Bonaventure, *Vigilia nativitatis Domini*, *sermo* 11, no. 3; Q IX:99; cf CA 3, 33).

[82] On the arguments of 'fittingness' (*convenientia*) in the theology of St Thomas, see G. Narcisse OP, *Les Raisons de Dieu: Argument de convenance et esthétique théologique selon St Thomas d'Aquin et Hans Urs von Balthasar* (Fribourg, 1997).

[83] Cf ST 3a q. 28, a. 1.

eternally in His Divinity by the Father without a mother is conceived in time in His humanity by the Mother without a father.[84] It is not the Virginal Conception that makes Christ the Son of God: He is Son from eternity through His generation by the Father in the Godhead. No, His Virginal Conception is a fitting outward sign and expression, in His manhood, of the eternal generation. As Pope John Paul II teaches us, 'The fact that Jesus did not have an earthly father, because He was generated "without human intervention", sets out clearly the truth that He is the Son of God, so much so that even when He assumes human nature His Father remains exclusively God.'[85] Even in His humanity, Jesus' only Father is God.

Secondly, the Virginal Conception is fitting because it reveals God the Son's special characteristic of being the Word of the Father, the concept of the Father's mind. Now an 'interior word' or concept is conceived in the mind without any corruption of the mind. 'Since, therefore, the flesh was so assumed by the Word of God as to be the flesh of the Word of God, it was fitting that it should also be conceived without corruption of the Mother.'[86] As the conceiving of an idea is a spiritual act, so the conceiving of the Word in the womb of the Virgin is an incorporeal operation of the Trinity. Such conceiving does not in itself corrupt but rather perfects the mind, and so likewise the Word, when He is

[84] As Louis Thomassin says: 'Since there are two births of one and the same Word, one in divinity, the other in humanity, the former eternal, the latter temporal, this imitation, like all temporal imitations of the eternal, had to be as clear as possible. Therefore, as He was in the one case born of the Father without a mother, so in the other He had to be born of a Mother without a father, of a Virgin Father and thus of a Virgin Mother, in both cases virginally and without corruption' (*Dogmata theologica*, vol. 3, new ed. [Paris, 1886], p. 186).

[85] General audience address, 28 Jan. 1987.

[86] ST 3a q. 28, a. 1.

conceived in human nature, does not corrupt but confirms and consecrates the virginity of His Mother. The Virgin herself conceives the Word in her own mind before conceiving Him in her flesh, that is to say, the Word exists in Mary by faith as an interior word (a word of the Word), before He exists in her in flesh, as the Father's Word made man.[87]

Thirdly, the Virginal Conception blends harmoniously with both the personal property of the Holy Spirit and the works generally attributed to Him. His property is to be the Love of the Father and the Son: in the Holy Spirit, the Father and the Son love each other, and in the Holy Spirit, They love us.[88] When, therefore, the Father in His love for mankind gives us His Son in human flesh, it seems only right that that flesh should be fashioned by Him who is personal Love in the Godhead. Christ is conceived, not through the fleshly love of a husband for his wife, but through the spiritual love of the Spirit-Love for the whole human race. Thus the only Spouse by whom Mary conceives is divine, God the Holy Spirit.

Fourthly, the Virginal Conception, at the dawn of the new creation, is a beautiful verification of the world's dependence for its coming to be and continuing to be on the omnipotence of the Triune God. 'If you believe God could make the heavens, the sun, the stars out of nothing, if you believe that He could fashion the earth, the seas, the animals, this visible world in all its array, if at length He could create man out of dust, why do you maintain that He could not give [Christ] to an undefiled Virgin by the work and power of God?'[89] Belief in the Virginal Conception is ruled out in advance only by those who hold the deistic view that the natural order of the cosmos, though brought into existence

[87] See pp. 176f.
[88] See pp. 142f., 185f.
[89] St Maximus of Turin, *Homilia 7 De nativitate Domini* 2; PL 57:238D.

by God, does not depend upon Him for its conservation and
for the activity of every agent within it. But in fact the
natural order of the cosmos, as a structure of secondary
causes, is entirely dependent upon Him for its being and
activity. God, the First Cause, causes secondary causes to
cause: He works in them in such a way that they also have
their own proper working.[90] Anything that is not God is
caused by God, including those things that we call actions.
Were there some positive thing that we could do independently of God, then God would not be the first and universal cause. Thus, when in His wisdom God so wills it, He can
do by Himself, without secondary causes, what secondary
causes usually do in dependence on Him, or He can produce effects that are entirely beyond the powers of secondary
causes.[91] Such effects, in the two cases, are what we call miracles.[92] And when God in His wisdom and love chooses by
His own power to produce in the womb of Mary the effect
that is naturally produced by male seed, that effect is called
the miracle of the Virginal Conception. In relation to the
matter supplied by the Mother, the conception of the Son is
natural, for, like every other child, His body is fashioned out
of her blood, but in relation to the active principle, the
conception is miraculous, for the maternal matter is fertil-
ized, not by male seed, but by the Holy Spirit.[93] To the
confounding of all materialism and determinism, the Virginal Conception, like every other miracle, demonstrates
that the cosmos is not a closed system but an open order,
ever dependent upon God in all it is and does, ever ready to
receive from Him fresh influxes of His power. But unlike
any other miracle, the Virginal Conception shows the crea-

[90] Cf ST 1a q. 105, a. 5.
[91] Ibid., a. 6.
[92] Ibid., a. 7.
[93] ST 3a q. 33, a. 4.

ture so open to the Creator, so *capax Dei*, that, in dependence upon Him, it can welcome Him, *she* can welcome Him, into personal union with a created nature.

Fifthly, the Virginal Conception is harmonious with the perfection of the Son's sacred humanity and with His Headship as New Adam.[94] Human persons, conceived of male seed, contract in their conception the guilt of Original Sin inherited from the Old Adam. But the Divine Person of the Son of God is absolutely sinless, and He assumes human nature at His conception in order to deliver men from sin; He is the Lamb of God who takes away the sin of the world (cf Jn 1:29). He could not, therefore, be conceived into Adam's nature by the means through which we are conceived not only into Adam's nature but also into Adam's sin.[95]

> The bodily origin of Christ [says Scheeben] must be so arranged that He thereby truly enters into relationship with the [human] race, yet at the same time is not dependent on the first Head and his sinful influence. He must instead stand out as the new superior Head of the race by virtue of His mode of origin, and be introduced into the race as the source of its reformation and recreation from above by an act of God analogous to the creation of the first parents of the race.[96]

The Incarnate Word is the *New* Adam, who comes to 'make all things new' (Rev 21:5). As St Irenaeus would have it, in bringing us Himself, the Son of God brought 'all newness',[97] for He came to recreate, from within, the world that was originally created by Him but had fallen into the oldness of sin and death and captivity to the devil. It was not

[94] 'Jesus is conceived by the Holy Spirit in the Virgin Mary's womb because He is the New Adam, who inaugurates the new creation' (CCC 504).

[95] Cf ST 3a q. 28, a. 1.

[96] Scheeben, *Handbuch der katholischen Dogmatik*, vol. 2, p. 923.

[97] *Adversus haereses* lib. 4, cap. 34, no. 1; PG 7:1083C.

fitting, therefore, for Him to enter this world in the old dilapidated way. The Son of God 'enters this most lowly world', says St Leo the Great, 'born in a new order, by a new birth . . . conceived by a virgin, born from a virgin, without the fleshly desire of a father, without injury to the integrity of His Mother. Such an origin was fitting for the future Saviour of men, so that He might possess the nature of human substance and yet be spared the defilements of human flesh.' [98] By the newness of His human conception, the Son of God begins to deliver men, says St Bede, from the 'harmful oldness' (vetustas) that Adam inflicted upon His descendants by His sin.[99] An ordinary conception brings into existence one more wounded human person, another heir of Adam's sin, a 'child of wrath' (cf Eph 2:3) and estranged from God. But the Virginal Conception ushers into human nature an already existing Divine Person, the beloved Son, consubstantial with the Father, who comes to reconcile men with God 'in one body by the Cross' (cf Eph 2:16). Between the Virgin-born Son and the rest of mankind there is no difference in human nature, in *what* He and we are: He is consubstantial with us in our humanity. But, because of *who* He is, there is a difference in *how* He comes to be what He is as man.[100] From His Blessed Mother, our Lord takes the nature

[98] *In nativitate Domini, sermo* 2, no. 2; SC 22B:78. St Gregory of Nyssa likewise says: 'O wonderful thing! The Virgin becomes a mother and remains a virgin. Behold the new order of nature' (*In diem nativitatis Salvatoris*; PG 46:1136A).

[99] *Homilia 1 in festo Annuntiationis Beatae Mariae*; PL 94:9A.

[100] 'According to nature,' says St Maximus the Confessor, our Lord's humanity 'is the same as ours, but according to the generation without seed [*asporía*] it is not the same, since this human nature was not that of a mere man but belonged to the One who for our sakes became man' (*Epistola* 1; PG 91:60c). St Cyril of Alexandria likewise says: 'For since He is immutable and unalterable by nature as God, the living and subsisting Word of the Father, He did not form the body united to Himself from His own nature, but rather took it from us, and not from sleep and pleasure by the work of a man, but from the Holy

but not the guilt of man.[101] Since the Virginal Conception
inaugurates the eternal Word's re-creation of the cosmos, it is
most fitting that it should be the work, in a special way, of
the Holy Spirit. When God through His Word created the
world, the Spirit of God spread His wings above the waters
(cf Gen 1:2). When the Father sends the Word to make the
world anew, the Holy Spirit overshadows a woman. Again,
just as the Holy Spirit formed the Old Adam's body from the
virgin earth and animated it with a rational soul, so now the
same Spirit forms the New Adam's body from the Virgin
Mary and animates it with a rational soul.[102] As St Augustine
says, '"Truth is sprung out of the earth", Christ who said, "I
am the Truth", is born of a virgin. . . . Truth is sprung out of
the earth, flesh born of Mary.'[103] The Blessed Virgin, says St
Aelred, is the 'paradise of pleasure from the beginning,
wherein [God] placed man whom He had formed (cf Gen
2:8)'.[104] He concludes from this truth that, if we want the
New Adam to dwell in our hearts, we must prepare a Mary-
like Paradise for Him there. 'May the Spirit be there, the

Virgin in a new and strange manner and beyond the laws of nature' (*Contra
Iulianum*, lib. 6; PG 76:929A).

[101] St Leo, *In nativitate Domini, sermo*, no. 3; SC 22B:80. St Thomas says: 'It
was not possible in a nature already corrupt for flesh to be born from intercourse without incurring the infection of Original Sin. That is why Augustine
says: "In that union", namely, the marriage of Mary and Joseph, "the nuptial
intercourse alone was lacking, because in sinful flesh this could not be done
without fleshly concupiscence, which arises from sin, and without which He,
who was to be without sin, wished to be conceived' (ST 3a q. 28, a. 1). St
Thomas is not arguing that sexual concupiscence in the conjugal act is in itself
a sin (though it *can* be, when, for example, the couple have an intention
opposed to the good of offspring—see Suppl. 49, 5), but that in every human
being affected by Original Sin, even the holiest, it is a disorder caused by the
action of Adam. It is from this disorder that our Lord wished His human
conception to be free.

[102] Cf St Ambrose, *Expositio evangelii secundum Lucam* lib. 4, no. 7; SC 45:152.

[103] *Sermo* 185, cap. 2, no. 2; PL 38:998.

[104] *Sermo* 38, *In annuntiatione Domini*, no. 2; CCCM 2A:312.

fount unfailing, who waters us with His spiritual grace, with compunction, devotion, and all spiritual sweetness.' [105]

Sixthly, the virginal manner of our Lord's conception is a wonderful elevation of womanhood, of the daughters of the Old Eve, through the 'Mother and Maiden' who is the New Eve. It was a woman *alone* who represented our race in saying Yes to the Incarnation, a woman *alone* who served as the material source of our Lord's humanity. Thus both sexes are honoured by the mystery of the Incarnation: 'He wanted to assume the male sex in Himself and deigned to honour the female sex in His Mother. . . . Do not despair, males: Christ deigned to be male. Do not despair, females: Christ deigned to be born of a female.' [106] Scheeben sets out the good reasons that God had for honouring the two sexes in these two distinct ways:

> It is not by chance that it was precisely the male sex which was chosen for the highest elevation of nature, but the female sex for the elevation of the person. For nature hypostatically united to God had to represent God in His ruling position and as Bridegroom of the creature, a representation that the male sex alone could achieve. But the highest elevation of a created person into communion with God finds its expression in the relationship of the Bride to the Bridegroom, and for that reason it is naturally represented in the female sex. [107]

Seventhly, the Virginal Conception resonates in the loveliest way with the purpose of the Incarnation, which is nothing less than the divinization of men through their rebirth as the adopted sons of God. By the wisdom and love of God, the exemplary cause of the saving effect was supplied in the way the Saviour Himself was conceived. In the words of St Augustine, quoted by St Thomas, 'It was necessary that our

[105] Ibid., no. 18; CCCM 2A:317.
[106] St Augustine, *Sermo Denis* 25, no. 4; PL 46:935.
[107] *Handbuch der katholischen Dogmatik*, vol. 2, p. 922.

Head, by a conspicuous miracle, be born in the body of a virgin, to signify that His members would be born of the Virgin Church in the Spirit.'[108] The natural Son's human conception is the model and source of the divine rebirth of the adopted sons: of both the Head and the members it is true, though in different ways, that they are 'born, not of blood, nor of the will of the flesh, nor of the will of man, but of God' (cf Jn 1:13).

Before leaving the subject of the Virginal Conception, we should consider the question of St Joseph's reaction to the mystery. According to some of the Father and Doctors of the Church, Joseph wanted to 'put [Mary] away privately', not because he was ignorant of the Virginal Conception and suspected her of adultery, but because he already knew she had conceived by the Holy Spirit and felt unworthy to live in her presence. In his commentary on St Matthew's Gospel, St Thomas summarizes the argument as follows:

> Joseph had no suspicion of adultery, for he was well aware of Mary's chastity. He had read in Scripture that a virgin would conceive. . . . [H]e also knew that Mary was descended from David. It was easier, therefore, for him to believe that this had been fulfilled in her than that she had committed fornication. And so, regarding himself as unworthy to live under the same roof with someone of such sanctity, he wanted to put her away privately, as Peter said, 'Leave me, Lord, for I am a sinful man' (Lk 5:8).[109]

[108] *De sancta virginitate*, no. 6; PL 40:399, cited in ST 3a q. 28, a. 1. St Leo likewise says: 'For every man re-born, the water of Baptism is like a virginal womb, since it is the same Spirit filling the font who also filled the Virgin; thus the sin that a holy conception there did away with, the mystical washing here removes' (*In nativitate Domini, sermo* 4, no. 3; SC 22B:114).

[109] *Lectura super Matthaeum*, cap. 1, lect. 4. In her *Revelations*, St Bridget attributes these words to our Lady: '[A]fter I gave my consent to God's messenger, Joseph, seeing my womb enlarged by the power of the Holy Spirit, was exceedingly afraid. It is not that he suspected me of anything untoward, but simply that he remembered the words of the prophets when they foretold the

The purity of St Joseph is second only to that of our Lady. The eyes of his chaste soul were never blind to the chastity of his immaculate spouse. 'There is no doubt', says Denys the Carthusian, 'that the interior grace, sanctity, and chastity of Mary shone forth wonderfully and powerfully, not only in her face, but in the bearing and deportment of her body, so much so that anyone diligently considering her manner of life could not suspect her of fornication or any other sin.' [110]

The Virginity of Our Lady in Giving Birth to Her Son

It is of divine faith for Catholics to hold that our Lady not only conceived the divine Word as man 'without seed, by the Holy Spirit' but also gave birth to Him 'without corruption'.[111] According to the Church's Doctors, this freedom from corruption means that the God-Man leaves His Mother's womb without opening it (*utero clauso vel obsignato*), without inflicting any injury to her bodily virginity (*sine violatione claustri virginalis*), and therefore without causing her any pain.[112] Pope St Leo the Great teaches the doctrine of our

---

birth of the Son of God from a virgin, and reckoned himself unworthy of serving such a mother, until the angel in a dream commanded him not to be afraid but to serve me with charity' (*Revelationes*, lib. 7, cap. 25, new ed., vol. 2 [Rome, 1628], p. 239f.). For a fuller discussion of this issue, see I. de la Potterie SJ, *Marie dans le mystère de l'alliance* (Paris, 1988), pp. 87ff.; and J. M. McHugh, *The Mother of Jesus in the New Testament* (London, 1975), pp. 164ff.

[110] *Enarratio in evangelium secundum Matthaeum* cap. 1, a. 3; DCOO 11:17AB.

[111] Cf Lateran Council (649), can. 3; DS 703. St Augustine says that 'the Virgin conceived without male seed, gave birth without corruption, and remained in integrity after childbirth' (*Sermo* 215, no. 3; PL 38:1073).

[112] Cf ST 3a q. 35, a. 6. See also Scheeben, *Handbuch der Katholischen Dogmatik*, vol. 2, p. 939. The recusant divine Matthew Kellison summarizes the argument as follows: '[T]he pain of the Mother in giving birth is caused by the opening of the passages through which the child comes out. Now Christ was born and came forth from a closed womb and so did not cause His Mother pain' (*Commentarii ac disputationes in Tertiam partem Summae theologiae S. Thomae Aquinatis* [Douai, 1633], p. 329).

Lady's virginity *in partu* in his famous *Tome*, which was read and approved at the Council of Chalcedon: 'Mary brought Him forth, with her virginity preserved, as with her virginity preserved she had conceived Him.' [113] The *Catechism* speaks of our Lady's virginity being preserved 'even in the act of giving birth to the Son of God' (*etiam in partu Filii Dei*) and quotes the strong reaffirmation of the dogma by the Second Vatican Council: 'Christ's birth "did not diminish his mother's virginal integrity but sanctified it".' [114] In 1992, on the sixteenth centenary of the Council of Capua, Pope John Paul II vigorously proclaimed the virginity of our Lady *in partu*, comparing our Lord's birth from the 'intact virgin' with His Resurrection from the 'intact tomb'.[115] This faith, so boldly affirmed by popes and councils, is beautifully enunciated in the liturgical prayers of Christian West and East. In the Byzantine liturgy, on the feast of her Synaxis, the Theotokos speaks thus to her Child: 'As thou hast found my womb, so thou hast left it.' [116] And, on Christmas Day, the Church

[113] Cf DS 291.

[114] CCC 499, quoting LG no. 57. In his commentary on *Lumen gentium*, Monsignor Gérard Philips, who was a *peritus* at the Council and played a key role in the drafting of the Constitution, writes: 'Quite a few of the Fathers asked for an unambiguous declaration not only to affirm the Virginal Conception of Jesus—which the Christian faith has never doubted—but also fully to safeguard the aphorism *Virgo ante partum, in partu et post partum*. The Council thought that the terminology it employed could suffice for this end, without going into biological details. One thing is certain: this virginity, in its threefold aspect, is not taught as a personal privilege of Mary; for the whole Tradition it constitutes a *Christological* datum. *In coming into this world in order to save it, the Son of God did not harm this world in any way*. This is the idea that quite a few of the Fathers of the Church defended against the attacks of authors they described as heretics' (*La chiesa e il suo mistero: Storia, testo e commento della* Lumen gentium, new ed. [Milan, 1993], p. 544).

[115] *L'Osservatore romano*, Eng. ed. (10 June 1992), 13ff. See my book *Christ Is the Answer: The Christ-Centred Teaching of Pope John Paul II* (Edinburgh, 1995), pp. 32f.

[116] Synaxis of the Mother of God, *Menaion*, p. 292. St Proclus of Constantinople likewise says: 'He came from the womb just as He had entered

herself directly addresses our Lady: 'According to His good pleasure, by a strange self-emptying, He passed through thy womb, yet kept it sealed.' [117] The Roman rite is no less explicit: 'Blessed Mary, Mother of God, whose womb abideth intact, has today given birth to the Saviour of the world.' [118] Moreover, throughout the Christmas Octave, a special *communicantes* in the Roman Canon commemorates 'that most sacred night [or day] in which the inviolate virginity of Blessed Mary brought the Saviour into this world'.

Isaiah prophesied that the Mother of Emmanuel would be a virgin not only in conceiving Him in the womb (*Ecce virgo concipiet*) but also in bringing Him forth from the womb (*et virgo pariet*, cf Is 7:14). The angel Gabriel tells our Lady, in words that in the Greek have a strange syntactical structure, 'The Holy (*agion*) which shall be born of thee shall be called the Son of God' (Lk 1:35). It is hard to parse the neuter adjective. Some scholars have argued that it should be taken adverbially, as a description of the way in which our Lord's birth is holy, that is, sanctified and sanctifying. This seems to be the sense of St Cyril of Jerusalem's statement: 'His birth was pure, undefiled.' [119] The Fathers find types of the virginity *in partu* in Ezekiel's prophecy of the closed gate of the Temple (cf Ex 44:2) and in the 'garden enclosed' and 'fountain sealed up' of Solomon's canticle (cf Song 4:12).[120] The

---

through the ear; as He was conceived, so He was born. He entered without passion, and He went out without corruption, as the prophet Ezekiel says (Ezek 44:21)' (*Oratio* 1, no. 10; PG 65:692A).

[117] Feast of the Nativity, *Menaion*, p. 274.

[118] Fifth responsory, Matins of Christmas Day (*Breviarium romanum* [1962]).

[119] *Catecheses* 12, no. 32; PG 33:765A. The interpretation I am proposing here has been argued in detail by I. de la Potterie SJ in *Marie dans le mystère de l'alliance*, p. 65.

[120] ' "A garden enclosed, a fountain sealed up" (Cant 4:12), whence flows the river of which Joel speaks (Joel 3:18), which waters the torrent of cords (or thorns), of the cords by which they were tied or of the thorns which choaked the seed of the father of the family. This is the East Gate, as Ezekiel says (44:2),

reverence and modesty shown by the Fathers towards this beautiful mystery is in stark contrast with the prying crudeness of the heretics. St John Chrysostom, for example, is content to assert the fact of the miraculous preservation of our Lady's virginity during childbirth and refuses to delve into the details.[121] It was probably the Arian controversy that brought the miraculous birth to the forefront of the Catholic mind. That controversy was concerned chiefly with the true Divinity of the Son, and thus with His eternal generation from the Father. However, the Fathers found it necessary to bring His temporal birth into the discussion. The Arians, especially in the radical Eunomian party, were rationalists, presuming to enclose God in a definition. Against such arrogant folly, the Fathers cited the miracle of the Virgin Birth: How can men claim to have fathomed the infinite abyss of the divine and eternal generation of the Word from the Father when even His human and temporal birth from the Virgin is such an enigma?[122]

In the late fourth century, the doctrine of the virginity *in partu* was denied by Jovinian, a monk turned playboy, whose attack on the maidenly motherhood of Mary was part of a

---

ever closed, ever clear, either covering within itself or bringing forth from itself the Holy of Holies, the Gate through which the Sun of Justice, our High Priest according to the order of Melchizedek, goes in and comes out' (St Jerome, *Epistola* 48, no. 21; PL 22:510). 'O mystery! I see miracles, and I proclaim the Godhead: I perceive sufferings, and I do not deny the humanity. For Emmanuel opened the doors of nature as man, but as God did not break through the bars of virginity' (St Proclus of Constantinople, *Oratio* 1, no. 10; PG 65:692A). According to St Modestus of Jerusalem, the Ever-Virgin Theotokos is the 'sealed fountain . . . by whom the paradise of the orthodox Church is watered' (*Encomium in dormitionem SS. Dominae nostrae Deiparae semperque Virginis Mariae*, no. 6; PG 86B:3292C).

[121] 'Although I know that a virgin this day gave birth, and I believe that God was begotten before all time, yet the manner of this generation I have learnt to venerate in silence, and I accept that this is not to be probed too curiously with wordy speech' (*In salvatoris nostri Iesu Christi nativitatem oratio*; PG 56:388).

[122] Cf St Augustine, *Sermo* 195, no. 1; PL 38:1017–1018.

wider campaign against the consecrated state of virginity. Jovinian's heresy was condemned by synods held in Rome and Milan. The Synod of Milan, under the chairmanship of St Ambrose, invoked the words of the Apostles' Creed, *natus ex Maria Virgine*, which imply that the very act of giving birth to her Son, not just her conceiving of Him, was maidenly in its manner.[123]

The chief objection raised by the heretics to the virginity *in partu* is that, in the eyes of its adversaries, it makes our Lord's human birth and thus His human nature itself seem unreal. Does the doctrine not betray Gnostic or Manichean disdain for the flesh? Was it not a Gnostic, Valentinus, who taught that the Son of God merely 'passed through' His Mother, as through a channel?[124]

In reply to this objection, we must again invoke the distinction made within the Tradition between *what* Christ is as man and *how* He comes to be man: as St Leo says, just because His conception and birth (how He comes to be

---

[123] 'Christ . . . being God came to earth in an unusual way, as He was born from the immaculate Virgin. . . . But they say perversely: she conceived as a virgin, but she did not give birth as a virgin. So a virgin could conceive, but a virgin could not give birth, though the conception always precedes and the birth follows. . . . They should believe the Apostles' Creed, which the Roman Church always guards and preserves. . . . This is the Virgin who has conceived in the womb, the Virgin who has brought forth her Son. For thus it is written: "Behold, a virgin shall conceive and bear a son" (Is 7:14); for he says not only that a virgin shall conceive, but also that a virgin shall bring forth. For what is the gate of the sanctuary, that outer gate looking towards the East, which remains shut (Ezek 44:1f.)? Is not this gate Mary, through whom the Saviour entered this world . . . who conceived and brought forth as a virgin?' (*Ep.* 42. 4–6; PL 16:1125A–1126A).

[124] Tertullian (155–223), though defending and expounding the Virginal Conception as a primordial dogma of the faith, denies the virginity *in partu*, apparently in order to affirm the reality of the Saviour's birth against the Docetists: 'If as a virgin she conceived, in her childbearing she became a wife. For she became a wife by that same law of the opened body, in which it made no difference whether the violence was of the male let in or let out: the same sex performed that unsealing' (*De carne Christi* cap. 23; PL 2:790B).

man) are miraculous, it does not follow that His human
nature (what He is as man) is dissimilar to ours.[125] In the
manner of His human birth, says St Thomas, Christ wants to
reveal the truth not only of His humanity but also of His
Divinity. That is why 'He mingled marvellous things with
humble ones. Thus, to show His body was real, He is born of
a woman, but to show His divinity, He is born of a virgin,
for, as St Ambrose says in his hymn on the Nativity, "Such
birth befits the God of all." '[126] The heretic Valentinus denied
that the Son of God took anything from His Mother,
whereas the Church confesses that He is man 'from the
substance of His Mother',[127] that His flesh is fashioned by the
Holy Spirit from His Mother's pure blood. The virginity *in
partu* is a miracle of the bodily order, a cherishing and beau-
tifying of the Virgin's flesh. Such a miracle would be of no
interest to the Gnostics or Manicheans, who despised the
body and sought for it no splendour. The preservation of
virginity *in partu* manifests a God who not only creates the
biological realm but also descends to its depths in person.
Our Lady's virginity is a quality of her soul as well as of her
body. But the rational soul is the substantial form of the
human body, making it to be what it is, the body of a human
being. It is therefore fitting that its beauty should be manifested through the beauty of the body. We could even say
that the virginity *in partu* is a kind of divinely instituted

[125] The miraculous manner of our Lord's temporal birth does not alter His
human nature or make that birth any less real or human. St Leo gives us a
singularly clear statement of the two moments of our Lady's virginal childbearing: 'He was begotten by a new kind of birth: conceived by a virgin, He was
born of a virgin; without the carnal concupiscence of a father, without harm
to the integrity of the Mother.' 'Although Christ is born of the Virgin's womb,
and His birth is miraculous, His nature is not different from ours. True God,
He is equally true man, and there is no lie in either of the two substances' (*In
nativitate Domini, sermo* 4, no. 3; SC 22B:104).
[126] ST 3a q. 28, a. 2.
[127] See the Athanasian Creed (DS 76).

sacrament of the virginity in Mary's soul. The matchless maidenhood is both corporeal and spiritual. As St Bernard says, 'She was a virgin in body, a virgin in mind, a virgin in profession, a holy virgin in spirit and body.' [128]

But why was it necessary for the Son of God to be born as man in a way that would not injure the integrity of His Mother's virginity? The necessity is again one of fittingness, of harmony and thus of beauty, like the need to fit a third and a fifth alongside the root to achieve the lovely consonance of a major chord. The virginity *in partu* is what is needed for Christ's human birth to be in accord with the rest of His work in creation and redemption. St Thomas and the other Doctors of the Church hear the following harmonies in the mystery:

First, a birth without corruption is in harmony with the personal property of the person who was born, namely, the Word of God. Now 'a word is not only conceived in the mind without corruption, but also comes out of the mind without corruption.' [129] St Hilary answers the Arian charge that if the Father generates the Son eternally from His essence, He must be thereby diminished in His essence, by arguing that the same Son was born as man from His Mother without damaging her bodily integrity. He then draws this conclusion: 'Surely divine law requires us not to regard as impossible with God something that was possible by His power in man.' [130] Cardinal Bérulle argues that, since the temporal birth is a kind of image of the eternal, the perfections of the latter should so

---

[128] St Bernard cited by St Bonaventure (see *De annuntiatione Beatae Virginis Mariae, sermo* 2; Q IX:660). St Thomas says that the hymen pertains to virginity only *per accidens*, and that its rupture by any means other than sexual pleasure is no more destructive of virginity than the loss of a hand or foot (cf ST 2a2ae q. 152, a. 1, ad 3). However, he also holds that bodily integrity belongs to the perfection of virginity (see *Quaestiones quodlibetales* 6, q. 10, prol).

[129] ST 3a q. 28, a. 2.

[130] St Hilary, *De Trinitate* lib. 3, cap. 19; PL 10:87.

far as possible be mirrored in the former: 'Jesus is the Son of
the Father; He proceeds from His Father's bosom without
opening it. This bosom remains eternally closed despite the
procession and mission of the Son of God in the world. He
also wants to proceed from the virginal womb of His Blessed
Mother. This womb remains closed as before, symbolized by
the Enclosed Garden and the Sealed Fountain, and by the East
Gate through which God passes.' [131]

Thus the preservation of integrity in the human body of
the Mother mirrors the preservation of immutability in the
divine nature of the Son who is born. As St Augustine says,
'Before He became, He was; and because He was omnipotent, He could become while remaining what He was. He
made a mother for Himself, while He was with the Father;
and when He became [man] from the Mother, He remained
in the Father. How could He cease to be God in beginning
to be man, He who granted His Mother not to cease be a
virgin when she gave birth?' [132]

Secondly, the miracle of the Virgin Birth is in wonderful
harmony with the saving purposes of the Incarnation of the
Word. St Thomas argues that, since the Son of God became
man to take away our corruption, it was not fitting for Him
to corrupt the virginity of His Mother by being born.[133]
Thus, as St Gregory of Nyssa once wrote, the fruitful maidenhood of Mary is like a rock upon which death is dashed.[134]
It proves that this fallen world is not destined to be for ever a

---

[131] Pierre de Bérulle, *Opuscules de piété*, new ed. (Grenoble, 1997), p. 188.

[132] St Augustine, *Sermo* 186, cap. 1, no. 1; PL 38:999.

[133] 'The Lord Jesus Christ came to take away our maladies, not to contract
them; to bring a remedy to our vices, not to succumb to them. . . . That is
why it was necessary for Him to be born in new conditions. . . . It was
necessary that the integrity of the One being born preserve the pristine virginity of the one who gave birth . . .' (St Leo, *In nativitate Domini, sermo* 2, no. 2;
SC 22B:78).

[134] Cf *De virginitate*, cap. 13; PG 46:377D.

closed system of corruption. When He is born of a Virgin
and rises from the dead in the flesh, the Divine Word breaks
the cycle of Adam's decay. That is why the Fathers compare
the sealed womb of the Virginal Birth with the sealed tomb
of the Resurrection, or His passage from the womb to His
entering through closed doors into the Upper Room.[135] The
Son of God is born as man of the Virgin, suffers, dies and
rises again as man, in order to halt the decline of mankind
into dust. Christ's body, in leaving the closed womb, did not
have the subtlety it would have when it passed through the
closed doors; it was in a state of mortality, not yet in that of
glory. However, as a miracle of the bodily order, the coming
forth of the Infant Word from the Virgin's closed womb
was a foretaste of that definitive transfiguration of the flesh
which took place for Him on the third day after His death
and for us will occur on the last day of all human history.
The Divine Word is made flesh to restore man, disfigured
through Adam's sin, to beauty, the beauty of grace in his soul
and the beauty of glory in His body. He, therefore, takes
the way of beauty when He comes into the world. God is
born of the Virgin, says the Franciscan Doctor, 'not by opening, not by corrupting, since "this gate shall be shut" for
ever; "it shall not be opened, and no man shall pass through
it" (Ezek 44:2), but by making it fruitful and beautiful
[*fecundando et decorando*]'.[136] The Franciscan poet sings of the
same truth:

> Without break of the seal, the beautiful Son is born,
> With its gates still fastened, of His palace He takes His
> leave.

---

[135] 'In the flesh He was born, coming forth as small through a closed womb,
and in that same flesh He was resurrected and came in as great through closed
doors' (St Augustine, *Sermo* 215, no. 4; PL 38:1074).

[136] St Bonaventure, *In nativitate Domini, sermo* 12; Q IX:100A.

Unfitting would it surely be for Divine Power
To do violence to His home and hospice [*casa
    albergata*].[137]

Thirdly, the virginity *in partu* is in harmony with the
commandments. God, who commanded us to honour our
parents, did not want to 'diminish the honour of His Mother
by being born'.[138] Even in the way He is conceived and born,
God the Son shows He is faithful to His own law: He
honours His Mother, because when He leaves her womb He
does not destroy the physical seal of her virginity. The outward sign of the Virginal Conception remains intact when
Christ is born. The Virginal Birth is thus further proof of the
courtesy of God, of His *curtayse* love, as Lady Julian of Norwich would say.[139] The Father's Word and Wisdom 'orders all
things sweetly' (cf Wis 8:1), that is, with an infinite delicacy
and tact. That is why, in taking flesh from the Virgin, He
does not employ her as a passive instrument but, with divine
chivalry, invites and inspires her active consent. As He enters
Mary's womb, so He leaves it—without hurt or harm of its
maidenly wholeness. 'He came all so *still*/ To His Mother's
bower. . . .' The guarding of His Mother's virginity in childbirth was not necessary by an absolute necessity, as if God
were unable to act otherwise, and yet it is a lovely and
entirely congruous gift bestowed by the Son upon the
Mother. Almighty God can do what no other child can do:
He can choose His Mother and the manner in which He
enters and leaves her womb.

Our Lord Jesus, who was with the Father before He was
born of His Mother, chose not only the Virgin of whom He
was born, but also the day on which His Birth took place.
Men subject to error very often choose days. . . . No one,

[137] *Laude*, no. 32; ed. F. Mancini (Rome, 1974), p. 88.
[138] Cf ST 3a q. 28, a. 2.

however, can choose the day of his birth. But Christ the Lord was able both to create and to select the day of His birth.[140]

Fourthly, since our Lord is born as man and later dies and rises again in order to bring us the fullness of joy with Him in Heaven (cf Jn 15:11), it is fitting that He should bring joy, not pain, to His Mother when He comes forth from the womb.

> The pain of childbirth is caused by the opening of the passages through which the child comes out. Now, as we said above, Christ came out of the closed womb of His Mother, and so no violent opening of the passages took place. Thus there was no pain in the birth nor corruption, but only gladness that the God-Man should be born into the world, as Isaiah says: 'It shall bud forth and blossom, like the lily, and shall rejoice with joy and praise' (Is 35:1f.).[141]

The Son of God makes His birth a cause of gladness, not of sadness, for His Mother, so that she can say with the prophet Habakkuk, 'I will rejoice in the Lord, and I will joy in God my Jesus' (Hab 3:18).[142] Thus, by His gifts to her of joy, the divine Babe makes His Mother 'the lyre of His melodies'.[143] He comes to wipe away every tear from our eyes. Suffering, when offered up in faith and love in union with Christ, can be a beautiful apostolate, but in itself it is an evil and is never multiplied by God without good cause. According to St John Damascene, the pains that our Lady was spared in Bethlehem she endured on Calvary; the birth

[139] *A Book of Showings to the Anchoress Julian Norwich*, part 1, Short Text, chap. 3, ed. E. Colledge OSA and J. Walsh SJ (Toronto, 1978), p. 211.

[140] St Augustine, *Sermo* 190, cap. 1, no. 1; PL 38:1007.

[141] ST 3a q. 35, a. 6.

[142] Cf St Bonaventure, *In nativitate Domini, sermo* 3; Q IX:111B.

[143] *Des heiligen Ephraem des Syrers Hymnen de Nativitate (Epiphania)* 15; CSCO, *Scriptores Syri*; GT, E. Beck OSB (Louvain, 1959), p. 146.

of the Head was in joy, but the birth of the Mystical Body was in sorrow.[144]

Fifthly, the virginal manner in which Holy Mother Mary brings forth Christ the Head of the Mystical Body in the flesh anticipates the virginal manner in which Holy Mother Church brings forth the members of the Body by water and the Holy Spirit. As St Augustine says:

> The only-begotten Son of God deigned to take upon Himself a human nature drawn from a virgin so that He might thus link a spotless Church to Himself, its spotless Founder. . . . Since the virginity of His Mother was in no way violated in the birth of Christ, He likewise made His Church a virgin by ransoming her from the fornication of demons.[145]

Our Lady's Lifelong Virginity

The Fifth Ecumenical Council, Constantinople II (553), calls our Lady *aeiparthenos, semper virgo*, 'ever-virgin', the title with which she is acclaimed in the liturgies of both East and West.[146] According to the teaching of the Church, after conceiving and giving birth as a virgin, the Mother of God remained for ever a virgin. Her marriage to St Joseph was a true one, endowed with all the goods of marriage, but it was never consummated. She and her spouse most chaste lived together in perfect and perpetual continence. The so-called brethren of the Lord mentioned in the Gospels are, therefore, not the physical children of Mary and Joseph but close relatives from the extended family. In the early centuries, the perpetual virginity of our Lady was denied by such heretics as Jovinian, Helvidius and the so-called Antidicomarianites and defended with chivalrous zeal by, among others, St

---

[144] Cf St John Damascene, *De fide orthodoxa*, lib. 4, cap. 14; PG 94:1161D.

[145] *Sermo* 191, cap. 2, no. 3; PL 38:1010.

[146] Cf DS 447; CCC 499.

Ambrose, St Jerome and St Augustine. In 1555 Pope Paul IV
condemned the denial of the perpetual virginity by rational-
istic Protestants.[147]

One of the signs of the perpetual virginity of our Lady in
Scripture is our Lord's entrusting of His Mother to the care
of St John. From Origen onwards, Catholic exegetes have
argued that this shows that, after the death of Joseph, there
was no one else within the immediate family to look after
Mary, and that she therefore conceived no child but Jesus.[148]
In the Tradition of the Church, from the earliest days, our
Lady has been called '*the* Virgin', suggesting that virginity
was her defining attribute and permanent state. At the beginning of the second century, St Ignatius of Antioch presents
the virginity of Mary as an indispensable truth of the Faith, a
deep mystery that eludes the grasp of the devil's mind, 'to be
cried aloud' but 'hidden from the prince of this world'.[149]

The Fathers and Doctors are agreed that our Lady's words
at the Annunciation—'How shall this be done, because I
know not man?'(cf Lk 1:34)—signify that, before the arrival
of the angel, she has already resolved to remain a virgin
throughout her life.[150] Many authors believe this resolution to
have been, from the beginning, a formal and absolute vow of
virginity. St Thomas takes a slightly different view. In the Old
Law, he says, both men and women were required to get

[147] Cf *Cum quorumdam hominum*; DS 1880.

[148] Cf Origen, *Commentaria in Ioannem*, tom. 1, no. 6; PG 14:32.

[149] Cf *Epistola ad Ephesios* no. 19; ed. J. B. Lightfoot, *The Apostolic Fathers*, vol.
2, section 1 (London, 1885), pp. 76f.

[150] 'She would surely not have said that, if beforehand she had not vowed her
virginity to God' (St Augustine, *De sancta virginitate* 4, 4; PL 40:398; cf *Sermo*
225, no. 2; PL 38:1097; St Gregory of Nyssa, *In diem natalem Christi*; PG
46:1140ff.). According to Pope John Paul II, our Lady's question 'How shall this
be done, because I know not man?' proves that 'by a voluntary choice she
intended to remain a virgin. . . . The expression she used, with the verb in the
present tense, reveals the permanence and continuity of her state' (General
audience address, 24 July 1996).

married and have children, because the worship of the true God was to be spread through the physical increase of God's people. For this reason, before her betrothal to Joseph, Mary did not vow virginity absolutely, but she did desire it, and vowed it conditionally, the condition being, 'If it be pleasing to God'. After it had been made known to her that it was pleasing to God,[151] and before the Annunciation, she and St Joseph together made the vow absolutely.[152]

In the Old Testament, lifelong virginity was not generally esteemed as a religious state of life. The vocation of the righteous Israelite, man or woman, was to marry and to have a large family, in order to swell the numbers of the chosen people. Faced with dying without marriage and offspring, Jephthah's unmarried daughter bewails her virginity (cf Judg 11:38). Now both before and during the earthly lifetime of our Lord, there were signs of a more positive attitude towards virginity as a religious state. The great prophets of the desert, Elijah and St John the Baptist, were unmarried, and in the mysterious Essenes and Therapeutae we find whole communities devoted to prayer and asceticism.[153] However, Pope John Paul II insists that we must not interpret our Lady's desire or vow of virginity in this merely sociological way:

> The unique privilege of the Immaculate Conception influenced the whole development of the young woman of Nazareth's spiritual life. Thus it should be maintained that Mary was guided to the ideal of virginity by an exceptional inspiration of that same Holy Spirit who, in the course of the

[151] St Bonaventure suggests that our Lady vowed her virginity only through divine inspiration (or following an angelic revelation) and after St Joseph had assured her that he would honour and guard her virginity (cf *4 Sent.* d. 28, q. 6; d. 30, q. 2; Q IV:696, 710). St Thomas says that our Lady was 'divinely assured that Joseph was of like mind, and so she could accept marriage with him without danger' (*4 Sent.* d. 30, q. 2, a. 1b, ad 3).

[152] Cf ST 3a q. 28, a. 4, ad 1.

[153] See Philo, *De vita contemplativa*.

Church's history, would spur many women to the way of
virginal consecration. . . . Filled with the Lord's exceptional
gifts from the beginning of her life, she was oriented to a
total gift of self—body and soul—to God, in the offering of
herself as a virgin.[154]

The Pope suggests that our Lady accepted motherhood with
the same divinely infused bridal love with which she desired
virginity:

Mary accepted her election as Mother of the Son of God,
guided by spousal love, the love that totally consecrates a
human being to God. By virtue of this love, Mary wished to
be always and in all things 'given to God' (*Deo donata*), living
in virginity. The words 'Behold the handmaid of the Lord'
express the fact that from the outset she accepted and understood her own motherhood as a total gift of self, a gift of her
person to the service of the saving plans of the Most High.
And to the very end she lived her entire maternal sharing in
the life of Jesus Christ, her Son, in a way that matched her
vocation to virginity.[155]

Our Lady, the perfect Daughter of Zion, gives God that
pure bridal love to which His people had been called, but
which they had signally failed to give. The prophets condemned the chosen people for playing the harlot by consort-
ing with the other nations and their gods (cf Hos 2:1ff.), and
yet they never abandoned hope for a virginal Jerusalem over
which God would rejoice as a bridegroom rejoices in his
bride (cf Is 62:5). In vowing virginity, Mary discloses her
desire to be that pure bride of God.

Mary herself wanted to be the personal image of that absolutely faithful bride, totally devoted to the divine Bridegroom, and therefore she became the beginning of the new

[154] General audience address, 24 July 1996.
[155] Cf *Redemptoris Mater*, no. 39.

Israel in her spousal heart. [Her question 'How?' signifies] I am a virgin devoted to God, and I do not intend to leave my spouse, because I do not think that God wills it—He who is so jealous of Israel, so severe with anyone who betrays Him, so persistent in His merciful call to reconciliation! Mary is well aware of her people's infidelity, and she wants personally to be a bride who is faithful to her most beloved divine Spouse.[156]

But how could our Lady allow herself to be betrothed and married if she had already made a vow of virginity, at least in desire? Would such a vow not have made the marriage invalid? In answer to the first question, it must be said that our Lady accepted marriage, as she embraced virginity, in obedience to the Father and under the inspiration of the Holy Spirit. It was, says St Thomas, 'by the intimate impulse of the Holy Spirit that our Lady was willing to be married, trusting that by divine help she would never come to carnal union. Still, she left this to the will of God, and so she suffered no harm to her virginity.'[157] Moreover, our Lady and St Joseph both gave the consent that makes a marriage: they consented to union in marriage but 'not expressly to sexual union, except with the condition, "were it to please God"'.[158] In other words, had it pleased God that our Lady and St Joseph should have had conjugal relations, they would then have done His will in that way, just as now they do so by vowing their lifelong virginity.

Why, if she was to be for ever a virgin, did God want His Mother to be married? St Thomas says that it was fitting for His own sake, for His Mother's sake and for our sake. *For His own sake*: to protect Him from being rejected by unbelievers as illegitimate, to ensure that He had a genealogy of the kind

---

[156] General audience address, 4 Dec. 1991.
[157] Cf ST 3a q. 29, a. 1, ad 1.
[158] Ibid., q. 29, a. 2.

that was then customary (running through the male line), to conceal Him from the attacks of the devil and to give Him the care of St Joseph. *For His Mother's sake*: to save her from scandal and from stoning as an adulteress, to protect her good name and to give her the care of St Joseph. *For our sake*: among other reasons, so that St Joseph's testimony might add supporting proof that Christ was born of a virgin; to provide us with a sign of the Church universal, which is both a virgin and yet married to one husband, namely, Christ; and, since our Lady was both married and virgin, to honour in her person the two Christian states of life, virginity and marriage.[159] St Ambrose again underlines the chivalrousness that God showed our Lady: even though He was born of a Virgin, He wanted the Virgin Mother to be married, because He 'preferred men to doubt His own origin rather than His Mother's innocence. He knew the extreme delicacy of a virgin's modesty, how easily it is questioned, and He was not willing that our faith in His birth be strengthened at the cost of dishonour to His Mother.'[160]

The objections to the perpetual virginity of our Lady raised by heretics over the course of the centuries include the following:

First, St Matthew tells us that 'before they came together, she was found with child, of the Holy Ghost' (Mt 1:18). According to the heretics, the phrase 'before they came together' implies that at some later time Mary and Joseph did come together, that is, have conjugal relations. St Jerome offers a linguistic solution to this apparent difficulty: 'The preposition "before",[161] though it often indicates consequent events, sometimes refers to things that have only been

---

[159] Ibid., q. 29, a. 1.

[160] *Expositio evangelii secundum Lucam*, lib. 2, no. 1; SC 45:70; cited in ST 3a q. 29, a. 1, ad 2.

[161] He is thinking of Latin, but his remarks apply to both Greek and Hebrew.

thought about beforehand. Moreover, the things thought about do not necessarily take place. So if someone says "I set sail before lunch in the port", it does not mean that he had lunch in the port after setting sail, but that he was thinking about having lunch in the port.' Again, says Jerome rather naughtily, if we say 'before Helvidius repented, he was cut off by death', we do not mean that he had the opportunity of repenting after death. And so, when St Matthew says, 'Before they came together, she was found with child, of the Holy Ghost', he does not mean that subsequently they did come together, but at the very time when the world thought they would soon be living together as man and wife, Christ was conceived by the Holy Spirit, and so they did not subsequently come together.[162]

Another apparently troublesome text is Matthew 1:25: 'He knew her not till she brought forth her first-born son.' Does this not imply that after the birth he did 'know' her? This statement can be interpreted in a number of ways. St John Chrysostom argues that the 'knowledge' referred to here is not carnal but intellectual knowledge: before she gave birth, St Joseph did not know Mary in the sense that he did not realize how wonderful she was. Other Fathers believe it refers to the sense knowledge of ocular sight. Just as the Israelites could not look at Moses while he was speaking with God, because his face shone with so much glory, so Joseph could not look upon Mary while she glowed with the radiance she carried within. The most commonly favoured resolution of the difficulty concentrates on the word 'till', which, whether in Hebrew or Greek, has two distinct meanings in Scripture. Sometimes it refers to a definite period of time, as, for example, when St Paul says that the law was 'set because of transgressions, until the seed should come to whom He made

---

[162] *De perpetua virginitate B. Mariae*, no. 4; PL 23:185cf.

the promise' (Gal 3:19). Or it can refer to an indefinite period of time. When, for example, our Lord says that He will be with us 'till the consummation of the world' (cf Mt 28:20), He does not mean that He will then leave us but rather that He will be with us always, both before and after the end of the world. And so here the evangelist means that St Joseph always honoured the purity of our Lady, both before the birth of her Son and afterwards.[163]

Why do the Evangelists call Jesus the 'first-born son' of Mary (cf Mt 1:25; Lk 2:7)? These words are an enigma, for Blessed Mary is ever-virgin and has no other physical children, before or after conceiving Jesus. However, when we expound the text according to the mind of the Church and with the help of her Fathers, worry gives way to wonder. The first aid to understanding is again provided by St Jerome. Every only child is a firstborn; what you need to be firstborn is to lack siblings who precede you, not to possess siblings who succeed you.[164] But why does the sacred author choose such a problematic term? Because in the mind of Israel it was not a problematic term but a profound title, with many levels of meaning in the vocabulary of faith: the firstborn male, of men or cattle, belongs in a special way to God. 'Sanctify unto me every firstborn that openeth the womb among the children of Israel' (Ex 13:2). The unprecedented offspring is an object uniquely precious, a gift of God's goodness that deserves to be offered back in gratitude. This attitude is presupposed by the sacrifice of Isaac: the firstborn is a candidate for consecration, the sacred victim par excellence. But even that statement does not reach far enough into the mystery of the firstborn. Before the institution of the Aaronic priesthood, the eldest son of each family served as priest. In the Jewish way of thinking, then, to say 'firstborn' is to suggest dedica-

[163] Ibid., no. 6; PL 23:189AB.
[164] Ibid., no. 10; PL 23:192B.

tion to God in a twofold sense, both the destiny of a victim and the dignity of a priest. When Luke the Gentile, carefully reproducing the Jewish way of thinking, tells us that our Lady 'brought forth her firstborn son', he is imparting one of the chief truths of Divine Revelation: the Child of the Virgin, only born and therefore firstborn, is the fulfillment of all the worship of the Old Covenant. The only Son of God and Mary is the definitive Priest and ultimate Victim.

According to St Paul, the Lord Jesus is 'first-born' in a more than legal way: He is the 'first-born from the dead' (cf Rev 1:5), 'the first-born among many brethren' (cf Col 1:18). He is the firstborn Son of God, the Only-Begotten of the Father, Son by nature, who in the flesh He assumed is the first to be born to the new life of the Resurrection. Through our Baptism, we are His members and brethren and so become reborn sons of God, sons by grace with the hope of being sons in glory, in the Resurrection. St Bede quotes St John, 'But as many as received Him, He gave them power to be made the sons of God' (Jn 1:12), and makes this comment: 'He is rightly called the "first-born" of these [adopted sons of God], because in dignity He comes before all the sons of adoption, even those who preceded by birth the time of His Incarnation.' [165]

Several times in the New Testament we hear of the 'brothers' of the Lord (cf Mt 12:46; Jn 2:12). One man is singled out for special mention as 'the brother of the Lord', namely, James (cf Gal 1:19). Do these titles not imply that Mary and Joseph had other children? Not at all. It is *de fide*, of divine and Catholic Faith, to hold that the brothers of the Lord were *not* His blood brothers, but some other kind of close relative. St Jerome says that some people think that they were

---

[165] St Bede, *Homelia* I, 5, *In vigilia nativitatis Domini*; CCSL 122:35. On primogeniture and priesthood, see St Thomas, *Super ad Hebraeos* cap. 2, lect. 3.

children of St Joseph by another marriage. (This was the position of a few of the Fathers, most notably St Epiphanius in the fourth century.) However, St Jerome himself takes a different line. He is confident that St Joseph was a virgin[166] and that the brethren of our Lord were His cousins on His Mother's side, the sons of a sister or some other close kinswoman of our Lady. He shows that Scripture recognizes more than one sort of brother, four sorts in fact: by nature, by stock, by kindred, and by affection. Jacob and Esau, like James and John, are brothers by nature, because they are born of the same parents. All the Jews are brothers by stock because they are members of the same race or tribe, the children of Abraham (cf Deut 15:12). Abraham and Lot are brothers by kindred, that is, members of the same extended family (cf Gen 14:14). King David refers to those who are brothers by affection, who 'dwell together in unity' (Ps 132:1).[167] The brethren of the Lord are brethren in the third sense, as Abraham and Lot were brothers; they were related to our Lord in the extended family as His cousins. Classical Greek has a word for cousin, *anepsios*, but Aramaic and Hebrew do not, and it is the Semitic way of speaking and thinking about kinship that is reflected in the Greek of the New Testament. Biblical Hebrew had a special name for the son of someone's father's brother, but for other kinds of cousin it had to fall back on cumbersome phrases such as 'the son of the brother of his mother'.[168]

What proof is there that these brothers of the Lord were in fact cousins? St Jerome's argument runs as follows. The most prominent of the so-called brothers of the Lord is St James,

[166] *De perpetua virginitate B. Mariae*, no. 23; PL 23:203AB.

[167] Ibid., no. 14; PL 23:196C–198B.

[168] See *The Dictionary of Classical Hebrew*, ed D. J. A. Clines, vol. 1 (Sheffield, 1993), pp. 173ff., which confirms the truth of St Jerome's analysis of the range of meaning of the Hebrew word for 'brother'. St Luke, though a Gentile, takes great care in the way he renders Semitic patterns of thought and speech.

the first Bishop of Jerusalem and the author of the Epistle
that bears his name. Two other men named James are mentioned in the New Testament: St James the Great, one of the
Twelve, son of Zebedee (whose feast the Church celebrates
on 25 July) and St James the Less, son of Alphaeus, who is
also one of the Twelve (and whose feast is celebrated with St
Philip in May). Now there is no doubt that St James the
Great and St James the Less are two different individuals. But
why, if there were three prominent men named James in the
apostolic Church, is one of them called 'James the Less', a
nickname that implies a comparison between two? St Jerome
concludes that St James, son of Alphaeus, and St James,
brother of the Lord, are one and the same person.[169] But why
is James, son of Alphaeus, called our Lord's 'brother'? St
Jerome's answer is as follows. In Matthew 13:55 we hear of
four 'brothers' of our Lord: James and Joseph, Simon and
Jude. Later, in the Passion narrative, St Matthew mentions a
Mary who is the mother of James and Joseph (cf Mt 27:56).
Now, according to St Jerome, this Mary was the wife of
Alphaeus, the father of James the Less. In St John's Gospel
this same Mary is described as 'His Mother's sister, Mary of
Clopas' (Jn 19:25). Thus if Mary, wife of Alphaeus, mother
of the Apostle St James the Less, is our Lady's sister, her sons
are our Lord's first cousins and, according to the Aramaic
custom, would be referred to as His 'brothers'. But why is
Mary, wife of Alphaeus, called 'Mary of Clopas'? St Jerome
was not sure. He thought that Clopas could be this Mary's
father's name or clan name or another form of her husband's
name, Alphaeus. It is this second interpretation that is most
likely, because Clopas and Alphaeus are two possible tran-
scriptions of the same Aramaic name.[170]

[169] Cf *De perpetua virginitate B. Mariae*, no. 15; PL 23:198.
[170] Cf McHugh, *The Mother of Jesus in the New Testament*, p. 225. Canon
McHugh has further refined St Jerome's theory: he argues that 'brothers' means

Our Lady has a single physical Son but a multitude of spiritual sons, sons in the Holy Spirit. Jesus, from the Cross, entrusted Mary to the devotion of John and John to the protection of Mary. Our Lady's Motherhood was thus enlarged: mothering of the Head was now extended into a mothering of the members. Christ our Lord is both eternally begotten of God the Father in His Divinity and born in time of the Blessed Virgin in His humanity. According to nature, therefore, He has both a Father and Mother: the heavenly Father in His divine nature and the Virgin Mother in His human nature. Now we who are the members of His Mystical Body, who with Him are like one mystical person, share by supernatural grace in both of these relations: in Christ we have God as our Father and Mary as our Mother; we are sons-in-the-Son of God and Mary.

> Just as in natural and corporeal generation [says St Louis de Montfort] there is a father and a mother, so in supernatural and spiritual generation there is a Father who is God and a Mother who is Mary. All the true and predestined children of God have God as Father and Mary as Mother, and he who does not have Mary as Mother does not have God as Father.[171]

Jesus is indeed Mary's firstborn son, for in Him and through Him we become her and His Father's adopted sons.

St Thomas says that the 'detestable' error of Helvidius, who taught that our Lady and St Joseph had conjugal relations after the birth of Christ, disparages both the Divine Persons of the Trinity and the two human persons of Mary and Joseph. First, it 'detracts from the perfection of Christ. Just as according to His divine nature He is the Only-Begotten of

---

'foster brothers', first-cousins who were regarded as brothers. Unlike Jerome, McHugh thinks these 'brethren of the Lord' were cousins on St Joseph's rather than on our Lady's side (ibid., pp. 234–54).

[171] *Traité de la vraie dévotion à la Sainte Vierge*, no. 30; in *Oeuvres complètes de St Louis-Marie Grignion de Montfort*, ed. M. Gendrot (Paris, 1966), pp. 502f.

the Father, as His Son who is perfect in all ways, so it was also fitting that He should be the only-begotten of His Mother, as her most perfect bud.' Secondly, the denial of our Lady's perpetual virginity offends the Holy Spirit, for the Virgin's womb was His sanctuary, 'in which He fashioned the flesh of Christ. It was therefore not fitting that it should be violated by some other through intercourse with a man.' St Ambrose asks pointedly, 'Would the Lord Jesus have chosen for His Mother a woman who would defile the heavenly chamber with the seed of a man, that is to say, someone incapable of preserving her virginal chastity intact?'[172] Thirdly, the suggestion that our Lady and St Joseph had conjugal relations 'detracts from the dignity and sanctity of the Mother of God. She would have seemed most lacking in gratitude if she had not been content with so great a Son, and if by her own accord she had wanted to lose by sexual intercourse the virginity that had been miraculously preserved in her.' Fourthly, this heresy is an insult to St Joseph, because it accuses him of the extreme presumption of attempting to violate the pure Maiden who had conceived by overshadowing of the Holy Spirit. 'It would have been for Joseph himself an act of the greatest presumption if he had tried to defile her whom, by the angel's revelation, he knew to have conceived God by the Holy Spirit.'[173]

Fatherhood Renewed

The Arian father-god provided heavenly endorsement for the tyranny of earthly rulers, at home as well as at court. He was a projection onto the skies of the old pagan *paterfamilias*, towering with terrifying superiority over his sons. By contrast, the true God the Father, revealed by God the Son made

---

[172] *De institutione virginis* 6, 44; PL 16:317.
[173] Cf ST 3a q. 28, a. 3.

man, the Father in whose image all paternity is created, issues a challenge to the old heathen vice of paternal domination and writes a charter for the new Christian virtue of paternal devotion. The first embodiment of that virtue was St Joseph, who was a true father to the Lord Jesus, not in the flesh but by law and affection. In his Apostolic Exhortation *Redemptoris custos*, Pope John Paul II teaches us that by giving Joseph to Mary as husband and thus to Jesus as foster father, God the Father revealed His saving plan to transfigure with new beauty His original gifts of marriage and family life. He wanted the Ever-Virgin Mother of His Son to be a married woman, because, through His Son made man, He raised up marriage to the dignity of a sacrament. He wanted that same Son, 'God from God and Light from Light, [to enter] into human history through the family',[174] because He wanted to sanctify the family afresh. The eternal Word is made flesh to make all things new, including the family and all its essential relations—fatherhood, motherhood and childhood. The first man to receive that Christian grace of transfigured fatherhood is St Joseph.

> In this family, Joseph is the father: his fatherhood is not one that derives from begetting offspring; but neither is it an 'apparent' or merely 'substitute' fatherhood. Rather, it is one that fully shares in authentic human fatherhood and the mission of a father in the family. This is a consequence of the hypostatic union: humanity taken up into the unity of the Divine Person of the Word-Son, Jesus Christ. Together with human nature, all that is human, and especially the family— as the first dimension of man's existence in the world—is also taken up in Christ. Within this context, Joseph's human fatherhood was also 'taken up' in the mystery of Christ's Incarnation.[175]

[174] John Paul II, *Letter to Families*, 2 Feb. 1994, no. 2.
[175] *Redemptoris custos*, no. 21.

High among the gifts that God the Father lavished upon
the sacred humanity of the Son was the person of St Joseph.
God did not want His Virgin-born Son to share human life
without experiencing the love of a human father, and so
He called and sanctified a son of David to be the instrument
of that divine paternal love whereby the Father loves the
Son within the Godhead. As a physical act, fathering a child
lasts but a moment, but as a spiritual vocation it is a perpetual effort and joy. Although the virgin Joseph knew nothing of the first, he excelled in the second, for he received
from the heavenly Father graces proportionate to the task
of bringing up the Only-Begotten made man. Thus, in
spirit, Joseph, son of Jacob, became a more perfect father
than his own father, or indeed any man, had ever been or
would be.

5. The Mystery of the Maiden and Mother

The Wisdom of God is foolishness to the wisdom of the
world, and the wisdom of the world is foolishness with God
(cf 1 Cor 1:20). Now our Blessed Lady is the Mother of
eternal Wisdom Incarnate, and that Wisdom's most perfect
created image. It is not surprising, then, to discover that
throughout the centuries worldly wisdom has attacked the
Son through a cowardly campaign against the Mother. The
Gnostics denied the reality of our Lord's sacred humanity
by claiming that He merely passed through His Mother 'as
through a channel'. The Nestorians divided the one Jesus into
two different persons and so would not acknowledge Mary as
Mother of God. The Helvidians and Jovinianists disparaged
the call of our Lord to the consecrated life by denying
the perpetuity of the virginity of our Lady, the Queen of
Virgins. The Protestants of the sixteenth century, rejecting
all human cooperation with God, ignored our Lady's earthly

fiat and refused to invoke her heavenly intercession. The Liberal Protestants and Modernists, repudiating all conception of Christianity as a religion revealed from above, sought to dismiss as myth those truths that speak most clearly of the divine origin of Christianity's founder. The matchless Mother and Maiden is a great mystery, eternal Wisdom's highest created refulgence, and so in every age she is attacked by those who will not imitate her own humility and surrender their minds to the transcendent truth of God.

> Since she proceeds so wonderfully from the incomprehensible abyss of the divine wisdom and omnipotence [says Charles de Koninck], is it surprising that the world finds it so hard to accept all the words that magnify the greatness and glory of Mary? . . . How can this pure creature, so weak in her nature, be clothed with all the power that God has deigned to manifest? 'The foolishness of God is wiser than the wisdom of men, and the infirmity of God is stronger than the strength of men' (1 Cor 1:25). Is the Blessed Virgin, in her blackness and her beauty, not the touchstone of the divine Wisdom? *Cunctas haereses sola interemisti*—You alone have abolished all the heresies.[176]

The man who would be orthodox, who desires to conform his mind to the wisdom of God and His Church, must contemplate in love the Maiden Mother who is Wisdom's very throne. True devotion to her, the kind of devotion displayed in the old English carol, is the surest way to intimate union with her Son.

> I sing of a maiden
> That is makeles;
> King of all kings
> To her Son she ches.

---

[176] *Ego Sapientia: La Sagesse qui est Marie* (Montreal, 1943), pp. 125f.

He came all so still
To His Mother's bowr,
As dew in April
That falleth on the flower.

Mother and maiden
Was never none but she;
Well may such a lady
Godes Mother be.

IV

'BORN TO RAISE THE SONS OF EARTH'

The Purpose of the Temporal Birth of Christ

> Mild He lays His glory by,
> Born that man no more may die,
> Born to raise the sons of earth,
> Born to give them second birth![1]

God the Son was made flesh and born of the Virgin Mary to
a great end: 'for us men and for our salvation'.[2] 'This day',
sing the angels, 'is born to you a *Saviour*, who is Christ the
Lord' (Lk 2:11). Now the saving purpose for which Christ
the Lord is born among men would seem to be threefold.[3]
First, He comes to reveal the truth about God and man: 'For
this was I born, and for this came I into the world, that I
should give testimony to the truth' (Jn 18:37). Secondly, He
is born to 'make all things new' (cf Rev 21:5) by delivering
the sons of Adam from the 'oldness' of sin and death.
Thirdly, the Father sends the Son, 'made of a woman . . . that
we might receive the adoption of sons' (Gal 4:4) and thus
become 'partakers of the divine nature' (2 Pet 1:4), sharers in
the life of the Blessed Trinity. In sum, we might say that the

---

[1] 'Hark! The Herald Angels Sing', by Charles Wesley et al. (EH 24).
[2] Cf the Niceno-Constantinopolitan Creed (DS 150).
[3] Cf ST 3a q. 40, a. 1.

Infant Word *makes the truth manifest, makes the old new, and makes men divine.*

The high purposes for which the Saviour is born are not attained merely by the fact of His being born. While our Lord does indeed merit special graces for us on the first Christmas Day, He does not communicate them until He has performed His last and greatest meritorious act on Good Friday and risen from the tomb on Easter Sunday. Whatever secret of redeeming love the Crib of Christ may contain, it is not unlocked without the key of the Cross. The Cradled God will, one day, be the Crucified. The eternal Word is conceived and born as man, like every other man, in order to enter human life, but the goal of His earthly life, the magnetic 'hour' to which His every human act is drawn, is the glorifying of the Father by His atoning death upon the Cross.

1. *Redeeming Love from the Crib to the Cross*

In the sacred art of Christendom, the Crib is often shown in its relation to the Cross. In the West, especially from the twelfth century, the manger is made to look like an altar [see art plate 3]. This suggests a twofold typology, in relation both to the Sacrifice of the Cross and to the Sacrifice of the Mass: the Christ Child is already Priest and Victim, as He will be on Calvary and as He will remain, to the consummation of the age, under the sacramental species.[4] Swaddling clothes are frequently wound crosswise round the Holy Child,[5] and in some images a column stands within the stable as a symbol of

[4] A strikingly beautiful example can be seen in the tympanum of the right portal of the west front of Chartres. Our Lady is in repose upon a bed, but the child is laid out upon an altar [see art plate 3].

[5] Ibid., p. 75.

the scourging at the pillar.[6] The artists of the later fifteenth
century, both south and north of the Alps, show a tiny, thin
and naked infant lying helpless on the ground before the
Virgin in prophecy of His lying, thirty-three years later, dead
and awaiting burial.[7] In Byzantine icons of the Nativity, the
swaddling clothes resemble the shroud in the icons of the
Resurrection, and the stable cave, with its black interior,
recalls both the empty Tomb and the jaws of Hell. Paul
Evdokimov derives a theological lesson from this cross-
referencing within the iconic tradition:

> [T]he sombre triangle of the cave, opening up dark depths, is
> Hell. In order to reach the abyss and become the 'heart of
> creation', Christ mystically places His birth at the bottom of
> the chasm where evil stagnates in its ultimate density. Christ is
> born in the shadow of death. The Nativity inclines the heav-
> ens down to Hell, and we contemplate, lying in the manger,
> 'the Lamb of Bethlehem who has conquered the Serpent and
> given peace to the world'.[8]

The Incarnate Word, now humbled unto infancy, will later
be humbled unto death, even death on the Cross. Other
men die because they are born, but the God–Man is born in
order to die.[9] God the Son, without ceasing to be immortal in
His divine nature, freely assumed human nature in a mortal
condition, so that on the Cross He might suffer and die in

[6] For example, see art plate 4 in this book, or the Bladelin altar of Roger van
der Weyden (c. 1452/1453; Schiller, plate 205).

[7] See the three Nativities—by Piero della Francesca, Hugo van der Goes,
and Geertgen tot Sint Jans—reproduced by John Drury in *Painting the Word:
Christian Pictures and Their Meanings* (New Haven, 2000), pp. 69, 79, 80. I am
grateful to my friend Mr Lionel Gracey for introducing me to this interesting
book. These paintings are reproduced again here as plates 5, 6 and 2.

[8] P. Evdokimov, *L'Art de l'icône: Théologie de la beauté* (Paris, 1970), p. 232.

[9] As St Gregory of Nyssa says: 'He did not suffer because He had been born;
no, it was because of death that God chose to be born' (*Oratio catechetica* 32; PG
45:80A).

atonement for the sin of the race of which He is Head.[10] And, in taking on human nature, He travels through the successive stages of human life from conception to the last breath: 'the first beginnings of infancy, and bodily growth, and suffering even unto death on the Cross'.[11] Thus faith in the Christmas mystery and faith in the Easter mystery are wedded by an indissoluble bond. Those who will not confess the Crib cannot accept the Cross and the Tomb, as Pope St Leo the Great argues in the case of the Manicheans: 'They have no share in the re-birth brought by Christ who deny Him to have been born bodily of the Virgin Mary. Thus, by not believing in His true birth, they do not accept His true Passion; and Him whose true burial they will not confess they deny has truly been resurrected.'[12] Both natures and births of the one Person of the Word are, therefore, necessary if man is to be saved. Only if Christ is true and perfect God can He save the human race, but only if He is true and perfect man can the human race make His saving grace its own.[13] 'Were

[10] The one Christ, says St Gregory Nazianzen, is 'passible according to the flesh, impassible according to the divinity' (*Epistola* 101, no. 15; SC 208.42). The very thought of mortality in the Immortal throws St Leo to the ground in stupefaction: 'That the Son of God, who is of one essence, though not one person, with the Father and the Holy Spirit, should become a partaker of our lowliness and be willing to be one of the passible, one of the mortal [*unus passibilium, unus . . . mortalium*], is a wonderful thing, inspiring a holy fear' (*In nativitate Domini, sermo* 5, no. 1; SC 22B:122). Leo is very blunt: there is *nothing* to be said in mitigation of the error of the Manichees. 'In their diversity, dearly beloved, all the other heresies deserve to be condemned. Nevertheless, each presents, under certain aspects, an element of the truth.' For example, though Arius 'did not see the eternal and immutable divinity in the unity of the Trinity, he did not deny it in the essence of the Father'. But 'in the infamous theory of the Manichees, however we look at it, there is absolutely nothing that one can accept' (*In nativitate Domini, sermo* 4, no. 5; SC 22B:116ff.).

[11] *In nativitate Domini, sermo* 10, no. 2; SC 22B:188.

[12] Ibid., *sermo* 4, no. 4; SC 22B:114.

[13] 'If He were joined to a creature, man would never be deified. Man cannot be deified unless the Son is true God. Man would never have been brought into the Father's presence had it not been His true and natural Word who put

He not true God,' says St Leo, 'He would bring no remedy; were He not true man, He would furnish no example.' [14] This is the truth that by their gifts the Magi confess: gold and frankincense signify Him who is God and King, but myrrh is a sign of Him who is man and mortal. [15] And these mysteries of self-abasement that the Catholic mind apprehends by faith, the Catholic heart embraces by devotion: 'We venerate Him in the Crib, we venerate Him on the Cross, we venerate Him in the Tomb. Devoutly we embrace Him made a tender babe for us, all covered with blood for us, deathly pale for us, laid in the tomb for us.' [16] The human infirmities of the Son of God in the Crib already anticipate the pains and anguish of the Cross. He has humbled Himself to be in truth, without pretending, a helpless, speechless babe. He cries when He is hungry and sleeps soundly when He has been fed. All these human limitations and disabilities God the Son Himself has freely assumed out of His great love for mankind, just as later, by that same love, He will endure in His Passion a pain in body and in soul surpassing all the pain of the world.

The Cross casts a long shadow over the Crib. No sooner is Jesus born than Herod wants Him dead (cf Mt 2:13). Simeon prophesies that the sign of the Son will be contradicted and the soul of the Mother pierced with a sword (cf Lk 2:34f.). Caryll Houselander wrote a whole treatise called *The Passion of the Infant Christ* in which she traced the many resemblances between the Nativity and the Passion:

---

on the body. And just as we would not have been delivered from sin and the curse of sin if the flesh taken by the Word had not been by nature human flesh (for we can have nothing in common with a being that is foreign to us), so, likewise, man would not have been deified if He who was made flesh had not been by nature from the Father and His true and proper Word' (St Athanasius, *Oratio 2 contra Arianos*, no. 70; PG 26:296AB).

[14] *In nativitate Domini, sermo* 10, no. 2; SC 22B:188.

[15] See p. 340.

[16] *In nativitate Domini, sermo* 5, no. 2; L–R 4:267.

On Calvary he is set between two thieves. In Bethlehem He
is set between two animals. On Calvary He is poor with the
poverty of destitution. In Bethlehem He is poor with the
poverty of destitution. He is deprived of His home in Nazareth, the cradle made ready for Him is empty: 'The foxes
have holes and the birds of the air their nests; but the Son of
Man hath not where to lay His head' (Lk 9:58; Mt 8:20). . . .
On Calvary He was stretched and straightened and fastened
down to the Cross. In Bethlehem He was stretched out
and straightened and fastened in swaddling-bands. On Calvary He was lifted up, helpless, and held up for men to look
upon. In Bethlehem He was lifted up, helpless, to be gazed
upon.[17]

From Mary of Nazareth's undefiled womb to Joseph of
Arimathea's unused tomb, the Son of God continues on His
course in human flesh, His single-minded and wholehearted
voyage of obedience to the Father and of love for mankind.
Since the end lies hidden in the beginning and the begin-
ning becomes clear at the end, it is not out of place for the
Church's preachers to slip in a mention of the Cross and
Resurrection on Christmas Day and of the Incarnation and
Nativity during Holy Week and Eastertide.

> It is fitting, brethren, that on the day of our Lord's Nativity
> you should also hear about the day of our Lord's Resurrec-
> tion. For just as the only-begotten God deigned to be born
> for us, so He deigned in the flesh to die for us, and He
> deigned also to rise again. . . . Conceived in the womb, He
> was made a sharer of our death; rising from the tomb, He has
> made us sharers of His life.[18]

The Crib of the Virgin Birth, the Cross of the Atoning
Sacrifice, and the Empty Tomb of the Bodily Resurrection

---

[17] *The Passion of the Infant Christ* (London, 1949), pp. 60f.
[18] St Fulgentius of Ruspe, *Sermo 2, De duplici nativitate Christi*, no. 8; PL
65:729B.

represent the first moments and the final hour of the work by which, in a created human nature, the uncreated Word, through whom all things were made, repairs the world damaged by Adam's sin. 'Between His birth and death,' says St Ephrem, 'He placed the world in the middle;/ By [His] birth and death, He revived it.'[19] The Byzantine liturgy looks upon the Infant Word as the principle of the transfiguration of the whole material universe:

> Thou hast come, O Resurrection of the nations,
> To bring back the nature of man from its wanderings,
> Leading it from the hills of the wilderness to a pasture
> rich in flowers.
> Do thou destroy the violent strength of the murderer
> of man,
> O thou who in thy providence hast appeared as man
> and God.[20]

St Bernard argues that, while the Nativity of our Lord contains spiritual treasures in profusion, the believer can lay hold of them only through the merits of His Passion. We 'seek in His Passion what He brought us at His Birth, for it was in His Passion that the coffer was broken and the treasure it contained poured out as the price of our salvation'.[21]

The Child in the Manger is already both Priest and Victim. As Mary and Joseph and the shepherds gaze upon Him, He, at His soul's fine point, gazes upon the heavenly Father and renders Him His whole assumed humanity, in its childhood simplicity: 'Lo, I have come to do thy will, O God.'

> With a perfect will [says Dom Marmion], Christ accepted
> that sum of sorrows which began with the lowliness of the

[19] St Ephrem the Syrian, 'Twenty-First Hymn on the Nativity', in *Hymns*, ET (New York, 1989), p. 177.

[20] Matins, Feast of the Nativity, *Menaion*, p. 281.

[21] *In nativitate Domini, sermo* 1, no. 8; L-R 4:250f.

Manger only to be ended by the ignominy of the Cross. From His entrance into this world, Christ offered Himself as Victim: the first action of His life was a sacerdotal act. What creature is able to measure the love that filled this sacerdotal act of Jesus? Who is able to know its intensity and describe its splendour? The silence of adoration can alone praise it in some degree.[22]

2. The Infant Word Makes Truth Manifest

The Babe of Bethlehem is the *Verbum infans*, the Divine Word who has become a human babe, an *in-fans*, naturally incapable of speech.[23] But He is also the *Verbum infans revelans*, the Wisdom that comes forth from the mouth of the Most High,[24] pouring out the 'great light' of truth upon 'the people that walked in darkness' (cf Is 9:2). The Child-God, said a poor mad poet, comes 'at once our utmost doubts to clear,/ And make our hearts with wonder wild'.[25] Despite, or rather through, His infancy, He imparts the salvific doctrine of the Gospel. He is the Father's eternal Word, and so His every human act and experience, even His silences, speak volumes about both God and man. As St Ignatius of Antioch says, 'What He achieved by His silence was worthy of the Father.'[26] And St Bernard adds: this infancy, this speechlessness, 'is not mute': *Infans quidem est, sed Verbum infans, cuius ne ipsa quidem infantia tacet.*[27] In fact, the silence of the Infant

[22] Columba Marmion, *Christ in His Mysteries*, new ed. (London, 1939), p. 80.
[23] See p. 160.
[24] See the antiphon *O Sapientia*.
[25] Christopher Smart, 'The Presentation of Christ in the Temple', in *Selected Poems of Christopher Smart*, ed. K. Williamson and M. Walsh (London, 1990), p. 149.
[26] *Epistola ad Ephesios*, no. 15, in *The Apostolic Fathers*, ed. J. B. Lightfoot, vol. 2, section 1 (London, 1885), p. 69.
[27] *In nativitate Domini, sermo* 5, no. 1; L-R 5:266. Blessed Guerric of Igny says: 'This Child seems to know nothing, but it is he who teaches knowledge

Word is a most apt imitation of His divinely silent procession in the bosom of the Father.[28]

The Child-God manifests the truth by the objective eloquence of His infancy in its union with His Divine Person. The world hears nothing of His preaching: the ears of most Bethlehemites catch nothing but the wail of a newborn infant. But those who have the gift of faith—our Lady and St Joseph, the shepherds and the Magi—perceive in this crying, in these tears of God, the first articulation of the good news: 'The tears of Man in God alone,/ The joy of God in men was seen./ Two things so alien to each other,/ Or to the rule, had never been.'[29] In one way, the Infant Word teaches unconsciously, for one level of His human mind is still in its early days of formation, but in another way, in a higher sphere, He teaches, even in His infancy, both knowingly and willingly. As we have seen,[30] according to the teaching of the Schoolmen and the mystics, reaffirmed by Pope Pius XII in *Mystici corporis*, our Lord enjoys from His conception, because of the Hypostatic Union, certain wonderful perfections in His human intellect and will.[31] Even as an infant, at the summit of His soul, He gazes upon the face of the Father. In seeing Him, He sees every man for whom He has become incarnate and will lay down His life, and in seeing each one of us in the lofty reaches of His holy mind, He loves each one of us in the fiery depths of His Sacred Heart. St Paul refers to this doctrine when He speaks of the Son of God loving and delivering Himself up for him, Paul, upon the

---

to man and angel (Ps 93:10), He who is truly the God of the sciences, the Word and Wisdom of God' (*In nativitate Domini, sermo* 1, no. 2; SC 166:166f.).

[28] Cf Charles de Koninck, *Ego Sapientia: La Sagesse qui est Marie* (Montreal, 1943), p. 95.

[29] St John of the Cross, 'Romance IX: The Birth of Christ', in *Poems of St John of the Cross*, trans. Roy Campbell, new ed. (Harmondsworth, 1960), p. 93.

[30] See pp. 81f.

[31] See pp. 61f.

Cross (cf Gal 2:20). Now a love so particular presupposes a knowledge that is comparably personal, the human knowledge by Christ Crucified of that individual man who will at first persecute Him in His members but later preach Him to the Gentiles. Such human knowledge, of Paul and every individual member of the human race, could not have been acquired by our Lord through natural experience but was vouchsafed to Him supernaturally in the Beatific Vision, by which He saw God and in God all the things that God has created. It is, therefore, as what St Thomas calls a 'comprehender', a 'beholder', that on earth our Lord had intimate human knowledge of St Paul. Before Jesus touched Paul from Heaven, He had somehow already grasped him on earth. The Apostle seems himself to bear witness to this wondrous 'comprehension' by Christ. Writing to the Philippians, he says that he does not claim to have reached perfection, but that he presses ever onward, in the hope that he will come to comprehend even as he is 'comprehended by Christ Jesus (*comprehensus sum a Christo Iesu*)' (cf Phil 3:12).[32] Such comprehension will be possible to Paul only in the Beatific Vision, and so it was possible to Jesus as man only by the same Beatific Vision.

During His infancy, then, through the 'blessed science' in His human intellect, the Incarnate Word has intuitive knowledge of the Father and of each one of us, His creatures.[33] He

[32] I am indebted for this exegesis to Father François-Marie Léthel OCD, *Connaître l'amour du Christ qui surpasse toute connaissance: La Théologie des saints* (Venasque, 1989), pp. 249f. The 'comprehension' to which I refer here has the broad sense of 'attainment' rather than the narrow sense of 'containment' (see ST 1a q. 2, a. 7, ad 1).

[33] Charles de Foucauld, hermit of the Sahara and apostle of Tuaregs, once wrote that, by His enjoyment of the beatific vision in His human soul on earth, our Lord taught us to 'move through this world as if we were not of this world, without concern for exterior things, occupying ourselves only with one thing: to look upon, and to love, our heavenly Father, and to do His will' (*Écrits spirituels* [Paris, 1927], p. 55).

therefore knows what He is doing when He teaches by His silence. It may seem strange to our poor modern minds to ascribe such spiritual glories to a babe, but we should recall that they are not a precocious natural achievement, but a supernatural enlightenment that requires only childhood's receptivity for its presence in the mind of Christ. Light shines from the divine nature of the Word upon the summit of His human intellect in such a way that it does not interfere with natural growth on its lower slopes.[34] Thus, according to St Thomas, while enjoying a relative omniscience from His conception through the beatific and infused knowledge in His soul, our Lord also truly 'increases in wisdom' through a normal and natural 'experimental knowledge': like us, He gets to know the world by His senses, and from the data of sense experience He abstracts ideas or 'intelligible species'.[35] Therefore, as St Bonaventure says, while Jesus in His Nativity did as man know as many things when He was born as when He died, 'He had not *experienced* so many.'[36] Yes, in one way, He knows everything, and yet in another way, He learns, He discovers, He experiences wonder.[37] Indeed, we could say that no child has looked with such freshness of wonder upon the world. 'Our Lord did nothing that did not suit His age.'[38] For all the extraordinary perfections He enjoys, no child has been more exactly and purely childlike, just as no grown man has been more mature. He does not rush to grow up, itching to know things beyond Him. His infused knowledge is habitual, a store of ideas from which He draws only when His mission demands. His one desire is to be 'about the Father's

[34] 'The soul of Christ, which is a part of human nature, was perfected, by a light participated from the divine nature, for that blissful knowledge by which God is seen in His essence' (ST 3a q. 9, a. 2, ad 1).

[35] Cf ST 3a q. 12, a. 2.

[36] Cf *De sancto Marco evangelista, sermo* 2; Q IX:525.

[37] Cf ST 3a q. 12, a. 3; q. 15, a. 8.

[38] ST 3a q. 12, a. 3, ad 3.

business' (cf Lk 2:49), and only for the Father's glory does He reveal His own wisdom to the greybeards. In the Holy Child of Bethlehem, even in His human intellect, there is a twofoldness of perfection and infirmity, of glory and weakness.[39] No child's mind has been more humble, more open to learn and to gain knowledge of the world, and yet no child's mind has been raised up so high with such a crowning of wisdom, knowledge and understanding. This mysterious coincidence of omniscience and innocence contains an urgent lesson for those who do not confess faith in the Incarnate Word:

> The perfection of the Infant obviously has a deeper significance than fittingness to the Son of God and the Mother of God. Here is underlined a truth that marks the sharp difference between the pagan and the Christian world. For here is written, in capital letters of perfection, the truth that the infant, helpless though it be, is the equal on human grounds of any adult; and this from the first instant of its life. Where justice and charity are the bases of human life, this truth is evident; where physical strength is the foundation of human living, what chance has the infant?[40]

The Infant Word Reveals the Triune God

The Infant Word reveals God to us. As the Apostle says in the Epistle of the Mass of Christmas Day, 'God, who, at sundry times and in divers manners, spoke in times past to the fathers by the prophets, last of all, in these days hath spoken to us by His Son' (Heb 1:1f.). First, He reveals the Trinity of Persons in the One Divine Essence, not yet by His own words, but by the objective eloquence of His silent infancy, and by the words and actions of those who in His infancy are

[39] See pp. 62f.
[40] W. Farrell OP, *A Companion to the Summa*, vol. 4 (New York, 1949), p. 151.

His 'eyewitnesses and ministers' (cf Lk 1:2). Thus St Gabriel, who announces His conception and birth to our Lady, opens up those eternal processions in the Godhead which he, with the whole angelic host, beholds with joy in Heaven. '[O]bserve how the angel has declared the whole Trinity to the Virgin, making mention of the Holy Spirit [cf Lk 1:35], the Power [the Son, cf vv. 32, 35], and the Most High [the Father, cf v. 32], for the Trinity is indivisible.'[41] As we have seen, the temporal birth of Christ from the Virgin is an image of His eternal birth from the Father.[42] His birth on earth from the Mother without a father opens up for us His birth in Heaven from the Father without a mother. Those, then, who contemplate in faith and love the Saviour's human birth will be led by Him into deeper union with Him and His Father in the unity of the Holy Spirit. The only-begotten Son, who rests eternally in the bosom of the Father, has made Him known by His birth in time from the Virgin (cf Jn 1:18).

The Incarnate Son, asleep in the manger, reveals the Trinity's life of love, both the love that the Triune God is and the love He shows towards us. Without uttered words, by the very fact of His infancy united to His Divine Person, He displays the unbounded generosity of God's mercy, for the heavenly Father so loved the world, as we have already heard St Bonaventure say, that He gave 'not pennies but a Person, not a servant but the Son', and, in giving His Son, He lavished upon us 'all He was, all He had, all He could'.[43] In some mysterious way, this infant form, in all its fragile fini-tude, is an exquisitely appropriate instrument for disclosing the infinite attributes of God. 'O manifest infirmity,' cries St Augustine, 'O wondrous humility, in which all the greatness

---

[41] Theophylact, cited in CA 3, 34.

[42] See pp. 133f., 149f., 197f.

[43] *In vigilia nativitatis Domini, sermo* 1: Q IX:89–91.

of God lay hidden!'[44] Thus the holiness of God can be compared not only to the incandescence of a consuming fire, which causes penitent fear in the 'man of unclean lips' (cf Is 6:5), but also to the innocence of a cradled infant, which can inspire protective love in even the hardest of hearts. As a Church Father famed for his golden words said so beautifully:

[N]ature teaches us all the value and merit of infancy. Over what barbarity is infancy not victorious. . . . Fathers know it well, mothers feel it, everyone experiences it, man's very bowels bear witness to the fact. And so it was in infancy that He wanted to be born. He wanted to be loved, not feared.[45]

The revealing work of the Incarnate Word begins outside the womb in the silence and helplessness of childhood. He will not 'force His secrets upon us'.[46] When He made His glory visible on the mount of Transfiguration, it threw His apostles to the ground in holy fear (cf Mt 17:6). Thus might the manifestation of truth have been done from the beginning and throughout His sojourn on earth, but such a refulgent revelation, dazzling men into submission, was not the means chosen by the eternal Wisdom of God. He took the little way of self-emptying, inviting men to find Him in a human weakness that seems at first most opposed to His divine omnipotence. He revealed His truth and saved our race, says St Jerome, 'not by fulminating and thundering, but in tears in the Crib and in silence on the Cross'.[47] St Bernard

[44] *Sermo* 184, cap. 3, no. 3; PL 38:997.

[45] St Peter Chrysologus, *Sermo 118 in Epiphania*; PL 52:617A.

[46] Houselander, *Passion of the Infant Christ*, p. 31.

[47] *Epistola* 82, no. 1; PL 22:736. 'Surely if He had so willed it, He might have come moving the Heavens, making the earth to shake, and shooting forth His thunderbolts; but such was not the way of His going forth; His desire was not to destroy, but to save; and to trample upon human pride from its very birth, and therefore He is not only man, but a poor man, and has chosen a poor

of Clairvaux agrees with his predecessors among the Fathers: 'He has made Himself a little one; His Virgin Mother wraps His little body in swaddling clothes: how can you still tremble with fear? This should convince you that He comes not to destroy but to save you, to rescue and not to bind you.'[48] This tender Babe is the almighty Creator from whom I come, the awful Judge to whom I shall return. To save me from the fires of Hell, He has made Himself a little one, born of the Virgin Mary, indestructibly innocent, irresistibly loveable. How can I fail to kneel in penitence and worship by His cradle, laying bare before Him the destitution of my heart: *O puer dulcissime, Iesu bone,* 'O good Jesu, child most sweet!'[49] Thus by His Nativity and infancy, the Incarnate Son repudiates in advance all the heresies of false rigour, all the Calvinist cruelties of double predestination and the physical predetermination to sin, which disfigure the face of God and inspire a paralysing terror that does not even attain the dignity of a salutary and servile fear.

The Infant Word reveals the humility of God, for He is Himself God, omnipotent and infinite, but for our sake, He has made Himself a little child, tiny and weak. 'The immense God has become a child, an adorable little baby: astonishing mystery, the redemption of the pious, the glory of the humble, the judgement of the impious, the ruin of the proud.'[50] To honour this divine condescension, the Cistercians used to prostrate themselves when the announcement

---

mother, who had not even a cradle where she might lay her newborn Child; as it follows, "and she laid Him in a manger"' (St John Chrysostom, CA 3, 68).

[48] *In nativitate Domini, sermo* 1, no. 3; L-R 4:246. 'That is why at this, His self-manifestation to mortals, He preferred to show Himself as a child, to appear more loveable than terrible. He preferred for this moment to reveal that which could arouse love and to defer that which could inspire fear' (Blessed Guerric of Igny, *In nativitate Domini, sermo* 1, no. 2; SC 166:170).

[49] Ibid., no. 4; SC 166:172.

[50] Ibid., no. 2; SC 166:170.

of the Nativity was read from the Martyrology on Christmas Eve.[51] According to St Leo, humility was the chief instrument employed by God Incarnate in the defeat of the spiritual foes of man: '[T]he entire victory of the Saviour, that victory which conquered both the world and the Devil, began in humility and in humility was completed.'[52] This 'true and voluntary humility' was first manifested in His Mother's womb and then sustained all the way to the Cross: throughout His life on earth, He 'both chose and taught [it] as being His entire strength'.[53] When the Magi arrived in Bethlehem, they did not see the divine King of the Jews performing any great signs and wonders; they saw Him in all His simplicity, 'a tranquil and silent child, entrusted to His Mother's care', manifesting only one miracle: His humility.[54]

Both Lucifer and Adam fell by pride, and so only by humility can the first be defeated and the latter redeemed. Angels are pure spirits, and so their sin could not have been one of passion. It was in fact one of pride: the refusal to serve, to be subject to the greatest of all superiors, namely, God, their almighty Creator.[55] They wanted to be 'as God', not in equality, because, by their natural intelligence, they knew that such an aspiration was impossible. But they did seek to be as God 'by way of likeness'. Thomas gives two explanations of what this might mean: either the angels desired as a final end something they could attain by their own natural powers or, assuming they desired a supernatural end, they thought that even that exalted dignity could be reached by their own self-driven force.[56] They were captivated by

---

[51] Cf St Bernard, *In vigilia nativitatis Domini*, sermo 6, no. 5; L-R 4:238.

[52] St Leo, *In Epiphaniae solemnitate*, sermo 7, no. 2; SC 22B:278.

[53] Ibid., no. 3; SC 22B:280.

[54] Ibid., no. 2; SC 22B:278.

[55] Cf ST 1a q. 63, a. 2.

[56] Ibid., q. 63, a. 3.

their own beauty and refused to look higher towards the
infinitely greater supernatural beauty of the end to which
they were ordered, the Three-Personed Beauty of which
they were but a reflection. In a word, the devil and his
demons sought happiness in themselves. Theirs was the sin of
Narcissus: they fell in love with themselves.[57] The sin of
Adam, which he committed at the devil's instigation, takes
the same self-admiring path. Adam was a creature of flesh
and spirit, not a pure spirit, and yet, because of the preternatural gifts harmonizing his lower with his higher powers,
he could not sin through any disordered desire for a sensible
good. But he could and did sin through a disordered desire
for a spiritual good. Again, he was too intelligent to dream of
being equal with God by nature, but he could be deluded
into thinking he could take over from God the decision
about what was good and what was bad for him to do.[58]

So the sons of Adam have much to learn about humility:

> See, O man, what God became for you; recognize the lesson
> of surpassing humility taught by a teacher who, as yet, says
> no word. Once, in Paradise, you were so eloquent that you
> named every living thing; but for your sake, your Creator lay
> speechless and did not even call His Mother by her name. . . .
> Human pride brought you to such a depth that only divine
> humility could raise you up.[59]

The Holy Child strikes a blow against demonic pride,
both in Satan himself and in all his human cooperators. 'This
little Babe,' says St Robert Southwell, 'so few dayes olde,/ Is
come to ryfle sathans folde.'[60] The meek Lamb of God is the

---

[57] Cf St Bonaventure, *Breviloquium* pars 2, cap. 7; Q V:225.

[58] Cf ST 2a2ae q. 163, a. 2.

[59] St Augustine, *Sermo* 188, cap. 3, no. 3; PL 38:1004.

[60] St Robert Southwell, 'Come to Your Heaven, You Heavenly Quires', in
The Poems of Robert Southwell SJ, ed. J. H. McDonald CSC and N. P. Brown
(Oxford, 1967), p. 14.

militant Lion of Judah: 'The weakness of the Child in the
cave triumphs over the prince of this world. It binds the
strong man armed (cf Lk 11:21), takes captive the cruel
tyrant, delivers and sets us free from our captivity.'[61] The
omnipotent God by His infancy gives the lie to the Luci-
ferian ideology of the 'will to power'. St Bonaventure sees
the Child Jesus as the hammer of human pride and presumption, the divine prophet of righteous anger, of whom Elijah
and Jeremiah were but distant types.

> [A]gainst the vanity of the sciences you will find an infant
> without speech or chatter; against the vanity of riches you
> will find Him wrapped in swaddling clothes, not with cloth,
> not with skins, but only with rags, not with one but with
> several because of their poverty; against the vanity of digni-
> ties and honours, you will find Him placed in a manger, at
> the feet of animals.[62]

The littleness of the Child-God is a challenge to Adam's
arrogance: 'Are you still great in your own eyes now that
God has become small before your very eyes? . . . To give
you an example to follow, God, though He is the greatest of
all, made Himself the humblest and smallest of all.'[63] The
Infant Word confounds all intellectual vainglory. The self-
emptying of Eternal Wisdom puts to shame every tendency,
especially in the modern age, to make self, mere subjectivity,
the centre of metaphysics.[64] The taking of flesh by First
Truth is a reproach to all those who, in search of truth, would
shun man's frail body or despise his humble senses. The

---

[61] Blessed Guerric, *In nativitate Domini, sermo* 1, no. 2; SC 166:166f.

[62] St Bonaventure, *In vigilia nativitatis Domini, sermo* 12, no. 2; Q IX:102.

[63] Blessed Guerric, *In nativitate Domini, sermo* 1, no. 2; SC 166.168f.

[64] In *Three Reformers*, Jacques Maritain entitles his chapter on Luther
'L'Avènement du moi' [The Arrival of Self]: *Trois réformateurs: Luther, Descartes,
Rousseau* (Paris, 1925), p. 19. In Luther, western thought undergoes a new and
almost unprecedented turn to self.

Christmas mystery teaches us that, if our intellect is to find its final fulfillment in the vision of God Most High, our knees must be ready to bend low beside His cradle.

The Son of God became little to make us great, and yet He also became little to help us to be little, to be high in sanctity by becoming low in humility. Cardinal Bérulle says of the Holy Child that 'littleness is deified in His person, and He has sanctified it in others.' [65] Some of the Church's Doctors argue that by the fact of His own infancy the Son of God conveyed the lesson of His adulthood: '[U]nless you be converted, and become as little children, you shall not enter into the Kingdom of Heaven' (Mt 18:3). In order to teach us the 'little way' of going to Him in the Spirit, He took the little way when He came to us in the flesh.[66]

> O sweet and sacred infancy [says Blessed Guerric], you restore true innocence to men, infancy by which every age can return to blessed infancy (cf 1 Pet 2:2), being conformed to you not in littleness of members, but in lowliness of mind and in holiness of manners. Yes, sons of Adam, you are all very grand in your own eyes; your pride has turned you into enormous giants. But 'unless you convert and become like this little Child, you will not enter the Kingdom of Heaven' (cf Mt 18:3–4). 'I am the door', says this Child (cf Jn 10:7). If the height of men does not stoop, this lowly door will not admit them. It will, without doubt, 'crush the heads of many in the land' (Ps 109:6). Those who approach the door with

[65] Letter to Queen Mother, 18 Aug. 1628, no. 6; in *Correspondance du Cardinal Pierre de Bérulle*, ed. J. Dagens, vol. 3 (Paris, 1939), p. 406.

[66] 'Today a little child is born for us,' says St Bernard, 'so that man may no more presume to magnify himself, but that we may be rather converted and become as little children' (*In vigilia nativitatis Domini, sermo* 5, no. 3; L-R 4:231). 'Christ was not only born by a second birth, but also became a little child. "For a Child is born to us, and a Son is given to us" (Is 9:6). And He wanted to be born in a small place. Why? To teach you and the whole world that no one can enter the Kingdom of Heaven unless He becomes a little child' (St Bonaventure, *In Epiphania Domini, sermo* 1; Q IX:146).

heads held high will be pushed away and fall backwards, with broken heads.[67]

According to some exegetes, the little child whom our Lord presents as a model for imitation is Himself. He sets Himself in the midst of His disciples, as if to say, 'Unless you be converted, and become as *this* little child, *the little child that I was and am*, you shall not enter into the Kingdom of Heaven.' Jesus is Himself the chief and most perfect exemplar of the childlike virtues: He is humble, free from concupiscence, and does not remember enmities.[68]

The Infant Word Reveals the Mystery of Man

The God-Man reveals man as well as God. 'Only in the mystery of the Incarnate Word does the mystery of man truly become clear.'[69] To this proposition we can add another: 'Only in the mystery of the Infant Word does the mystery of infancy become clear.' What adults quickly forget from their childhood, what so often they fail to understand about their own little ones, is made vividly intelligible by the Infant Word. He who is the 'exegete of the Father' (cf Jn 1:18) is also the exponent of human childhood. 'The mute and speechless simplicity of this Child "makes the tongues of infants eloquent" (Wis 10:21), makes them speak "with the tongues of men and angels" (1 Cor 13:1), imparting to them tongues of fire.'[70]

The Infant Word reveals the truth about man and the childhood of man. The pagan world never fully perceived the spiritual beauty of childhood: 'child' was a synonym of

---

[67] Blessed Guerric, *In nativitate Domini, sermo* 1, no. 2; SC 166:166f.

[68] *Lectura super Matthaeum,* cap. 18, no. 1.

[69] Second Vatican Council, Pastoral Constitution on the Church in the Modern World, *Gaudium et spes* (1965), no. 22.

[70] Blessed Guerric, *In nativitate Domini, sermo* 1, no. 2; SC 166:166f.

imperfection, a brief stopover on the flight to full humanity.[71]
Only when God had deigned to become a child, to live out
His childhood without shortening the experience by a day,
did men discover weighty new reasons for revering the
youngest members of the human family. St Ephrem pictures
the little ones of the world rejoicing that at last their greatest
friend, the Child-God, has come: 'The children cry out:
"Blessed is He who became our brother and playmate in the
streets! O happy day, when we give praise with branches to
the Tree of Life, whose height has bent down to us children."'[72] St Bonaventure, disciple of the childlike Poverello,
argues in similar fashion: 'Christ became a child to exalt
children and make them kings. And so kings reigning on
earth, since they wanted to reign in Heaven, humbled themselves and came to a little child, that He might teach them
humility.'[73] And the exaltation of the child that He established by His own physical childhood, He confirmed by His
teaching on spiritual childhood. He singles out the child, the
young child, as the best available example of the dispositions
needed for entry into the Kingdom. It is artless babes, not
clever adults, who are the privileged recipients of His mysteries (cf Mk 11:25).

[71] 'But obviously, for Jesus, the condition of early childhood is by no means
a matter of moral indifference and insignificance. Rather, the ways of the child,
long since sealed off for the adult, open up an original dimension in which
everything unfolds within the bounds of the right, the true, the good, in a zone
of hidden containment which cannot be derogated as "pre-ethical" or "unconscious", as if the child's spirit had not yet awakened or were still at the animal
level—something it never was, not even in the mother's womb. That zone or
dimension in which the child lives, on the contrary, reveals itself as a sphere of
original wholeness and health, and it may be even said to contain an element of
holiness, since at first the child cannot yet distinguish between parental and
divine love' (Hans Urs von Balthasar, *Unless You Become Like This Child* [San
Francisco, 1991], p. 12).

[72] *Des heiligen Ephraem des Syrers Hymnen de Nativitate (Epiphania)* 8, 19;
CSCO, *Scriptores Syri*; GT, E. Beck OSB (Louvain, 1959), p. 54.

[73] *In Epiphania Domini, sermo* 1, no. 1; Q IX:146f.

Christ loves infancy [says St Leo], which He first assumed in soul and body. Christ loves infancy, the teacher of humility, rule of innocence, model for goodness. Christ loves infancy, towards which He directs the behaviour of older people, to which He leads back the aged, and those whom He exalts to the eternal kingdom He inclines towards His own example.[74]

The Infant Word Reveals the Truth about Poverty

The Infant Word reveals to man the truth about poverty— the counsel of consecrated poverty, the beatitude of spiritual poverty and the burden of material poverty. The Child Jesus teaches in weakness from the manger what the adult Jesus teaches by words on the mount (cf Mt 5:3). By choosing to be born in material deprivation, in a stable and as the foster son of a carpenter, He manifests the beauty of poverty when it is voluntarily undertaken for the Kingdom. By coming in obscurity, as a little and lowly Messiah, willingly without any outward Davidic glory,[75] He shows how blessed are they whom the Spirit moves to contempt of riches and, through humility, of the honours of the world.[76]

St Bernard extracts two lessons—one ascetical, the other moral and social—from the voluntary poverty of the Word. First, he shows how the Christmas mystery teaches man that

[74] St Leo, *In Epiphaniae solemnitate, sermo* 7, no. 3; SC 22B:280.

[75] 'He did not come with pomp but in poverty and need' (St Bonaventure, *In dominica 1 Adventus, sermo* 3, no. 2; Q IX:28).

[76] St Thomas says that some of the beatitudes were given us by our Lord for removing the impediment of a happiness based on pleasure. One way in which you can live a life of pleasure is through having an abundance of external goods, whether riches or honours. Now, you can detach yourself from riches and honours either by virtue, so that you use them in moderation, or, in a more excellent way, by a gift (of the Holy Spirit), so that you despise them altogether. 'Hence the first beatitude is: "Blessed are the poor in spirit," which may refer either to the contempt of riches, or to the contempt of honours, which results from humility' (ST 1a2ae q. 69, a. 3).

spiritual wealth lies hidden within material want when it is adopted freely for the love of God who assumed it freely for the love of man. The birthday of the Saviour is the birthday of the evangelical counsel of poverty:

> There was one treasure He could not find [in Heaven], namely, the treasure of poverty, of which there was on earth an abundance and a superabundance, although man was unaware of its worth. It was, therefore, for the sake of this treasure that the Son of God came down from His throne on high, in order to choose it for Himself and by His appreciation to make it precious in our own eyes. Adorn, then, O Zion, adorn thy bridal couch, but let it be with the ornaments of poverty and humility. These are the swaddling clothes that best please Him; these, as Mary bears witness, are the silks with which He delights to be clothed.[77]

The saints follow the poor Christ in poverty. They conform themselves to the homeless Son of Man, who in the stable in Bethlehem had to sleep where the oxen feed and in the lanes of Galilee lacked even the lodging of the foxes (cf Lk 9:58). They see that the poverty of Christ is more than material. The physical deprivations are the outward signs of the metaphysical. As we saw above, the Son of God assumes human nature with the limitations essential to what is created and bodily and with infirmities 'in the likeness of sinful flesh' (cf Rom 8:3). When He is conceived and born as man, He retains the radiance of His Divinity, but He does not allow it to shine with any visible glamour. 'Look at the eternal Word,' says Father Faber, 'first in the bosom of the Father, and then in the bosom of Mary, and say whether a lower depth of poverty can be conceived.'[78] The physical self-impoverishment and the metaphysical self-emptying seem strangely appropriate as an expression in the humanity of the self-giving by

---

[77] St Bernard, *In vigilia nativitatis Domini, sermo* 1, no. 5; L-R 4:201.
[78] *Bethlehem*, p. 378.

which, in the Divinity, the Son exists with the Father in the unity of the Holy Spirit. Neither as God nor as man does the Son live by grasping (cf Phil 2:6). Trinitarian love is therefore well expressed by the poverty of the Master, and Christian charity is well served by the poverty of the disciple. Evangelical poverty, like the other counsels, removes the things that make the perfection of charity more difficult.[79] It is not impossible for the rich man to enter the Kingdom of Heaven, just harder: he is more encumbered, more distracted—fearful of losing what he has or hopeful to gain even more. That is why, as St Thomas says, 'the man who is poor in his cell and rich in his conscience' can sleep more soundly than 'the rich man in his purple'.[80] If we want to take the heavenward path, we would do well to imitate the manner in which the Son of God took the earthward path in Nazareth and Bethlehem. Something of the same poverty attaches to His sacramental presence in the Holy Eucharist. It is hard to think of any mode of presence among men more humbling, more radically poor, than substantial presence beneath the appearance of bread.

St Bernard also sees in the poverty of the Crib a summary of the Church's social doctrine. God reveals His love of the poor by becoming one of the poor Himself.

> His poor swaddling clothes suggest nothing consoling to those who 'wish to walk in long robes'. The manger and the stable have no comforting lesson for those who 'love the first seats in the synagogues'. Perhaps they will say they are satisfied to let all this consolation go to those who 'wait with silence for the salvation of God', to those who mourn, and to those who are clad in the livery of the poor. Let them know, therefore, that none but these will be consoled by the angels. It is to the 'shepherds watching and keeping the

[79] Cf ST 2a2a q. 184, a. 3.
[80] *Contra impugnantes* pars 2, cap. 6.

night-watches over their flock' that the joy of the new light is
announced, and it is for them, so we are told, that the
Saviour is born.[81]

The Christmas mystery poses a threat to the ideologies
that would exploit the poor man—liberal capitalism, which
enslaves him to big business by the lure of prosperity, and
socialism and communism, which enslave him to the party
and the state and fill his mind with violent envy. As Chesterton says, '[t]here is in this buried divinity an idea of *undermining* the world.'[82] Belief in a God 'born like an outcast or
even an outlaw' re-casts from top to bottom 'the whole
conception of law and its duties to the poor and outcast'.
Once God has assumed the form of a servant, there can be
no more slaves. 'There could be and were people bearing
that legal title, until the Church was strong enough to weed
them out, but there could be no more of the pagan repose in
the mere advantage to the state of keeping it a servile state.'[83]
When the King of Kings takes upon Him the form of a
servant, He subverts all species of political servility, whether
of the right or left, every estrangement of the human person
and the family from the independent activity and ownership
they need for a life worthy of man.

Those human beings whose sole goal in life is self-
enrichment are shamed by the self-emptying of the Son of
God. God reveals the wisdom of a 'preferential love'[84] for the
poor by choosing to become one of the poor Himself, and
He exposes the folly of an 'immoderate love of riches'[85] by
forgoing certain perfections of His human nature and certain
privileges in the circumstances of His human life:

[81] *In nativitate Domini, sermo* 5, 5; L-R 4:269.
[82] G. K. Chesterton, *The Everlasting Man*, new ed. (San Francisco, 1993), p. 181.
[83] Ibid., p. 173.
[84] See CCC 2448.
[85] See CCC 2445.

Brethren, the tears of Christ cause me shame and sorrow. I was playing out of doors in the street, while sentence of death was being passed upon me in the privacy of the royal council chamber. But the King's only-begotten Son heard of it. And what did He do? He left the palace, took off His crown, dressed Himself with sackcloth, scattered ashes on His head, bared His feet, and wept and lamented because His poor slave was condemned to death.[86]

The Son of God appeared in poverty at His first coming, because at His Second Coming He will judge us on the charity we have shown towards the poor (cf Mt 25:35ff.). Those who worship Christ in the states of His humility— whether in the manger or the monstrance—will be well trained for finding and serving Him in the unprepossessing persons of the poor. '[A]s long as you did it to one of these my least brethren, you did it to me' (Mt 25:40). 'He makes Himself poor,' says the Little Flower, 'so that we may be able to do Him charity. He stretches out His hand to us like a beggar, so that upon the sunlit Day of Judgement, when He appears in His glory, He may be able to utter, and we to hear, the loving words: "Come, blessed of my Father, for I was hungry." ' [87]

3. The Infant Word Makes New the Old

The Infant Word makes the old new, and, through the liturgy of the Christmas season, he communicates the graces of renovation to His Church:

Grant, we beseech thee, almighty God, that the new Nativity of thine Only-begotten in the flesh may deliver us whom an old servitude holds fast beneath the yoke of sin.[88]

[86] *Sermo* 3, no. 4; L-R 4:260.
[87] Letter to Céline, 2 Aug. 1893; in *General Correspondence*, vol. 2, ET (Washington, D.C., 1988), p. 808.
[88] Collect of the Third Mass of Christmas Day, *Missale romanum* (1962). 'O Lord, who by the wondrous birth of thy Son hast put away the old nature of

Every Christmas, the Church and all her members feel the aftershock of this newness. As Chesterton points out, the happiness of Christmas 'is not a state; it is a crisis'. We keep vigil, sing Mass at midnight. 'Everything is so arranged that the whole household may feel, if possible, as a household does when a child is actually being born in it.'[89] It is, as always, the children who grasp what is really going on. '[Children] have the serious and even solemn sense of the great truth; that Christmas is a time when things happen; things that do not always happen.'[90] In one way, says Chesterton, Christmas is very simple, but in another it is very complex, 'the simultaneous striking of many notes; of humility, of gaiety, of gratitude, of mystical fear, but also of vigilance and of drama'.[91]

'Oldness' is often used in Sacred Scripture as a metaphor for the corrupting effects of sin. For example, St Paul urges the Ephesians to 'put off, according to former conversation, the old man, who is corrupted according to the desire of error' (Eph 4:22). The figure of speech is fitting. When any material thing is new, it has 'integrity and power and beauty',[92] but when it gets old, it tends to fall to pieces and to lose its original force and charm. As a man ages, he advances towards death: 'That which ageth and groweth old is near its end' (Heb 8:13).[93] In preparation for its final dissolution in

---

our manhood, grant that by this Sacrament of thy Nativity we may be restored unto newness of life' (Postcommunion of the Second Mass, *Missale romanum* [1962]).

[89] *The Spirit of Christmas: Stories, Poems, Essays*, ed. Marie Smith (London, 1984), p. 22.

[90] Ibid.

[91] *The Everlasting Man*, in The Collected Works of G. K. Chesterton, vol. 2 (San Francisco, 1986), p. 312.

[92] Cf St Thomas, *4 Sent.* d. 17, q. 1, a. 1c.

[93] '[O]ldness is a way to corruption': St Thomas, *Super secundam epistolam ad Corinthios*, cap. 4, lect. 5.

the grave, the body becomes weaker and more subject to
disease; youthful energy and good looks fade into a distant
memory; we end up, as the poet says, 'sans teeth, sans eyes,
sans taste, sans everything'.[94] Something similar happens to
the soul because of the habits of sin. As St Thomas says,
'through sin, power and spiritual beauty are lost';[95] sin causes
oldness, because it corrupts 'the good of nature'.[96] It was the
Old Adam who brought into the world the oldness of sin,
and through sin came death and the old age that is its herald
(cf Rom 5:12). There is, then, a twofold oldness inherited
from Adam—guilt and punishment.[97]

Blessed Guerric says that '"unto us a boy is born", by a
temporal nativity, in order to make us new (innovandis).'[98] St
Gregory Nazianzen likewise sees Christmas as a 'festival of
re-creation'.[99] The Son of God is conceived as man by the
Holy Spirit and born as man of the Virgin precisely so that
He may make all things new, to repair and restore the world,
which was created through Him and which Adam by his sin
aged and deformed. St Irenaeus uses the Pauline doctrine of
'recapitulation': the Son of God sums up and gives a new
beginning to the whole cosmos by His Incarnation, birth,
life, death and Resurrection. Some of the Fathers speak of
this work of renovation as one of 'rejuvenation'. The eternal
Son comes to bestow the grace of regeneration as God's sons
on the fallen sons of Adam, the grace of rejuvenation on a
race that has grown old and grey in sin and death. We are
born as sons of Adam for mortal life, for a life that ends with

[94] William Shakespeare, As You Like It, act 2, scene 7, line 139.

[95] See St Thomas, Super epistolam ad Colossenses, cap. 3, lect. 2.

[96] Super epistolam ad Romanos, cap. 6, lect. 2.

[97] Cf St Thomas, 3 Sent. d. 15, q. 2, a. 3c; Compendium theologiae, lib. 1, cap.
236; Lectura super Matthaeum, cap. 26, lect. 4.

[98] In nativitate Domini, sermo 1, no. 1; SC 166:164.

[99] Cf Oratio 38, no. 4; PG 36:316B. Cf O. Casel OSB, 'Die "Neuheit" in den
Weihnachtsorationen', Liturgische Zeitschrift 4 (1931–1932), 83–87.

death, but we are reborn in Christ as sons of God for eternal life. St Leo the Great, for example, says that 'if He had not summoned human oldness to a new beginning by his birth, death would have reigned from Adam to the end.'[100] Representing the East, we might cite the great Byzantine preacher and poet St Andrew of Crete: 'God on earth, God from Heaven, God among men, God carried in the Virgin's womb, whom no place could ever confine. . . . And so our first formation receives a new re-formation, and the aged world lays aside the oldness caused by sin.'[101] The Only-Begotten of the Father is born of the Virgin Mary to rescue us from the twofold oldness of guilt and punishment, by giving us grace for the justification of our souls and glory for the resurrection of our bodies. On the Last Day He will come to conform our lowly bodies to be like His glorious body (cf Phil 3:21). Then the heavens and the earth will be remade; God will wipe the tears from our eyes (cf Rev 21:1, 4); and the great Lamb will say, 'Behold, I make all things new' (Rev 21:5). But this wonderful renewal, which will be completed on the Last Day, at the beginning of the great and unending Eighth Day, was inaugurated on Lady Day and Christmas Day, in the Incarnation and human birth of the Son of God:

> A marvellous wonder has this day come to pass. Nature is made new, and God becomes man. That which He was, He has remained, and that which He was not, He has taken upon Himself, while suffering neither confusion nor division.[102]

As we saw above, the manner of His human conception and birth is new, virginal and miraculous, as a sign given by

---

[100] St Leo, *In nativitate Domini, sermo* 5, no. 5; SC 22B:132.

[101] *In annuntiatione Beatae Mariae*; PG 97:884A.

[102] Tone Eight, Great Vespers, Synaxis of the Mother of God, *Menaion*, p. 291.

God that here He is doing that 'new thing' prophesied by Isaiah: 'a way in the wilderness and rivers in the desert' (cf Is 43:19).

> [T]he Child that lies in the Crib came to make us children, because 'only children enter the Kingdom of Heaven' (cf Mt 18:3), and all our growth in Him 'unto the measure of the age of the fulness of Christ' (cf Eph 4:13f.) is a process of becoming ever younger, until all the weary old age of this mortality is consumed in the eternal childhood of immortality, where alone we are fully restored to the 'image and likeness of God', who, though He is 'the Ancient of Days' (cf Dan 7:9), knows no old age. He is 'older than all and younger than all' [St Augustine].[103]

Our Lord's objective work of renewal is completed only with His death, Resurrection and Ascension, but it begins in His birth. His bodily infancy is a most wonderful sign, indeed the exemplary and instrumental cause, of the spiritual infancy, the new childhood of God, which He comes to bestow upon us. 'Blessed be the Child', sings St Ephrem, 'that has made men young again today. . . . Old men cry out: "Blessed be the Child who rejuvenated Adam!" Adam was sad when he saw how old and feeble he had become. . . . Blessed be the Child through whom Adam and Eve gained new youth.' [104] To begin with, in this life, He rejuvenates our souls by His grace, but at the end He will make our bodies young again by His glory. The Son of God, having risen from the dead in His human body, is for ever a young man. His body is sustained through its perfect submission to His soul in an unending vigour, with powers of movement surpassing beyond all measure the prowess of

---

[103] Erich Przywara SJ, 'Advent und Weihnacht', *Frühe religiöse Schriften* (Einsiedeln, 1962), p. 283.

[104] *Des heiligen Ephraem des Syrers Hymnen de Nativitate* 3, 1; CSCO 187, *Scriptores Syri* 83; GT, E. Beck OSB (Louvain, 1959), p. 18; 7, 11, p. 49.

even the best-trained athlete in his prime. And this youth-fulness of body will be communicated to us, His members:

> It is written: 'Until we all meet . . . unto a perfect man, unto the measure of the age of the fulness of Christ' (Eph 4:13). Now Christ rose again in the age of youth, which, so Augustine says, begins at about the age of thirty. Therefore, others, too, will rise again in the age of youth. Further, man will rise again in the greatest perfection of nature. Now human nature has its most perfect state in the age of youth. Therefore all will rise again at that age.[105]

The metaphor of oldness is neither an insult to the elderly nor a licence for the young. The newness that Christ brings, first for the soul and later for the body, is supernatural. When old Simeon takes the Infant Messiah into his arms, and the aged prophetess speaks of Him 'to all that look for the redemption of Israel' (cf Lk 2:28ff.), they prove themselves to be among the first recipients of the rejuvenating grace of Christ.[106] They know the truth of St Bernard's words: He is 'the New Man who can never become old, who brings into true newness of life those whose bones have all grown old (cf Ps 31:3)'.[107] Simeon and Anna have an eagle-like youthfulness of soul that puts to shame the spiritual decrepitude of those chronologically younger people, such as Herod, who lack the saints' perfection of childlike hope in the Child-God.

---

[105] 4 Sent. d. 44, a. 3a, sed contra.

[106] Blessed Guerric, In purificatione Beatae Mariae Virginis, sermo 3, no. 1; SC 166:340f.

[107] St Bernard, In vigilia nativitatis Domini, sermo 6, no. 6; L-R 4:239.

4. The Infant Word Makes Man Divine

The Wonderful Exchange

The Fathers and Doctors see the Incarnation as establishing a 'wonderful exchange' between God and man: He takes what is ours so that He may give us what is His. 'The whole reason for the Incarnation', says St Bonaventure, 'is the salvation of soul and flesh. . . . God, the Word of God, through the flesh He assumed, established an exchange [*commercium*], a union, in order to ennoble our nature.'[108] The term 'wonderful exchange' (*admirabile commercium*) emerges about the time of the Council of Ephesus, though the idea is much older.[109] On the Octave Day of Christmas it is used in an antiphon that goes back to the age of the Fathers:

> *O admirabile commercium! Creator generis humani, animatum corpus sumens, de Virgine nasci dignatus est: et procedens homo sine semine largitus est nobis suam Deitatem.*

> O wonderful exchange! The Creator of the human race, taking upon Him a body ensouled, has deigned to be born of the Virgin, and, coming forth as man, He has lavished on us His Godhead.[110]

St Paul presents the exchange as a motive for the Corinthians' generosity towards the poor of Jerusalem: 'For you know the grace of our Lord Jesus Christ, that being rich He became poor for your sakes; that through His poverty you might be rich' (2 Cor 8:9). St Irenaeus, disciple of a disciple of the beloved disciple of the Lord, wields it as an argument

---

[108] *In nativitate Domini, sermo* 2, no. 2; Q IX:108B.

[109] See M. Herz on *sanctum commercium* in *Münchener theologischen Studien* 2.15 (Munich, 1958), 24ff, 70ff.

[110] Antiphon of the first psalm at Lauds, *Breviarium romanum* (1962); antiphon of the first psalm of Vespers, *Liturgia horarum* (1970).

against the Gnostics: 'The Word of God . . . became what
we are in order to make us what He is.' [111] Later, St Proclus,
champion of our Lady's divine motherhood in the Constantinople of Nestorius, says that the Blessed Virgin is the
'market of the saving exchange'. [112] In her womb God con-
ducted an 'awesome transaction' (*phrikton synallagma*), out of
all proportion to human trading. [113] There is no equivalence
between the opulence of what is given and the indigence of
what is taken. St Augustine likewise speaks of an 'amazing
barter and divine exchange'. [114] It is amazing because God
truly 'gets nothing out of it'. He, who is infinite in His
perfections, is neither enhanced nor diminished by the taking
of our finite frailty. But we paupers are enriched with a pearl
beyond price:

> An absolutely wonderful exchange! Taking flesh, you lavish
> divinity, an exchange contracted out of charity not greed.
> Truly, to the glory of your indulgence and wholly to the
> profit of my indigence. You are indeed a merciful Child
> whom mercy alone made a child. [115]

Such is the largesse of our God. The eternal Word takes
upon Him the poverty of our humanity and gives in exchange the riches of His Divinity. 'He who gives riches
becomes poor, for He assumes the poverty of my flesh, that I
may assume the riches of His divinity. He that is full empties
Himself, for He empties Himself of His glory for a short

---

[111] *Adversus haereses*, lib. 5, prol.; PG 7:1120B.

[112] *Oratio* 1, no. 1; PG 65:681A.

[113] Ibid., no. 8; PG 65:688D–689A.

[114] *Enarratio in psalmum 30*, no. 3; PL 36:231.

[115] Blessed Guerric, *In nativitate Domini*, sermo 3, no. 1; SC 166:188. St
Thomas invokes the Christmas antiphon: 'It was no small thing that the Son of
God came to us and assumed our flesh, but for our great advantage. By so
doing He established a kind of exchange, that is to say, He assumed an animated body and deigned to be born of the Virgin in order to lavish on us His
divinity' (*In symbolum Apostolorum*, a. 3).

while that I may have a share in His fulness.' [116] This stupendous transaction begins in the Virgin's womb, when the Son
empties Himself and takes the form of a slave, and continues
all the way up to the summit of Calvary and down into the
pit of Sheol, the furthest extremity of our slavish poverty.
Mortal life He takes, risen life He gives; manhood He assumes, Godhead He bestows—His Father to be our Father,
His Spirit to be the transfiguring Comforter of our souls.
The upshot of this exchange is nothing less amazing than the
deification of man: God is made man so that men might be
made gods. The lowering of the Creator makes possible the
elevation of the creature.

Partakers of the Divine Nature

Deification, the sharing of the Christian in the very life of
God, is the special gift for which the Church prays throughout the Christmas season. 'To be made partakers of the
Divinity to which our humanity was united in the Person of
Christ, and to receive this divine gift through this humanity
itself—such is the grace attached to the celebration of today's
mystery.' [117] For example, in the Secret of the Mass of Midnight, according to the older Roman rite, the priest prays
that 'we may, through this sacred exchange, be found in the
likeness of Him in whom our substance is made one with
thine'.[118] The Byzantine liturgy is struck by the sublime irony
of Providence, by which Adam's arrogant aspiration for divinity is fulfilled, beyond all expectation, through God's assumption of humanity: 'Taking man's form, thou hast now
bestowed upon him the joy of becoming godlike: for it was

[116] *Oratio* 38, no. 13; PG 36:325C.
[117] Marmion, *Christ in His Mysteries*, p. 116.
[118] Secret, Midnight Mass, *Missale romanum* (1962).

in hope of this that of old we fell from on high into the dark depths of the earth.' [119]

The Greek words *theôsis* and *theopoiêsis*, 'divinization', 'deification', are not found in the New Testament, but the concept, expressed in synonymous phrases, belongs to the essence of the apostolic preaching. As the *Catechism of the Catholic Church* teaches us, summing up the Church's unchanging Faith, the grace of our Lord Jesus Christ 'introduces us into the intimacy of Trinitarian life. . . . [It] is the gratuitous gift that God makes to us of his own life, infused by the Holy Spirit into our soul to heal it of sin and to sanctify it. It is the *sanctifying* or *deifying grace* received in Baptism.' [120] When we are baptized, we are made the members and co-heirs of Christ (cf 1 Cor 6:15; Rom 8:17) and thereby receive, from the overflow of His grace, a share in His divine Sonship, 'the power to be made the sons of God' (cf Jn 1:12ff.). Those who live 'in Christ' are truly a 'new creation' (cf 2 Cor 5:17) and are caught up into the intimacy of Trinitarian life: the Father sends the Spirit of His Son into their hearts, enabling them to cry 'Abba, Father' (cf Gal 4:6). As the three Divine Persons dwell in each other by nature, so They dwell in us, and we dwell in Them, by grace. This is the intention with which our Lord prays on the eve of His Passion: 'That they all may be one, as thou, Father, in me, and I in thee, that they also may be one in us' (Jn 17:21). Transfiguring familiarity with the Trinity is already a reality by faith and charity in this life but will be perfected in the life

---

[119] Feast of the Nativity, *Menaion*, p. 279. St Bonaventure expresses a similar insight in one of his Christmas sermons: 'What did you desire, O Adam, if not to be as God (cf Gen 3:5)? What did you desire, proud Lucifer, if not to be like unto God (cf Is 14:14)? Still it never entered into your desire to be gods. The creature never desired to be God. Yet this, above all desire, has taken place, for God is man, and man is God. What is there sweeter, more loveable, more inspiring of trust?' (*In vigilia nativitatis Domini, sermo* 12, no. 2; Q IX:101).

[120] CCC 1997, 1999; cf Jn 4:14; 7:38–39.

to come by face-to-face vision: 'Dearly beloved, we are now the sons of God, and it hath not yet appeared what we shall be. We know that when He shall appear, we shall be like to Him, because we shall see Him as He is' (cf 1 Jn 3:1ff.). The 'redemption of our body' in the Resurrection will be the final revelation of our adoptive sonship, our entry 'into the liberty of the glory of the children of God' (cf Rom 8:19ff.). Thus, as children of God, members of Christ and temples of the Holy Spirit, we are 'partakers of the divine nature' (2 Pet 1:4).

The doctrine of deification is the predilection of the Greek Fathers, but it is by no means their exclusive property.[121] All the Fathers and medieval Doctors hold and teach it with a common mind. So universal was the doctrine that it could be cited as a premise when the Fathers were arguing against the Arians.[122] As always, St Thomas can serve as spokesman for the Tradition: 'The only-begotten Son of God, wanting to make us sharers of His divinity, assumed our nature, so that He, made man, might make men gods.'[123] The sanctifying grace that Christ merited by His Passion, the grace that overflows from Him as Head of the Church and is conferred in all seven of His Sacraments, is 'a participation in the divine nature'.[124] By grace we are made 'godlike',[125] 'gods by participation',[126] and in glory in Heaven, we attain supernatural beatitude 'by divine power, according to a certain participation in the Godhead'.[127]

We can misunderstand the deifying effects of grace both

[121] See I.-H. Dalmais OP, 'Divinisation'; DS 3:1376ff.

[122] See p. 132.

[123] St Thomas Aquinas, *Officium de festo Corporis Christi*, pars 3, no. 3.

[124] Cf ST 1a2ae q. 112, a. 1. Grace is 'nothing other than a certain participated likeness of the divine nature' (ST 3a q. 62, a. 1).

[125] Cf *2 Sent.* d. 26, a. 4, ad 3.

[126] Cf ST 1a2ae q. 3, a. 1, ad 1.

[127] Cf ST 1a2ae q. 62, a. 1.

by defect and by excess. The temptation on one side is to play it safe and reduce the mystery to more manageable proportions, to make it something tamely moral and external, a mere metaphor for a certain kind of conduct. Against such nervous reductionism, we must insist that the 'participation in the Godhead' that Christ won for us in His mysteries and bestows upon us in His Sacraments is physical and formal, a new, transfigured life for the essence of our souls. Grace acts in the manner of a formal cause: as whiteness makes something white, so grace makes our souls divine.[128] Thus, what we are, as sanctified by grace, is godlike. However, we must be on guard against lurching to the other extreme and turning Christian deification into a hideous replica of pagan pantheism. The divine nature is not communicated to us substantially, as it is within the Trinity, or personally, as it is in the Incarnation, but accidentally, as an accidental form or quality perfecting the substance of the soul.[129] When our Lord assures His disciples that, as the Father has loved Him, He has loved them (cf Jn 15:9), He does not mean He wants them to 'be God by nature or united to God in person', but only that they should have 'a likeness of these things, namely, be gods by the participation of grace'.[130] Deifying grace does not abolish our creatureliness nor does it alter our human nature or destroy our personalities, but rather fulfills our personalities, perfects our nature, and preserves our creatureliness. The grace that makes us pleasing to God is not God but an effect of God, 'created grace', a supernatural quality that elevates our souls, endowing them with a radiance that reflects the beauty of the Trinity.

[128] Cf ST 1a2ae q. 110, a. 2, ad 1. 'By grace the soul takes on a Godlike form [anima per gratiam conformatur Deo]' (ST 1a q. 43, a. 5, ad 1).

[129] Cf ST 1a2ae q. 110, a. 2, ad 2; 3a q. 2, a. 10, ad 2.

[130] Lectura super Ioannem, cap. 15, lect.2.

The key word in the theology of deification is *participation*, which St Thomas defines as follows: 'To participate is, as it were, to take part. Therefore, when something receives in a particular way what belongs to something else in a universal way, the former is said to "participate" in the latter.'[131] When we say that man by grace participates in the Godhead, we do not mean that he takes a part of God, for God has no parts and is incapable of change. The partiality is on the side of the creature. Being divine by participation means that what in the sanctifying God is essential, infinite and complete is found in the sanctified soul in an accidental, finite and partial form. In this way, sanctifying grace gives us a share in the Godhead as it is in itself, as it subsists in the three Divine Persons. As Father Garrigou-Lagrange says: 'Just as the Godhead in itself is communicated to the Son through eternal generation, so the Godhead as it is in itself is participated in by the just, especially the blessed, through divine adoption.'[132] Within the Godhead, the Father knows Himself in the Son, and the Father and the Son love each other in the Holy Spirit. By the created gift of grace, we are caught up into this intimate knowing and loving. Our souls, just by being created by God in His image, already mirror the processions within the Godhead, but, by grace and charity and the gifts of the Holy Spirit, this resemblance is raised up to an incalculably higher level: we know and love the Divine

[131] St Thomas, *In De hebdomadibus*, lect. 2. 'In other words, when we find a quality or perfection possessed by a given subject in only partial rather than in total fashion, such a subject is said to participate in that perfection' (J. F. Wippel, *The Metaphysical Thought of Thomas Aquinas: From Finite Being to Uncreated Being* [Washington, D.C., 2000], p. 96f.). The classic works on participation in St Thomas are: C. Fabro, *La nozione metafisica di partecipazione secondo S. Tommaso d'Aquino*, new ed. (Turin, 1950); and L. B. Geiger, *La Participation dans la philosophie de St Thomas d'Aquin* (Paris, 1942).

[132] R. Garrigou-Lagrange OP, *De gratia: Commentarius in Summam theologicam S. Thomae 1a2ae qq. 109–114* (Rome, 1950), p. 109.

Persons with a kind of experimental, firsthand directness. As St Thomas loves to say, in connection with the Gift of Wisdom, quoting Denys, we 'suffer the things of God'.[133] Alongside grace comes charity, which gives our wills a fiery likeness to the Holy Spirit, the Love of the Father and the Son, and the Spirit's Gift of Wisdom, which with the other gifts accompanies grace and charity, bestows on our intellects a brightness like that of the Father's eternal Wisdom, the 'Love-breathing Word'.[134] This, then, is the supernatural life, in grace and in glory: as the Venerable Father Arintero puts it, it is 'a resemblance of and participation in the inner life of God, One and Three'.[135]

Intimate Contact with the Divine Persons

Sanctifying grace gives us the contact of close friendship with each of the Divine Persons. Now there are two ways we can think of sanctifying grace: *entitatively* (to use the jargon), in itself, as a quality in some subject; and *intentionally*, in relation to the object with which it enables the subject to have contact. When we look at grace in the first way, as a created gift perfecting our souls, we have to conclude that it is an effect produced by all three Divine Persons, for all works outside the Godhead are common to the whole Trinity. Since it is the Triune God that is the principal efficient cause of the grace of adoption in our souls, it is the whole Trinity that *makes* the adopted sons of God.[136] However, when we consider grace intentionally, we have to say, with Cardinal Journet, that it 'leads to God as He is in Himself, to the Three Divine Persons

---

[133] ST 2a2ae q. 45, a. 2.

[134] Cf ST 1a q. 43, a. 5, ad 2.

[135] Juan Arintero OP, *The Mystical Evolution in the Development and Vitality of the Church*, vol. 1, ET, new ed. (Rockford, 1978), p. 44.

[136] ST 3a q. 23, a. 2.

as really distinct from each other'.[137] The glorious destination of grace, the object towards which the sanctified soul stretches out, is 'the very nature of God subsisting in the Three Divine Persons, attained equally no doubt, but without confusion and in their proper singularity'.[138] By grace we know the Incarnate Son as Brother, Head and Bridegroom, and therefore with His Father as our Father and Their Holy Spirit as the Guest and Comforter of our souls.

Divinizing adoption

Divinization is a divinizing adoption: we become by grace what Christ is by nature—not just God but God *the Son*. The

[137] C. Journet, *L'Église du Verbe incarné*, vol. 2, *La structure interne de l'Église: le Christ, la Vierge, l'Esprit Saint*, new ed. (Paris, 1999), p. 457. Journet derives the entitative/intentional distinction from St Thomas: 'Charity can be considered in two aspects: according to its being in the subject, and then it is measured by the capacity of the one who receives it . . . [and] according to its inclination to the object, and then it has no measure' (*1 Sent.* d. 3, q. 2, a. 3, ad 5). Journet also quotes John of St Thomas: '[A]lthough grace is an effect caused by the whole Trinity and comes from God inasmuch as He is one, nevertheless the movement and tendency of the creature do not stop at the gifts of grace, they go on to the Divine Persons who are thereby manifested to them . . . in such a way that it is the Divine Person Himself who is given and sent to the creature, and not only His gifts, even though the Person is neither given nor sent without them' (*In 1a q. 43*, disp. 17, a. 3, no. 16; see Journet, *L'Église*, pp. 459f.).

[138] Journet, *L'Église*, p. 462. By grace, says St Thomas, 'we are assimilated to that divine nature by which the Father and the Son are one' (*Lectura super Ioannem* cap. 17, lect. 5). The Venerable Juan G. Arintero OP offers this valuable clarification: 'The works of grace are not like those of nature. The latter, as realized *ad extra*, are referred to the substantial unity of the divine omnipotence and are common to the Three Persons, however much they may be appropriated to one or other of Them according to our way of speaking. But the works of grace, since they make us enter into the joy of the Lord, into the intimate and secret life of the Divinity, and into friendly and familiar fellowship with the Father, the Son, and the Holy Ghost, raise us up to a participation in those ineffable communications which are effected *ad intra*, in the very bosom of God' (*The Mystical Evolution in the Development and Vitality of the Church*, vol. 1, ET [St Louis, 1950], pp. 140f.).

Lord Jesus is the true and natural Son;, we are sons by grace and adoption. St Athanasius, perhaps the supreme Doctor of divinization, sets out the distinctions in rhythmic prose:

> The Son of God was made the Son of Man in order that the sons of men, the sons of Adam, might be made the sons of God. The Word, begotten of the Father in Heaven in an ineffable, inexplicable, incomprehensible, and eternal manner, came to this earth to be born in time of the Virgin Mary, the Mother of God, so that they who were born here below might be born again from above, that is, of God. . . . He is the Son of God by nature, we by grace; He has become the son of Adam through His goodness and graciousness, while we are sons of Adam by nature.[139]

The adoption of men by grace is common to the whole Trinity, but it can be linked to each of the persons in particular, 'to the Father as its author, to the Son as its model, and to the Holy Spirit as the one who imprints upon us the likeness of this model'.[140] It is the Father who regenerates us in the likeness of His only-begotten Son by the working of the Holy Spirit.[141]

Divinized in Christ

The only way for us men to share the Divinity of the Trinity is to be united to the humanity of the Son. St Thomas says

[139] *De incarnatione contra Arianos* 8; PG 26:996AB.

[140] Cf ST 3a q. 23, a. 2, ad 3.

[141] 'In brief, the Father regenerates us for eternal life and makes us share in His very own nature in order to make us like to the image of His only-begotten Son [cf Rom 8:29]; the Son gives us the power to become sons of God and His own brothers and co-heirs; and both together call us and translate us from death to life by communicating to us Their Spirit of Love [cf 1 Jn 3:14], who vivifies us with that life of grace which is the seed of glory and imprints upon us the seal of Christ' (Arintero, *Mystical Evolution*, vol. 1, p. 147).

that it should not surprise us to know that the whole of Christian Faith is centred on two great realities, 'the divinity of the Trinity and the humanity of Christ . . . because the humanity of Christ is the way we reach the divinity'.[142] No one comes to the Father except through the Son (cf Jn 14:6). As God, with the Father and the Holy Spirit, the Lord Jesus is the principal efficient cause of our deification, and as man He is its instrumental and meritorious cause. Since by deifying grace we are the adopted sons of God, we can also say that Christ, as the natural Son of God, is the exemplary cause.[143] Moreover, this deifying grace is poured out upon us, through the humanity of the Son and from the Divinity of the Trinity, in the Sacraments of the Church. At the font and the altar, in the confessional or on his sickbed, through the hands of the bishop or the lips of the bride, the Christian man reaps the profits of the 'wonderful exchange' transacted in Bethlehem. By the grace of the virtues and gifts in the Sacraments, we paupers share in the divine riches of our Head and King.

Divinizing Incorporation

Our adoption and thus our deification are the effects of being living members of Jesus Christ. We first became such members when we were baptized. Our membership was then strengthened in Confirmation, completed in the Eucharist and restored, after grave sin, by Penance. By the grace of the Sacraments we are made members of the Son and therefore sharers in His Sonship, sons–in–the–Son. Once inserted into

---

[142] *Compendium theologiae* lib. 1, cap. 2.

[143] The grace of adoption, 'since it comes to us through the Incarnation, not of the Father or the Spirit, but of the Son, is marked by a very special filial character, which constitutes an eminent privilege of the age of the new law, and which is imprinted on the whole Church' (Journet, *L'Èglise*, p. 485).

the Body, as limbs alive with the divine life of the Head, we
are like one person, one man, with Him, and God the Father
looks upon us with something of the gaze with which He
beholds the Only-Begotten.

> If, then, the human race, in analogous fashion, likewise be-
> comes the Body of Christ, and its members become the
> members of God's Son, if the divine person of the Son of
> God bears them in Himself as His own, then, with due
> proportion, must not the divine dignity of the Son of God
> flow over to men, since they are His members? Must not
> God the Father extend to these members the same love as
> that which He bears for His natural Son, must He not em-
> brace them in His Son with one and the same love, inasmuch
> as they belong to Him? Must He not communicate to the
> Son's mystical members the same divine holiness and
> splendour with which He adorns the human nature of the
> Son? Must He not raise them to infinite heights and place
> them next to His Son on the latter's own thrones?[144]

Deification and the Christmas Mystery

It would seem that the deifying grace of our adoption is
more fittingly connected with the Easter mystery than with
the Christmas mystery. After all, the grace of our adoption
was merited by our Lord in His Passion. We first receive that
grace in the Sacrament of Baptism, in which we share
Christ's death and burial in order to be raised up to newness
of life in Him (cf Rom 5:3ff.). That is true. Still, our adoption can also, indeed must also, be seen as an effect of the
Christmas mystery. Our rebirth into divine life is modelled
on the Saviour's birth into human life. The divinization of
man begins with his regeneration by water and the Holy
Spirit in Baptism. As St Leo says:

[144] M. J. Scheeben, *The Mysteries of Christianity*, ET (St Louis, 1946), pp. 377f.

[T]oday's feast renews for us the sacred beginnings of Jesus born of the Virgin Mary, and as we worship the birth of our Saviour, we discover that we are celebrating our own origin. The generation of Christ is the origin of the Christian people, and the birthday of the Head is the birthday of the body. Although each is called in turn, and all the sons of the Church are distinct by succession of time, nevertheless, the whole mass of the faithful spring from the font of Baptism. Just as they are crucified with Christ in His Passion, raised with Him in His Resurrection, and placed at the Father's right hand in the Ascension, so they are born with Him in the Nativity.[145]

By the grace of our Baptism, we participate in those two births of Christ, the eternal and temporal, which are the themes of the first and third Masses of Christmas Day. The participation in the two is a single reality, for, as we have seen, the temporal and human birth from the Virgin is an image, the most perfect image, of the eternal and divine begetting by the Father. We are truly 'born of God' (cf Jn 1:13). The Father regenerates us in the likeness of the only-begotten Son. Whereas the begetting of the eternal Son by the Father is by the necessity of nature, the begetting of the adopted sons is by the freedom of grace. 'For of His own will hath He begotten us by the Word of truth' (Jas 1:18).

With the Word [writes Dom Marmion], we can say 'O Father, I am thy son, I came out from thee.' The Word says it necessarily, by right, being essentially God's own Son; we only say it by grace, as adopted sons; the Word says it from all eternity; we say it in time, although the decree of this predestination is eternal; for the Word, this language denotes a relation of origin with the Father; with us, there is added a relation of dependence. But for us, as for Him, there is a true sonship: we are, by grace, God's children. The Father wills

---

[145] *In nativitate Domini, sermo* 6, no. 2; SC 22B:138ff.

that, despite our unworthiness, we should give Him the name of 'Father' [cf Gal 4:6; 1 Jn 3:1].[146]

When the Holy Spirit lavishes His grace on someone who lacks it, He brings Christmas and Easter into the soul, resurrection in the form of rebirth. Gracelessness is always spiritual deadness, whatever the cause of the lack, whether through that deprivation of grace which is an effect of Adam's sin or that loss of grace which is an effect of my sin. In their different ways, the newly baptized and the newly absolved are equally newborns: they are born anew into Christ; Christ is born anew in them. Deification can therefore be described as both our share in the life of the Trinity and as the Trinity's living presence in us. In the souls of the just, the three Divine Persons make Their home, the Father begetting the Son, and the Father and the Son breathing forth the Holy Spirit. Our Lord promises this mystical inhabitation by grace and charity when He says, 'If anyone love me, he will keep my word. And my Father will love him, and we will come to him and will make our abode with him' (Jn 14:23).

Some of the Fathers distinguish between a conception of the Word in the soul by faith and a birth of Christ by charity. St Ambrose says that we are not all like 'Mary, conceiving Christ by the Holy Spirit [and] giving birth to the Word, for some people abort the Word before they give birth. . . . Do the will of the Father if you want to be a mother of Christ.'[147] Ambrose has in mind the text from Matthew, in which our Lord says that 'whoever does the will of my Father in Heaven is my brother, and sister, and mother' (Mt 12:50). These words do not disparage our Blessed Lady; on the contrary, they reveal her towering grandeur. She more than any other created person does the will of the heavenly

---

[146] Marmion, *Christ in His Mysteries*, p. 46f.

[147] *Expositio evangelii secundum Lucam* 10, 24–25; CCSL 14:352f.

Father, and her heart is so Catholic, so dispossessed of itself
by grace, that she can open up her motherhood for the
Church and the individual Christian to share. And the glorious paradox is that that sharing is itself a motherly act. As I
said in my book *Redeemer in the Womb*: 'She shows herself to
be our Mother by drawing us, through her intercession, into
her motherhood of faith and obedience. Mary mothers us
into mothering Christ.'[148] It is through the intercession of
Mary our Mother that God our Father brings Christ to birth
by the grace of the Holy Spirit. A Jesuit poet sums up a long
tradition of mystical theology when he writes:

> Of her flesh He took flesh:
> He does take fresh and fresh,
> Though much the mystery how,
> Not flesh but spirit now
> And makes, O marvellous!
> New Nazareths in us,
> Where she shall yet conceive
> Him, morning, noon, and eve;
> New Bethlems, and He born
> There, evening, noon, and morn—
> Bethlem or Nazareth,
> Men here may draw like breath
> More Christ and baffle death;
> Who, born so, comes to be
> New self and nobler me
> In each one and each one
> More makes, when all is done,
> Both God's and Mary's Son.[149]

[148] John Saward, *Redeemer in the Womb: Jesus Living in Mary* (San Francisco, 1993), p. 115.

[149] 'The Blessed Virgin Compared to the Air We Breathe', in *The Poems of Gerard Manley Hopkins*, ed. W. H. Gardner and N. H. MacKenzie, new ed. (London, 1970), p. 95.

The soul of the deified person is a spiritual Bethlehem, a house of the Bread of Life, a cave that shines with the light of 'God's and Mary's Son' newborn. This spiritual birth, according to the theological and liturgical traditions of the Church, is the theme of the second Mass of Christmas Day, the Mass of the Dawn. Daybreak is a mingling of light and dark, and so too, according to St Thomas, is the birth of Christ in the just.[150] As something that happens in time, it is relatively easy for time-bound creatures to understand and is therefore like light; but as something spiritual, it is hard for the fleshly to grasp and is therefore more like the dark. The Introit of the Mass refers to this twilight mystery of our deification when it says, 'Light this day shall shine upon us, for a Child is born to us, and the government is upon His shoulder, and His name shall be called Wonderful, Counsellor, God the Mighty, the Father of the world to come, the Prince of Peace' (Is 9:2, 6).

Raising the Sons of Earth

The fulfillment of our deification is in the eternal Christmas of Heaven, when we hope at close hand to behold the begetting of the Son by the Father and the breathing forth of the Spirit by the Father and the Son.[151] Already by grace we are sons-in-the-Son (cf 1 Jn 3:2), and when Christ comes to raise the dead, we shall be transformed even more perfectly into His likeness (cf Phil 3:21), for then the perfection of God's image in our souls will overflow into our flesh. This final fulfillment of God's adopted sons, through the redemption of their bodies, is the liberation for which the whole created order groans (cf Rom 8:21ff.). This is the consumma-

---

[150] Cf ST 3a q. 83, a. 2, ad 2.
[151] Cf Venerable Pope Pius XII, *Mystici corporis*, no. 79.

tion of the great joy that was inaugurated in the cave in Bethlehem and first announced from the skies above Bethlehem's fields.

> Born that man no more may die,
> Born to raise the sons of earth,
> Born to give them second birth!

V

'ONCE IN ROYAL DAVID'S CITY'

The Time and Place of the Saviour's Birth

> Once in royal David's city
> Stood a lowly cattle shed,
> Where a Mother laid her baby
> In a manger for His bed.
> Mary was that Mother mild,
> Jesus Christ her little Child.[1]

Matter matters to the Christian, and so, too, do matters of when and where. Time and space, like the visible universe to which they belong, were created by God and are therefore good, very good. 'In the beginning' God makes the time of day out of the separation and union of light and dark, and the place of earth from the gathering of the waters and the surfacing of dry land (cf Gen 1:5–9f.). Thus, already as someone who believes in the creation of the world by God, the Christian has reason for respecting questions of dating and location and has no reason at all for reviling them.[2] But, as someone who believes in the assumption of human nature by

---

[1] Hymn by Mrs C. F. Alexander (EH 605).

[2] Spontaneously, out of its very heart, Christianity has generated historians such as Eusebius of Caesarea and St Bede the Venerable. In addition to his history of the English Church and people, Bede also wrote two philosophico-theological treatises on time, *De temporum ratione* (CCSL 123B) and *De temporibus* (CCSL 123C).

God, the Christian has even higher motives for venerating time and place: they have become the sanctuary of God's presence, the stage of His saving action. That is why the faithful of Jesus Christ love 'royal David's city', where He was born, and revere the day and year, in all their particularity, when the birth took place: '*Once* in royal David's city'.

But Gnostics and Manicheans do not have any time for time, nor can they find a place in their systems for place. They regard the spatiotemporal, material world as the trick of a malevolent deity and therefore feel contempt for those who fuss with maps and clocks. Evelyn Waugh gives an example of this dualistic disdain in his novel about St Helena, the mother of Constantine. The Empress, who is not yet a Christian, is at a meeting attended by the grand Roman ladies of Trèves. The speaker is a Gnostic sage, 'quite the latest thing in Higher Thought'. He turns out to be Helena's old tutor, the eunuch Marcias. Having dazzled his audience with stories about Sophia and the Aeons of light, the lecturer agrees to answer questions. Someone asks for clarification of some small detail. Then Helena puts up her hand and, 'in clear, schoolroom tone', asks, 'When and where did all this happen? And how do you know?' Marcias dismisses the difficulty of his former pupil: 'These things are beyond time and space. Their truth is integral to their proposition and by nature transcends material proof.' The enlightened eunuch has only pity for someone so hopelessly locked into time and space, the prison walls of the material world. Helena's questions— 'When? Where? How do you know?'—are 'a child's' questions. The Empress does not deny the charge: 'That is why your religion would never do for me, Marcias. If I ever found a teacher, it would have to be one who called little children to him.' Later in the day Helena sends for the Christian scholar Lactantius and debriefs him about the lecture: 'I couldn't understand a word he said. It's all bosh, isn't it?'

Lactantius leaves Helena in no doubt: 'All complete bosh, your Majesty.'³ Helena may not yet be a Christian, but her no-nonsense mind is already well disposed for receiving the grace of Christian Faith. She is repelled by the Gnostic inter- mediaries and their complicated lessons for the learned, but her heart reaches out in expectation of the true God who reveals His mysteries to children. The down-to-earth daugh- ter of King Coel of Colchester has no desire to fly from the flesh to the high spheres of Pseudo-Gnosis but seems ready to welcome a God who would descend into flesh and redeem the lowly sites and seasons of earth. And when the time of her own life has run its course, her Catholic Faith, by a sure instinct, seeks out the places hallowed by God's incarnate presence, even the wood to which His body was nailed. St Helena discards the bosh and twaddle of myth for the beauty and truth of the Gospel.⁴

Following, then, the regal path of St Helena, we shall meditate in this chapter on the time and place in which Christ was born. Like St Thomas, we shall consider, accord- ing to the literal sense of the Gospel texts, the appropriate- ness of this special moment of history and this particular patch of earth. But we shall also consider their spiritual sense, that is, those other realities of Divine Revelation to which, by God's providence, this time and this place refer.

1. The Place of Our Saviour's Birth

'Every sensible body', says St Thomas, 'has a natural aptitude to be in some place.'⁵ All material substances have extension,

³ Evelyn Waugh, *Helena: A Novel* (Boston, 1950), pp. 121ff.
⁴ 'Early writers divide the credit for [the] foundation [of the first church of the Nativity] between Constantine himself and his mother the Empress Hel- ena' (R. W. Hamilton, *The Church of the Nativity, Bethlehem: A Guide* [Jerusalem, 1947], p. 11).
⁵ *In Physica* lib. 3, lect. 9, no. 2.

that is, parts set alongside each other in space. That is why the Divine Word cannot take upon Him a true human body without taking up position in a certain place. But, in coming to be here as man, He did not move from where He exists eternally as God. The Son of God comes down from Heaven, 'not as if His divine nature ceased to be in Heaven, but because He began to be in a new way here below, that is, in the assumed nature'.[6]

The first place in which the Son of God lived on earth was the womb of His Mother, whose home was in Nazareth in Galilee.

> His first step is in Nazareth, and His first repose is in the Virgin of Nazareth. This is the first step of the Son of God in coming into the world. This is His first dwelling-place, when He takes flesh in the Virgin and reposes in her womb for the space of nine full months.[7]

Carried in His Mother's womb, the Incarnate Son moves on to the hometown of Elizabeth and Zechariah. Then, after the nine months of waiting are ended, He comes forth and finds Himself in Bethlehem, the city of David. Here 'He makes Himself visible to our eyes, and displays Himself to the sight and enjoyment of His people; the angels come and fall down at His feet, the shepherds hasten to Him, the kings come.' In the Church of the Nativity, the second downward step of the Son of God into this world is commemorated with a silver star bearing the inscription *Hic de Virgine Maria Jesus Christus natus est*, 'Jesus Christ was born of the Virgin Mary *here*'—here on the site of the stable cave, in Bethlehem, in the land of Judea, in an obscure corner of the vast Roman empire. 'Look, in this little hole in the ground the Creator of the heavens was born. *Here* He was wrapped in swaddling

---

[6] ST 3a q. 5, a. 2, ad 1.
[7] Pierre de Bérulle, *Vie de Jésus*, chap. 6, nos. 21f.; OCB 433–34.

clothes; *here* He was seen by the shepherds; *here* He was pointed out by the star; *here* He was adored by the wise men.'[8] In the Byzantine liturgy, the Church addresses these places as if they were persons and urges them to welcome Christ, the Word through whom all things at first were made, who now comes at last in the flesh to make all things new:

> Make ready, O cave; the Virgin draws nigh to give birth. Be glad and rejoice, O Bethlehem, land of Judah, for from thee our Lord has shone forth as the dawn. Hearken, ye mountains and hills and all ye lands round about Judea: for Christ comes in His love for mankind, to save the man He fashioned.[9]

Judea

The Son of God is born as a Jew in Judea, the land in southern Palestine reoccupied by the Jews after their return from Babylon. St Bernard notices that the evangelist adds the phrase 'of Judea' when he announces the birth in Bethlehem, for this birth is the fulfillment of the promise once made about Judea to the Fathers: 'The sceptre shall not be taken away from Judea, nor a ruler from his thigh, till He come that is to be sent, and He shall be the expectation of nations' (Gen 49:10).

> Salvation is indeed from the Jews, but it extends to the ends of the earth. 'Judah', it says, 'thee shall thy brethren praise. Thy hands shall be on the necks of thy enemies' (Gen 49:8), which we never read concerning the original Judah, but which we do see fulfilled in Christ. For He is the lion of the tribe of Judah, concerning whom it is added: 'Judah is a lion's whelp; to the prey', it says, 'my son, thou art gone up'

---

[8] *Epistola* 46, no. 10; PL 22:490.
[9] Forefeast of the Nativity of Christ, *Menaion*, p. 201.

(Gen 49:9). The great predator is Christ, who, before He knows how to call anyone father and mother, has plundered Samaria.[10]

The Lamb of God is the Lion of Judah. He assumes the nature, not of any species of the Seraphim, but of the seed of Abraham (cf Heb 2:16). In fidelity to the law that He Himself imposed upon Abraham and His descendants, He is circumcised on the eighth day (cf Lk 2:21; Gen 17:10) and becomes bar mitzvah, a son of the commandment, in his twelfth year (cf Lk 2:42). The flesh of the Son of God is fashioned from Jewish blood, more exactly from the immaculate blood of the Hebrew maiden Mary. Physically through her and legally through Joseph, He has kinship with the Patriarchs and the Prophets: the Son of God and Son of Mary is Son of David, Son of Abraham (cf Mt 1:1). Quoting the Apostle, who said that 'of the Jews according to the flesh is He who is over all things, God blessed for ever' (Rom 9:5), St Thomas reminds us that God the Son is only 'of the Jews' through the Blessed Virgin.[11] The back He gave in His Passion to the smiters, and the cheeks He gave to 'those who pulled out the beard' (cf Is 50:6), are the back and the cheeks He received 'from Mary of the tribe of Judah, and what He received from Jewry He gave to Jews to strike and flog'.[12] The Fathers have no doubt: our Lord is 'of the seed of David by the birth He has from Mary'.[13] Jesse is the root, David the tree, Mary the branch and Jesus the flower the branch

[10] *In vigilia nativitatis Domini, sermo* 1, no. 4; L-R 4:200f.

[11] Cf ST 3a q. 35, a. 4.

[12] St Eulogius of Alexandria, *Sermo in ramos palmarum* 10; PG 86B:2930.

[13] St Irenaeus, *Adversus haereses* lib. 3, cap. 16, no. 3; PG 7:922B. Even earlier in the second century, St Justin Martyr says that the Son of God is 'born, by the will of the Father, of a virgin of the race of Abraham, of the tribe of Judah, and of the stock of David' (*Dialogus cum Tryphone Iudaeo* no. 43; PG 6:568A). St Leo calls our Lady 'the royal Virgin of David's stock' (*In nativitate Domini, sermo* 1, no. 1; SC 22B:68).

brought forth. St Matthew traces the genealogy through St Joseph not only because God wanted to ratify a Jewish custom but also because He 'preferred to be called "the carpenter's son" rather than allow His Mother to be stoned on suspicion of adultery'.[14] According to the Law, a man must marry within his own tribe (cf Num 36:6f.). Thus, if Joseph is of the house and lineage of David, then so, too, is Mary, and so, too, through Mary, is Jesus.[15] Moreover, by calling Him 'Son of Abraham' as well as 'Son of David', the Evangelist ascribes to Christ the perfection of all the sacred offices of the Old Testament, for Abraham was prophet and priest, while David was prophet and king.[16]

Jewry, the land and the people of the Jews, is blessed above all others, for from them comes Christ according to the flesh (cf Rom 9:5). As Cardinal Bérulle says: 'Just as this people is miraculous in its birth, originating as it does from two barren people, so it is miraculous in its progress and conservation.' The Holy Land is promised and given to them 'not so much for the people themselves as for the Messiah who is to be born among them, that is, to receive Him and give Him a lodging on earth, to be the seat of His empire, and to be as it were the centre of His law, of His state, and of His myster-

[14] *Rationale* lib. 6, cap. 13, no. 14; 140A:185.
[15] *Lectura super Matthaeum*, cap. 1, lect. 4. Baldwin of Canterbury, twelfth-century Cistercian and Archbishop of Canterbury, says that, since the Blessed Virgin was of the seed of David, her Divine Son could be seedlessly of that same Davidic seed (see *Sermo* 13, *In annuntiatione Sanctae Mariae*, no. 42; CCCM 99:206).
[16] 'He . . . calls Christ the Son of both [Abraham and David], to show that in Him was fulfilled the promise made to both. Also because Christ was to have three dignities: king, prophet, priest. Now Abraham was prophet and priest: priest, because God says to him, "Take a heifer" (cf Gen 15:9); and prophet, because the Lord said to Abimelech concerning him, "He is a prophet, and shall pray for thee" (cf Gen 20:7). David was king and prophet, but not priest. He is therefore expressly called the Son of both [Abraham and David], so that the threefold dignity of His forefathers might be recognized by hereditary right in Christ' (St John Chrysostom, CA 1, 11).

ies'. From the call of Abraham onwards, the very being of the Hebrews is prophetic: it speaks to the world of the one true God and His loving plan for man's salvation:

> The whole state of the Jews is prophetic, predictive, announcing, publishing in the world the world's salvation. The whole body of this republic is turned into a voice and speaks to the universe of the One who is to come to save it, and this whole people serves only to prepare the world to receive Him.[17]

When we look upon the Jews, then, we must see them in relation to Jesus, who is their Messiah and glory and the light to lighten the Gentiles:

> Abraham is His father; this people are His subjects; this promised land is His dwelling place and first empire. With this thought in mind, let us cast a glance of love and respect at this land, for it is the land of Jesus: it is the land where He is to live and to die, the land where He wants to establish His glory. If He is to be announced, it will be in Nazareth; if He is to be born, it will be in Bethlehem. If He is to be offered and presented to the eternal Father, it will be in the Temple. If He is to live, it will be in Judea. If He is to be nursed and raised, it will be in Galilee. If He is to die, it will be in Jerusalem; if He is to go up into Heaven, it will be on the Mount of Olives. If He is to establish His glory and His empire, it will be in the house of Jacob, in the family of Judah. If He is to give the Law to the universe, it will be from Sion: 'The Law shall come forth from Sion' (Is 2:3).[18]

With sorrow, not anger, Bérulle recalls that Judea did not recognize the blessing, the privilege of matchless grandeur, that was bestowed upon her: she did not know the time of her visitation (cf Lk 19:44). From the eyes of Jesus Himself

---

[17] *Vie de Jésus*, Préambule, chap. 21; OCB 425.
[18] Ibid., chaps. 18 and 19; OCB 424f.

her foolish blindness will draw tears that promise final redemption:

> One day your woe will draw tears from the eyes of your
> Saviour and Lord. In the midst of His triumph He will forget
> Himself and His glory, in order to remember you and your
> woe, and He will say one day with tears: 'If thou also hadst
> known, and that in this thy day, the things that are to thy
> peace' (Lk 19:42).[19]

It is precisely because the existence of the Jews is prophetic
(this people would not exist were it not for their election by
God) that the ungodly in every age have waged war against
them. Take the case of Hegel. Though not strictly atheistic,
his grandiose system is pantheistic in its general tendency.
God, Absolute Spirit, is inseparable from the process of the
world. By contrast, the revelation made to the Jews affirms
before all else that the Lord God of Israel is not the world or
a part of the world but the transcendent Creator of the world
and everything in it. Such a religion, to which even the
ethnic existence of those who profess it bears witness, is of
necessity an affront to the totalitarian pantheism of Hegel.
Almost alone among twentieth-century scholars, Balthasar
perceived and exposed this systematic anti-Semitism at the
heart of Germany's most influential philosopher of the nineteenth century:

> [T]his reconciliation of the Greek spirit with the Gospel has
> one precondition: the complete elimination of the Jewish
> dimension. In his insatiable and hateful polemic against the
> Old Testament, Hegel pursues the one thing for which he
> has no use in his otherwise all-reconciling system: the sovereign
> and lordly elevation of God above the world, who acts,
> elects and rejects in complete freedom of will; and thus he
> has no use either for the distinctively Old Testament form of

[19] Ibid.

the divine glory: the *Kabôd*. . . . 'The Jewish principle of opposition' pulls God and the world apart.[20]

What the Hebrew nation did imperfectly as God's people, the Hebrew maiden Mary does perfectly as God's Mother: by the virginity of her soul and body, she manifests 'the sovereign and lordly elevation of God above the world', or, as she herself sings, she 'magnifies the Lord' and the mighty things He can do when a humble handmaid lets Him act within her (cf Lk 1:46ff.). In thought and reality, the Blessed Virgin of Nazareth, our Lady of Zion, Israel's fairest flower, is inseparable from her people. Those who would cut off Jesus from the Jews, who would oppose, as Luther opposed, Law and Gospel, are led inevitably to weaken the bond of Jesus with Mary.[21] It comes as no surprise, therefore, to discover that post-Hegelian Biblical criticism is marked by both an a priori rejection of the Virginal Conception and a tendency to exaggerate the discontinuity between the Old and New Testaments.[22] Anti-Semitic prejudice and the anti-Marian impulse regularly coincide in the Protestant mind. Once again it is Balthasar who has perceived the truth of this matter:

[20] *Glory of the Lord: A Theological Aesthetics*, vol. 5, *The Realm of Metaphysics in the Modern Age*, ET (San Francisco, 1991), pp. 579–80.

[21] In his treatise on *How Christians Regard Moses* (1525), Luther writes: '[I]f anyone confronts you with Moses and his commandments, and wants to compel you to keep them, simply answer, "Go to the Jews with your Moses; I am no Jew". . . . I dismiss the commandments given to the people of Israel': *Luther's Works*, vol. 35, *Word and Sacrament*, ed. E. T. Bachmann, I, ET (Philadelphia, 1960), p. 166. It is interesting to note that, in his early sermons on the Magnificat (1521), in which a devotion to our Lady and a willingness to invoke her intercession are still evident, there is also a much more kindly view of the Jews than will be displayed later: 'Tell them the truth in all kindness' (ibid., vol. 21, *The Sermon on the Mount and The Magnificat*, ed. J. Pelikan, ET [St Louis, 1956], p. 355).

[22] This tendency is noticeable in the enormously influential *Theological Dictionary of the New Testament*, whose editor, the Lutheran scholar Gerhard Kittel, was an enthusiastic Nazi.

Something else is characteristic of the Protestant deficiency: the absence of Mariology is parallel to that Lutheran rift between the Law and the Gospel which in the long run implies anti-Semitism.

He then restates the truth presupposed by his negative judgment about Protestantism as a positive judgment about Judaism and our Lady:

In Mary . . . the *whole faith of Israel*, beginning with the unprecedented faith of Abraham, is gathered, a faith that tends toward Christ and remains a paradigm for Christians. . . . Woman, as Synagogue-Mary-Church, is the inseparable unity of that which makes it possible for the Word of God to take on the being of the world, in virtue of the natural-supernatural fruitfulness given to her.[23]

The unity-in-difference between Creator and creature, which 'Synagogue-Mary-Church' reveals, is the truth against which the whole of German Protestant thought, from Luther to Hegel, sets its face. During the Middle Ages, among those who invoked the Lily of Israel and Star of Jacob, the true Rebecca and Rachel, the antitype of Miriam, anti-Semitism could only ever be an aberration, a deplorable reversion to a sub-Christian, indeed pre-Christian prejudice. However, in the modern age, once Law and Gospel have been estranged and love for the Messiah set at odds with devotion to His Mother, anti-Semitism can be erected, as it was by Luther and Hegel, as a fundamental principle of philosophy and theology. The medievals most disposed to devotion to our Lady were often those most inclined to the defence of her people. St Bernard, the eloquent panegyrist of Mary, was also an heroic protector of the Jews. To this day, Bernard is a name honoured in Israel in remembrance of the

---

[23] 'Mary–Church–Office', in *A Short Primer for Unsettled Laymen*, ET (San Francisco, 1985), pp. 89f.

noble Gentile who in 1146 rose up from his sickbed to stop the persecution of the Jews of the Rhineland.[24] Rabbi Joshua Ben-Meir remembered him as saying, 'Touch not the Hebrews. Speak to them with kindness, for they are of the flesh and bone of the Messiah: to harm them is to wound the Saviour in the apple of His eye.'[25] Something similar happened at the beginning of the twentieth century. In the years when the French people were violently divided on the Dreyfus question, Léon Bloy, the apostle of devotion to our Lady of La Salette, gave a Mariological explanation for the gravity of the sin of hatred of the Jews: 'Anti-Semitism . . . is the most horrible blow that our Lord has received in His everlasting Passion. It is the bloodiest and the most unforgivable, because He receives it on the Face of His Mother and from the hand of Christians.'[26] William of Newburgh, a medieval English Augustinian much influenced by the Cistercians, in his commentary on the Song of Songs, presents our Lady as in a special way the mother and advocate of her people, the old Israel:

[T]he merits of the merciful Mother greatly plead for the salvation of the people of Israel. Think of the great persistence of pious prayers with which she daily intercedes with her almighty Son for her race. She doubtless forgets that her sweet Son was so cruelly killed by them, and considers only that the Victim of salvation was taken from them. 'Remember, my Son,' she says, 'that from them thou didst take the flesh in and by which thou didst work salvation in the midst

[24] Cf *The Letters of St Bernard of Clairvaux*, no. 393, To Henry, Bishop of Mainz; ET by B. Scott-James, new ed. (Stroud, 1998), p. 465.

[25] Cited in M. R. Simon, OCSO, *The Glory of Thy People: The Story of a Conversion* (New York, 1954), p. v. Father Simon, a convert from Judaism, dedicates his book to St Bernard, 'Father of Contemplatives and Protector of Jews' (ibid.).

[26] *Journal*, vol. 2, 1907–1917 (Paris, 1999), p. 114.

of the earth, and that they whose flesh thou didst not disdain must partake of thy spiritual goods.' [27]

Bethlehem

The Son of God was born as man in Bethlehem, 'royal David's city'. Eight centuries before, Micah had prophesied the glory that was coming to this humble town: 'And thou, Bethlehem, Ephrata, are a little one among the thousands of Juda; out of thee shall He come forth unto me that is to be the ruler in Israel; and His going forth is from the beginning, from the days of eternity' (Mic 5:2). St John Chrysostom points out the exactness of the prophecy: Micah says that the Messiah will 'come forth' out of Bethlehem, for Christ is born there but does not stay there.[28] 'Micah, in agreement [with the other prophets], reveals the One who came from Bethlehem and Judea and was destined from eternity to be the ruler in Israel, through whom the transformation (*katallagê*) of the cosmos takes place, when He purges us of our sins and guides us to a better destiny.' [29]

In Bethlehem the Incarnate Word continues what He began in Nazareth, the transfiguration of the cosmos that was brought into being, and is ever conserved in being through Him. Listen to the praise it receives from St Romanos, the prince of Greek hymnody:

> Bethlehem has re-opened Eden. Let us go and see. We have delights in a hidden place (cf 1 Chron 9:18). In the cave, we shall regain the goods of Paradise. There appeared the unwatered root whence flowered forgiveness. There again was

[27] J. C. Gorman, ed., *William of Newburgh's Explanatio sacri epithalamii in matrem sponsi: A Commentary on the Canticle of Canticles* (Fribourg, 1960), p. 152.

[28] Cf CA 1, 71.

[29] Cosmas Indicopleustes (sixth-century Christian geographer), *Christian Topography*, bk. 5, no. 147; SC 159:215.

found the undug well that David once sought for refreshment. There a virgin, by her childbearing, quenched the thirst of Adam and the thirst of David. Let us hasten to the place where the little Child is born who is God before the ages.[30]

For the sake of the Child who is God before the ages, the saints love Bethlehem. St Jerome called it 'the most glorious place on earth'.[31] His spiritual daughter, St Paula, swore that in the cave of the Nativity, 'with the eyes of faith', she had seen 'the Infant wrapped in swaddling clothes, the Lord crying in the manger, the Magi worshipping, the star shining down, the devoted foster-father, and the shepherds coming by night to see the word that had come to pass (cf Lk 2:15)'.[32] When St Francis spoke of the Lord Jesus, he would often call Him simply 'the Babe of Bethlehem', and when he uttered the word 'Bethlehem', his voice was more like the bleating of a sheep.[33]

If the saints, who have orthodox and living faith in Christ, love Bethlehem, the heretics, who lack faith, despise or overlook it. In the middle of the fifth century, Pope St Leo the Great wrote to Juvenal, Bishop of Jerusalem, rejoicing that Juvenal had returned to orthodoxy but grieving over his previous lapse into the heresy of Eutyches, who taught that in Christ the divine nature swallowed up the human. What Juvenal had done was nothing less than the denial of our Lord Jesus Christ according to the flesh (cf 2 Jn 7). Now St Leo goes on to say that a Christian who lives in Jerusalem, as Juvenal does, has even less excuse than others do for falling into the Monophysite heresy, since 'he is taught to know the power of the Gospel not only by the statements in texts but also by the testimony of places.'

[30] St Romanos the Melodist, *Hymn 1 on the Nativity*;, no. 1; SC 110:50.

[31] *Epistola* 58, no. 3; PL 22:581.

[32] *Epistola* 108, *Ad Eustochium*, no. 10; PL 22:884.

[33] See p. 35.

Make use, therefore, beloved brother, of these invincible proofs of the Catholic faith and defend the preaching of the Evangelists by the testimony of the holy places in which you live. In your country is Bethlehem, in which the Saviour, the Child born of the Virgin of the house of David, has shone forth, whom, wrapped in swaddling clothes, the manger of the crowded inn received.[34]

Eternal Wisdom Incarnate had some good reasons for wanting to be born in Bethlehem. St Thomas mentions two of them. First, He wanted to be born in the city where David was born 'so that the promise [made to David] would be shown to have been fulfilled from the very place of his birth'. Secondly, as St Gregory the Great says, ' "Bethlehem" means "house of bread". Now it is Christ Himself who said, "I am the Living Bread, which came down from Heaven" (cf Jn 6:41).'[35] The City of David is thus the birthplace of the Eucharist. 'The place He was born', says St Bede, 'is rightly called the "House of Bread", because He came down from Heaven to earth to give us the food of heavenly life and to satisfy us with the flavour of eternal sweetness.'[36] Since the Church contains within her the Bread of Life, she can be called 'the perpetual Bethlehem'.[37]

Through the Holy Eucharist every Catholic church becomes a Bethlehem. Each is a mystery of a real but hidden presence. In the manger the Son hid His Godhead beneath the dwindled form of infancy, and on the altar, beneath the lowly species of bread, even His manhood eludes the gaze of men. In both states of humility the eternal Son does deeds of infinite grandeur.

---

[34] *Epistola* 139, nos. 1- 2; PL 54:1105A.

[35] Cf ST 3a q. 35, a. 7.

[36] *Homelia* I, 6, *In Nativitate Domini*; CCSL 122:40.

[37] *Des heiligen Ephraem des Syrers Hymnen de Nativitate (Epiphania)* 25, no. 6; CSCO 187, *Scriptores Syri* 83; GT, E. Beck OSB (Louvain, 1959), p. 117.

The Infant Jesus, the joy of the Father and our joy, is for ever there, and in Him the Father declared, with rare expletive, that He was *well* pleased. Still, on the altar and in the tabernacle, the Babe of Bethlehem is increasing the glory of the Father. Still is He giving breadth and space to His Father's love by the multitude of the redeemed. Still is He furnishing His Father with new opportunities of communicating His Paternity to new children and in new graces. . . . Still is every Mass illustrating all the Father's perfections in that work of His predilection, the work of abbreviating His long, eternally spoken, and unbrokenly uttered Word.[38]

In his commentary on St Matthew's Gospel, St Thomas gives another reason for our Lord's choice of a birthplace. Bethlehem was chosen for the Nativity, as Jerusalem was chosen for the Passion, in order to avoid worldly glory, for worldlings like grand places for their birth, but not for their suffering. Thus our Lord reveals His wisdom as well as His humility. He is born in Bethlehem, the least among the thousands of Judea, 'in order to confirm His teaching and to show its truth, for if He had been born in some great city, the power of His teaching would have been ascribed to human power'.[39] The very smallness and obscurity of Bethlehem help to dispose the minds of men for perceiving the grandeur and clarity of Christ's teaching and for discovering the source of its authority in the truth of His Divinity. In the *Summa*, St Thomas quotes, in support of this claim, a sermon attributed to Theodotus of Ancyra and preached at the Council of Ephesus:

Had He chosen the great city of Rome, men would have reckoned that the change in the world was due to the power of her citizens. Had He been the Emperor's son, they would have ascribed His success to imperial power. But that we

[38] *Bethlehem*, pp. 487f.
[39] *Lectura super Matthaeum*, cap. 2, lect. 2.

might acknowledge that it was the Godhead that transformed the world, He chose a poor young woman to be His Mother and a birthplace even poorer.[40]

At Ephesus, the Fathers reaffirmed, against Nestorius, the Catholic truth that the Child born of the Virgin is not a mere man raised up to divine glory but the true God, the almighty Word, who has humbled Himself to human infirmity.[41] It was fitting, therefore, for Theodotus to preach about the power of the Son's Divinity transforming the world through the humble circumstances of His human life. Even before He will show it through the effects of His grace in the saints, Christ reveals, in the mystery of His own birth, that 'power is made perfect in infirmity' (cf 2 Cor 12:9).

The Stable Cave

Our Lord is born in the little town of Bethlehem, and within that little town He is born outside of a proper house, in a 'lowly cattle shed', for 'there was no room in the inn' (Lk 2:7). According to St Bede, the humiliations of His birthplace are freely assumed for the sake òf the 'wonderful exchange':

> He who sits at His Father's right hand finds no room in an inn, that He might prepare for us in His Father's house many mansions. He is born, not in His Father's house, but in an inn and by the wayside, because through the mystery of the Incarnation He was made the way by which to bring us to our country, where we shall enjoy the truth and the life.[42]

[40] ST 3a q. 35, a. 7, ad 3.

[41] 'It was not that an ordinary man was first born of the Blessed Virgin, on whom afterwards the Word came down. No, what we say is that, having been united to the flesh from the womb, [the eternal Word] has undergone birth in the flesh, making the birth in the flesh His own' (*Epistola 2 ad Nestorium*; DS 251).

[42] CA 3, 68.

St Bede, who never left his native Northumbria, has left us a vivid description of the place of the Nativity taken from an account written by Adamnan, Abbot of Iona:

> Bethlehem, the city of David, is situated on a narrow ridge, compassed with valleys on every side. . . . In the east corner there is a kind of natural grotto. Its outer part is said to be the place of our Lord's Nativity; the inner is called the manger of the Lord. The interior of the cave is covered with precious marble over the place where our Lord is said to have been born, and above it stands a great church of the Blessed Virgin Mary.[43]

The cave mentioned by Bede was the kind of fissure in the rock that farmers in many cultures have used as shelter for their animals. The earliest reference to this stable cave of the Nativity is in the writings of St Justin Martyr, who was a Palestinian Christian of the second century.[44] Each new generation in the local Church retained and passed on the memory of where the Saviour was born. 'In Bethlehem they show you the cave where He was born', says Origen, 'and in the cave the manger where He was wrapped in swaddling clothes . . . and the rumour in those places, even among the enemies of the faith, is that this is indeed the cave in which Jesus was born, He whom Christians worship and admire.' [45] Long after the birth, during the reign of Hadrian, the cave of the Nativity, like the other holy places, suffered the humiliation of being used for heathen fertility rites—in the case of Bethlehem, in honour of the lover of Venus, Adonis, who was slain by a wild boar.[46] And so, for nearly a century, before

---

[43] *Historia ecclesiastica gentis anglorum* lib. 5, cap. 16; PL 195:256C.

[44] '[W]hen the Child was born in Bethlehem, since Joseph could not find a lodging in that village, he took up his quarters in a certain cave near the village; and while they were there, Mary brought forth the Christ and placed Him in a manger, and here the Magi who came from Arabia found Him' (*Dialogus cum Tryphone Iudaeo* no. 78; PG 6:657D–660A).

[45] Origen, *Contra Celsum* lib. 1, cap. 51; PG 11:756A.

Helena's work of purgation and reclamation, Providence permitted the place of the Saviour's Virgin Birth to be defiled by heathen depravity. Now every example of the divine permission of human wickedness is always an inscrutable mystery, and so we should not expect in this life to perceive all of the good that God was able to bring out of this evil done by man. But this much at least should be evident: the profanation of Bethlehem proves this fallen world's desperate need for the truth and grace of Jesus Christ and the devil's determination to expropriate what is good and to use it for his own wicked ends.

St Gregory of Nyssa regards the cave as an outward sign of that inward state of fallen human nature which the Son of God has become man in order to heal or overcome: 'The Lord is born in a cave? Think of it as representing our life, blind, dark, and subterranean, in which One is born who shows Himself to men sunk in darkness and the shadow of death.' [47] Talk of caves makes one think of Plato and the metaphor of the cave in the *Republic*. Schooled by Aristotle and St Thomas, we know that that passage does not offer an adequate account of the permanent nature of human knowing, but we cannot deny that it is an apt description of the present *condition* of human knowing. As we struggle to attain the truth, it may well seem as if we are only glimpsing flickering shadows on the wall. The fallen mind of man is

[46] 'From the time of Hadrian to the reign of Constantine, for about one hundred and eighty years, there was an image of Jupiter in the place of the Resurrection. On the rock of the Cross the pagans placed and worshipped a marble statue of Venus. The authors of the persecution reckoned that they would destroy our faith in the Cross and Resurrection, if the holy places were polluted by idols. And over our dear Bethlehem, the most glorious place on earth, of which the Psalmist sings, "Truth has sprung from the earth", the grove of Thamuz, that is, of Adonis, cast its shadow, and in the cave, where once the Christ Child cried, the lover of Venus was bewailed' (*Epistola* 58, no. 3; PL 32:581).

[47] *Oratio in diem natalem Christi*; PG 46:1141C.

not, as Luther thought, altogether bereft of the truth, but it has been wounded through Adam's loss of the preternatural knowledge with which he was originally endowed, and so it finds it hard to apprehend even naturally accessible religious and moral truth. Even for those truths, we have a moral need for the brilliance of Divine Revelation.[48] And so the presence in the cave of the Father's Word and Splendour is the beginning of the enlightening of this benighted world. 'And the light shines in darkness, a darkness which was not able to master it' (Knox Jn 1:5).

In Byzantine art, the cave in the icons of the Nativity is made to resemble the jaws of Hades in the icons of the Descent into Hell [see art plate 7]. The same semicircle of darkness reappears in the icons of the Baptism of our Lord. Against all naturalistic perspective, the river Jordan is painted as a vertical backdrop of black-blue. Thus the descent of the Father's beloved Son into the waters of the Jordan appears as an announcement and promise of His descent into the waters of death.[49] At the beginning of His public ministry, in obedience to the Father and in docility to the Holy Spirit's prompting, the sinless Son-made-man accepts from John's hands a baptism intended for sinners. Likewise, later, when the work of preaching and healing is ended, He takes upon Himself the vast mass of human wickedness in order to make atonement for it by the outpouring of His most precious blood.

The Manger

A manger, a trough for the feeding of livestock, was the only cradle that Mary could find for her newborn Child, the

---

[48] Cf First Vatican Council, Dogmatic Constitution on the Catholic Faith, *Dei Filius*, cap. 2; DS 3005.

[49] See L. Ouspensky and V. Lossky, *The Meaning of Icons*, ET, new ed. (Crestwood, 1982), pp. 157–65, 180–88.

Incarnate Creator: 'And she brought forth her firstborn Son and wrapped Him up in swaddling clothes and laid Him in a manger, because there was no room for them in the inn' (Lk 2:7). According to St Bede, our Lord willed this makeshift bed as a type of the Eucharist: 'It was on account of the chief Sacrament that, when He was born, He chose as a throne for Himself a manger, where animals usually come to feed. He was already leaving a hint that at the most sacred table of the altar He would refresh all the faithful with the mysteries of His Incarnation.'[50] When it comes to the words 'and laid Him in a manger', the Gloss adds the comment, 'that is, the Body of Christ upon the altar'.[51] A late fourteenth-century diptych from the Meuse-Rhine region depicts the Holy Child asleep in a sheaf of corn.[52] The message is plain: just as God the Son once took upon Himself the humble form of infancy and was cradled in a manger, so now the same Son, true God and true man, makes Himself present, is offered by the priest and received by the faithful, beneath the humble form of bread. St Bonaventure quotes the Gloss and draws from it an important conclusion: 'He is placed in a manger, that is, "on the altar", where Christ in the species of bread is offered in His divinity and humanity. Thus He is food or bread not only by reason of His divinity, but also by reason of His humanity. He lies in the manger like hay for the simple.'[53] Day by day, therefore, in the Most Holy Sacrament of the Altar, the sons of the Church can 'find the Child wrapped in swaddling clothes and placed in a manger'.[54] As an expression of the continuity between the Eucharist and

[50] St Bede, *Homilia* I, 6, *In nativitate Domini*; CCSL 122:41f.

[51] *Glossa in evangelium Lucae*; PL 114:896.

[52] G. Schiller, *The Iconography of Christian Art*, ET, vol. 1 (London, 1971), fig. 184.

[53] *In Epiphania Domini*, sermo 3; Q IX:158A.

[54] Cf Blessed Guerric of Igny, *In nativitate Domini*, sermo 5, no. 5; SC 166:234.

the Incarnation, it was once a custom at Midnight Mass in St Mary Major's in Rome to lay the consecrated Host in the relic of the Crib.[55] Many medieval representations of the Nativity make the manger look like an altar, as if to say, 'The divine Child lying here is already a priest, already designated as the victim by whose self-oblation atonement will be made for all the sins of mankind.'

2. The Time of Our Saviour's Birth

Time is bound up with change. Aristotle defines it as the 'number [or measure] of movement [or change] according to before and after',[56] or even more succinctly as 'the principle of corruption'. Wherever there is movement or change, there is succession, the shift from past to future: what could be, now is, and what was, is no more. St Augustine confessed that he could not say what time was, but he knew enough to assert that 'if nothing passed, there would be no past time; and if nothing were going to happen, there would be no future time; and if nothing *were*, there would be no present time.' The present moment stands between two kinds of non-being: the past, which no longer is, and the future, which is not yet. The present does not rest, even for a moment. If it did, if it ceased to pass into the past, it would be, not time, but eternity, the now that stands still. As the poet suggests, we have to 'gather . . . rosebuds while [we] may', because 'Old Time is still a-flying'.[57] That is why Augustine said of time that 'it tends to non-being'.[58] The passing of days and minutes is the persistent confirmation of

[55] Schiller, *Iconography*, vol. 1, p. 63.

[56] ST 1a q. 10, a. 1; cf Aristotle, *Physics* 4, 11; 220a25.

[57] Robert Herrick, 'To the Virgins, to Make Much of Time', in *The Poetical Works of Robert Herrick*, ed. L. C. Martin (Oxford, 1956), p. 84.

[58] *Confessiones* lib. 11, cap. 14, no. 17; PL 32:816.

our essential creaturely frailty, that abyss of non-being over which our being is poised by the conserving act of God. He Who Is, the Pure Act, is eternal and unchangeable; we who are not, who were created out of nothing and are ever poised between the two nothingnesses of past and future, are temporal and changeable.[59]

And into what St Bede called 'the fleeting and wave-tossed course of time'[60] came the changeless and everlasting Word. Without abandoning His eternity, He took upon Himself our temporality in order to make us temporal men partakers by glory of the eternity that is His with the Father and the Holy Spirit. 'O Word, who dost exist before time, through whom time was made, who wast born in time even though thou art life eternal: thou dost call those who exist in time and make them eternal.'[61] As Pope John Paul II says:

> God's revelation implants itself into time and the annals of history. The Incarnation of Jesus Christ took place in the 'fullness of time' (Gal 4:4). Therefore, two thousand years

[59] Even the angels do not altogether transcend time. If we look simply at what they are, at the incorruptible spirituality of their nature, then we are forced to conclude that they do not change and therefore have no past or future. But if we take account of the angels' acts of understanding and affection, if we remember that first the angels were created in a state of pilgrimage and probation, and that only after their choice for or against God, did they rise up to Heaven or fall down into Hell, then we cannot fail to see that the angels know change and are therefore subject to a kind of time. According to St Thomas, spiritual creatures *in their natural being* are measured by what he and the other Schoolmen call 'aeviternity' (*aevum*), in which the unchangeable is joined to the mutable; *in their acts of understanding and affection*, in which there is succession, they are measured by time; and *in their enjoyment of the Beatific Vision*, they participate in the divine eternity (see ST 1a q. 10, a. 5, ad 1). Father P.-M. Emonet OP says of a hyacinth: 'Being temporal, its being is an apparition between two nothingnesses—the nothingness of before and the nothingness of after' (*The Dearest Freshness Deep Down Things: An Introduction to the Philosophy of Being*, ET [New York, 1999], p. 71).

[60] F. Wallis, ed., *Bede: The Reckoning of Time*, cap. 71 (Liverpool, 1999), p. 249.

[61] St Augustine, *Enarratio in psalmum 101*, no. 10; PL 36:1311.

after that event, we judge it necessary forcefully to assert: 'In the Christian faith, time has a special gravity'. It is within time that the whole work of creation and salvation is brought to light; and it emerges clearly above all that, with the Incarnation of the Son of God, our life is even now a foretaste of the fulfilment of time which is to come (cf Heb. 1:2).[62]

In the Eternal Word Incarnate time is redeemed (cf Eph 5:16). He is 'yesterday and today, the beginning and the end, Alpha and Omega, and to Him belong the times and all the ages'.[63] Christ our Lord leads the ages of man to their final end, to that Last Day which will be the beginning of the unending eighth day of risen glory. In the General Judgment, the complex fabric of human history, all the intricate interweavings by which Providence in each hour brings good out of the evil done by creatures, will be disclosed as a tapestry of the utmost beauty. And even now, when the Last Day remains a hope for the future, time, through the Incarnation, possesses a new depth and dignity. 'Behold, now is the acceptable time; behold now is the day of salvation' (2 Cor 6:2). Having touched the hem of Eternity in Christ, the passing moments of time, which seem to confront us so cruelly with our frailty, become sacraments of God's mercy and might.[64] Here and now His will must be done; here and now His grace is available for the doing.

The evangelists fix the time of our Saviour's birth within an identifiable period of human history: 'in the days of King

[62] *Fides et ratio*, no. 11. In his encyclical for the new millennium of Christianity, the Holy Father says: 'The Incarnation of the Word, culminating in the Easter mystery and the gift of the Spirit, is the pulsating heart of time, the mysterious hour in which the Kingdom of God came to us (cf Mk 1:5), indeed took root in our history, as the seed destined to become a great tree' (*Novo millennio ineunte*, no. 5; cf *Tertio millennio adveniente*, no. 10).

[63] The prayer at the blessing of the Paschal Candle, *Missale romanum* (1962 and 1970).

[64] On the 'sacrament of the present moment', see Jean-Pierre de Caussade SJ, *Self-abandonment to Divine Providence*, ET, new ed. (London, 1961).

Herod' (Mt 2:1; cf Lk 1:5), in the reign of the Roman
Emperor Caesar Augustus (cf Lk 2:1), when Quirinius was
governor of Syria (cf Lk 2:2). The Roman Martyrology, in
the edition of Baronius, sets this moment within the great
context of universal history:

> In the five thousand one hundred and ninety-ninth year of
> the creation of the world, from the time when God in the
> beginning created the heaven and earth; the two thousand
> nine hundred and fifty-seventh year after the Flood; the two
> thousand and fifteenth year from the birth of Abraham; the
> one thousand five hundred and tenth year from Moses, and
> the going forth of the people of Israel from Egypt; the one
> thousand and thirty-second year from the anointing of David
> the King; in the sixty-fifth week according to the prophecy
> of Daniel; in the one hundred and ninety-fourth Olympiad;
> the seven hundred and fifty-second year from the foundation
> of the city of Rome; the forty-second year of the rule of
> Octavianus Augustus, all the earth being at peace, in the sixth
> age of the history of the world, Jesus Christ, eternal God,
> and the Son of the Eternal Father, desiring to sanctify the
> world by His most merciful coming, being conceived by the
> Holy Ghost, and nine months having passed since His con-
> ception [*here the voice is raised and all kneel*], is born as man, in
> Bethlehem of Judea, of the Virgin Mary. The Nativity of our
> Lord Jesus Christ according to the flesh.[65]

The whole of mankind, both the nations that claim the
name Christian and those to which the Gospel must still be
preached, numbers the years from the human conception and
birth of the Son of God. The present system for the record-
ing of history was invented by the sixth-century Scythian
monk Dionysius Exiguus, but the man who first applied it to
the writing of history was the eighth-century English monk
St Bede the Venerable. In his history of the English people

---

[65] C. Baronius, *Martyrologium romanum*, new ed. (Venice, 1601), p. 696.

and Church, he dates the year in which each event takes place before or after 'the Incarnation of our Lord'.[66]

Since He is God, an eternally existing Divine Person, our Lord can do what other men cannot do: He can choose the time of His birth on earth. Now we can be sure that that time was the very best, the most fitting, of times.

> The difference between Christ and other men is that other men are born subject to the necessity of time, whereas Christ, as Lord and creator of all times, chose for Himself the time in which He was born, as He chose also the place and the Mother. And because 'what is from God is ordered' (Rom 13:1) and fittingly disposed, it follows that Christ was born at the most fitting of times.[67]

The Age

According to an interpretation St Bede inherited from the Fathers and bequeathed to the Middle Ages, our Lord was born at the beginning of the sixth and final age of human history, the last day of the great week of the centuries.[68] The seventh day is the eternal Sabbath enjoyed already by the blessed in Heaven, and the eighth is the unending day of the righteous that begins with the resurrection of their bodies at the end of time.[69] The sixth epoch was in a way both the youth and the old age of the world.[70] The number six, says St Bonaventure, is in many respects the sign of the Saviour. He came in the sixth age, but then He was conceived in the sixth

[66] *Historia ecclesiastica gentis anglorum* lib. 1, cap. 2, et passim; PL 95:25cff.

[67] ST 3a q. 35, a. 7.

[68] 'The Lord wanted to be born at the end of the year to show that He was coming in the last age of the world' (*Rationale* lib. 6, cap. 13, no. 2; 140A:181).

[69] Cf St Augustine, *De diversis quaestionibus LXXXIII*, q. 64, no. 2; PL 40:55. See also *De Genesi contra. manichaeos* lib. 1, cap. 23, no. 40; PL 35:191; Wallis, *Bede*, cap. 66, pp. 158ff; cap. 71, pp. 246ff.

[70] Cf St Augustine, *Retractationes* lib. 1, cap. 26; PL 32:626.

month after the conception of the Baptist, suffered on the sixth day of the week, and hung on the Cross at the sixth hour of the day. Moreover, the sixth month after the Baptist's conception was March, the month in which, according to the traditional dating, man and the world were created. Thus new creation corresponds to old, 'restoration matches the first condition', and the prophet's words are fulfilled: 'For as the new heavens and the new earth, which I will make to stand before me, saith the Lord, so shall your seed stand, and your name. And there shall be month after month, and Sabbath after Sabbath' (Is 66:22f.).[71]

The Best and the Worst of Times

The eternal Word brought a Second Spring for the whole cosmos He created, a renewal for all the times of the history of which He is Lord. But, to begin with, He brought His newness to the age of Caesar Augustus, the time when as man He was conceived and born of the Virgin. These were the best of times and the worst of times, a new and seemingly imperishable age of gold and yet an old and collapsing age of clay.

> It was the best sort of paganism [says Chesterton] that wore the laurels of Rome. It was the best thing the world had yet seen, all things considered and on any large scale, that ruled from the wall of the Grampians to the garden of the Euphrates. It was the best that conquered; it was the best that ruled; and it was the best that began to decay.[72]

It was the best of times. The world was at peace under the rule of Roman law. This peace in the political order, the *pax*

---

[71] Cf *Commentarius in evangelium S. Lucae* cap. 1, v. 26, no. 41; Q VII:20.

[72] *The Everlasting Man*, new ed., in The Collected Works of G. K. Chesterton, vol. 2 (San Francisco, 1986), p. 285.

romana, was a suitable accompaniment to the human birth of Him who is peace in His very person: 'The very Author of Peace and Maker of time sent ahead of Him a time of peace, and so, on His appearing in the flesh, He opened the gate of light and proclaimed the joys of eternal peace, first to the House of Jacob, that is, the people of Israel, and then to all the nations which streamed towards Him.'[73] The prevalence of peace was practically useful as well as symbolically meaningful, because it enabled the first emissaries of the Gospel to travel with ease across national borders.[74] Thus, through the Incarnation of the Son, the Holy Spirit reveals the Providence of the Father at work in the history of Rome. Without realizing it, the great Roman generals and emperors—Pompey, Caesar, Augustus—helped to prepare the world for Christ. Cardinal Bérulle seems to see the noblest of the Romans marching in a line that leads to Christ: 'This unity of empire that they establish on earth exists only to dispose the earth to receive and to believe in the unity and truth of its God. This universal peace tends to a single goal, to suffer thee to be born in peace and to do thee homage as Prince of Peace.'[75]

The preceding half-century had been a golden age in Latin literature. In the person of Cicero, Rome had a statesman who was also a philosopher and the prince of Latin prose. Virgil brought Latin poetry to perfection, singing with a sweetness and a sadness to rival the melodies of the Greeks. In his *pietas* and in his reverence for reality, especially for the tearfulness of things, he stands for that noble heathenism which will most readily be baptized and transformed.

And yet it was the worst of times. Pagan antiquity could not connect theory with practice, philosophy with ethics and

---

[73] St Bede, *Homelia* I, 6, *In nativitate Domini*; CCSL 122:38.
[74] Ibid.
[75] *Vie de Jésus*, Préambule, no. 22; OCB 426.

religion. Even though Roman reason perceived many of the naturally knowable religious and moral truths of religion, Roman will did not translate them into conduct: as St Paul says, addressing the Church in Rome, 'when they knew God, they have not glorified Him as God or given thanks' (Rom 1:21). There were wise men in Rome, as there had been wise men in Athens, who had the feeling, as Chesterton puts it, that there is 'something higher than the gods',[76] one true God beyond the many gods. The most intelligent men in pagan antiquity felt shame before the obscenities of the deities of the myths. And yet, as St Augustine points out in *The City of God*, still they offered sacrifice at the gaudy shrines.[77] 'Did Plato,' asked Bossuet, 'with his eloquence that the world deemed divine, upset a single altar where those monstrous deities were adored?'[78]

It was in the home, in the attitudes to marriage, family and childhood, that the best and worst of the ancient Romans was to be seen. They treasured *pietas*, devoted loyalty to one's parents and kin. They recognized that the family was the foundation of human society. Augustus introduced long-lasting laws to curb adultery and encourage marital fidelity. And yet the Romans filled their homes with many evils. Husbands could divorce wives, wives could divorce husbands, 'with relative freedom'.[79] Cicero, for all his lofty moralizing, divorced Terentia, his wife of thirty years, in order to marry Publilia, a wealthy girl of fifteen, whom he later discarded.[80]

---

[76] Ibid., 107.

[77] Cf *De civitate Dei* lib. 8, cap. 12; PL 41:236–37.

[78] 'Discours sur l'histoire universelle', in *Oeuvres: Textes établis et annotés par l'abbé Velat et Yanne Champailler* (Paris, 1961), p. 897.

[79] Cf S. Treggiari, *Roman Marriage: Iusti Coniuges from the Time of Cicero to the Time of Ulpian* (Oxford, 1991), p. 475.

[80] Juvenal mentions a woman who had eight husbands in five autumns, a record worthy of commemoration on a tombstone (*Satire* 6, 230).

Worst of all, the Romans of the last century B.C. and first century A.D. showed little respect for their children. They were often devoted parents, but though they had rejected the ritual sacrifice of children in religion, they thought nothing of exposing those of their little ones who were disabled or reckoned unwanted. There are expressions of affection for young children in the writings of Roman authors—for example, Catullus' picture of 'little Torquatus . . ./ Stretching out his little hands/ From his mother's lap'[81]—but such tenderness is rare. The deaths of little ones seem to have been accepted mostly with impassivity; indeed, the Romans disapproved of parents who displayed excessive grief.[82] A work such as the medieval poem *Pearl*, which describes a father's sorrow at the death of his small daughter and his vision of her bliss in Heaven, is unthinkable in the culture of pagan antiquity. Abortion was widely practised, by rich and poor alike. There were no legal restrictions against it at the time our Lord was born. In this respect, the age of Augustus in Rome is no worse than the golden age of Athens. It comes as a shock to the Christian reader of Plato and Aristotle to find, alongside all the splendour of truth that enlightened Augustine and Aquinas, the recommendation that 'defective offspring' be killed.[83] Plato saw the child as an inferior being, to be classed with slaves and beasts,[84] while Aristotle supported the state's right to fix a limit on the size of families and recommended early abortion whenever a child was conceived above the authorized number.[85] Roman satirists and moralists sometimes condemn abortion but usually out of suspicion that abortion conceals adultery or in protest against

[81] *Gai Valeri Catulli Veronensis liber*, no. 61, ll. 212ff.
[82] S. Dixon, *The Roman Family* (Baltimore and London, 1992), p. 107.
[83] Cf Plato, *Republic* 460c, 461bc; Aristotle, *Politics* 1335b.
[84] *Republic* 431c; *Theaetetus* 171e.
[85] Cf *Politics* 1335b.

the mother's usurping of the father's right to decide the fate of his offspring, rather than through a belief in the unborn child's human dignity. An honourable exception is Seneca, who praises his mother to the shame of those women who extinguish the new life within their wombs.[86] The Roman family in these years was small, deliberately limited by choices against the child, whether contraception, abortion or infanticide.

The women of Augustan Rome seem troubled and troubling. Augustus himself is said to have made a speech in praise of the wife who is 'chaste, domestic, a good housekeeper, a rearer of children',[87] but Juvenal, in his Sixth Satire, following a Greek literary convention that goes back to Hesiod, launched a brutal attack on the sex that he regarded as anything but fair. He alleged that all the women he knew, whether beautiful or ugly, young or old, embodied some flagrant vice or folly. They were habitually deceitful in all their dealings, inevitably unfaithful as wives. Marriage, he concluded, was a mantrap. Juvenal paints a dark picture of feminine corruption unrelieved by the light of feminine nobility. He is clear-sighted in his denunciation of moral ugliness, but he seems blinded from the recognition of moral beauty. When misogyny reappears in the West, it will do so through reversion to this pagan sensibility. By contrast, Catholic Christianity—through the God-Man's gift of the Sacrament of Matrimony and through devotion to His Blessed Mother—will from the beginning work against the climate of contempt for women.

Fatherhood in ancient Rome also presents a grim spectacle. The Roman *paterfamilias* was an absolute monarch, endowed by the positive law with the rights of life and death over his children (*ius vitae necisque*). Immediately after the

[86] Cf *Ad Helviam matrem: De consolatione*, no. 16.
[87] Cf Cassius Dio, *Roman History* 56, 3.

birth of a child, the midwife would place the newborn on the ground for the father to raise up as an indication that he wanted the child to live and to be brought up under his roof. If the child was handicapped or of doubtful paternity, then the father could order his destruction.[88] It was the Christian Emperors Constantine and Justinian who, for the first time in the history of Rome, outlawed infanticide as a monstrous crime. The old Greek view that a man's bond with his wife was inferior to his friendship with other men also persists in the Rome of the last century B.C. Cicero writes to Atticus, 'I am so forsaken by all that my only time of repose is spent with my wife, my little girl, and sweet Cicero [Junior].'[89] At first hearing, it sounds as if Cicero is rejoicing in his family life, but closer reading reveals that he is complaining of being so neglected by his male friends that he is forced to spend his free time at home. This cult of male friendship could and did degenerate into perversion. In his *Satires* Juvenal describes with disgust the homosexual subculture of the Roman nobility, including the sodomitic 'marriage' of one of the Gracchi. This is the moral evil that the Apostle singles out as epitomizing the moral bankruptcy of the Gentiles (cf Rom 1:26ff.).

The Son of God brings purgation and transformation, death and resurrection, to the pagan Roman world. All that was beautifully true and good the Infant Word fulfilled, while what was hideously false and evil He expelled—through the decrees of councils and emperors, through Christian marriage and family life, through the preaching and example of the saints. Chesterton describes this Christmas revolution in a poem from the years of his youthful confusion:

> And so long is the sign in heavens
> In the east the unquenchable gleam

---

[88] Cf Suetonius, *De vita Caesarum: Divus Claudius*, 27, 1:

[89] *Ad Atticum*, lib. 1, ep. 18.

Still the babe that is quickened may conquer
The life that is new may redeem,
Ho, princes and priests, have ye heard it?
Grow pale through your scorn,
Huge dawns sleep before us, stern changes,
— A child is born.[90]

As the modern Western world turns away from Jesus
Christ, it is salutary to take up the invitation made by Pope
Leo XIII on the nineteenth centenary of the Incarnation and
remind ourselves of what the world was like before Jesus
Christ came in the flesh:

> What kind of life is it from which Jesus Christ . . . is ex-
> cluded? What kind of morality and what manner of death are
> its consequences can be clearly learnt from the example of
> nations deprived of the light of Christianity. If we but recall
> St Paul's description (cf Rom 1:24–32) of the mental blind-
> ness, the natural depravity, the monstrous superstitions and
> lusts of such peoples, our minds will be filled with horror
> and pity. . . . Pride would not mislead, nor indifference ener-
> vate, so many minds, if the divine mercies were more gener-
> ally called to mind, and if it were remembered from what an
> abyss Christ delivered mankind and to what a height He
> raised it. The human race, exiled and disinherited, had for
> ages been daily hurrying into ruin, involved in the terrible
> and numberless ills brought about by the sin of our first
> parents, nor was there any human hope of salvation, when
> Christ Jesus our Lord came down as the Saviour from
> Heaven.[91]

[90] 'The Song of the Cradle', in The Collected Works of G. K. Chesterton,
vol. 10A, Collected Poetry, ed. A. Mackey (San Francisco, 1994), p. 170.
[91] Pope Leo XIII, Tametsi (1900), no. 3.

The Occasion: The Census of the World

St Luke reports the occasion of our Lord's birth with the exactness of the historian:

> And it came to pass that in those days there went out a decree from Caesar Augustus that the whole world should be enrolled. This enrolling was first made by Cyrinus [Quirinius], the governor of Syria. And all went to be enrolled, every one unto his own city. And Joseph also went up from Galilee, out of the city of Nazareth, into Judea, to the city of David, which is called Bethlehem; because he was of the house and family of David (Lk 2:1–4).

In choosing such a time, with its discomforts, for His human birth, the God-Man displays, says St Bede, ' a very great condescension' on His own part and thereby bestows upon us a very great blessing:

> He paid tribute to Caesar, so that He might grant us the grace of perpetual freedom. The Son of God, as man, did service to a king who was ignorant of submission and service to God, so that He might thereby give us a pattern of humility. He indicated how much we should by charity serve each other, since He Himself did not shrink from paying service to a king who was ignorant of true charity.[92]

The submission to the census is a continuation of the wonderful exchange of the Incarnation. From the Son of God's acceptance of registration in the Empire of Rome comes the chance for His members to be signed up for the Kingdom of Heaven:

> O King of all [sings the Byzantine Church], wishing man to be enrolled in the book of life, thou hast enrolled thyself according to the law of Caesar. As a stranger hast thou come

---

[92] St Bede, *Homelia* I, 6, *In Nativitate Domini*; CCSL 122:40.

unto thine own, calling back to Heaven those who were unhappily estranged from Paradise.[93]

The Season: Winter

Jesus is born 'in the bleak midwinter', when 'frosty wind made moan' and 'earth stood hard as iron'.[94] St Ephrem sees a great fittingness in the coming forth of Him who is Life in the season that is a kind of death:

In December, when the nights are long, the endless Day has arisen. In winter, when all creation is deep in gloom, Beauty has come forth to bring His good cheer to the cosmos. In winter that makes the earth barren, virginity has learnt to give birth.[95]

The Divine Word Incarnate came forth from the warmth of His Mother's womb into the physical cold of the Judean midwinter and into the moral cold of the fallen world. Father Faber puts it beautifully: 'The Sacred Heart of the Babe of Bethlehem has come to be the vast central fire of the frozen world.'[96] Chesterton has the same insight: 'Never we know but in sleet and snow,/ The place where the great fires are.'[97] The bearing of the cold of winter by the Word Incarnate is an anticipation of His bearing of the sin of the world. 'He chose the harshness of winter for His birth, so that from then on He might bear the affliction of the flesh for us.'[98] In December, in the cold season when man most feels his mortal frailty, the eternal Son comes to invigorate us with the

[93] Forefeast of the Nativity, *Menaion*, p. 210.
[94] Poem by Christina Rossetti, now widely sung as a hymn (EH 25).
[95] *Des heiligen Ephraem des Syrers Hymnen de Nativitate (Epiphania)* 4, nos. 119–21; GT by E. Beck, CSCO, *Scriptores Syri* 83 (Louvain, 1959), p. 32.
[96] *Bethlehem*, p. 132.
[97] Chesterton, 'A Child of the Snows', in Collected Works, vol. 10A, p. 152.
[98] ST 3a q. 5, a. 8, ad 3.

new youth of adoption by the Father and to warm us with
the blaze of the Holy Spirit. Under the influence of its
usurping prince, the world is chilled by the north wind of
cupidity, but by the flight of the Dove from the Heart of the
Prince of Peace, the world is warmed by the south wind of
charity. In the winter of discontent, the Infant Word bears
His Bride a promise of the delights of spring still to come:
the winter of poor Eve will soon be ended and the rain over
and gone (cf Song 2:11f.). But He warns her that first, on
Golgotha, a terrible 'pruning' must be done (cf v. 12), of
which the hardships of the manger are but the slightest har-
binger; only thereafter will the flowers of the Resurrection
appear in our land.

The Redeemer of time is born at the time of the winter
solstice. At the very moment night begins to shorten and day
to lengthen, the Light of the World, the Sun of Justice,
reveals His intention to make men 'grow in the divine light,
"to enlighten them that sit in darkness and in the shadow of
death" (cf Lk 1:79)'.[99] John the Forerunner is born at the
summer solstice, Jesus the Messiah near the winter one. But
that is just as well, because John confessed that he had to
decrease, just as Jesus had to increase (cf Jn 3:30). He was not
the Light but came to bear witness to the Light (cf Jn 1:7).

The spiritual meanings hidden in the timing of the Nativity bring home to us once more that the transformation of
the cosmos is in train. This is not just any birth, not even the
birth of a great saint or hero, but the temporal birth of the
Creator and Lord of all time. He takes trouble with time,
weaves history into a tapestry in which seeming clashes of
colour shine in a perfect blend.

> He chose the day He had created as the day on which He
> would be created [i.e., born in a created nature], just as He

[99] Ibid.

was made of the Mother whom He made. The day He chose
was the one on which the light begins to increase; this
symbolizes the work of Christ, who renews our inner man
day by day. The birthday of the eternal Creator in time had
to be in harmony with His temporal creation.[100]

But, of course, it must be so: the Creator is born as man in
order to make all creation new.

The Day

During the Great Jubilee of 2000, it was often said in the
popular press that we cannot be certain about the exact date
of the birth of Christ. That was already the view of Clement
of Alexandria in the early third century, who seems unaware
of any firm tradition on the subject.[101] True, in the same
period, St Hippolytus gives the date as the twenty-fifth of
December in the forty-second year of Augustus, but this
particular passage (in his commentary on Daniel) is of dubi-
ous authenticity.[102] The text known as *De Pascha computus*,
which dates from 243 and is printed among the works of St
Cyprian, states that our Lord was born on 28 March, three
days later than what was already established by the mid-third
century as the date of His Crucifixion and would eventually
be settled on as the date of His conception.[103] The author of
the *De Pascha computus* may mean by 'born' what St Matthew
means when he reports the angel as telling Joseph that 'that
which is *born in her* is of the Holy Ghost' (Mt 1:20), namely,
'conceived', for conception, the first stage of human generation, is birth *in* the womb, while parturition is birth *from* the

[100] St Augustine, *Sermo* 186, cap. 3, no. 3; PL 38:1000.
[101] Cf *Stromata* lib. 1, cap. 21; PG 8:888. L. Duchesne's discussion of the date
of our Lord's birth is still the classical text to which scholars refer: *Christian
Worship: Its Origin and Evolution*, ET, new ed. (London, 1923), pp. 257ff.
[102] Cf *Commentaire sur Daniel* 4, no. 23; SC 14:306.
[103] Cf *De Pascha computus*, no. 20; CSEL 3/3:267.

womb.[104] This interpretation is confirmed by the fact that the *De Pascha computus* presents as a type of the 'birth' of Christ the 'making' of the sun on the fourth day of creation (cf Gen 1:16). Now, while it is hard to see how the birth of Christ is a making, His conception is the making of His human body. The sun begins to be on the fourth day of creation, while the already existing Son of God begins *to be man* at the first moment of conception.

The most ancient authority for the liturgical commemoration of the Nativity on the twenty-fifth of December is the so-called Philocalian Calendar, drawn up in Rome in 336. About fifty years later, in a homily preached on that day in Antioch, St John Chrysostom says that the feast was introduced at Antioch just ten years or so before. He is confident that the liturgical date of our Lord's birthday is also the historical one. The Roman Christians, he says, have been celebrating the feast for a long time and according to an ancient tradition. They are in a better position than anyone else to know the right date, because the acts of the Judean census, taken by command of Augustus, are stored in the public archives in Rome.[105] Modern scholars do not share the ancient Doctor's certitude. They argue that the Christians of Rome chose the date in order to counteract the popularity, and to Christianize some of the themes, of the pagan 'Birthday of the Invincible Sun' celebrated in honour of the winter solstice. The message would be that Christ is the true and eternal sun and Son, the Sun of Justice, who arises with healing in His wings (cf Mal 4:2).[106] Another view is that the dating of our Lord's conception (and thus of His birth)

[104] See p. 152f.

[105] *Homilia in diem natalem Domini nostri Iesu Christi*, nos. 1–2; PG 49:351–53.

[106] It seems less likely that Christmas was intended to compete with the Roman Saturnalia, which ended on the twenty-third of December (Duchesne, *Christian Worship*, p. 261).

developed out of a tradition about the date of the Crucifixion. According to Tertullian, our Lord suffered and died
on the eighth day before the Kalends of April.[107] St Hippolytus in his Paschal table assigns the Passion to a year in which
the fourteenth day of the Jewish month of Nisan coincided
with the twenty-fifth day of the Roman month of March.[108]
This same date was also the official Spring equinox. The
death of Christ therefore fell on the day when, according to
both Jewish and Christian Tradition, God created Heaven
and earth (cf Gen 1:1).[109] Duchesne argues that, once the
date of our Lord's death was known, the date of His conception could have been deduced through an instinctive conviction that Christ must have lived on earth, from conception to
last breath, for a complete number of years. 'The Incarnation
must, therefore, like the Passion, have taken place on the
twenty-fifth of March, and as the Incarnation was reckoned
from the first moment of the conception [by] Mary, the birth
of Christ must have taken place on the twenty-fifth of December.'[110]

[107] 'In the month of March, at the time of Passover, on the eighth day before
the Kalends of April, on the first day of unleavened bread . . . the whole
synagogue of the sons of Israel killed Him' (*Adversus Iudaeos* no. 8; PL 2:616B).
The date of 25 March for the conception of our Lord is given also by St
Augustine (cf *De Trinitate* lib. 4, cap. 5, no. 9; PL 42:894).

[108] Cf *Canon paschalis*; PG 10:877–78.

[109] See Duchesne, *Christian Worship*, pp. 251–53.

[110] Ibid., p. 263. Many other events of salvation history were thought to have
taken place on the twenty-fifth of March: 'This day is numbered among the
chief festivals, because the beginning of the whole Christian religion is dated
from it. On this day the world ruined by sin was restored to life by the Passion
of Christ. On this day, too, John the Baptist was beheaded, and on this day
James, the brother of John, had his head chopped off. On this sacred day, as the
whole Church today celebrates, the Incarnation of Christ was announced by
an angel. We read that on this day, at the very hour when the first man was
created in paradise, the Son of God, the New Man, was conceived in the
Virgin's womb. She was the Paradise of fruit, the *fons hortarum*, because in her
sprang forth the Tree of Life, and from her the fount of wisdom flowed forth

Some of the Fathers believed that our Lord's birth could be dated exactly through the dating of the birthday of the Baptist. The Annunciation took place in the 'sixth month' of the pregnancy of St Elizabeth (cf Lk 1:26). Now it is evident from the Gospel that our Lord was conceived immediately after the Virgin had said her *fiat*, and so, since human pregnancy lasts nine months, it follows that our Lord was born fifteen months after the conception of his cousin, St John the Baptist. If we can date the conception of the Forerunner, we can date the birth of the Messiah. St John Chrysostom says that it must have been during the fast of the seventh month (cf Lev 23:24), on 24 September, the Day of Atonement, that Zechariah, while officiating, encountered the angel and Elizabeth, though barren, conceived John (cf Lk 1:8ff.). Now the angel Gabriel came to the Virgin Mary 'in the sixth month' of Elizabeth's pregnancy. Our Lord was therefore conceived on the twenty-fifth of March and born on the twenty-fifth of December.[111]

The Eighth Day

On the eighth day after His birth, Jesus, like every other male child of the Hebrews, was circumcised. St Bonaventure sets out the reasons why the Lord of all submitted to the law that He Himself had imposed upon Abraham and his sons:

[T]o commend the Old Law against Faustus [the Manichean], who said that it was not from God. 'For I say that

---

and poured out all its delights, in whom are hid all the treasures of wisdom and knowledge (cf Col 2:3). It is also the tradition that at the very hour at which Adam ate of the forbidden tree, Christ, hanging on the Cross, drank the vinegar mixed with gall, and at the hour at which the Lord cast out man from Paradise, Christ brought the thief into it. All this, according to the Tradition of the Church, took place today' (Honorius of Autun, *In annunciatione Sancta Mariae*; PL 172:901D–903A).

[111] See L. Thomassin, *Traité des fêtes de l'Église* (Paris, 1683), p. 228.

Christ Jesus was minister of the circumcision for the truth of God, to confirm the promises made unto the Fathers' (Rom 15:8). To show in Himself the reality of the flesh against the Manichean who said that He had an imaginary body. . . . To give us an example of humility and obedience and conformity to others. . . . To invite an evangelical circumcision of the spiritual and bodily senses. To begin our redemption by a first shedding of blood. . . . Mystically, the eight days of the circumcision signify the seven gratuitous virtues, and the eighth is final perseverance in them.[112]

St Thomas sees the circumcision as a 'wonderful exchange', or rather as an extension of the exchange established by the Incarnation itself. As the Son of God 'was made man and circumcised in the flesh, not for Himself, but to make us gods by grace, and that we might be circumcised spiritually, so, again, for our sake He was presented to the Lord, that we might learn to offer ourselves to God'.[113] The acceptance by the sinless Son of God of a rite instituted for the sinful sons of Adam and Abraham looks towards the final term of the wonderful exchange: the Incarnate Word's work of vicarious atonement on the Cross, His bearing, in order to bear away, of the sins of mankind:

Christ, though He is without sin, voluntarily took upon Himself our death, which is the effect of sin, in order to deliver us from death, and to make us to die spiritually unto sin. Likewise, even though He had not contracted Original Sin, He took upon Himself circumcision, which was a remedy against Original Sin, in order to deliver us from the yoke of the Law, and to accomplish a spiritual circumcision in us. His plan was, in a word, to take on the shadow in order to carry out the reality.[114]

[112] *In circumcisione Domini, sermo* 4; Q IX:140.
[113] ST 3a q. 37, a. 3, ad 2.
[114] Ibid., q. 37, a. 1, ad 3.

It is fitting, then, that on the Feast of the Circumcision the antiphon *O admirabile commercium* should be sung.

> We celebrate Christ's coming to men on the day of His nativity; we celebrate the coming of men to Christ on the Octave. This is easily discernible in the antiphons that are sung in the morning office. On the Nativity of the Lord, the first antiphon, *Genuit puerpera Regem*, tells of the pure birth of the Lord; on the Octave the first antiphon says *O admirabile commercium*. When it says *commercium*, it shows that something is given and received. Christ gave us His divinity and received our humanity. What He gave we worship on the Nativity, and what He took we worship on the Octave.[115]

St Cyril of Alexandria sees the eighth day of the circumcision as an anticipation of the eighth day of the Resurrection, after which Christ would give His apostles the commission to convey to the world a spiritual circumcision, when He said, 'Go and teach all nations, baptizing them.'[116] St Bede looks beyond the eighth day of the Resurrection of the Head to the unending eighth day of the risen glory of the elect:

> His Resurrection prefigures the resurrection of each one of us, in both flesh and spirit. Christ has taught us by being circumcised that our nature must both now in itself be purged from the stain of vice, and at the last day be restored from the plague of death. And as the Lord rose on the eighth day, that is, the day after the seventh (which is the Sabbath), so we also after six ages of the world and after the seventh, which is the rest of souls, and is now carrying on in another life, shall rise as on the eighth day.[117]

[115] Amalarius of Metz, *De ecclesiasticis officiis*, lib. 5, cap. 32; PL 105:1223A.
[116] CA 3, 78.
[117] Ibid.

Christmas Day and the Cosmos

Christmas is a 'feast . . . of re-creation'.[118] By His Incarnation and human birth, the Father's eternal Word inaugurated His mission of raising to a new beauty the spatiotemporal world that was created through Him at the beginning and later disfigured by Adam's sin. He comes, in the words of the Martyrology, to 'consecrate the world'.[119] The cosmic consecration will be complete only on the Last Day, when our bodies are redeemed and the whole material order is 'delivered from the servitude of corruption' (cf Rom 8:21). Then the time of this world will pass into the participated eternity of the eighth day, and the whole vast space of the universe, from our humble little planet to the grandest of the galaxies, will be made into a 'new heaven and earth' (cf Rev 21:1). And this most marvellous transfiguration began with the virginal conception and birth of the Father's Only-Begotten. In the Byzantine liturgy, the Church depicts the cosmos as a living person transported by the hope for restoration that lies in the crib:

> When the creation beheld thee born in a cave, who hast hung the whole earth in the void above the waters, it was seized with amazement and cried: 'There is none holy save thee, O Lord.' O merciful Lord, making manifest the figures of thine ineffable Incarnation, thou hast unfolded visions and breathed forth prophecies; and now thou art come and hast fulfilled them, being born in the flesh from a pure Maid in the city of David. Earth has spread out its wide spaces and receives the Creator, as He receives from angels glory, from Heaven the star, from the shepherds praise, from the Magi gifts, and acknowledgement from the whole world.[120]

---

[118] Cf St Gregory Nazianzen, *Oratio* 38, no. 4; PG 36:316B.

[119] See p. 306.

[120] Forefeast of the Nativity, *Menaion*, p. 205. This text echoes the one already quoted above: 'What shall we offer thee, O Christ, who for our sakes hast appeared on earth as man? Every creature made by thee offers thee thanks.

From the Gnostics of the second century to the Modernists of the twentieth, heresy has been scandalized by the particularities of the Incarnation. By contrast, Catholic orthodoxy venerates, to the glory of the Incarnate Word, the times and places of His coming among us in the flesh. This is strikingly evident in the Gospel of St John. The very evangelist who soars eaglelike into the eternal truths of our Lord's Divinity is the one who most lingers over the temporal details of His humanity, the *factum*, so to speak, of the *Verbum caro*.[121] It is in the fourth Gospel that we hear, for example, about the five porticoes of the pool by the Sheep Gate (cf Jn 5:2), the season (winter) when Jesus walked in Solomon's portico (cf Jn 10:23), the weight of the pure nard used by Mary to anoint the feet of Jesus (cf Jn 12:3), the name of the high priest's slave (cf Jn 18:10), the positioning of the cloths in the empty tomb (cf Jn 20:7). The evil spirit in his pride loathes everything bodily and therefore tempts men into despising or doubting the bodily truths of Divine Revelation (the Virgin Birth, the Resurrection, the miracles, the Real Presence) as well as all the spatial and temporal circumstances of our Saviour's earthly life and works.[122]

The angels offer thee a hymn; the heavens a star; the Magi, gifts; the shepherds, their wonder; the earth, its cave; the wilderness, the manger: and we offer thee a Virgin Mother. O pre-eternal God, have mercy upon us' (ibid., p. 254).

[121] '*Verbum caro* FACTUM *est*. In writing this, my mind will persist in translating it: The Word made flesh is a FACT' (Vincent McNabb OP, *Some Mysteries of Jesus Christ* [London, 1941], p. 8).

[122] 'In his fury, the devil "sweeps down a third of the stars of heaven, and casts them to the earth" with sovereign scorn, finding them meaningless. *The fact that the devil holds matter in scorn explains many things. He did not accept that God be Creator of a world which includes matter. He wants a God who is only Light. He wants only justice. Being only "intellectual" he pleads justice above all else. He is "cerebral", with a cold, purely metallic intellect, for he has lost love and contemplation*' (Marie-Dominique Philippe OP, *Wherever He Goes: A Retreat on the Gospel of John* [Laredo, 1998], p. 95).

The Catholic Christian cannot vilify but is called instead to venerate the particularities of the Christmas mystery. From this determinate time and this specific place, even from the confines of His cradle, Redeeming Love begins the restoration of the universe.

> Once in royal David's city
> Stood a lowly cattle shed,
> Where a Mother laid her baby
> In a manger for His bed.
> Mary was that Mother mild,
> Jesus Christ her little Child.
>
> And our eyes at last shall see Him,
> Through His own redeeming love,
> For that Child so dear and gentle
> Is our Lord in Heaven above;
> And He leads His children on
> To the place where He is gone.[123]

---

[123] Hymn by Mrs C. F. Alexander (EH 605).

VI

'TO THE GENTILE WORLD DISPLAY'D'

The Manifestation of the Newborn Christ

> Holy Jesu, in thy brightness
> To the Gentile world display'd
> With the Father and the Spirit
> Endless praise to thee be paid.[1]

God the Son was made true man at the very moment the
Blessed Virgin uttered her *fiat*, but while He lay hidden
within her body, neither she nor any other earthly creature
could *see* Him in His human form. Only when our Lady had
brought Him forth could she gaze upon His sweet face and
hold His tiny body in her arms.[2] Thus, while Nazareth was

---

[1] From the hymn 'Bethlehem! Of Noblest Cities' (a translation of
Prudentius' *O sola magnarum urbium*) by Edward Caswall (WH 25).

[2] 'At the Annunciation, God was indeed given to Mary and Mary was
indeed given to her God, but the gift remained very hidden. The presence
remained imperfect, for presence demands that the beings who are in one
another's presence are perfectly distinct, face to face, that the two can truly lead
the same life. The unity of knowledge and love, even when this knowledge and
love are divine, are not sufficient for a complete presence, especially in the case
of those who have bodies. We need a physical presence, a look that is like a
reflection, the living expression of this unity of knowledge and love. The
distinguishing characteristic of birth is precisely that it fulfils this complete
differentiation of the body of the child from that of his mother, thus enabling
the child to become present to his mother. That is why it is not joy that is
dominant at the Annunciation, but silent desire in expectation of a promise to

the site of the Son's Incarnation, Bethlehem was the scene of His visible appearing, the manifestation of God newborn in human nature: 'Today the Word of God appears clothed in flesh, and what has never been seen by the eyes of man can now be touched by his hands.'[3] Holy Jesus first displays His brightness to our Lady, St Joseph and the shepherds, who are all of the Jewish race, and then, twelve days later, He shows Himself to the Gentiles in the persons of the Magi. Thus, on both days, the twenty-fifth of December and the sixth of January, God incarnate is manifested to men, though it is only the later of the two feasts that bears the official name Epiphany or Theophany. St Augustine distinguishes them as follows:

> On the first occasion, He who existed as God with His Father without a beginning was born as man of a human mother. To flesh He was manifested in the flesh, because flesh could not see Him as He existed in spirit. On that day, which is called His Nativity, Jewish shepherds saw Him. On this day, whose proper name is the Epiphany, meaning Manifestation, Gentile Magi adored Him. His coming was announced to the shepherds by angels, to the Magi by a star. The angels dwell in the heavens that the stars adorn. Hence, to both the shepherds and the Magi, the heavens have shown forth the glory of God (cf Ps 18:2).[4]

Here, then, are the instruments and recipients of the manifestation of the God-Man. To the shepherds and the Magi, by means of the angels and the star, the Father's 'Only-begotten appeared in the substance of our mortality'.[5] Each of these luminous realities, though only briefly mentioned in

---

be fulfilled' (Marie-Dominique Philippe OP, *Mystère de Marie: Croissance de la vie chrétienne* [Nice, 1958], pp. 144f.).

[3] St Leo, *In nativitate Domini, sermo* 6, 1; SC 22B:124f.

[4] St Augustine, *Sermo* 204, no. 1; PL 38:1037.

[5] Preface of the Epiphany, *Missale romanum* (1962 and 1970).

the Gospels, is worthy of study and meditation, and to that
end the first part of this chapter is devoted. In the second
half, a darker, more troubling side of the Christmas mystery
must be considered. The Epiphany in Bethlehem is a strange
mingling of light and shadow. The Dayspring from on high
shines upon a world darkened by sin and death and subservi-
ence to the powers of night. The great God-Man is made
known to a few men but remains hidden from most. Some
welcome and worship Him, while others plot His destruction. Innocent hearts blaze with the flame of love, and yet
corrupted minds fill up with the smoke of hate. Even in His
infancy, in the very act of being manifested, the face of the
Man of Sorrows is 'as it were hidden and despised' (Is 53:3).[6]
That is why, having contemplated the holy angels and men
who made the Saviour known, we must confront the unholy
angels and men who conspired to have Him killed.

1. The Shepherds

Manifestation to the Few

In his treatise 'On the Manifestation of the New-born
Christ', St Thomas helps the eyes of our mind to perceive
the simple brilliance of Eternal Wisdom shining through the
strange complexity of His earthly epiphany. He can think of
several good reasons why the Saviour's birth should not have
been divulged to the whole of mankind.

> First, if all men had known who Jesus was from the begin-
> ning, He would not have been able to redeem us by His
> Cross, for, as the Apostle says, 'if they had known it, they
> would never have crucified the Lord of glory' (1 Cor 2:8).[7]

[6] This text is quoted in the *sed contra* of ST 3a q. 36, a. 1.

[7] At the time of the Passion the Jewish leaders knew our Lord to be the
Messiah promised in the Law, and guessed He might be the true Son of God,

Both the religious leaders of the Jews and the demons knew that our Lord was the Messiah promised in the Law, but of His Divinity they were ignorant. No creature, with full knowledge, would attempt the madness of putting God Incarnate to death.[8]

Secondly, the displaying of Christ's radiance to all men by 'manifest signs' would not only diminish the merit of faith but also deprive it of its essential character, which is unseenness, 'the evidence of things that appear not' (cf Heb 11:1).[9] Our Lord wants us in this life to walk in the darkness of faith and only in the life to come to attain the light of vision. If we want to rest for ever beneath the sunlight of the Lamb, we must allow our intellects to be prepared and purified, emptied out and mortified, by the obscurity of faith.[10] That is why the Holy Eucharist is par excellence the 'mystery of faith', for there, beneath the sacramental species, not only is the Godhead in hiding, as it was in the Crib and on the Cross, but the manhood, too, 'steals from human ken'.[11]

The third reason why the glory of Christ was not revealed to all men during His infancy is that they would then have doubted the reality of His humanity. The Son of God

---

but this 'conjectural knowledge was darkened in them by envy and by desire for their own glory, which seemed to them to be lessened by the excellence of Christ' (cf St Thomas, *Super primam epistolam ad Corinthios* cap. 2, lect. 2).

[8] Cf ST 3a q. 47, a. 5.

[9] Cf ST 2a2ae q. 1, a. 4.

[10] St John of the Cross argues that all three of the theological virtues 'void the faculties': 'Faith causes darkness and a void of understanding in the intellect, hope begets an emptiness of possessions in the memory, and charity produces the nakedness and emptiness of affection and joy in all that is not God' (*The Ascent of Mount Carmel*, bk. 2, chap. 6, no. 2; trans. K. Kavanaugh OCD and O. Rodriguez OCD, *The Collected Works of St John of the Cross*, new ed. [Washington, D.C., 1979], p. 119).

[11] Cf St Thomas's Eucharistic hymn *Adoro te devote* in the version by Gerard Manley Hopkins, 'Godhead Here in Hiding, Whom I Do Adore' (WH 72).

wanted to be man not just truly and perfectly, through the
assumption of a complete and concrete human nature, but
also credibly, through the assumption of that human nature
in a condition that would strike men as human beyond all
doubt.[12] The Incarnation is not a charade. Having decided
to take the 'little way' into human life, the humble path of
infancy, the Son of God wants to be, and to be seen to be, a
totally real human baby. We are saved by faith in both the
Divinity and the humanity of Christ. It was necessary, therefore, for Christ's birth to be made known to men in such a
way that the proof of His Divinity should not be prejudicial
to the perception of His humanity. The God-Man was
therefore manifested through creatures rather than through
Himself. The shepherds and the Magi saw Him in the
weakness of infancy and so were convinced that He was
true man. However, through the singing of the angels and
the shining of the star, they learned that He was true
God, the eternal Son sent as true man and Messiah by the
Father.[13]

The Divine Word adapted His manifestation in the flesh to
the state and condition of the persons who received it. The
pious Jews, such as Simeon and Anna, were spiritual people,
well used to being instructed by 'the inward impulse of the
Holy Spirit', and therefore needed no sensible sign. But the
shepherds and the Magi were absorbed with material things,
with rounding up sheep and tracking down planets, and so
they needed to be led through an accessible outward sign, the
Christmas star or the appearance of angels in visible form,
to the ineffable mystery of the Word made flesh. In both
cases, the sign was in the heavens, for the birth of Christ
itself is a mystery at once heavenly and earthly. However,

[12] Cf ST 3a q. 36, a. 1.
[13] Cf ibid., a. 4.

only the shepherds received the message directly from an angel, because as Jews they were familiar with the idea of angelic visitations.[14]

Why did God choose shepherds to be the first audience of the Christmas cantata of the angels? Five reasons become apparent from a study of the Tradition, two pertaining to the literal meaning of the shepherds, three to their typological function. The historical facts, which fit well with the saving plans of God, are first that they were Jews and secondly that they were poor. As types, they point to Christ Himself, the bishops of His Church and the Christian soul that contemplates Him in faith and love.

The Simplicity of the Shepherds

It is fitting that the birth of the God-Man should be manifested in the first place to Jewish shepherds, because His and His apostles' later preaching is directed first to 'the lost sheep of the house of Israel' and only afterwards to the Gentile world (cf Mt 10:5f.). It is also beautifully appropriate that the Saviour who brings blessedness to the meek and poor in spirit (cf Is 61:1ff.; Mt 5:3ff.) should reveal Himself to shepherds, who are 'the most simple, most humble, and most innocent of men'.[15] As Chrysostom says, the angel did not deliver the good news to the Scribes and Pharisees, who were eaten up with pride and envy, but to 'simple men living in the ancient practices of Moses and the Patriarchs'. From this we may conclude that 'there is a certain road which leads

[14] Ibid., a. 5.

[15] These words are taken from the commentary on the Third Part written by the recusant divine Matthew Kellison: *Commentarii in tertiam partem Summae theologiae* (Douai, 1633), p. 337. For a brief biography of Kellison, see G. Anstruther OP, *The Seminary Priests: A Dictionary of the Secular Clergy of England and Wales, 1558–1850*, vol. 1, *Elizabethan, 1558–1603* (Ware and Durham, 1968), pp. 193f..

by innocence to philosophy.'[16] The love of wisdom is the passion of the humble heart. The humble man is wise because he recognizes the truth about himself and his utter dependence upon God in both the natural and the supernatural orders. When a man is humble and united to the Trinity by charity, the Holy Spirit pours into his soul, however lacking he may be in letters, the great gift of supernatural wisdom. And even in the acquisition of natural wisdom, humility is a great help: it protects the mind from the vices of curiosity and intellectual pride.

Humility, simplicity, straightforward fidelity: these are the principles of the philosophy of the shepherds, '[w]hose wealth's their flock, whose wit to be/ Well read in their simplicity'.[17] It should not surprise us, therefore, that, when the Mother of God summons modern man to turn from the world's false wisdom to the true wisdom of her Son, it is so often to shepherd boys and girls that she makes herself seen and heard.[18] With Jesus, Mary praises the Father for hiding His mysteries from the wise and prudent and revealing them to little ones (cf Mt 11:25).

The Shepherds and the Good Shepherd

The shepherds kneel not only as ambassadors of the Jews and the humble but also as icons of the humble King of the Jews, whom they worship. What these men do for their occupation has something in common with what the Father has sent the Son to do for all men's salvation. They are shepherds of dumb sheep, just as He is the 'shepherd and bishop' of the

[16] CA 3, 69. Cf ST 3a q. 36, a. 3, ad 4.
[17] Richard Crashaw, 'In the Holy Nativity of Our Lord God: A Hymn Sung as by the Shepherds', in *Carmen Deo Nostro: Sacred Poems by Richard Crashaw*, ed. J. R. Tutin (London, 1897), p. 19.
[18] For example, at Fatima.

immortal souls of men (cf 1 Pet 2:25). The Lamb asleep in the manger is the good Shepherd who will lay down His life for the flock (cf Jn 10:11ff.), the great Pastor of the sheep, whom the Father will bring again from the dead (cf Heb 13:20).

> And while the angels in the sky
> Sang praise above the silent field,
> To shepherds poor the Lord most high,
> The one great Shepherd, was revealed.[19]

Shepherds and Pastors

The shepherds of Bethlehem are also types of the shepherds of the Catholic Church, that is, of the bishops, who act in the person of the one great Shepherd of the sheep. The Church's pastors, too, must be ready to share with others the truths they have contemplated: 'The shepherds did not hide in silence the hidden mysteries they had come to know by divine influence, but they told whomever they could. Spiritual shepherds in the Church are appointed especially for this purpose: to proclaim the mysteries of the Word of God.'[20] St Bede points to the dogmatic precision of the shepherds' words: 'As men who were truly watching, they said, not "Let us see the Child", but "the Word" which has come to pass, that is, the Word which was from the beginning. Let us see how it has been made flesh for us, since this very Word is the Lord.'[21] In this respect, too, they are an example to the Church's official teachers: they have an enthusiasm, a restless yearning, for the Word. The shepherds, being simple men,

---

[19] Sedulius' hymn *A solis ortus cardine*, which is sung at Lauds during the Christmas Octave. This is the version by J. Ellerton (EH 18).

[20] St Bede, *Homelia* I, 7; CCSL 122:49

[21] CA 3, 74.

are interested not in myths and make believe but in truth and reality, in the true Word of God, who has really been made flesh for the world's salvation.

Shepherds and Mystics

According to St Bonaventure, the shepherds' words, *Transeamus*, 'Let us go over to Bethlehem, and let us see this Word that is come to pass' (cf Lk 2:15), can be taken in a spiritual sense as 'the words of contemplatives contemplating the Incarnation of Christ'. The passing over is fourfold, as is the seeing, for which the passing over is a preparation.[22] Before the Christian soul can see the Word of God, it must pass from ignorance to wisdom, from guilt to penitence, from penitence to abundant justice, from misery to glory.[23] And the seeing of the Word is also of four kinds. The first is the recognition, by those who have passed from ignorance to wisdom, of the reflection of the Creator in His creatures. Secondly, those who have passed from guilt to penitence see God, in the human nature He has assumed, by the light of faith. Thirdly, those who have passed from penitence to abundant justice see God, by a supernatural perception, in human conscience. Fourthly, those who have passed from this earthly place of pilgrimage to the fatherland in Heaven see God, by the light of glory, in His essence and nature.[24] Thus the shepherds of Bethlehem, by their hastening from the fields to the stable, prefigure every movement and transition in the spiritual life of the Christian. Ascetical and mystical theology turns out to be the science of the simple.

[22] *In nativitate Domini, sermo* 1, no. 2; Q IX:103.
[23] Ibid.; Q IX:103–4.
[24] St Bonaventure, *In nativitate Domini, sermo* 1, schema; Q IX:106.

Pastoral Poetry

The Adoration of the Shepherds confirms an intuition that is common to all the great poets of the West, from Theocritus and Virgil to Spenser, Shakespeare and John Clare: the shepherd is a man specially blessed. However morally flawed individual shepherds may be, the shepherding life in general has qualities that resemble some of the noblest virtues and human acts, qualities that, in fact, dispose a man for the acquisition of the virtues and the performance of the acts. Fortitude and temperance, even a kind of asceticism, are demanded of those who must brave wild weather and harsh hillsides. The shepherd has the privilege of solitude and silence, the setting most conducive to contemplation. Even in his labour, he has the leisure that is the basis of all culture and art. He has the opportunity to see what busy men so often fail to notice, the grandeur of God in His creation.

2. The Angels

The truth manifested to the shepherds is not just the presence of a baby in a manger (which is evident enough) but the identity of the baby: this baby, this real human infant, is the eternally begotten Son of the Father (which is a vast mystery, well hidden). The person who is manifested in the flesh is a Divine Person, the second Hypostasis of the Blessed Trinity. The solemnity of the Epiphany is the day on which the Father's 'Only-begotten, who is co-eternal with [Him] in [His] glory, appeared before our eyes in the reality of our corporeal flesh'.[25] Now since it is the human birth and human nature of *God* that are manifested, it is fitting that angels, who are God's most immediate servants, should do the manifest-

[25] The special *communicantes* in the Roman Canon for the Epiphany of Our Lord: *Missale romanum* (1962 and 1970).

ing. And it is also fitting that 'the brightness of God' should have 'shone round about them' (cf Lk 2:9), for the One whose birth they announce is in Himself the 'brightness of [the Father's] glory' (cf Heb 1:3).[26] The song of the angels, 'Glory to God in the highest, and on earth peace to men of good will' (Lk 2:14), imparts the same lesson: the eternal Word, now new born as man, is in Himself the glory of God and peace towards men.[27] By singing of peace, the angels reveal the final saving purpose of the Saviour's birth and their own most sincere desire, namely, that the sons of Adam should be their 'companions in the heavenly Jerusalem, that is, in the vision of perpetual peace'.[28]

3. The Magi

The Origin and Identity of the Magi

The name Magi is of Persian origin, as, perhaps, were the men who bore it.[29] St Matthew tells us that they came to Jerusalem 'from the East' (cf Mt 2:1), which is thought by many exegetes to have been Persia, though some suggest Babylon and Arabia or even the regions on the eastern borders of Judea.[30] Chrysostom says that it was fitting for the Christian Faith to arise where the sun rises each day, 'for faith is the light of the soul'.[31] Scripture does not supply us with the personal names of the Magi, or even with an exact indication of their number. However, Tradition teaches us

[26] ST 3a q. 36, a. 5, ad 1.

[27] CA 3, 72.

[28] St Bede, *Homelia* I, 6; CCSL 122:42.

[29] *Magos* may come from the name for the priestly class in Akkad.

[30] Cf ST 3a q. 36, a. 3, ad 3. Gold, frankincense and myrrh were the traditional products and gifts of the Arabians; see M.-J. Lagrange OP, *Évangile selon Saint Matthieu*, new ed. (Paris, 1948), p. 20.

[31] Cited in ST 3a q. 36, a. 3, ad 3.

that there were three of them, one for each of the gifts mentioned in the Gospel (cf Mt 2:11), and that their names were Balthasar, Caspar and Melchior.[32] Their relics are venerated in the cathedral church of Cologne.

According to St Jerome, there were three classes of magus in the ancient Near East: some were practitioners of demonic magic, others were experts in astronomy and the science of nature, while a third group was a caste of ascetical priests. Jerome assures us that our Magi were of the second kind, sober students of the stars.[33] The great Dominican exegete Father Lagrange holds the same view.[34] St Augustine is not troubled by the thought that they may have been wizards, for the whole point of their story is that, like the Bishop of Hippo himself, they turn from their wickedness to Christ: 'As clumsiness is the chief note in the rusticity of the shepherds, so ungodliness stands out in the profanities of the Magi. This Cornerstone joined both to Himself, for He chose the foolish for the confounding of the wise and came to call, not the just, but sinners, so that the proud might not boast nor the weak despair.'[35] Salvation is for all sorts and conditions of men, and so, too, is the Epiphany of the Saviour. He was manifested to the wise and powerful (the Magi as kings) as well as to the simple and lowly (the shepherds); both to the righteous (Simeon and Anna) and to sinners (the Magi as wizards); to men (the shepherds, the Magi, and Simeon) but also to women (Anna). Thus He shows that 'no condition of men is excluded from Christ's salvation.'[36]

[32] *Collectanea*; PL 94:541CD.
[33] *Commentaria in Danielem*, cap. 2, v. 2; PL 25:498CD. In several places in the Greek Bible, *magos* is used in a pejorative sense to mean 'magician' (e.g., Dan 1:20; 2:2, 10; 4:4; Acts 13:6ff.).
[34] Lagrange, *Évangile*, p. 21.
[35] *Sermo* 200, no. 3; PL 38:1030; cited in ST 3a q. 36, a. 3, ad 2.
[36] ST 3a q. 36, a. 3.

The Magi and the Preaching of the True Faith

The restricted manifestation of Christ at His birth foreshadowed the more extensive revelation that would come later. Epiphany looks towards the Public Ministry, the Paschal Mystery and the post-Pentecostal preaching of the Church.

> [A]s in the later manifestation, the first announcement of the grace of Christ was made by Him and His apostles to the Jews and afterwards to the Gentiles, so the first to come to Christ were the shepherds, who were the first-fruits of the Jews, as being near to Him; and afterwards came the Magi from afar, who were 'the first fruits of the Gentiles', as Augustine says.[37]

The Magi show true faith and real love towards the Incarnate Son. The Holy Spirit moves them to seek the newborn Messiah and, when He is found, to worship Him as God.[38] As Chrysostom says, in words quoted by Aquinas:

> If the Magi had come in search of an earthly King, they would have been disconcerted at finding that they had taken the trouble to come such a long way for nothing. Consequently, they would have neither adored nor offered gifts. But since they sought a heavenly king, though they found in Him no signs of royal pre-eminence, yet, content with the testimony of the star alone, they adored: for they saw a man, and they acknowledged a God.[39]

The Magi are endowed with divine and catholic faith, and the gifts they bring are an abridgement of its articles. What the Fathers would later state in explicit formulation, the

[37] Ibid., ad 1; and q. 36, a. 8.

[38] 'And therefore, as the devotion and faith of the nations is without any error through the inspiration of the Holy Spirit, so also we must believe that the Magi, inspired by the Holy Ghost, acted wisely in paying homage to Christ' (ST 3a q. 36, a. 8).

[39] Cited in 3a q. 36, a. 8, ad 4.

treasures of the Epiphany affirm by implication: 'Gold as to
a king, frankincense as sacrifice to God, myrrh as embalming
the body of the dead'.[40] The Holy Infant is the one eternal
Son in two natures, the Divine Saviour, at once kingly and
sacerdotal, who comes to conquer Satan's pride and atone
for Adam's sin. The three gifts poured out at His feet refute
all the heresies later pitted against His person:

> In the offering of frankincense [says St Fulgentius], the
> Arians are confounded who claim that sacrifice must be
> offered to the Father alone. In the offering of myrrh, the
> Manicheans are confounded who do not believe that Christ
> truly died for our salvation. In the gold both are con-
> founded, because the Manicheans do not believe Him to
> have been born of the seed of David according to the flesh,
> while the Arians try to ascribe a natural servitude to the
> Only-begotten God. . . . In these same gifts, Nestorius, too,
> is confounded. He tried to divide Christ into two persons,
> but now he sees the Magi humbly offering, not certain gifts
> to the God and other gifts to the man, but the same gifts to
> the one God-Man. . . . This oblation of the Magi also re-
> futes the madness of Eutyches . . . for he abolishes the truth
> of those gifts, when he seeks to preach one nature in
> Christ.[41]

In the texts of the Byzantine liturgy, the Mother of God
finds a dogmatic meaning even in the geographical movements of the Magi. She compares the strange journey from
the East to the infinitely stranger journey of God the Son
from Heaven to earth:

> The pure Virgin spoke in wonder, as she heard the Magi
> standing together before the cave, and she said to them:
> 'Whom do ye seek? For I see that ye have come from a far

[40] St Gregory the Great, *Homiliae in evangelia* lib. 1, hom. 10, no. 5; PL
76:1112D.
[41] *Sermo 2, De duplici nativitate Christi,* no. 10; PL 65:756E–57A.

country. Ye have the appearance, but not the thoughts, of Persians; strange has your journey been, and strange your arrival. Ye have come with zeal to worship Him who, journeying as a stranger from on high, has strangely, in ways known to Himself, come to dwell in me, granting the world great mercy.'[42]

Ever sensitive to the significance of numbers, St Augustine argues that the twelve days between the Saviour's birth and His adoration by the Wise Men represent the sacred multiple formed from applying Catholic faith in the Three in One to the four corners of the Gentile world:

> [The Gentiles] come, not from one part of the world only, but, as the holy Gospel according to Luke says, 'from the East and from the West, from the North and from the South' (13:29), to sit down with Abraham and Isaac and Jacob in the Kingdom of Heaven. And so, by the grace of the Blessed Trinity, the whole earth, from its four corners, is called to faith. By this reckoning, when you multiply four by three, you get the sacred number of the Apostles, twelve. That is a sign of the salvation of the whole world, from its four corners, in the grace of the Trinity. . . . Perhaps this was the reason why, twelve days after the birth of Christ, the Magi, the first fruits of the Gentiles, came to see and to worship Christ, and were found worthy not only to receive their own salvation but also to symbolize the salvation of all the Gentiles.[43]

The Adoration of the Magi

When the Wise Men enter the house and find 'the Child with Mary, His Mother', they fall down and adore Him (cf Mt 2:11). Their simple gesture is instructive for every

---

[42] Forefeast of the Nativity, *Menaion*, p. 200.
[43] St Augustine, *Sermo* 204, cap. 3, no. 3; PL 38:1036.

succeeding generation in the earthly Church. According to St Bonaventure, the house in which Christ is to be found *corporeally* is the womb of the Blessed Virgin; *spiritually*, the faithful soul; *sacramentally*, the Church militant; and *eternally*, the house of the heavenly court.[44] The Magi provide the believer with a noble example of devotion to the Incarnate Son in His several dwelling places, that is, to Jesus in the womb and arms of Mary, Jesus in the Sacred Host, and Jesus in the hearts of His saints. The 'falling down' of the Magi is particularly instructive. We, too, should fall down, bow one knee or even (in solemn exposition) two, when we enter the house of the Church Militant and find the great God-Man substantially present, yet humbly hidden, beneath the sacramental species. Of all the ways in which He is present on earth, this is the most excellent and the most deserving of our love.[45]

Ambassadors of the Wise

The Wise Men were the ambassadors of all who have employed natural reason to attain the truth about the human person, the universe, the very being of things. Alongside their material gifts they laid down the first fruits of all the pagan wisdom that would later be taken up, in the service of the true religion, by the Fathers and Doctors of the Church. By the perception of their senses and the knowledge they acquired by study, as well as by the supernatural lights they received from God, the Magi discovered the physical presence of the Incarnate Logos, whom they then worshipped. Thus they proved that 'though faith is above reason, there can never be any conflict between faith and reason, since it is the very same God that reveals mysteries and infuses faith

---

[44] St Bonaventure, *In Epiphania Domini, sermo* 2; Q IX:151B.
[45] Cf Pope Paul VI, *Mysterium fidei*, nos. 38–39.

who endows the human mind with the light of reason: God cannot deny Himself nor can truth contradict truth.'[46]

The Metaphysics of the Manger

When Christ was born, philosophy was reborn. Supernatural faith in Him does not contradict natural reason, but it does lead it to perfection. Pope John Paul discusses this perfection in his encyclical *Fides et ratio*. The first aspect is subjective: faith in Christ enlightens the mind of the philosopher. '[F]aith purifies reason. . . . As a theological virtue, faith liberates reason from presumption, the typical temptation of the philosopher.' Once armed with Christian humility, the philosopher will 'find courage to tackle questions that are difficult to resolve if the data of Revelation are ignored'.[47] The human mind has not been intrinsically corrupted through the Fall, as if it had lost its capacity to apprehend the truth, but it has been wounded and so finds it difficult to attain the great naturally knowable truths of religion and morality. Reason needs healing and reclamation.

The second aspect of reason's perfection by faith is objective: faith in Christ enlarges the content of philosophy. 'Revelation clearly proposes certain truths which might never have been discovered by reason unaided, although they are not of themselves inaccessible to reason.'[48] One such truth, cited by Chesterton in his book *St. Thomas Aquinas*, is the dignity of the human body. He argues that it was precisely St Thomas's faith in the Word made flesh, in the crucified Word risen in the flesh from the tomb, that gave his reason new reasons for heeding what Aristotle had to say about 'the

---

[46] Cf First Vatican Council, Dogmatic Constitution on the Catholic Faith, *Dei Filius* (1870), chap. 4; DS 3017.

[47] *Fides et ratio*, no. 76.

[48] Ibid.

senses, and the sensations of the body, and the experiences of the common man'.

> The Body was no longer what it was when Plato and Porphyry and the old mystics had left it for dead. It had hung upon a gibbet. It had risen from a tomb. . . . Plato might despise the flesh; but God had not despised it. . . . After the Incarnation had become the idea that is central in our civilization, it was inevitable that there should be a return to materialism, in the sense of the serious value of matter and the making of the body. When once Christ had risen, it was inevitable that Aristotle should rise again.[49]

The Incarnation of the Word in a general way and the infancy of the Word Incarnate in a specific way open new doors for philosophy. More exactly, it is the *wonderfulness* of these revealed mysteries that inaugurates a renaissance of reason. According to Aristotle, wonder is the beginning of knowledge and thus of wisdom.[50] Now eternal Wisdom incarnate, the Infant Word, is most wonderful and opens up new paths for human reason, even in its natural operation. The Incarnation is thus an expansion and empowerment of the human mind in its admiration of the truth. It is the central and greatest marvel of the world. As St Thomas says in words we quoted in an earlier chapter, 'Of all the works of God this surpasses reason more than any other, since one cannot conceive of God doing anything more wonderful than that true God, the Son of God, should be made true man.'[51] Faith in true God made true man enhances reason's

---

[49] *St. Thomas Aquinas*, new ed., in The Collected Works of G. K. Chesterton, vol. 2 (San Francisco, 1986), p. 493. Chesterton argues that St Thomas by his use of Aristotle did what St Francis did by his veneration for nature: '[T]hey both reaffirmed the Incarnation, by bringing God back to earth' (ibid., p. 428).

[50] Cf Aristotle, *Metaphysics* 982b17; 983a12; St Thomas, *In libros metaphysicorum* lib. 1, lect. 3.

[51] SCG 4, 27.

capacity for surprise and gives it a new motive for pressing on to the summit of metaphysics. As Balthasar says, '[B]ecause of that final securing of reality which the believer who encounters God in Christ experiences, the theological vision makes it possible for the first time for the philosophical act of encounter with Being to occur in all its depth.'[52] When the Logos, the divine reason through whom all things were made, enters this world as an infant, He confirms by a supernatural light what human reason can already glimpse by its own natural light, namely, that the universe is the work of a supreme and transcendent Intelligence, and that the being of finite things, so beautiful and yet so fragile, is the gift of the first and necessary Being. Balthasar's suggestion seems to be confirmed by a fact in the history of philosophy: it was the Christian believer Thomas, not the pagan Aristotle or Muslim Avicenna, whose reason grasped the importance of the real distinction of essence and existence in creatures and their real identity in God.[53] Only when He Who Is has revealed Himself, through the Incarnation of the Son, as the Trinity in Unity can human reason proceed to the task of developing a philosophy of *esse*. As Pope John Paul II says in *Fides et ratio*:

> The mystery of the Incarnation will always remain the central point of reference for an understanding of the enigma of human existence, the created world and God himself. The challenge of this mystery pushes philosophy to its limits, as reason is summoned to make its own a logic that brings down the walls within which it risks being confined.[54]

---

[52] *The Glory of the Lord: A Theological Aesthetics*, vol. 1, *Seeing the Form*, ET (San Francisco, 1982), p. 146.

[53] 'The truth of the matter is that, notwithstanding these earlier manifestations, it remained for St Thomas to put the doctrine of the real distinction into proper focus and to give systematic development to the consequences emanating from it' (H. D. Gardeil OP, *Introduction to the Philosophy of St Thomas*, vol. 4, *Metaphysics*, ET [St Louis and London, 1967], p. 204).

[54] *Fides et ratio*, no. 80.

The Incarnation of the Logos provokes man's mind to an unprecedented response of wonder, thereby opening up uncharted vistas for philosophy. The Christmas mystery inspires wonder not only at the God who humbled Himself to assume human childhood, but also at the human childhood elevated through its assumption by God. The joyful mysteries of Christ's childhood, from His conception by the Holy Spirit to His finding in the Temple, reveal as actual a possibility undreamed of by the ancients: a child is the wisest of all; indeed, a child, the Child Jesus, is the divine Wisdom of which all human wisdom is but an image.[55] This is the truth to which the Magi testify. Balthasar, Caspar and Melchior kneel by the crib as the delegates of Socrates, Plato and Aristotle, and indeed of all the philosophers of the West and East. They offer the Christ Child their treasures, but they also confess their poverty: 'We are the three Wise Men of yore,/ And we know all things but the truth.'[56] 'So very simple is the road,/ That we may stray from it.'[57]

When uncreated Wisdom becomes a child, when through the Hypostatic Union His childlike soul is filled with all the treasures of created wisdom (cf Col 2:3), then at last do all childhood's intellectual and spiritual capacities begin to reveal themselves to men. If childhood can serve as an instrument of uncreated Wisdom, an instrument united to His Divine Person, it would seem to follow that there is some quality in childhood, even in us human persons, in peculiar harmony with uncreated Wisdom and therefore with the created wis-

---

[55] Children can be prodigiously good at mathematics but not metaphysics. Why? Because mathematical reasoning, though abstract, deals with things that can be imagined, whereas metaphysical reasoning is of a higher degree of abstraction altogether, dealing as it does with purely intellectual things (see St Thomas, *Sententia libri ethicorum* lib. 6, lect. 7).

[56] 'The Wise Men', in The Collected Works of G. K. Chesterton, vol. 10A, *Collected Poetry*, ed. A. Mackey (San Francisco, 1994), p. 186.

[57] Ibid., p. 187.

dom of philosophy. After the first Christmas Day, in the light
of Christ's own teaching, 'Unless you be converted and become as little children' (Mt 18:3), Christians begin to wonder
about childhood. Consider St Augustine, who had a fascination with babies, at once tender and sober, that has no precedent in his pagan philosophical mentors. You will look in
vain in Plotinus for anything remotely like Augustine's
description of his own infancy in the *Confessions*: 'I was
welcomed by the comforts of human milk.'[58] The philosophers who were blind to childhood's dignity are men who,
like Augustine himself before his conversion, were not
'humble enough to hold the humble Jesus as [their] God'.[59]

Chesterton, like Augustine, was a Christian in whom the
Christ Child stirs wonder about all human childhood.

> And to us, though we wrestle and travail
> Though we fancy and fret and disprove
> Still the plumes stir around us, above us
> The wings of the shadow of Love
> Still the fountains of life are unshattered
> Their splendour unshorn
> The secret, the marvel, the promise
> —A child is born.[60]

Among the things that Chesterton found wonderful about
children was their own sense of wonder. In his essay on Baby-
Worship he argues that the astonishment we feel in the presence of any baby mirrors the astonishment that the baby has
in the presence of the world. We worship the baby, and the
baby by his wide eyes instructs us. The strange gravity of
the infant of three months leads us back to the splendour of
the real, the beauty of being:

---

[58] *Confessiones* lib. 1, cap. 6, no. 7; PL 32:661.
[59] Ibid., lib. 7, cap. 18, no. 24; PL 32:745.
[60] 'The Song of the Cradle', in Collected Works, vol. 10A, p. 170.

It is the gravity of astonishment at the universe, and astonishment at the universe is not mysticism, but transcendent common sense. The fascination of children lies in this: that with
each of them all things are re-made, and the universe is put
again upon its trial. . . . There is always in the healthy mind
an obscure prompting that religion teaches us rather to dig
than to climb; that if we could once understand the common
clay of earth, we should understand everything. Similarly, we
have the sentiment that if we could destroy custom at a blow
and see the stars as a child sees them, we should need no
other apocalypse. This is the great truth which has always lain
at the back of baby-worship, and which will support it to the
end. . . . We may scale the heavens and find new stars innu-
merable, but there is still the new star we have not found—
that on which we were born.[61]

Chesterton regards the child as a realist in the strict philosophical sense: he knows things existing independently of his
mind, and he is amazed at them. Looking back on his own
childhood, GKC remembered 'a sort of white light on everything', a light that had 'a sort of wonder in it, as if the
world were as new as myself; but not that the world was
anything but a real world'.[62] And in one of his finest poems
he prayed that, if God were to grant him a long life, he
would still, even in his second childhood, 'stare at everything;/ As I stared once at a nursery door/ Or a tall tree and
a swing.'[63]

If St Thomas Aquinas is the greatest of philosophers, it
may well be because he kept to the end that unaffectedness of
astonishment he had when he was a little boy and bothered

[61] 'A Defence of Baby-Worship', *The Defendant*, new ed. (London, 1907),
pp. 147f.
[62] *Autobiography*, new ed., in Collected Works, vol. 16 (San Francisco, 1988),
p. 53.
[63] 'A Second Childhood', in Collected Works, vol. 10A (San Francisco,
1988), p. 250.

everyone with the question 'What is God?' His last confession before death, so we are told, was like that of a five-year-old, in its simplicity as well as in its purity. It is fitting, therefore, that Chesterton should make the Angelic Doctor the spokesman of the common sense, not only of the sane man but of the simple child.

> When a child looks out of the nursery window and sees anything, say the green lawn of the garden, what does he actually know; or does he know anything? . . . A brilliant Victorian scientist delighted in declaring that the child does not see any grass at all; but only a sort of green mist reflected in a tiny mirror of the human eye. . . . Men of another school answer that grass is a mere green impression on the mind; and the child can be sure of nothing except the mind. . . . St Thomas Aquinas, suddenly intervening in this nursery quarrel, says emphatically that the child is aware of *Ens*. Long before he knows that grass is grass, or self is self, he knows that something is something. Perhaps it would be best to say very emphatically (with a blow on the table), 'There *is* an Is.' [64]

The child knows that there *is* an Is. What he knows first of all is being, for being (*ens*) is the proper object of the intellect.[65] His mind is receptive of the glorious reality of the world, and he is amazed *that* things are, even before he knows exactly *what* they are. That is why he tends to be captivated by anything—for example, by the wrapping of his Christmas presents rather than by the toys they contain. The child in the garden knows that the grass *is*, but his wonder at this apparently ordinary thing seems to indicate that he is surprised that

[64] *St. Thomas Aquinas*, new ed., in Collected Works, vol. 2, pp. 528–29.

[65] 'The first thing conceived by the intellect is being, because everything is knowable only inasmuch as it actually exists. Hence, being is the proper object of the intellect, and is thus the first intelligible, just as sound is the first audible' (ST 1a q. 5, a. 2; cf SCG 2, 83; 2, 98).

it should be at all. 'If mountains rose on wings to wander', say Chesterton and the child, 'They were no wilder than a cloud.' [66] Now from such childlike amazement at being, at the extraordinariness of the ordinary, flows the whole of metaphysics and natural theology.

> Looking at Being as it is now, as the baby looks at the grass, we see a second thing about it; in quite popular language, it *looks* secondary and dependent. Existence exists; but it is not sufficiently self-existent. . . . The same primary sense which tells us it is Being, tells us that it is not perfect Being; not merely imperfect in the popular controversial sense of containing sin or sorrow, but imperfect as Being, less actual than the actuality it implies. For instance, its Being is often only Becoming, beginning to Be or ceasing to Be; it implies a more constant or complete thing of which it gives in itself no example. That is the meaning of that basic medieval phrase, 'Everything that is moving is moved by another.' [67]

In order to prove the existence of God according to the five ways of St Thomas, all you need are the first principles of reason, the evidence of your senses, and your childhood's sense of wonder. Chesterton mentions the first way, the argument from motion, but the child leads us also to the third way, the argument from contingency. [68] The swing, the tree, my mother at the nursery door: all of them truly *are*, and yet they might not be. They depend for their existence on the Necessary Being who does not depend on them or on anything else. [69] They do not exist by their very nature. They have or share in being, but they are not their own being. They must, therefore, be caused by the First Being, who exists most perfectly, not by sharing or having being, but

[66] 'The Mystery', in Collected Works, vol. 10A, p. 240.
[67] *St. Thomas Aquinas*, in Collected Works, vol. 2, p. 533.
[68] Cf ST 1a q. 2, a. 3.
[69] Ibid.

absolutely, by being being, *ipsum esse per se subsistens*.[70] This is the 'sublime truth' about Himself that God taught Moses: His very essence is to exist.[71] The child himself may not draw these grand conclusions, but his amazement at the universe provides the modest but indispensable premises.[72]

4. The Star

The star of Bethlehem was a bright reality in the heavens, not just a bright idea in the evangelist's mind. Since St Matthew wrote under divine inspiration, he could not have made the mistake of saying that a star guided the Magi, when in fact it did not; nor would the Spirit of Truth have moved him, in an otherwise historical narrative of the Saviour's birth, to throw in an apparently factual statement that was in truth a figure of speech. Matthew searches through the Old Testament for prophecies of the events he describes, but in each case it is evident that it is the actuality of the event that motivates the search for the prophecy, not the availability of the prophecy that forces the invention of the event. St Thomas, following Chrysostom, argues that the star, though a

[70] Ibid., q. 44, a. 1; q. 3, a. 4.

[71] Cf SCG 1, 22.

[72] One of Chesterton's most eloquent statements of his—and indeed St Thomas's—philosophy of being is in his book on Chaucer: 'There is at the back of all our lives an abyss of light, more blinding and unfathomable than any abyss of darkness; and it is the abyss of actuality, of existence, of the fact that things truly are, and that we ourselves are incredibly and sometimes almost incredulously real. It is the fundamental fact of being, as against not being; it is unthinkable, yet we cannot unthink it, though we may sometimes be unthinking about it; unthinking and especially unthanking. For he who has realized this reality knows that it does outweigh, literally to infinity, all lesser regrets or arguments for negation, and that under all our grumblings there is a subconscious substance of gratitude. That light of the positive is the business of the poets, because they see all things in the light of it more than do other men': *Chaucer*, new ed., in The Collected Works of G. K. Chesterton, vol. 18 (San Francisco, 1991), pp. 172–73.

real one, was not one of your common or garden stars.[73] It was not, as some early writers thought, a comet, because comets do not appear in the daytime and are unvarying in their course. However, in its signification, it has something in common with the comets, because the heavenly Kingdom of Christ 'shall break in pieces, and shall consume all the king-doms [of the earth], and itself shall stand for ever' (Dan 2:44).[74]

Why did the Magi associate the new star with the birth of the Messiah in Judea? It may be that they had read the prophecy of Balaam: 'A star shall rise out of Jacob' (Num 24:17). The Messianic hopes of the Jews were well known in the Gentile world.[75] Since the Christmas star did not seem to belong to the known order of the cosmos, they concluded that it must be the extraordinary star that, according to the expectation of the Jews, would herald the coming of their King and Saviour. St Augustine suggests that angels may have revealed to the Magi that the star was a sign of the birth of Christ, while St Leo is more enthralled with God's illumina-tion of their intellects: '[B]esides the outward form which aroused the attention of their corporeal eyes, a more brilliant ray enlightened their minds with the light of faith.'[76]

The shining of the star in celebration of Christ's birth has a similar purpose to the shading of the sun in mourning at His death (cf Lk 23:44f.). These spectacular signs in the heavens were needed to support faith in the power of our Lord's Divinity at those two moments of His earthly life when the believer is most conscious of the weakness of the assumed humanity. This is the argument of St Maximus of Turin as quoted by St Thomas: 'If you disdain the manger, raise your

[73] ST 3a q. 36, a. 7.
[74] Ibid.
[75] Lagrange, Évangile, p. 23.
[76] Cited in ST 3a q. 36, a. 5, ad 4.

eyes a little and gaze on the new star in the heavens, proclaiming to the world the birth of our Lord.' This establishes the major premise. The Angelic Doctor supplies the minor and the conclusion: 'But in His Passion yet greater weakness appeared in His manhood. Therefore, there was need for yet greater miracles in the greater lights of the world.' [77]

Theological reason can add a further argument to the ones made by St Thomas. The work of redemption is the renewal, not the replacement, of the work of creation. That is why the whole cosmos is even now looking forward to the final 'revelation of the sons of God' and the 'redemption of our body' (cf Rom 8:21, 23). When the risen Son conforms our lowly bodies to be like His glorious body (cf Phil 3:21), He will transfigure the whole bodily universe of which they are a part. There will be 'a new heaven and a new earth', for the Lamb will by then have made new every corner of the cosmos (cf Rev 21:1ff.), and the last enemy, the death of the body, will be destroyed (cf 1 Cor 15:26). Now this world-renewing victory was promised and inaugurated by the Incarnation and Paschal Mystery of the Son of God. It is fitting, therefore, that His Crib and Cross should be acclaimed by the great lights of the cosmos, the star above Bethlehem and the darkened sun above Calvary.

Although the star of Bethlehem was a reality, not a mere symbol, it did have a spiritual as well as a literal meaning. First and foremost, it signified Christ Himself, of whose coming the prophet said, 'A star shall rise out of Jacob' (Num 24:17). As the Church prays to her Spouse in the Byzantine liturgy, 'O Master who has risen as a Star out of Jacob, thou hast filled with joy the watchers of the stars, who interpreted wisely the words of Balaam, the soothsayer of old.' [78] In the

---

[77] Ibid., q. 44, a. 2, ad 3.
[78] Feast of the Nativity, *Menaion*, p. 273.

Middelburg altarpiece, Rogier van der Weyden expresses this typology in painted form by showing the Magi gazing at the Infant Jesus framed within a sun-like star in the sky.[79] St Bonaventure can think of several ways in which the newborn Christ should be compared to a star: 'He was most radiant in the purity of universal cleanness . . . most beautiful in the loveliness of universal grace . . . most noble in the liberality of universal clemency . . . most efficacious in the fruitfulness of universal beneficence.'[80]

St Peter Damian sees the star as a symbol of our Lady. Stars have three characteristics: they are fiery, bright and clear, they send out their beams upon the earth and they shine down upon us at night. Each of these stellar qualities is to be found in the Mother of God:

> The Virgin Mary was of a fiery nature, for she is that fiery bush in which the Lord appeared to Moses, which seemed to blaze out, but was not burnt up (cf Ex 3). The Virgin appeared with child, but she was not consumed with the fire of lust. Again, in herself she is splendid and radiant, so much so that it is written of her in the Song of Songs: 'Who is she that cometh forth as the morning rising, fair as the moon, bright as the sun?' (Song 6:9). She sends out from herself the ray of light that penetrates to the secret places of the heart. . . . And just as the ray of light comes from a star, while the star retains its integrity, so the Son came forth from the Virgin while her virginity remained inviolate, as the prophet Ezekiel says: 'This gate shall always be shut, and no man shall pass through it, but the Lord alone shall enter by it' (Ezek 44:2). A star shines at night, and the Virgin, too, shone in a singular way in the night of this world, as is written of her: 'Thou alone hast destroyed all the heresies in all the world.'[81]

---

[79] Cf S. Kemperdick, *Rogier van der Weyden* (Cologne, 1999), p. 63.
[80] *In nativitate Domini, sermo* 7; Q IX:115f.
[81] *Sermo 1, In Epiphania Domini*; PL 144:508AC.

According to St Bonaventure, the historical star has a number of complementary spiritual senses: it stands for Sacred Scripture, which is the *exterior* star that leads us onwards to Christ; for the Blessed Virgin Mary, who is the *superior* star that leads us up to Christ; and for the grace of the Holy Spirit, which is the *interior* star that leads us into Christ.[82]

5. The Holy Innocents

Christmas is light with a sense of wonder, yet heavy with the sounds of war. It bears a message of peace, but, as Chesterton says, it throws down 'a challenge and a fight'.[83] The peace that passes all understanding, the divine peace that the Christ Child gives and is, can only be fully enjoyed by men of goodwill when the battle against mankind's ancient foe has been fought and won. This is the victory for which the eternal Word was born and manifested in the flesh. 'For this purpose the Son of God appeared, that He might destroy the works of the devil' (1 Jn 3: 8). As the Byzantine Church sees it, the very infancy of her Bridegroom strikes a blow against the pride of the fallen created spirit:

> The enemy and deceiver was wounded when he saw God laid in a poor and narrow manger as a babe, and by the hand of God was he cast down, for our salvation who sing: O God our Deliverer, blessed art thou.[84]

The Infant God is, therefore, in danger as soon as He has been born, from the devil as principal agent and from Herod as instrument. Three kings from foreign Persian lands afar rejoice with 'exceeding joy' and adore the Prince of Peace, but the King of Judea is 'exceeding angry' and resolves to

---

[82] *In Epiphania Domini, sermo* 1; Q IX:150.
[83] *The Everlasting Man*, new ed., in Collected Works, vol. 2, p. 315.
[84] Forefeast of the Nativity, *Menaion*, p. 208.

destroy Him. Joseph, being warned in a dream, takes the
Child and His Mother and escapes into Egypt, but Herod, in
his wrath, orders the killing of all boys of two years and
under (cf Mt 2:16). According to St Thomas, these troubles,
permitted by God, are in strange accord with the birth of His
Son in the flesh; indeed, they are the extension of His
Epiphany:

> First, because thereby the heavenly dignity of Christ is mani-
> fested. As St Gregory says: 'After the birth of the King of
> Heaven, the king of the earth was troubled, doubtless be-
> cause earthly grandeur is confounded when heavenly majesty
> is disclosed.' Secondly, because thereby Christ's power as
> judge is foreshadowed. As St Augustine says in a sermon on
> the Epiphany: 'What will His tribunal as judge be like when
> His cradle as infant struck terror into proud kings?' Thirdly,
> because it foreshadowed the overthrow of the devil's king-
> dom. As Pope St Leo says in a sermon on the Epiphany: 'It
> was not so much Herod in himself who was troubled as the
> devil in Herod. For Herod thought Him to be a man, but the
> devil thought Him to be God. Each feared a successor to his
> kingdom: the devil a heavenly successor, Herod an earthly
> successor.' But this was a groundless fear, because Christ had
> not come to have an earthly kingdom on earth, as Pope St
> Leo says, addressing Herod: 'Your kingliness does not attract
> Christ, nor is the Lord of the world content with the paltry
> power of your sceptre.' [85]

The Holy Innocents do not strictly manifest Christ, but
they certainly bear Him witness—as the Roman liturgy says,
'not by speaking, but by dying'.[86] Their witnessing death—
their martyrdom—has an objective glory that transcends the
defects in the subjective state of their humanity. They enjoy
an affinity with Jesus by race, sex, age and place: like the

[85] ST 3a q. 36, a. 2, ad 3.
[86] The Collect of the Feast of the Holy Innocents, *Missale romanum* (1962).

Creator in the cradle, they are baby boys of Bethlehem. Each is a kind of icon of the Messiah. The fact that they are confused with Him proves the reality of the human infancy of the Only-Begotten of the Father, and the fact that once they somehow confessed Him and now partake of His glory in Heaven reveals that Christ is the Saviour of all men, including infants. As Pope St Leo the Great says in one of his sermons for Epiphany: 'He crowned the infants with a new glory, and by His own early days He consecrated the beginnings of little ones, so that He might teach us that no man is incapable of the divine mystery.'[87] In Baptism even a newborn is made a new creation (cf 2 Cor 5:17). He dies with Christ and rises up to divine life in Him (cf Rom 6:1ff.). Original Sin, the death of the soul, is remitted, and the divine life of grace infused. Even the smallest neophyte, the newborn newly baptized, is a member of Christ, an adopted son of God, a temple of the Holy Spirit, a 'partaker of the divine nature' (2 Pet 1:4). The young Christian in the cradle bears the character of Christ upon his soul and is filled with the grace of the virtues and gifts of the Holy Spirit. He is a deified person, and if by some tragedy he dies prematurely, he goes directly to Heaven to sing with the angels.

> In the case of the children whom Herod killed, He showed the innocence and humility of the kind of people who would, in their turn, die for Him. The two years of age of these children signified the number of the precepts upon which 'depend the whole Law and the Prophets' (Mt 22:40).[88]

---

[87] *In Epiphaniae solemnitate, sermo* 2, no. 3; SC 22B:224.
[88] St Augustine, *Sermo* 202, no. 2; PL 38:1034.

Innocence from Bethlehem to Beaconsfield

G. K. Chesterton was one of several great Catholic writers of the turn of the twentieth century who had a mysteriously ardent devotion to the Holy Innocents, the victim flock of Christ. The two most important others are St Thérèse of Lisieux and Charles Péguy. All three were born within eighteen months of each other. The Little Flower wrote a play *The Flight into Egypt* and meditated often and at length on the Heaven of the Innocents unmerited by any adult good works. Two years before he died fighting for France in the Great War, Charles Péguy composed his epic poem on the *Mystère des saints innocents*, those 'simple children [who] play with their palm and martyrs' crowns'. Chesterton himself returns many times to the mystery, both in his poetry and in *The Everlasting Man*. In the poem 'The Neglected Child', for example, he describes how the 'Teachers in the Temple' chided our Lady for losing her Son for a time, yet 'made their notes; while naked/ And monstrous and obscene/ A tyrant bathed in all the blood/ Of men that might have been.'[89]

God gave Gilbert Chesterton, Thérèse Martin and Charles Péguy a charism of prophetic insight into the drama of the century lately ended. They perceived, decades before the industrialization of murder in the concentration camps and abortion mills, that modernity's attempt to suppress Christ would end with a new slaughter of the innocents. There was to be an out-Heroding of Herod. With regard to birth control, Chesterton argued that it is always and in all circumstances, objectively and in practice, an act of hostility towards the child. The very name was dishonest, concealing as it did, behind words of clinical cleanness, the squalid alliance of hatred and lust. 'They insist on talking about Birth Control

---

[89] Collected Works, vol. 10A, p. 84.

when they mean less birth and no control.' [90] The man and the woman must have their pleasure, but the child, at all costs, *must not be.* Chesterton realized that the contracepting couple no longer see the child as a beautiful person, the fruit of love and gift of God, but as a horrible thing to be avoided, a disaster to be averted. This is the outlook of Herod in the heat of his passion and of Lucifer in the cold of his pride.

The Dragon is desperate to devour the Child of the Woman and, in Him, every child (cf Rev 12:4). The King hates the infants, because any one of them might be his rival. The Evil One hates the little ones, because they remind him, in their innocence, of the Lamb by whom he is vanquished. The child is small and humble, the divinely appointed model of Christian discipleship, but Satan is grand and haughty, the implacable foe of the follower of Christ. In Paul Claudel's play *La nuit de Noël 1914*, the spirit of a soldier killed in the defence of France welcomes the souls of the children who have been massacred by the enemy: 'Come, holy innocent souls! Come witnesses of Jesus Christ, come, tender lambs whom the cruel Herod has immolated, not for any evil you have done, but *solely out of hatred for the God of whom you are the image.*' [91] And one of his comrades says, 'There is nothing the devil abominates so much as a little child.' [92] Thus, in every age, but perhaps in this more than any other, human wickedness is seen at its most diabolical in crimes against the child. [93] What the devil once tempted Herod to begin, he has now persuaded whole cultures to continue.

What shield can guard us from these evils? What sword can strike down our spiritual foes? Only the arms that God alone

[90] *The Thing,* new ed., in The Collected Works of G. K. Chesterton, vol. 3 (San Francisco, 1990), p. 170.

[91] Paris, 1915, p. 18.

[92] Ibid., p. 19.

[93] See my book *The Way of the Lamb: The Spirit of Childhood and the End of the Age* (Edinburgh, 1999).

can supply: divinizing grace, the theological virtues, the gifts of the Holy Spirit and the Mother through whose intercession all these blessings are poured out. Devotion to Blessed Mary Ever-Virgin is Christendom's God-sent protection from the forces that defile purity and destroy the child. Where she is truly honoured, the infant has a cradle and the family a sheltering roof. Where she is forgotten or defamed, the façade of Christian culture soon crumbles, might crushes meekness, and lust smothers love.

> Where she is driven out, the ghost of Herod steps in, and the people are bemused by the Idumean's dreams of dominion and glory, feastings in newly built palaces and deeds of violence in dark cellars, and in their hearts awaken Herod's hatred of his own offspring and his fear of children. And the old visions come up again, of goddesses of the fruitfulness of the earth, the breaking of the buds, and the fall of the leaf. Each one presses her own child to her breast, ready to fight for it against the others. The children of Leto draw the bow again, and there is no mercy for the sons and daughters of Niobe. So let us follow the children who sing at the top of their voices: *Adeste, fideles, / Laeti triumphantes, / Venite, venite in Bethlehem.* And when we give each other our Christmas presents in His name, let us remember that He has given us the sun and the moon and the stars, the earth with its forests and mountains and oceans and all that lives and moves upon them. He has given us all green things and everything that blossoms and bears fruit—and all that we quarrel about and all that we have misused. And to save us from our own foolishness and from all our sins He came down to earth and gave Himself. *Venite adoremus Dominum.*[94]

We must at all costs imitate the Magi and find the Child God with His Mother in the house of His true Church, and having found Him, we must ask Mary to help us render Him

---

[94] Sigrid Undset, *Reflections on Christmas and Twelfth Night* (London, 1932), p. 41f.

the gift that pleases Him best, 'a contrite and humbled heart' (cf Ps 50:19). The Cradle of Redeeming Love conveys no other truth, confers no other grace, than that truth and that grace which together make up the 'Little Way', of which the Mother of Redeeming Love is the purest realization. Our Blessed Lady, if we allow her, will lead us to a humble love of Jesus wherever He is to be found: in the Sacred Host, in the person of His Vicar, in all those little ones whom the Dragon seeks to devour. This love, the Holy Spirit's most precious gift of charity, is co-redeeming, the means through which the Virgin-born Son has always most clearly displayed His brightness to the Gentiles and will at last overthrow Lucifer and all the Herods of history.

> Holy Jesu, in thy brightness
> To the Gentle world display'd
> With the Father and the Spirit
> Endless praise to thee be paid.

CONCLUSION

Containing Everything: Mystic Nativity

When Gilbert Chesterton was a boy, he loved to walk from his home in Kensington to Trafalgar Square, and there, in the National Gallery, he would sit and stare at the 'Mystic Nativity' of Botticelli [see art plate 8]. By one of those strange prophetic intuitions that from time to time lightened the darkness of his troubled youth, he felt that somehow this painting contained everything:

> Do you blame that I sit hours before this picture?
> But if I walked all over the world in this time
> I should hardly see anything worth seeing that is not
>   in this picture.[1]

The 'Mystic Nativity', or rather the mysterious Nativity that it depicts, does indeed contain everything worth seeing; it radiates the beauty of the earth that delights the eyes of pilgrims, but it also shows something of the super-beautiful realities that give bliss to those who behold them in Heaven. It is not surprising to learn that this painting gladdened the heart of the young Chesterton. A great joy, an infectious merriment, overflows from the Divine Infant and the Mother who adores Him. Angels dance and play, as Dante says they do,[2] in the sight of the Thrice-Holy God, whose presence in

---

[1] 'The Nativity of Botticelli', in The Collected Works of G. K. Chesterton, vol. IOA (San Francisco, 1994), p. 64.

[2] Cf *Paradiso* canto 28, line 26.

the Empyrean is symbolized by a golden disk in the sky. Here is the final cause of the human birth of the Son of God: the entry of intellectual creatures into the beatitude of the Trinity. And here, too, is the final happiness, the glorious fulfillment, of which the Feast of Christmas is a foretaste.

This Christian icon, this page from the Bible of the Poor, serves as a summary of the argument of this book. Such a deployment is in keeping with the painter's own intentions. Botticelli painted the 'Mystic Nativity' to be a comprehensive affirmation of Catholic faith and hope. Its symbols are meant to provide a key to the understanding of the violent and confused times in which he lived, a salutary shock for the high and mighty in their presumption and a consolation for the weaker brethren in their fears. At the top of the canvas, Botticelli wrote a testimony in Greek:

> I, Alessandro, painted this picture, at the end of the year 1500, in the troubles of Italy, in the half-time after the time, according to the eleventh [chapter] of St John [Revelation], during the release of the devil for three and a half years. Then He shall be bound in the twelfth [chapter], and we shall see [him buried] as in this picture.

1. A Tale of Two Cities: Bethlehem and Florence

Within a picture of the birth of Christ in the city of David, Botticelli concealed a message of hope for the rebirth of Christendom in the city of Dante. He finished work on the canvas on the last day of the Florentine year 1500, that is, on 24 March 1501,[3] at the middle point of the second millennium of Christianity and at the end of a decade of confusion. After the death of Lorenzo de' Medici in 1492 and the

---

[3] At that time, in many places, the civil year began with the solemnity of the Annunciation, 25 March, which was also thought to be the day on which God created the world (see above, pp. 320f.).

expulsion of his son Pietro two years later, the preaching of the Dominican friar Savonarola had brought the city of Florence a second spring in religion and morality. But then, in 1498, Savonarola was executed, and by 1500 Italy was on the edge of disaster. The French King Louis XII had captured Milan. Cesare Borgia, the Pope's nephew, was trying to push out the boundaries of the Papal States. Savonarola had prophesied just such a winnowing of Church and state, but he also held out the hope that death and destruction would be followed by restoration. The French King might prove to be a second Charlemagne, who would convert the heathen and bring back peace to Christendom. But first Italy must endure the second woe prophesied by the seer of Revelation, the unloosing of the devil for three and a half years. Only then would the renovation begin.[4] From Christ, through His Blessed Mother, graces of conversion would fall upon the souls of men, and again above Florence, as once over Bethlehem, the angels would sing peace on earth to men of goodwill, and the demons would slink back into Hell.

2. A Tale of Two Comings

Botticelli's Greek inscription refers to the book of Revelation and therefore to the Second Coming of Christ in glory on Doomsday, but the painting itself depicts the First Coming of Christ in humility on Christmas Day. Like the Fathers, Botticelli was doubtless struck chiefly by the contrasts between the two comings: 'At His first coming He was wrapped in swaddling clothes in a manger; at His second coming He will be robed in vestments of heavenly light.'[5] But he and they did not ignore the continuities. It is the same Divine Person, the

[4] Ronald Lightbown, *Sandro Botticelli: Life and Work* (London, 1989), pp. 252f.
[5] St Cyril of Jerusalem, *Catecheses* 15, no. 1; PG 33:869A.

eternal Son, in the same human nature, who lies in the manger with the meekness of an infant and sits on the throne with the majesty of a judge. The Incarnate Word did not cast off His humanity when He ascended to the Father's right hand, nor will He lack it when He comes again. It is as Son of Man that the Son of God calls the sheep to bliss and sends the goats to everlasting fire (cf Mt 25:31ff.). By the mercy of God, men are to be judged by a man, that is, by the man who is God, 'for we have not a high priest who cannot have compassion on our infirmities, but one tempted in all things like as we are, without sin' (Heb 4:15).[6] Just as the justice to be deployed at the world's end was not absent from His mind at His own human beginning, so the mercy manifested on Christmas Day will fill His Heart on Judgment Day. 'So honoured is this earth,' says Cardinal Newman, 'that no stranger shall judge us, but He who is our fellow, who will sustain our interests, and has full sympathy in all our imperfections.'[7] From the pulpit of his canvas, Botticelli preaches no other Gospel: we need not be afraid, for the tremendous King

---

[6] 'Why does He call Him Son of Man rather than Son of God? One reason is that He will judge as Son of Man. "And He hath given Him power to do judgement, because He is the Son of Man" (Jn 5:27). There are three reasons for this. First, so that He may be seen by all. In the form of the divinity, He could only be seen by the good; therefore, if He is to be seen by all, He must be seen in the form of man. "Every eye shall see Him" (Apoc 1:7). The second reason is the merit of Christ, for He merited this by His Passion. "He humbled Himself, becoming obedient unto death, even to the death of the Cross, for which cause God also hath exalted Him" (Phil 2:8f.). The third reason is so that He may appear as the One destined to judge in the form in which He Himself was judged. "And O that a man might so be judged with God, as the Son of Man is judged with His companion" (Job 16:22). The fourth reason is that by the mercy of God men are judged by men. "For we have not a high priest who cannot have compassion on our infirmities, but one tempted in all things like as we are, without sin" (Heb 4:15). This [compassionate high priest] will be the Son of Man' (St Thomas, *Super Matthaeum*, cap. 25, lect. 3).

[7] 'The Incarnation', in *Parochial and Plain Sermons* (San Francisco, 1997), p. 252.

holding all history in His hand is the tender Babe, the compassionate and crucified High Priest. Lucifer, in all his sevenfold wickedness, is sent scuttling by the Lamb.[8]

The Christmas mystery, in Botticelli's vision, sums up the whole of Christianity: reveals or presupposes its chief dogmas, lays the foundations of its moral and social doctrine, opens a path to the highest reaches of its mysticism. The setting is the world of God's creation in all the beauty of green leaf and flower: the season is spring, not winter. The painter seems to be saying that the Son of God is born as man in order to make the cosmos new, to restore it to unblighted freshness. In the background is a dark wood, doubtless intended by the illustrator of the *Divine Comedy* to recall the *selva oscura* in which Dante once lost his way.[9] The world in which Christ is born is the lovely world of God's creation— yes, but Adam's sin has darkened and disfigured it. The devil holds it in thrall. The cave of the Mystic Nativity is reminiscent of the death that sin brought with it, of the tomb in which the body of the Saviour will be placed on Good Friday and of the black hole of Hades into which His soul will go down on Holy Saturday. His swaddling clothes look already like a shroud. The ass is marked with a prominent cross. To the left of the Holy Family, an angel points towards the coming bloody Sacrifice (and its unbloody renewal in the Mass) by a scroll that says, 'Behold the Lamb of God.' The Son of God has descended deeply into our midst, into our human nature and infant frailty, but He is ready, in obedience to the Father's plan for man's salvation, to plunge deeper still,

---

[8] There are seven demons in the painting. This number probably alludes to the seven heads of the Dragon (see Rev 12:3), which in turn symbolize the seven deadly sins.

[9] See *Inferno* canto 1, line 2. Botticelli did a series of illustrations for *The Divine Comedy*, ninety of which were assembled for an exhibition at the Royal Academy in London in the spring of 2001.

even into the pit of death. The Sun of Justice has come to shed His brightness upon the remotest thickets of the dark wood. Through the opening of the cave, behind the most distant trees, we can see the gleam of a new day: 'This day is the dawn of a new redemption, of the restoration of the old, and of everlasting joy.'[10] 'The people that walked in darkness have seen a great light' (Is 9:2).

The predominant colours in the painting are white, green and red, which symbolize the theological virtues of faith, hope and charity, the very foundations of Christian life.[11] Three angels in these colours kneel on the roof of the stable, while another three, in the same livery and with a scroll bearing the words 'Peace to men of good will', embrace the redeemed at the bottom of the picture. Botticelli here repeats the teaching of his spiritual master, Savonarola, in a Christmas sermon of 1494: 'If you wish to be at rest, seek Christ. Come to this Crib, seek none but Him, and you will find rest. Be well assured that you will never have peace until you come to this Crib and to this light of faith in Christ.'[12] Confirmation of that truth is to be found in the serene face of our Lady. Her eyes are placed at the geometrical centre of the painting, as if the painter were instructing us to share her gaze, to look, as she looks, with loving faith upon her Child and God. Our Lady's spouse most chaste, St Joseph, is the first to look with her at Jesus. He sits, with his back to us, in an attitude of

---

[10] Responsory at Matins of Christmas Day, *Breviarium romanum* (1962).

[11] In the pageant of Divine Revelation at the end of the *Purgatorio*, Dante presents the theological virtues in the symbolic form of three dancing ladies: '[T]he first so red of hue,/ She'd scarce be noted in the furnace-flare;/ The next appeared of emerald through and through,/ Both flesh and bone; the third of them did seem/ As she were formed of snowflakes fallen new' (canto 29, lines 121–26; ET by Dorothy L. Sayers [Harmondsworth, England, 1955], p. 301).

[12] F. Cognasso, ed., *Girolamo Savonarola: Prediche italiane ai fiorentini*, vol. 1, *Novembre e dicembre del 1494* (Perugia, 1930), p. 315.

self-effacing piety. Here is the model, the friend and father we need, for a worthy approach to Jesus and Mary.

As we look from left to right at the three men with the angels of the theological virtues, we notice a heightening of emotion, suggesting the different ways in which God may bestow these virtues upon men. The first figure on the left is calm and upright; he is the Christian who by God's grace has never wavered in hope. The second is somewhat more bowed; he is the believer who, like an Augustine, has received the grace of conversion and thereafter the great gift of perseverance unto death. The third figure is being saved from collapsing by the angel; he is a man saved by divine mercy at the eleventh hour, who, when other men thought him lost, made an act of the charity that covers many sins. The men are wearing olive wreaths, as are the men by the entrance to the cave. And the angels, both those on the ground and those above, all carry olive branches.[13] The olive is a symbol of the grace, virtues and gifts infused by the Holy Spirit.[14] The Son is born as man in order, after His death, Resurrection, and Ascension, to pour out the grace of the Holy Spirit, with the virtues and the gifts, through the Sacraments of His Church and thereby to lead men to the Father's house. Botticelli shows the angels pointing with their olive branches at the Incarnate Son, as if to show that from His meek and lowly Heart the healing oil of the Spirit flows out upon men: 'The school of the Holy Spirit is humble. And what is this school? It is the manger of Jesus. Go, then, and humble yourself at

[13] A Florentine who had lived through the Savonarola years would be reminded of the great procession on Palm Sunday (known in Florence as 'Olive Sunday'). Like the men in the picture, the children would have olive leaves on their heads and branches in their hands, and would cry out 'Long live Christ who is our King!' (see Lightbown, *Sandro Botticelli*, pp. 253f.).

[14] 'The grace of the Holy Spirit is symbolized by oil; that is why Christ is said to be anointed with the oil of gladness on account of the plenitude of the Holy Spirit that He possessed' (ST 3a q. 72, a. 2).

the holy manger. Be not ashamed of the infancy of Christ, for "in Him are hid all the treasures of wisdom and knowledge" (Col 2:3).'[15]

3. A Tale of Two Cities: Bethlehem and Jerusalem

The Incarnate Son of God was born in the little town of Bethlehem but died in the great city of Jerusalem. Eternal Wisdom thereby confounded the wisdom of the world, which prefers grand places for birth and obscure places for suffering.[16] His earthly life is one of ever-deepening humility, from infancy and silence and the lack of worldly acclaim to the humility of and exposure to the world's contempt. Only when He has loved His heavenly Father and human brethren 'unto the end' (cf Jn 13:1), into the depths of death and Hades, does He rise up into glory (cf Lk 24:26). And the path that He, the Head, has taken is the course to be followed by His members. We cannot reach our destination in the heavenly Jerusalem unless we make a start in Bethlehem, the spiritual city that is regeneration, humility and the House of Bread. The blessed have received rebirth through Baptism (in Water, Blood or Desire)[17] from the Passion of the Son of God but also somehow from His human birth. They conformed themselves to the Infant of Bethlehem by becoming little children in humility.[18] If they sinned gravely, they received the restoration of baptismal grace and a return to spiritual infancy in the Sacrament of Penance (or the desire

---

[15] Girolamo Savonarola, *Sermoni e prediche*, vol. 1 (Prato, 1846), p. 477.

[16] See p. 247.

[17] According to the Council of Trent, justification cannot take place 'without the washing of regeneration *or the desire for it*' (Sixth Session, Decree on Justification [1547], cap. 4; DS 1524). On martyrdom as the 'Baptism of Blood', see ST 3a q. 66, a. 12; and on the three 'Baptisms' of Water, Blood, and Desire, see 3a q. 66, a. 11.

[18] See pp. 248f.

thereof).[19] They entered the House of Bread and received, or desired to receive,[20] the divinizing flesh of the eternal Word. Yes, the citizens of the Jerusalem above know the secrets of the Bethlehem below.

Christmas is, in one way, the mystery of beginning, both for Christ and us, but in another way it already contains the end. The Infant Christ is a 'beholder' as well as a 'wayfarer'. He is not just setting out on a path that will lead Him to glory through suffering and death; already His human soul is glorified by the vision of the Father.[21] This little child on earth is Heaven's high King, the eternal Son sent by the Father from Heaven, and even as man, in His human mind and heart, He bears Paradise within Him. What He dies for, the opening up of the Beatific Vision to men, He as man already enjoys at His birth. Botticelli makes the Holy Child look upwards, to His human Mother but also to His heavenly Father. The great disk of the light of glory shines above the stable. Angels dance and embrace the righteous. *Gloria* is found *in excelsis* but also in *profundis*, for Heaven, the Sacred Heart of Heaven, lies amid the straw. 'Today', says Chrysostom, 'Bethlehem has imitated Heaven. Singing angels do duty for the stars, and in place of the sun the Sun of Righteousness, without circumscription, is embraced [in His Mother's arms].'[22]

---

[19] See L. Ott, *Fundamentals of Catholic Dogma*, ET, new ed. (Cork, 1963), p. 438.

[20] '[B]efore receiving a sacrament, the reality of the sacrament can be had through the very desire of receiving the sacrament. Accordingly, before actual reception of this sacrament [of the Holy Eucharist], a man can obtain salvation through the desire of receiving it, just as he can obtain salvation before Baptism through the desire of Baptism. . . . [T]he reception of Baptism is necessary for beginning the spiritual life, while the receiving of the Eucharist is necessary for its consummation. But he does not have to have it in the proper sense; it is sufficient for him to have it in desire, as an end is possessed in desire and intention' (ST 3a q. 73, a. 3).

[21] See pp. 61f., 81f., 242f..

[22] *In salvatoris nostri Iesu Christi nativitatem oratio*; PG 56:385.

Heaven dwelt on earth on the first Christmas Day, and on every Christmas Day Christ's faithful taste a little of the happiness of Heaven, the bliss of their Head. The Church cries out in her joy: 'This day the King of Heaven has deigned to be born of a Virgin, that He might bring back to Heaven man who was lost.'[23] By the dogmatic truth it proclaims, by the graces it imparts and by the festivities it has inspired, the solemnity of Christmas conveys to the Christian mind something of what beatitude means. Heaven is our true native land, our *patria*, the house of the heavenly Father. And if we have a place there, it is only because it has been prepared for us by the Father's Son, true God from true God, the One who made Himself homeless in Bethlehem so that men might find their home in Him in Heaven. Here is the final goal of the 'wonderful exchange' of Lady Day and Christmas Day, of Maundy Thursday and Good Friday: the sharing of Adam's race in the happiness of Heaven, the happiness of the Triune God. For what purpose does the God–Man give Himself to us in the House of Bread, the Bethlehem of the Eucharist, if not to get us to the Jerusalem of Paradise?

Gilbert Chesterton grasped these great truths. He was inspired to see that the happiness of Heaven is foreshadowed, year by year, in the happiness of Christmas in a Christian home. This was what he learned from the novels of Dickens: the joy of the house of the Father will be not altogether unlike the mirth of the house of Christmas. Chesterton said of Dickens that '[a]ll his books are Christmas books.'[24] They tend always to the same goal: the happiness of a married couple and their children around the fireside. All the depictions of wickedness and cruelty, the terrifying encounters

[23] First and Second Responsories of the Matins of Christmas Day, and Antiphon of the Second Vespers of Christmas Day: *Breviarium Romanum* (1962).
[24] Introduction to the Everyman edition of the *Christmas Books*.

in dark streets and on windswept moors, are contrived to enhance the relief of finding goodness and charity in a light-filled room at home. Other writers, said Chesterton, exaggerate despair and the spirit of death. 'Dickens is still the only man who exaggerates happiness. That is, he is the only person to be talked about at Christmas; because he is the only person who talked about Christmas as if it was Christmas, as if it was even more Christmas than it is.' Dickens was not a Catholic. He was 'separated', Chesterton reminds us, 'by centuries of misunderstanding from that mysterious revelation that brought joy upon the earth, but at least he was resolved to enjoy it. It is because Dickens did hand on that tradition of joy, even if it was only traditional, that his name can never be separated from that greater name to which he also was loyal, in an uncongenial time by an instinct that was almost inspiration.' [25] If Chesterton was an untrained Thomist, Dickens was an unconscious one, but then, so is every sane human being. The moral philosophy of St Thomas Aquinas is about happiness, beatitude, and how we men can attain it: not by vice but by virtue, not by self-seeking but by self-giving, not by cupidity but by charity. The literary art of Charles Dickens is built on the same conviction. There is this difference, though: St Thomas teaches us that consummate happiness, the bliss that neither moth nor rust can destroy, can be found only in the life to come, in the immediate and intuitive vision of the Triune God. Dickens, while not denying the grander doctrine, sets his sights chiefly on the happiness attainable in this world, the happiness of family life. But this humble and human Dickensian realism is Thomistic, too. Grace does not destroy nature, and glory in a certain way begins in grace. The Incarnation has most wonderfully ennobled the institution of the family—every

---

[25] 'Dickens and Christmas', radio broadcast to the USA, Christmas Day 1931.

husband and wife and their children. The Ever-Virgin Mary was a married woman, and so her Son began His human life within a family.[26] The Christian family, in the likeness of that Holy Family, is the domestic Church, not only the first cell of the Church Militant but also an anticipation of the Church Triumphant. It is not unreasonable, therefore, to see the joys, natural and supernatural, of the Christian family's Christmas celebrations as an anticipation of the happiness of Heaven.

A great saint of Ireland once said that the citizens of Heaven constitute a 'blessed family',[27] a family partaking of the blessed home life of the Trinity. If the family is the Church in miniature, then the Church is the family writ large. The celestial beatitude of the Church Triumphant is domestic bliss, the rejoicing of the *domestici Dei* (cf Eph 2:19). The Bride, the holy city, delights in her Bridegroom (cf Rev 21:2); the brethren of the Son rejoice in His Father and theirs, with His Mother and theirs (cf Jn 19:27; 20:17). The family of the blessed behold the Triune splendour of God streaming from the pierced flesh of the Lamb (cf Rev 21:23), and they behold, too, the beauty of the Virgin who gave Him temporal birth, Heaven's sun-clothed Mother and twelve-starred Queen (cf Rev 12:1). They behold, and they love; they love, and they are glad. On the day of resurrection the gladness and glory of their God-seeing souls will over-flow into their bodies. Then, at the marriage banquet of the Lamb, shall all good Christian men rejoice, with full-bodied mirth, in an eighth and eternal day that will be at once Christmas and Easter, in a new heaven and new earth that will be both Jerusalem and Bethlehem. 'What is Heaven

[26] See pp. 221f., 229f.

[27] 'Blessed family, / which dwells on high, / where the old does not groan/ nor the infant cry' (*De mundi transitu*, in *Sancti Columbani opera*, ed. G. S. M. Walker [Dublin, 1957], p. 184).

like?' a little girl once asked her daddy. 'It's like the happiness
we feel today,' he said, 'like Christmas, the birthday of Jesus,
and it lasts for ever and ever.'

> To an open house in the evening
> Home shall men come,
> To an older place than Eden
> And a taller town than Rome.
> To the end of the way of the wandering star,
> To the things that cannot be and are,
> To the place where God was homeless
> And all men are at home.[28]

[28] Chesterton, 'The House of Christmas', in Collected Works, vol. 10A, p.
140.

SCRIPTURE INDEX

SUBJECT INDEX

Abelard, Peter, 162
Abraham: Jesus as descendent of,
  226, 287–89, 287n13, 288n16;
  and Trinity, 145, 145n87
Adam: creation of, 157, 157n119;
  Jesus as New, 201–3, 201n94;
  and man's loss of knowledge,
  301; pride and, 249, 250, 251;
  and sin, 201, 249, 250, 251261
Adamnan, Abbot of Iona, 299
Advent, 28–30, 28n22, 33. *See also*
  Christmas season
Aelred of Ricvaulx, St, 58n36, 203
Aeterni Patris (Leo XIII), 50n10
Albert the Great, St, 83n129
Albigensian heresy, 103
almah, 192–93
Ambrose, St: Christmas hymn of,
  66; on Christ's human birth,
  211; on deification of man,
  278; on Eucharist, 27n17; on
  Luke's historical accounts, 191;
  and perpetual virginity of
  Mary, 218, 222, 229; as saint of
  Christmas, 34; and Synod of
  Milan, 210
Anastasia (martyr), 32
Anastasius of Sinai, St, 158
Andrew of Crete, St, 185n45, 262
Angelico, Fra, 64
angels: in Botticelli's 'Mystic Na-
  tivity', 367, 368; and manifesta-
  tions of newborn Christ, 328,

  331–32, 336–37; pride of, 249–
  50; time and, 304n59
Anna, 264, 331, 338
Annunciation: Gabriel and, 72,
  181, 208, 246, 321; gift of,
  327n2; Mary's vow of perpetual virginity, 218–21,
  218n150, 219n151; and nuptial
  mystery, 167–68
Anthony, St, 36
Antidicomarianite heresy, 217
anti-Semitism, 290–93, 291nn21,
  22
Apollinarian heresy, 89
Apostle. *See* Paul, St (The Apostle)
Apostles' Creed, 65, 184, 210,
  210n123
Arian controversy: and deification
  of man, 269; and Father, 135,
  209, 212, 229, 237n10; and
  gifts of Magi, 340; and Virgin
  Birth, 209, 212
Arintero, Juan, OP, 272, 273n138,
  274n141
Aristotle: on birth and nature,
  123; on body and senses, 343–
  44, 344n49, 345; and children,
  311; on mystery and human
  intellect, 48n3; on time, 303;
  on wonder, 344
art: and Botticelli's 'Mystic Nativity', 362–69; Byzantine iconography, 236, 301; of Crib and

402 CRADLE OF REDEEMING LOVE

head and members, 51–52, 71; on Virginal Conception, 153, 197, 203n101, 204–5; on Virgin Birth, 26, 212, 212n128, 213; and 'wonderful exchange', 266n115, 322. *See also Summa theologiae* (St Thomas Aquinas)

Thomas of Canterbury, St, 32

Thomassin, Louis, 133n43, 198n84

time: angels and, 304n59; Aristotle on, 303; Augustine on, 303; St Bede on, 304, 306–7; the eighth day and eternity, 307, 324. *See also* birth of Christ in time

Titus Bostrensis, 112

Torrell, Father J.-P, OP, 60n43, 94n163

Tridentine Breviary, 31n32

Trinity: and Christ's two births, 124–25, 124n9; and deification of man, 268–69, 270–72, 278; and eternal generation of Christ, 135, 142–48, 143n78, 144nn83, 84, 145n87; and Eucharist, 74–75, 74n94; and Fatherhood, 145–48, 145n87, 146n91, 147nn92, 94, 148n98; and incorporeal generation of Christ, 133, 133n43; and intellectual generation of Christ, 136–42, 138n59; and *logos/*Word, 136–37, 136nn53, 54, 140; and Mary, 173, 175–76, 181–82; meditation and worship of, 105; mysteries of, 72–75, 72n89, 74n94, 75n95, 90n151, 91n153; and Old Testament, 145, 145n87; and para-

doxes of temporal birth, 156–57; sanctifying grace and human contact with, 272–73, 273nn137, 138; and theandric action, 72n89, 90–91, 90n151, 91n153; and Virginal Conception, 185–86, 196–97, 199–200. *See also* Holy Spirit

Undset, Sigrid, 360

Unigenitus Dei Filius (Clement VI), 84–85

Valentinus, heresy of, 211

Vatican Council, First, 48, 108

Vatican Council, Second: John Paul II and, 77; Mary and Catholic Tradition, 111n215; and Scriptural inerrancy, 109; and teachings on mysteries of Christ, 69, 77, 108n205; and Virginal Conception, 207n114; and Virgin Birth, 207, 207n114

Veni, Redemptor gentium (St Ambrose), 66

Verbum supernum prodiens (St Thomas Aquinas), 60n42

Vincent de Paul, St, 65

Virgil, 38–39, 309

Virginal Conception, 184–206; and analogy of creation of world, 188; Augustine on, 203, 203n101, 204–5; and Byzantine Church, 185nn45, 46; Christ's sacred humanity and Headship as New Adam, 201–4, 201n94, 202nn98, 100; date of, 320, 320nn107, 110, 321; and divinity of the Son, 187, 187n54;